Cultural Competence in Sports Medicine

Lorin A. Cartwright, MS, ATC
Pioneer High School, Ann Arbor, Michigan

René Revis Shingles, PhD, ATC
Central Michigan University

Human Kinetics

Library of Congress Cataloging-in-Publication Data

Cartwright, Lorin, 1956-
  Cultural competence in sports medicine / Lorin A. Cartwright and Rene Revis Shingles.
    p. ; cm.
  Includes bibliographical references and index.
  ISBN-13: 978-0-7360-7228-1 (print)
  ISBN-10: 0-7360-7228-4 (print)
  1. Sports medicine--United States--Cross-cultural studies. 2. Cultural competence--United States. I. Shingles, Rene Revis, 1962- II. Title.
  [DNLM: 1. Cultural Competency--United States. 2. Sports Medicine--United States. QT 261 C329c 2011]
  RC1210.C365 2011
  362.19'71027--dc22

                                             2010017546

ISBN-10: 0-7360-7228-4 (print)
ISBN-13: 978-0-7360-7228-1 (print)

The Web addresses cited in this text were current as of April 2010, unless otherwise noted.

Acquisitions Editor: Loarn D. Robertson, PhD; **Developmental Editors:** Elaine H. Mustain and Jillian Evans; **Managing Editor:** Melissa J. Zavala; **Assistant Editor:** Casey A. Gentis; **Copyeditor:** Tom Tiller; **Indexer:** Nan Badgett; **Permission Manager:** Dalene Reeder; **Graphic Designer:** Joe Buck; **Graphic Artist:** Yvonne Griffith; **Cover Designer:** Bob Reuther; **Photographer (cover):** © Peggy Brisbane; **Photo Asset Manager:** Jason Allen; **Art Manager:** Kelly Hendren; **Associate Art Manager:** Alan L. Wilborn; **Illustrator:** Tammy Page; **Printer:** Sheridan Books

Printed in the United States of America   10 9 8 7 6 5 4 3 2 1

The paper in this book is certified under a sustainable forestry program.

Human Kinetics
Web site: www.HumanKinetics.com

United States: Human Kinetics
P.O. Box 5076
Champaign, IL 61825-5076
800-747-4457
e-mail: humank@hkusa.com

Canada: Human Kinetics
475 Devonshire Road Unit 100
Windsor, ON N8Y 2L5
800-465-7301 (in Canada only)
e-mail: info@hkcanada.com

Europe: Human Kinetics
107 Bradford Road, Stanningley
Leeds LS28 6AT, United Kingdom
+44 (0) 113 255 5665
e-mail: hk@hkeurope.com

Australia: Human Kinetics
57A Price Avenue
Lower Mitcham, South Australia 5062
08 8372 0999
e-mail: info@hkaustralia.com

New Zealand: Human Kinetics
P.O. Box 80
Torrens Park, South Australia 5062
0800 222 062
e-mail: info@hknewzealand.com

This book is dedicated to Robert Galardi and Bryan Westfield, two people who have taught me what diversity really means.

-Lorin

To my husband and partner Stan, our son Lamar, and in loving memory of my parents, Anthony and Betty G. Revis. This one is for you.

-René

Contents

Foreword   ix | Preface   xi | Acknowledgments   xiii

Foreword

In its report, Missing Persons: Minorities in the Health Professions, the Sullivan Commission on Diversity in the Health Workforce stated that while African Americans, Hispanic Americans, and American Indians constitute nearly 25 percent of the U.S. population, these three groups account for less than 9 percent of nurses, 6 percent of physicians, and only 5 percent of dentists. The Commission's report explained that "diversity in the health workforce will strengthen cultural competence throughout the health system," and that "cultural competence profoundly influences how health professionals deliver health care." Among the report's many recommendations was "key stakeholders in the health system should promote training in diversity and cultural competence for health professions students, faculty, and providers."

The challenges we face in the athletic training profession are the same as the health professions cited in the Sullivan Commission's report. The National Athletic Trainers' Association reports that 81 percent of the certified membership is Caucasian, 2.6 percent Black, 3 percent Hispanic, 3.6 percent Asian American and Pacific Islander, and less than 1 percent American Indian. The changing demographics of the U.S. population make it increasingly likely that certified athletic trainers will encounter a diverse patient population regardless of clinical practice setting. Indeed, the NCAA reports approximately 35 percent of all athletes in all divisions are of color, and essentially half of division I football and men's and women's basketball players are African American.

A culturally competent health care workforce that includes certified athletic trainers is also essential to addressing the challenge of health care disparities among African Americans, Hispanics, and low-income children and adults. The Center for Disease Controls' Office of Minority Health and Health Disparities has offered this guiding principle for improving minority health:

> "The future health of the nation will be determined to a large extent by how effectively we work with communities to reduce and eliminate health disparities between non-minority and minority populations experiencing disproportionate burdens of disease, disability, and premature death."

The concept of cultural competence also transcends one's ability to understand and communicate with a patient of a different racial or ethnic background. To be a culturally competent and aware athletic trainer requires an understanding of delivery of health care to all individuals, regardless of race, ethnicity, sexual identity, sexual orientation, religion, class, and ability—both physical and cognitive.

Cultural competence mandates that each and every one of us do all we can to help diversify the athletic training profession. The ethnic diversity of the health care professions is inextricably linked to the delivery of more effective health care and the reduction of health care disparities. We know that racial and ethnic health care providers are more likely to serve minority and medically underserved communities, thereby increasing access to care. Also, racial and ethnic minority patients report greater levels of satisfaction with care provided by minority health care professionals. We can promote diversity within our health care profession by embracing the many initiatives promoted by the Ethnic Diversity Advisory Committee and becoming more literate about diversity and inclusiveness in athletic training education and clinical practice.

Cultural Competence in Sports Medicine is a welcome and overdue contribution to the athletic training literature. The book will guide athletic training faculty, clinicians, and students through an exploration of cultural competence that includes definitions, information on various culture-related illnesses, and how the changing demographics of our country will influence delivery of health care. The book also facilitates a self-examination and exploration of one's own background, which is necessary to help recognize and addresses one's own biases. Ultimately, readers of *Cultural Competence in Sports Medicine* will develop the skills necessary for the effective delivery of culturally-based and competent health care delivery.

David H. Perrin, PhD, ATC
University of North Carolina, Greensboro

Preface

In 2001, the Office of Minority Health in the U.S. Department of Health and Human Services issued a report titled *National Standards for Culturally and Linguistically Appropriate Services* [CLAS] *in Health Care.* One intended use was for educators "to incorporate cultural and linguistic competence into their curricula and to raise awareness about the impact of culture and language on health care delivery. This audience would include educators from health care professions" (p. 4). In response, the National Athletic Trainers' Association revised its educational competencies for entry-level athletic trainers by including cultural competence—an area that had lacked strong teaching—as a professional behavior. In turn, our intent for this textbook is to help educators, particularly those in athletic training, expand their teaching into the area of cultural competence.

Indeed, the volume before you is a pioneering textbook that introduces the world of culturally competent health care. We present detailed information for all students who will be working with diverse populations. The book is divided into four main parts:

In part I, we help you better understand cultural competence and why it is important. Specifically, chapter 1 presents models and theories of cultural competence, including the process of cultural competence as applied to the delivery of health care services, which serves as the book's foundation and basis of organization. Chapter 2 presents a detailed description of cultural-bound syndromes and of complementary and alternative medicine, and chapter 3 discusses the influence of demographics and health disparities in health care.

In part II, we discuss cultural awareness. Chapter 4 helps you learn about factors affecting cultural competence, including race, ethnicity, class, gender, sexuality, religion, and spirituality. Chapter 5, in turn, helps you become aware of your own cultural health care issues, barriers, and biases, as well as ways in which you may tend to stereotype. Thus the book teaches you how to assess your cultural attitudes and behaviors.

In part III, we help you develop cultural knowledge. These chapters discuss various areas of the world in terms of two, or often three, cultures from each given area. For each culture, the discussion addresses demographic and cultural background information, a brief history of country of origin and immigration, primary languages and communication styles, family structure, daily living and food practices, spiritual or religious orientations, health care information, biocultural assessment, common sensitivities and conditions, beliefs about illness, preventive healing practices, symptom management, and treatments. This rich discussion allows athletic training students to glean key information for use in providing assessment, rehabilitation, and education based on each culture. Readers should also understand that first-, second-, and third-generation immigrants may have different expectations from one another. For example, first-generation

immigrants may be more inclined to believe in supernatural cures, whereas individuals who have been acculturated to the United States will likely not adhere to first-generation culture. Additionally, readers should remember that the information provided in this part may not apply to *all* people in a culture. Thus, we've included an icon near a clarifying statement to help readers be aware of this mindset before reading more about a particular culture.

In part IV, we provide you with strategies, tools, and models for developing culture-specific skills. You will learn various ways to conduct cultural physical assessments, including strategies for eliciting information from your patients. Part IV also teaches you about cultural encounters in the health care environment—providing culturally competent care to your patients is not enough; you must also learn to practice your craft in a diverse work setting.

As an athletic training student, it is critical for you to develop understanding of the role you play when working with patients. You must become familiar with the cultures of the populations with whom you will work—and learn how best to work with each person within each culture. You will also have to address your own personal biases and privileges in order to ensure that you can give the best care possible and be respected for your work.

You will see several recurring features to help you throughout the book.

- **Professionals in their own words:** Each chapter opens with a feature about a noted professional in a health field. These features present a variety of professionals discussing their experiences in varied settings.

- **Chapter objectives:** We explicitly state the objectives for each chapter to help you focus your learning.

- **What would you do if . . . ?** This segment gives students the opportunity to reflect on a cultural encounter and discuss it in the classroom setting.

- **Activities:** This feature allows students to practice what they have learned about cultural competence in terms of knowledge, skills, and attitudes.

- **Questions for review:** Important questions are asked at the end of each chapter in order to help students summarize the chapter's content.

- **Key terms:** These terms appear in boldface in the chapters and are defined in the glossary at the end of the book.

- **Appendix:** This material supports athletic training students by providing additional information about illnesses and conditions.

Acknowledgments

Everything happens for a reason. This book started five years ago with a chance meeting in a hallway at the NATA convention. God put René and I together to write this book based on that chance meeting. It started with a dream we both had, and it finishes with the involvement of so many people.

Thank you to Barb Hansen, for tedious hours of reading, rewriting, editing, encouragement, interest, and pride. I could not ask for a better person in my life.

To my family, for your love, support, and encouragement to finish: Louise Cartwright, Bert Cartwright, Rose Ann Cartwright, Gary Cartwright, Linda Cartwright, Bruce Cartwright, and Kathy Cartwright.

To Cindy Nordlinger for her artistic impression of the original maps. May God bless you with good health. I love you. Thanks to Jan Lauer for being a great friend and believing in my ability to educate. I'm truly blessed by your friendship.

-Lorin

Were it not for the grace of God, a strong faith, the many prayers that were always answered, and the contributions of many, the writing journey would not have been completed successfully. I thank you . . .

My family, mentors, and friends, particularly, Mr. Stan L. Shingles, Mr. Lamar Shingles, Mrs. Betty G. Revis (in memory), Mrs. Sheila R. Smallwood, Mr. Ricky Revis, and Dr. Yevonne Smith for your unwavering love, support, and encouragement.

The faculty and students in the Athletic Training Education Program at Central Michigan University, who when faced with the challenge of finding resources on cultural competence said, "you just need to write a book," so I did. Thanks for being the impetus. Special thanks to Ms. Adero Allen, Mr. Matt Branceleone, Ms. Mollie Coe, Ms. Ali Jeske, Mr. Alex Lundy, Ms. Ashley Reed, and Ms. Kelly Reid, who served as research assistants.

The women's writing group, Dr. Susan Griffith, Dr. Pamela Eddy, and Dr. Debbie Silkwood-Sherer, for teaching me that a project of such magnitude could be written in small increments. A special thanks to Dr. Laretta Henderson who would not let me off the hook. Thanks for being my inspiration.

-René

We thank the staff at Human Kinetics Publishing, in particular, Dr. Loarn Robertson, acquisitions editor, for your excitement about our project, guidance, and patience; Mrs. Jillian Evans, developmental editor; Mr. Tom Tiller, copyeditor, thanks for your expertise and exceptional feedback; and Mrs. Melissa Zavala, managing editor, for putting all the pieces together. Thanks for being on our team.

-Lorin and René

PART

I

Exploring Cultural Competence

Part I helps you gain a broader perspective on culture, cultural competence, and factors (e.g., demographics) that may affect the provision of culturally competent care. Chapter 1 establishes the importance of cultural competence and presents definitions from scholarly sources and leading organizations. It also addresses the theoretical underpinnings of cultural competence and highlights several models of cultural competence, including the process of cultural competence in the delivery of health care services developed by Dr. Josepha Campinha-Bacote. Her model—which includes cultural desire, cultural awareness, cultural knowledge, cultural skill, and cultural encounters—serves as the foundation and organizing principle of this text, and it is discussed in detail. The chapter also presents terminology and language commonly used to describe specific ethnic and racial groups.

Chapter 2 addresses various culture-related illnesses, beliefs, and health care practices that athletic trainers may encounter. Specifically, the chapter defines a number of culture-bound syndromes, which are presented by geographic region, then by country of origin or culture, in order to show their relationship to each other. Not all patients from a given culture will be familiar with or believe in the culture-bound syndromes, but athletic trainers should be aware of such practices in the event that a patient presents with symptoms. The chapter also includes a discussion of complementary and alternative medicine (CAM) practices and lays out four domains of such practices: mind–body medicine, biological-based practices, manipulative and body-based practices, and energy medicine.

Chapter 3 discusses changes in U.S. demographics associated with race and ethnicity, language, income and poverty, and insurance. It also addresses how these changes could affect health disparities—particularly, access to health care. The last part of the chapter focuses on several cultural competence techniques that may help alleviate health disparities.

Defining Cultural Competence

Learning Objectives

Upon completing this chapter, students will be able to do the following:

1. Define cultural competence
2. Explain the importance of developing cultural competence
3. Identify the models and theories of cultural competence
4. Describe the model of cultural competence used in this text
5. Define language and terminology commonly used to describe racial and ethnic groups

Frank E. Walters, PhD, ATC

Photographer: Broward Health

I am currently the director of sports medicine for Broward Health and the director of the Wellness Center at Broward General Medical Center in Fort Lauderdale, Florida. I direct a sports medicine program designed to care for secondary athletes affiliated with contracted secondary schools in Broward County. I supervise, evaluate, and coordinate the work of 27 athletic trainers.

Prior to my present position, I was the first coordinator of the athletic health care services for the Department of Athletics, District of Columbia Public Schools. Before working in the DC Public Schools, I was an assistant professor in the Department of Kinesiology at Texas A&M University. I also worked as the head athletic trainer at Prairie View A&M. In 1977, I started my career as a teacher and athletic trainer at Pharr San Juan Alamo High School and then moved to a similar position at MB Smiley High School in Houston, Texas.

I was born in Munich, Germany and grew up in Brooklyn, New York. I obtained a BS degree in physical education at Brooklyn College in 1977 and an MS degree in physical education with a concentration in athletic training in 1978 from Indiana State University. I received a PhD in physical education from Texas A&M.

I have been a certified athletic trainer since 1977. I am a member of the National Athletic Trainers' Association, the Southeast Athletic Trainers' Association, Athletic Trainers' Association of Florida, and the National Society of Black Athletic Trainers. I am a board member of the Board of Certification (BOC). I was also the first president of the National Society of Black Athletic Trainers. I have served as a member of several National Athletic Trainers' Association (NATA) committees.

I have received numerous awards, most notably the first Indiana State University Athletic Training Department's Outstanding Alumnus Award in 1994. In 2002, I was named the NATA's Ethnic Diversity Advisory Council's Bill Chisolm Professional Service Award honoree, and in 2003 and 2010 was presented with the NATA's Most Distinguished Athletic Trainer and Hall of Fame Awards, respectively.

I chose athletic training as a profession primarily because of my mentor, Bill Chisolm, who showed a genuine interest in me as a person and as a student. I am confident that part of Bill's interest had to do with my being an African-American student, considering there were very few Blacks in athletic training at that time. Bill was only the second African-American professor I had ever encountered and I was fascinated and impressed. While Bill mentored many other students, I am confident that he worked especially hard to encourage those who were ethnically diverse. I have made it a part of my personal and professional mission to continue in Bill Chisolm's footsteps by actively engaging ethnically diverse athletic training students and young professionals.

"No matter how people are packaged, they get up each day and go about the business of living" (Funderburg, 2006). While doing the business of living, people sometimes become ill or injured and may seek the services of a health care provider, such as an athletic trainer. What happens during the ensuing health care encounter may be mediated by culture, race, ethnicity, social class, gender, sexuality, and religion. The ways in which people are perceived, how they perceive others, and the ways in which they view the social world may also affect how they are treated, how they respond, and how they treat others in the health care environment. As athletic trainers, then, it is important that we be responsive to the needs of all patients, regardless of how they are packaged. One way to be responsive is to develop cultural competence.

WHAT IS CULTURAL COMPETENCE?

Developing **cultural competence** is a process in which an athletic trainer learns to appreciate and respect cultural differences and take them into consideration in order to care for patients in a culturally congruent manner (Purnell & Paulanka, 2008). Cultural competence also involves analyzing and criticizing systems of power and privilege (Andersen & Collins, 2007) that create inequities in health care and health care delivery. For example, if a provider establishes office or clinic hours of

9:00 a.m. to 4:30 p.m.—with time off for lunch from noon to 1:00 p.m.—one consequence is that people who work during those times (particularly hourly workers) thus face a systematic barrier to care. A person in this situation must decide if seeking health care is more important than receiving pay. Thus, if a large number of community members are hourly workers, then providing culturally competent care that meets the needs of the community may mean adjusting one's hours of operation to give patients better access to that care. Cultural competence can be developed, and doing so takes time, energy, and commitment; the process requires an active choice followed up with conscious effort.

Scholarly Definitions

Cultural competence has been defined by numerous scholars (Andrews & Boyle, 1995; Campinha-Bacote, 2002, 2007; Giger & Davidhizar, 2007; Leininger, 1978; Purnell & Paulanka, 2005, 2008; Spector, 2004) and organizations (Office of Minority Health, 2005). Although no universally accepted definition exists, many of the definitions address common themes. In terms of individual health care providers, two recurring themes are as follows: (a) recognizing one's own cultural attitudes, beliefs, and biases in order to better understand the patient's culture and health care practices, and (b) acquiring culturally based knowledge and skills in order to provide care in a culturally congruent manner. Other themes focus on the health care system (organizational cultural competence)—for example, being able to work effectively with colleagues from a diversity of cultures.

Here are two scholarly definitions of cultural competence:

- "[T]he ongoing process in which the health care professional continuously strives to achieve the ability and availability to work effectively within the cultural context of the patient (individual, family, community)" (Campinha-Bacote, 2007, p. 15).
- "[C]ulturally sensitive, culturally appropriate, [and] meeting the complex culture-bound health care needs of a given person, family and community" (Spector, 2009, p. 8).

Definitions from Professional Health Organizations

Various health care organizations have either defined cultural competence or identified it as a desirable value. Here are several examples.

- **Health Resources and Services Administration (Bureau of Primary Health Care):** Cultural competence is a set of attitudes, skills, behaviors, and policies that enable organizations and staff to work effectively in cross-cultural situations. It reflects the ability to acquire and use knowledge of the health-related beliefs, attitudes, practices, and communication patterns of clients and their families to improve services, strengthen programs, increase community participation, and close the gaps in health status between diverse population groups. Cultural competence also focuses on population-specific issues, including health-related beliefs and cultural values (the socioeconomic perspective), disease prevalence (the epidemiologic perspective), and treatment efficacy (the outcome perspective) (Bureau of Primary Health Care, 2000, p. 3).

• **Office of Minority Health (U.S. Department of Health and Human Services):** Cultural and linguistic competence is a set of congruent behaviors, attitudes, and policies that come together in a system or agency or among professionals and that enables effective work in cross-cultural situations. Culture refers to integrated patterns of human behavior that include the language, thoughts, communications, actions, customs, beliefs, values, and institutions of racial, ethnic, religious, and social groups. Competence implies having the capacity to function effectively as an individual and an organization within the context of the cultural beliefs, behaviors, and needs presented by consumers and their communities (Office of Minority Health, 2005).

• **National Athletic Trainers' Association (NATA):** NATA addressed cultural competence in the fourth edition of its educational competences, where cultural competence is listed as a foundational behavior of professional practice. Athletic trainers are expected to "understand the cultural differences of patients' attitudes and behaviors toward health care[;] . . . [d]emonstrate knowledge, attitudes, behaviors, and skills necessary to achieve optimal health outcomes for diverse patient populations[; and] . . . [d]emonstrate knowledge, attitudes, behaviors, and skills necessary to work respectfully and effectively with diverse populations and in a diverse work environment" (National Athletic Trainers' Association, 2006, p. 6).

Developing cultural competence is an ongoing process; it happens over time. This process involves developing cultural awareness, knowledge, and skills in order to treat all patients as uniquely as possible. Health care providers and health care organizations alike should participate in the process of developing cultural competence in order to minimize barriers to health care.

WHY IS CULTURAL COMPETENCE IMPORTANT?

The ethnic and racial composition of the United States is changing. However, the people who work in and study the health professions (e.g., athletic trainers, nurses, and occupational and physical therapists) have remained relatively homogenous. Now, however, more immigrants to the United States are from Central and South America and Southeast Asia, and fewer come from Europe. In addition, fewer Caucasians were born in recent years. As of the 2000 U. S. Census, growth in the American workforce involved an increase in women (while men declined), in people of color (i.e., African Americans, American Indians, Asian Americans and Pacific Islander Americans, and Latinos) (Clark & Weismantle, 2003), and in immigrants. Approximately 20 percent of the population now speaks a language other than

English (Lowe, 2008). Athletic trainers must be prepared for these demographic changes!

Cultural competence is important because, as stated in the National Standards on Culturally and Linguistically Appropriate Services (Office of Minority Health, 2001; see also the sidebar), "culture and language have considerable impact on how patients access and respond to health care services." Diverse populations should be ensured equal access to high-quality health care, and health professionals should "promote and support the attitudes, behaviors, knowledge, and skills necessary for staff to work respectfully and effectively with patients and each other in a culturally diverse work environment." As one speaker asked of athletic trainers during a keynote address, "How about the manner in which we interact with colleagues, athletes and patients who might be different from ourselves . . . ? Do we contribute to a welcoming environment" (Perrin, 2003)?

National Standards on Culturally and Linguistically Appropriate Services (CLAS)

The CLAS standards are primarily directed at health care organizations; however, individual providers are also encouraged to use the standards to make their practices more culturally and linguistically accessible. The principles and activities of culturally and linguistically appropriate services should be integrated throughout an organization and undertaken in partnership with the communities being served.

The 14 CLAS standards are organized by themes: Culturally Competent Care (Standards 1–3), Language Access Services (Standards 4–7), and Organizational Supports For Cultural Competence (Standards 8–14). Within this framework, there are three types of standards of varying stringency: mandates, guidelines, and recommendations as follows:

CLAS mandates are current Federal requirements for all recipients of Federal funds (Standards 4, 5, 6, and 7).

CLAS guidelines are activities recommended by OMH [the Office of Minority Health] for adoption as mandates by Federal, State, and national accrediting agencies (Standards 1, 2, 3, 8, 9, 10, 11, 12, and 13).

CLAS recommendations are suggested by OMH for voluntary adoption by health care organizations (Standard 14).

Standard 1

Health care organizations should ensure that patients/consumers receive from all staff members effective, understandable, and respectful care that is provided in a manner compatible with their cultural health beliefs and practices and preferred language.

(continued)

Standard 2

Health care organizations should implement strategies to recruit, retain, and promote at all levels of the organization a diverse staff and leadership that are representative of the demographic characteristics of the service area.

Standard 3

Health care organizations should ensure that staff at all levels and across all disciplines receive ongoing education and training in culturally and linguistically appropriate service delivery.

Standard 4

Health care organizations must offer and provide language assistance services, including bilingual staff and interpreter services, at no cost to each patient/consumer with limited English proficiency at all points of contact, in a timely manner during all hours of operation.

Standard 5

Health care organizations must provide to patients/consumers in their preferred language both verbal offers and written notices informing them of their right to receive language assistance services.

Standard 6

Health care organizations must assure the competence of language assistance provided to limited English proficient patients/consumers by interpreters and bilingual staff. Family and friends should not be used to provide interpretation services (except on request by the patient/consumer).

Standard 7

Health care organizations must make available easily understood patient-related materials and post signage in the languages of the commonly encountered groups and/or groups represented in the service area.

Standard 8

Health care organizations should develop, implement, and promote a written strategic plan that outlines clear goals, policies, operational plans, and management accountability/oversight mechanisms to provide culturally and linguistically appropriate services.

Standard 9

Health care organizations should conduct initial and ongoing organizational self-assessments of CLAS-related activities and are encouraged to integrate cultural and linguistic competence-related measures into their internal audits, performance improvement programs, patient satisfaction assessments, and outcomes-based evaluations.

Standard 10

Health care organizations should ensure that data on the individual patient's/consumer's race, ethnicity, and spoken and written language are collected in health records, integrated into the organization's management information systems, and periodically updated.

Standard 11

Health care organizations should maintain a current demographic, cultural, and epidemiological profile of the community as well as a needs assessment to accurately plan for and implement services that respond to the cultural and linguistic characteristics of the service area.

Standard 12

Health care organizations should develop participatory, collaborative partnerships with communities and utilize a variety of formal and informal mechanisms to facilitate community and patient/consumer involvement in designing and implementing CLAS-related activities.

Standard 13

Health care organizations should ensure that conflict and grievance resolution processes are culturally and linguistically sensitive and capable of identifying, preventing, and resolving cross-cultural conflicts or complaints by patients/consumers.

Standard 14

Health care organizations are encouraged to regularly make available to the public information about their progress and successful innovations in implementing the CLAS standards and to provide public notice in their communities about the availability of this information.

Office of Minority Health 2001.

Culturally competent approaches to health care have been reported as effective with patients when delivered with "the combination of language services, training of staff on cultural competence, culturally competent health promotion, and organizational support" (Taylor, 2005, p. 136). Thus, the importance of cultural competence has been recognized both by organizations (through their mission or position statements) and by the federal government (through the CLAS standards) (Taylor, 2005). Even so, the specific components of cultural competence still need to be studied, and the next section discusses the work of several scholars who have done so.

THEORIES AND MODELS
OF CULTURAL COMPETENCE

Cultural competence has its roots in transcultural nursing, which was founded in the mid-1960s by nursing theorist Madeleine Leininger (Giger & Davidhizar, 2007). Transcultural nursing is defined as a "humanistic and scientific area of formal study and practice which is focused upon differences and similarities among cultures with respect to human care, health (or well-being), and illness based upon the people's cultural values, beliefs and practices" (Giger & Davidhizar, 1999, p. 5). Leininger developed the theory of cultural care diversity and universality: "the phenomenon of care needs to be studied in depth and practiced within a cultural context, which culminates in culturally congruent care for health, well-being, or dying" (Boyle & Wenger, 2002, p. 200).

Giger and Davidhizar (2007) focused on cultural assessment when they developed their transcultural assessment model for use in nursing; it has also been employed as a theoretical framework in other health professions. The model identifies six cultural phenomena that must be considered when assessing the culturally unique individual: communication, space, social organization, time, environmental control, and biological variation (figure 1.1). For each phenomenon, Giger and Davidhizar have developed a series of associated questions and specific behaviors that are used during patient assessment.

Rachel Spector (2000) studied the interaction of health care providers with people holding different cultural health and illness beliefs. Her intent was to "help nurses and other providers be aware of and sensitive to the beliefs and needs of their patients" (p. xiii). Spector (2004) combined the Giger and Davidhizar (2007) transcultural assessment model with the cultural heritage model, which added culture, religion, and ethnicity to the mix (figure 1.2). Her model demonstrates how an individual with a unique cultural background, religion, or ethnicity can be affected by the six cultural phenomena called out in the Giger and Davidhizar model.

The Purnell model for cultural competence (figure 1.3) was developed to be used by all health professionals across varying practice settings (Lattanzi & Purnell, 2006; Purnell & Paulanka, 2008). Represented visually, the model is circular and contains four rings; the outermost represents global society, followed in turn by community, family, and (the innermost ring) the individual person. The organizing framework is represented in the center of the circle, which is divided into 12 pie-shaped wedges, each of which represents a cultural domain. The 12 domains include overview/heritage, communication, family roles and organization, work force issues, biocultural ecology, high-risk behaviors, nutrition, pregnancy, death rituals, spirituality, health care practices, and health care practitioners (Lattanzi & Purnell, 2006; Purnell & Paulanka, 2005, 2008). Below the circle is a "jagged line, which represents the nonlinear concept of cultural consciousness" (Purnell & Paulanka, 2003, p. 9).

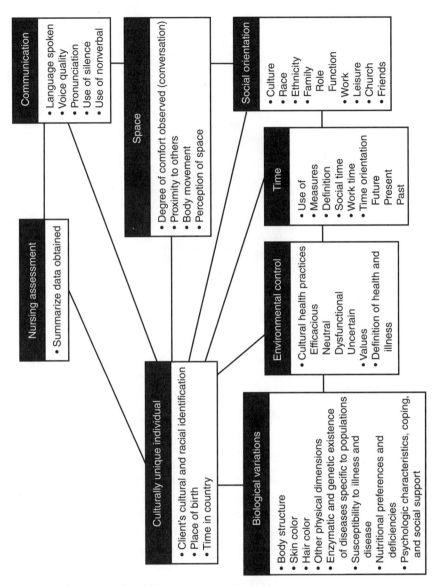

Figure 1.1 Giger and Davidhizar's transcultural assessment model.

This article was published *Transcultural nursing: Assessment and intervention*, 5th ed., J.N. Giger and R.E. Davidhizar, pg. 27, Copyright Elsevier 2007.

These models have many similarities and a few differences. Giger and Davidhizar's (2007) and Spector's (2009) models were developed as tools for cultural assessment of patients. Each of the cultural phenomena they identify is also represented in some aspect of Purnell's (Purnell & Paulanka, 2008) model. For example, the use of herbs and folk healers is included in environmental control under the Giger and Davidhizar and the Spector models, and in Purnell's model they are addressed in

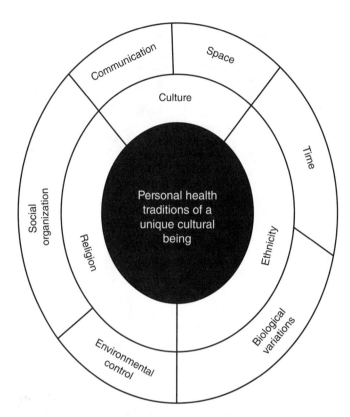

Figure 1.2 Spector's model of personal health traditions of a unique cultural being.

SPECTOR, RACHEL EL., CULTURAL DIVERSITY IN HEALTH AND ILLNESS, 7th Edition, © 2009, p. 8. Adapted by permission of Pearson Education, Inc., Upper Saddle River, NJ.

the category of health care practices and health care practitioners. Purnell's model also includes a patient cultural assessment and adds high-risk behaviors. Lastly, Purnell's model explicitly includes an assessment of health care providers—for example, work force issues and provider's level of cultural consciousness—whereas the other two models do not.

Josepha Campinha-Bacote's (2007) model—the process of cultural competence in the delivery of health care services—was developed in the context of transcultural nursing but intended for use by all health professionals. The model is also influenced by the professions of medical anthropology and multicultural counseling. It encompasses the "ongoing interpersonal approach to becoming culturally competent that is used for the application of transcultural knowledge" (Boyle & Wenger, 2002). Campinha-Bacote's model is used in this text as a framework for helping athletic trainers develop cultural competence. This model was chosen because it is broad and encompasses many aspects of the previously discussed models. For example, the assessment of a health care provider's level of cultural competence (Purnell &

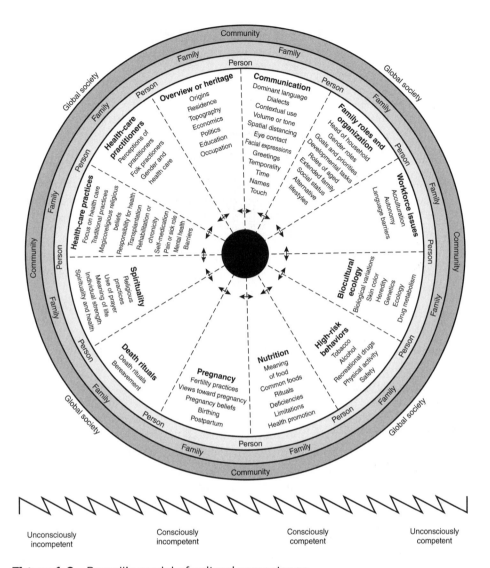

Figure 1.3 Purnell's model of cultural competence.

Reprinted, by permission, from L.D. Purnell and B.J. Paulanka, 2008, *Transcultural health care: A culturally competent approach*, 3rd ed. (Philadelphia, PA: F.A. Davis).

Paulanka, 2008) can be used as a part of cultural awareness. Likewise, the cultural phenomena (Giger and Davidhizar, 2007; Spector, 2009) and cultural domains (Purnell & Paulanka) can be engaged as part of cultural skill. Another reason for choosing Campinha-Bacote's model is that it goes a step further by including cultural encounters and, more important, cultural desire. This model in its entirety is discussed in the next section of this chapter, and each unit of the text addresses a different aspect of the model.

PROCESS OF CULTURAL COMPETENCE

Campinha-Bacote's model integrates five interdependent constructs: cultural awareness, cultural knowledge, cultural skill, cultural encounters, and cultural desire. Athletic trainers can engage or participate in any of the constructs, but they must address or experience each in order to internalize the process of cultural competence. The model makes six assumptions (Campinha-Bacote, 2007, p. 20):

1. Cultural competence is a process, not an event; a journey, not a destination; dynamic, not static; and it involves the paradox of knowing (the more you think you know, the more you really do not know; the more you think you do not know, the more you really know).
2. The process of cultural competence consists of five interrelated constructs: cultural desire, cultural awareness, cultural knowledge, cultural skill, and cultural encounters.
3. The spiritual and pivotal construct of cultural competence is cultural desire.
4. Variation occurs both within and across cultural groups.
5. Cultural competence is an essential component in providing effective and culturally responsive care to all clients.
6. All encounters are cultural and sacred encounters.

In Campinha-Bacote's (2007) model, the constructs of cultural competence are "pictorially depicted as a volcano, and, symbolically, when cultural desire erupts, it gives forth the desire to 'want to' (rather than have to) enter into the process of becoming culturally competent by genuinely seeking cultural encounters, obtaining cultural knowledge, possessing the skill to conduct culturally sensitive assessments, and being humble to the process of cultural awareness" (p. 16). Here are definitions of the constructs:

Cultural awareness involves an in-depth self-examination. The purpose is to explore one's personal and professional cultural values, beliefs, biases, and prejudices and how they affect clinical judgment. As has been found among women athletic trainers, one's perceived cultural advantages, disadvantages, and privileges may also affect how one interacts with patients (Shingles, 2001) and thus should be explored. Understanding one's self helps in the understanding of others.

Cultural knowledge encompasses three issues. The first involves learning about cultural values and health-related beliefs different from your own (particularly those present in and pertinent to the health care environment). The second involves learning about biological variations, health disparities between, and disease incidence among, groups and how best to address them. The third issue, treatment efficacy, involves obtaining information about how different ethnic groups respond to specific drugs (Campinha-Bacote, 2007). Treatment efficacy can be affected, for example, by environmental concerns (e.g., diet and nutrition), cultural beliefs and practices (e.g., use of herbal medicine or the athletic trainer's bias), genetics, and generic drug substitution (e.g., use of lactose as a drug filler).

Cultural skill is the ability to apply knowledge to collect relevant cultural data and perform a culturally based physical assessment (Campinha-Bacote, 2007).

Cultural encounter involves direct engagement in cross-cultural interactions. The purpose is to refine and modify one's beliefs about a cultural group and to prevent possible stereotyping. Cultural encounters should include an assessment of the patient's linguistic needs (Campinha-Bacote, 2007). It is also important to remember that not all individuals in a given racial or ethnic group will behave in the same way; an individuals' level of acculturation influences his or her beliefs and practices. Experiencing cultural encounters gives you a better understanding of such intragroup variation.

Cultural desire involves the health professional's motivation—developing a sense of wanting to, rather than having to, "provide care that is culturally responsive" (Campinha-Bacote, 2007). As a health professional, do you care enough about your patients to provide them with culturally competent services grounded in cultural awareness, cultural knowledge, and cultural skill honed through intentional cultural encounters?

Campinha-Bacote's model can be powerful for athletic trainers. It addresses what athletic trainers need to do for themselves through cultural awareness and cultural desire—what they need to learn about (cultural knowledge), apply to (cultural skill), and share with (cultural encounters) their patients. Part II of this book explores cultural awareness as defined by Campinha-Bacote. Part III addresses cultural knowledge in relation to specific ethnic and racial groups. Part IV explores cultural skill and cultural encounters.

TERMINOLOGY AND LANGUAGE

When talking about cultural competence, people invariably ask the following question: What do I call my patient? More specifically, they are asking what ethnic or racial term they should use. Such choices can be challenging because they are often fraught with assumptions about race, social class, gender, sexuality, and other differences. In this book, when referring to research, scholarship, or data put forth by scholars and other sources, the terminology they use in their work has been retained. When grouping people according to similar ethnic experiences, the following terms are used (the first letter of the ethnic or racial term is capitalized to reflect that the text is addressing a properly named group) (Andersen & Collins, 2007):

- African American is an ethnic and cultural term used to refer to an individual who identifies as an American "with origins in any of the Black racial groups of Africa" (National Center for Education Statistics, n.d., para. 3). African Americans are descendents of "people who were brought here [to the United States of America] as slaves from the west coast of Africa" (Spector, 1996, p. 191).

- Black is a racial term used to refer to an individual "...having origins in any of the Black racial groups of Africa." (National Center for Education Statistics, n.d., para. 3). It is an inclusive term used both for those who were born in the United States and for those who have immigrated to the United States (e.g., from the Dominican Republic, Haiti, Jamaica, and the West Indian Islands).

- The terms American Indian, Native American, Native People, and Indian (the term used varies by region) refer to an individual who identifies as "having origins in any of the original peoples of North America..., and who maintains cultural identification through tribal affiliation or community attachment" (National Center for Education Statistics, n.d., para. 3).

- Asian American and Pacific Islander American are ethnic and cultural terms used to refer to an individual who identifies as an American with "origins in any of the original peoples of the Far East, Southeast Asia, the Indian Subcontinent," (National Center for Education Statistics, n.d., para. 3) or the Pacific Islands. For example, persons may identify as Americans of Asian Indian, Chinese, Filipino, Japanese, Korean, Vietnamese, Guamanian, or Samoan decent.

- White is a racial term used to refer to an individual "having origins in any of the original peoples of Europe, North Africa, or the Middle East" (National Center for Education Statistics, n.d., para. 3). It is an inclusive term used both for those born in the United States and for those who have immigrated to the United States; it is used interchangeably with Caucasian.

- Caucasian is a cultural term used to refer to an individual who identifies as "having origins in any of the original peoples of Europe, North Africa, or the Middle East" (National Center for Education Statistics, n.d., para. 3). It is an inclusive term used both for those born in the United States and for those who have immigrated to the United States; it is used interchangeably with White.

- Hispanic refers to an individual who is Mexican, Puerto Rican, Cuban, Central or South American, or of another Spanish Culture or origin, regardless of race (National Center for Education Statistics, n.d.).

- Latino and Latina are ethnic and cultural terms used to refer to an individual who identifies as having Latino or Latin American heritage, regardless of ethnicity (Jamieson, 1995). Latinos may include individuals who are Mexican, Puerto Rican, Cuban, Central or South American, or of another Spanish Culture or origin, regardless of race (National Center for Education Statistics, n.d.).

- Middle Eastern is a general term used to refer to individuals who are Arab American (i.e., are members or descendants of Arab-speaking populations), Egyptian American, or Iranian American (those who speak Farsi or Persian) (Salimbene, 2005, p. 14). The U.S. Census counts Middle Easterners as White.

Periodically, the phrase *people of color* (rather than the term *minority*) is used as a collective voice for people who are African American or Black, Asian American or Pacific Islander American, Latino, or American Indian. The term *minority* is problematic because it may marginalize groups, identifying them as being somehow "less than" or "outside of the mainstream or dominant culture" (Andersen & Collins, 2007, p. xvii). At the same time, the phrase *people of color* can be differently problematic, since it categorizes entire ethnic and racial groups under one umbrella and thus may reflect less of a specific person's actual experiences (Andersen & Collins, 2007; Collins, 1994; Weston, 1991). The phrase may also depict Whiteness—or, more specifically, White people—as the unmarked (Frankenberg, 2008; Weston,

1991) normative center (Collins, 1994). For this reason, the phrase "non-White," which may be considered offensive, is not used. Would a woman be called a "non-man," indicating what she is not, rather than what she is (Tatum, 1997)?

Regardless of terminology, it is important to mention that the authors do not intend to make universal the unique and historical experiences of diverse people by grouping them in a category (Andersen & Collins, 2007). Categorization provides a means for discussing common experiences across different groups, allowing discussion and critical analysis of experiences of individuals and collective groups (Shingles, 2001). Similarly, for athletic trainers, it is important to think about how patients label or categorize themselves; if a group-identifying term is needed, the athletic trainer should ask the patient what term he or she prefers.

SUMMARY

According to Health Resources and Services Administration, "the process of integrating cultural competence into health care happens in different ways, at different levels, and in different settings " (2001). Cultural competence is a life-long journey that does not mean you are an authority on all cultures. Rather, it means that you are committed to respecting cultural differences, embracing similarities, and learning about and accepting that there are many world views on health and illness.

"Cultural competence is the ability to plan a safe and culturally effective" care plan for all people (Smallwood, 1997). Athletic trainers must become aware of the limitations of their cultural values, beliefs, and practices; obtain cultural knowledge; become open to cultural differences; and develop cultural skill. They must be willing to engage in cultural encounters and, above all else, *want* to (rather than have to) provide culturally competent care.

Learning Aids

What Would You Do If . . . ?

1. What if one of your colleagues called a young man a derogatory gay name after treating him?
2. What if your patient was a recent immigrant from France and she spoke English only as a second language?
3. What if you referred to your patient as Hispanic and he was offended because he preferred the term Latino?

Activities

1. Check out the U.S. Census at www.factfinder.census.gov (choose People in the left-hand column of options, then choose Race and Ethnicity) in order to determine the geographic areas of the United States where the majority of members of each of the following groups live: American Indians, Asian Americans, Blacks, Hispanics, and Whites. Then navigate the site to view information about the state in which you live. What are the racial, ethnic, gender, and income demographics?

2. Reexamine the CLAS standards listed earlier in the chapter (see pages 7-9), then choose one of the standards and brainstorm ideas about how it could be implemented in your health care profession.
3. Write your own definition of cultural competence.

Key Terms

Define the following key terms found in this chapter:

Cultural awareness   Cultural desire   Cultural knowledge
Cultural competence   Cultural encounter   Cultural skill

Questions for Review

1. Define cultural competence.
2. Why is it important to be culturally competent?
3. How is cultural competence developed?
4. List and explain the various theories of cultural competence.
5. What are the six assumptions and five constructs of Campinha-Bacote's model?
6. How are different racial and ethnic groups defined?

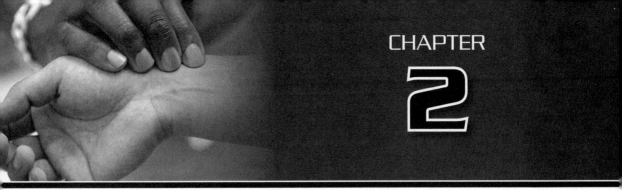

Cultural Beliefs and Practices

Learning Objectives

Upon completing this chapter, students will be able to do the following:

1. Define culture-bound syndromes
2. Define complementary and alternative medicine
3. Differentiate the domains of complementary and alternative medicine
4. Differentiate whole medical systems

Fabian J. De Rozario

I am the founder and CEO of Global Connect Enterprises LLC, a consulting and training firm that helps organizations and individuals tap into the power of connecting by understanding and making the most of cultural differences. I have presented workshops and keynote speeches in the areas of diversity, inclusion, communication, public speaking, personality styles, change management, and leadership at conferences, associations, Fortune 100 companies, and universities worldwide.

Photo courtesy of Fabian J. De Rozario

Groups and organizations that I have worked with include Delta Airlines, Cardinal Health, Pricewaterhouse Coopers, Radio Shack, PepsiCo, Philander Smith College, Marriott, Procter & Gamble, the U.S. Army Corps of Engineers, Capital One Bank, Abercrombie & Fitch, and CISCO. My 18 years of work and training experience spans higher education, association management, and private industry. Drawing on my experiences as an Asian immigrant to the United States, I use a presentation style that is interactive, engaging, and focused on enhancing personal skills to create world-class organizations.

I was born and raised in Malaysia and completed my secondary education at Fettes College in Edinburgh, Scotland. I arrived in the United States in 1982 and completed my bachelor's degrees in marketing and management, as well as a master's degree in parks and recreation administration at Southern Illinois University Carbondale. I have served in student services leadership and instructor positions at Northern Illinois University and the University of Arkansas at Little Rock. In Little Rock, I was named the first director of the University's Donaghey Student Center, a premier facility for student services, conferences, and fitness.

From 1998 to 2006, I served as director of U.S. university relations and director of global operations for the Golden Key International Honour Society and managed a budget of $3.7 million. Currently, I serve as an independent contractor consultant and lead facilitator with the Global Lead Management Consulting firm and with the Monster Leadership Program. I have received the Georgia Society of Association Executives President's Award and served as a board member for the group. I have also served as a faculty member of the National School of Recreational Sports Management and the Athletic Business Conference & Expo.

I am also active in the Asian community of Atlanta, which has the second-fastest-growing Asian population among U.S. cities. I am the co-founder and president of the Malaysian Association of Georgia and serve as secretary of the Asian/Pacific American Council of Georgia. I have been named an honoree of Who's Who in Asian American Communities in Georgia.

A patient's beliefs about the cause, signs, and symptoms of an illness or injury may not align with conventional Western medical diagnoses and treatment. The root of the problem may be based in cultural, spiritual, or folk beliefs and manifested in a physical, psychological, or emotional state. Likewise, patients' choices about how to seek care or treat themselves may not align with Western practices. As a result, athletic trainers need to be aware of various culture-bound syndromes that may present as general medical conditions or mental disorders as classified by Western medicine. Further, athletic trainers need to be aware of the complementary and alternative medicine (CAM) practices that their patients may be using. The purpose of studying culture-bound syndromes and CAM practices is to avoid misdiagnosing or mistreating patients.

CULTURE-BOUND SYNDROMES

Culture-bound syndromes are "features of an illness that vary from culture to culture" (Leff, as cited in Campinha-Bacote, 2003, p. 32). More specifically, appendix I of the American Psychiatric Association's *Diagnostic and Statistical Manual of Mental Disorders* (DSM-IV-TR) (2000) defines cultural-bound syndromes this way:

> recurrent, locality-specific patterns of aberrant behavior and troubling experience that may not be linked to a particular DSM-IV diagnostic category. Many of these patterns are indigenously considered to be "illnesses," or at least afflictions, and most have local names. . . . Culture-bound syndromes are generally limited to specific societies or cultural areas and are localized, folk, diagnostic categories that frame coherent meaning for certain repetitive, patterned, and troubling sets of experiences, and observations. (p. 898)

Athletic trainers must understand that many signs and symptoms of culture-bound syndromes are similar to other psychosocial and psychopathological conditions. It is critical to either identify and treat the culture-bound syndrome or refer the patient to another appropriate health care provider who can do so. For example, imagine a middle-aged, married Korean American woman from a lower economic class who reports symptoms of gastrointestinal distress (e.g., chronic indigestion, diarrhea, or constipation), hot flashes, headache or body ache, and feelings of helplessness or guilt. If the health care provider does not recognize the symptoms as possibly being hwa-byung (anger syndrome), then the patient may be misdiagnosed as having the flu, flulike symptoms, a stomach virus, or even depression. As a result, the patient may receive inappropriate treatment and culturally insensitive care. Similarly, a female athlete with a thin body build who runs cross country and has a history of multiple stress fractures and amenorrhea may have anorexia nervosa. This disorder, commonly seen among athletes, has origins in Western culture and other cultures undergoing Westernization (e.g., Japan), and it is believed to be a Western culture-bound syndrome (Andrews & Boyle, 2007). Keep in mind, however, that some groups may view the concept of a culture-bound syndrome as stereotypically imposed on them by a dominant culture. Thus it is critical to ask patients and family members if they think the presenting signs and symptoms are associated with or indicative of a particular culture-bound syndrome or folk illness.

The following descriptions of culture-bound syndromes from the DSM-IV-TR (American Psychological Association, 2000) are presented by geographic region or culture (Hall, 2006):

Culture-Bound Syndromes

East Asia

China and Taiwan

qi-gong psychotic reaction (China)—"acute, time-limited episode characterized by dissociative, paranoid, or other psychotic or nonpsychotic symptoms" (American Psychological Association, 2000, p. 902) that occur after participating in the health-enhancing Chinese folk practice of qi-gong.

shenjing shuairuo (China)—neurasthenia. Symptoms include "physical and mental fatigue, dizziness, headaches and other pains, concentration difficulties, sleep disturbance, and memory loss" (American Psychological Association, 2000, p. 902).

shenkui (China); also shen k'uei (Taiwan)—"marked anxiety or panic symptoms with accompanying somatic complaints for which no physical cause can be demonstrated. Symptoms include dizziness, backache, fatigability, general weakness, insomnia, frequent dreams, and complaints of sexual dysfunction (e.g., premature ejaculation and impotence). Symptoms are

(continued)

attributed to excessive semen loss from frequent intercourse, masturbation, nocturnal emission, or passing of 'white turbid urine' believed to contain semen. Excessive semen loss is feared because it represents the loss of one's vital essence and can thereby be life threatening" (American Psychological Association, 2000, p. 902).

Japan

imu (among the Ainu people in Sakhalin, Japan)—see *latah (Malaysia and Indonesia)*.

taijin kyofusho (Japan)—syndrome of intense fear that one's body, body parts, or bodily functions are displeasing, embarrassing, or "offensive to other people in appearance, odor, facial expression, or movement" (American Psychological Association, 2000, p. 903).

Korea

hwa-byung or wool-hwa-byung (HB)—folk syndrome "attributed to the suppression of anger" (Choi & Lee, 2007, p. 12). *Hwa* means "fire and anger" simultaneously, and *byung* means "illness," thus leading to the translations "fire illness" and "anger syndrome" (Roberts, Han, & Weed, 2006). "A variety of symptoms have been identified as indicative of HB. Pang (1990) describes the HB syndrome as involving gastrointestinal problems such as chronic indigestion, poor appetite, abdominal discomfort or pain, constipation, diarrhea, vomiting blood, and the feeling that there is a mass in the epigastrium. Additional somatic symptoms may include sensations of heat or hot flushes, heart palpitations, headaches, or body aches and pain (Park et al., 2001; Park, Kim, Schwartz-Barcott, & Kim, 2002). In addition to somatic symptoms, those afflicted with HB also present with psychiatric symptoms, including anxiety and depression, fear of impending death, general malaise, insomnia, feelings of helplessness, resentfulness, and guilt (Lin, 1983; Min, Lee, Kang, & Lee, 1987; Pang, 1990; Park et al., 2001, 2002)" (Roberts et al., p. 385).

shin-byung—syndrome "characterized by anxiety and somatic complaints (general weakness, dizziness, fear, loss of appetite, insomnia, and gastrointestinal problems)" (American Psychological Association, 2000, p. 902) followed by dissociation and experience of possession by ancestral spirits (American Psychological Association, 2000).

South and Southeast Asia

India, Sri Lanka

dhat and jiryan (India); sukra prameha (Sri Lanka); also shen k'uei (Taiwan)—semen-loss syndrome. Involves "severe anxiety and hypochondriacal concerns associated with discharge of semen" (American Psychological Association, 2000, p. 900).

Malaysia, Indonesia, and Thailand

amok (Malaysia)—"dissociative episode characterized by a period of brooding followed by an outburst of violent, aggressive, destructive, even homicidal behavior; typically seen in males" (American Psychological Association, 2000, p. 899).

bah-tschi, bah-tsi, and baah-ji (Thailand)—see *latah (Malaysia and Indonesia)*.

koro (Malaysia)—"episode of sudden, intense anxiety that the penis (or, in the rare female cases, the vulva and nipples) will recede into the body and possibly cause death" (American Psychological Association, 2000, p. 900).

latah (Malaysia and Indonesia)—"hypersensitivity to sudden fright, often with echopraxia, echolalia, command obedience, and dissociative or trance-like behavior" (American Psychological Association, 2000, p. 901). The Malaysian syndrome is more frequent in middle-aged women.

rok-joo (Thailand)—see *koro (Malaysia)*.

Philippines

mali-mali and silok (Philippines)—see *latah (Malaysia and Indonesia)*.

Africa

North Africa

zar (Ethiopia, Somalia, Egypt, Sudan, and elsewhere in North Africa, Iran, and other Middle Eastern Societies)—experience of spirit possession. Symptoms may include dissociative episodes accompanied by "shouting, laughing, hitting the head against a wall, singing, or weeping. Individuals may show apathy and withdrawal, refusing to eat or carry out daily tasks, or may develop a long-term relationship with the possessing spirit" (American Psychological Association, 2000, p. 903).

Sub-Saharan Africa

boufée delirante (West Africa and Haiti)—"sudden outburst of agitated and aggressive behavior, marked confusion, and psychomotor excitement. It may sometimes be accompanied by visual and auditory hallucinations or paranoid ideation" (American Psychological Association, 2000, pp. 898-900).

brain fag or brain fog (West Africa)—"condition experienced by high school or university students in response to the challenges of schooling. Symptoms include difficulties in concentrating, remembering, and thinking. . . . Additional symptoms center on the head and neck and include pain, pressure, tightness, blurring of vision, heat, or burning" (American Psychological Association, 2000, p. 900) and may be described as "brain fatigue."

(continued)

Mediterranean and Middle East

mal de ojo (Spain and Latin America)—the **"evil eye."** The evil eye is a glance believed to be capable of creating illness. "Symptoms include fitful sleep, crying without apparent cause, diarrhea, vomiting, and fever in a child or infant" (American Psychological Association, 2000, p. 901).

nevra (Greece)—see *nervios (Latin America)*.

sangue dormido (Portuguese Cape Verdeans)—literally means "sleeping blood." Symptoms include "pain, numbness, tremor, paralysis, convulsions, stroke, blindness, heart attack, infection, and miscarriage" (American Psychological Association, 2000, p. 902).

Latin America and the Caribbean

Caribbean

falling out or blacking out (Caribbean and southern United States)—episodes characterized by sudden collapse and fainting, often with hysterical blindness (American Psychological Association, 2000).

Latin America

ataque de nervios—idiom (i.e., expression) of distress reported principally among Latinos from the Caribbean but also among many Latin American and Latin Mediterranean groups. "Symptoms include uncontrollable shouting, attacks of crying, trembling, heat into the chest rising to the head, and verbal or physical aggression" (American Psychological Association, 2000, p. 899). Ataque de nervios frequently occur as a result of a stressful family event—especially the death of a relative, but also a divorce or fight with a family member (American Psychological Association, 2000).

bilis and colera (Latin America)—idiom of distress and explanation of physical or mental illness as a result of extreme emotion, which upsets the humors (described in terms of hot and cold.) Bilis and colera specifically implicate anger in the cause of illness (American Psychological Association, 2000).

locura (Latin America)—severe, chronic psychosis (American Psychological Association, 2000).

mal de pelea (Puerto Rico)—see *amok (Malaysia)*.

nervios (Latin America)—"Idiom of distress . . . referring to a general state of vulnerability to stressful life experiences and to a syndrome brought on by difficult life circumstances. [Symptoms may be very broad but commonly include] emotional distress, . . . headache, . . . irritability, stomach disturbance, sleep difficulty, nervousness, easy tearfulness, inability to concentrate, tingling sensations, and dizziness" (American Psychological Association, 2000, p. 901).

susto (principally Latinos in the United States and Latin America)—folk illness "attributed to a frightening event that causes the soul to leave the body and results in symptoms of unhappiness and sickness" (American

Psychological Association, 2000, p. 903). Symptoms are extremely variable and may occur months or years after the supposedly precipitating event. Alternate names include *"espanto, pasmo, tripa ida, perdida del alma,* and *chibih"* (American Psychological Association, 2000, p. 903).

United States, Canada, and Western Europe

anorexia nervosa (North America and Western Europe)—severe restriction of food intake, associated with morbid fear of obesity. Other methods may also be used to lose weight, including excessive exercise. This disorder may overlap with symptoms of bulimia nervosa (American Psychological Association, 2000).

bulimia nervosa (North America and Western Europe)—binge eating followed by purging through self-induced vomiting or use of laxatives or diuretics. Associated with morbid fear of obesity, this disorder may overlap with symptoms of anorexia nervosa (American Psychological Association, 2000).

Southern United States

rootwork (Caribbean and southern United States)—illness as the result of hexing, witchcraft, voodoo, or the influence of an evil person. "'Roots,' 'spells,' and 'hexes' can be 'put' or placed on other persons" (American Psychological Association, 2000, p. 902) in order to cause a variety of psychological or emotional problems until they are taken off by a root doctor (American Psychological Association, 2000).

spell (southern United States)—"trance state in which individuals experience communication with deceased relatives or with spirits" (American Psychological Association, 2000, p. 903).

Native American, Arctic, and Polynesian Peoples

Native Americans

ghost sickness (American Indian groups)—"preoccupation with death and the deceased, sometimes associated with witchcraft. . . . Symptoms may include bad dreams, weakness, feelings of danger, loss of appetite, fainting, dizziness, fear, anxiety, hallucination, loss of consciousness, confusion, feelings of futility, and a sense of suffocation" (American Psychological Association, 2000, p. 900).

iich'aa (Navajo)—see *amok (Malaysia).*

Eskimos and Arctic

pibloktoq (Greenland Eskimos)—"abrupt dissociative episode accompanied by extreme excitement of up to 30 minutes duration and frequently followed by convulsive seizures and coma lasting up to 12 hours" (American Psychological Association, 2000, p. 901).

Polynesia

cafard or cathard—see *amok (Malaysia).*

Evaluating and treating patients from diverse cultures can be challenging, particularly when the athletic trainer and patient are from different racial, ethnic, or cultural groups. In order to provide appropriate care or referral in such cases, the athletic trainer needs to understand the patient's signs and symptoms within the relevant cultural context. This list and description of culture-bound syndromes can serve as a resource for understanding and identifying signs and symptoms that may be described by patients during the history-taking portion of a physical assessment.

Although the DSM-IV-TR provides a description of culture-bound syndromes, it does not indicate how to treat them. As Simons (2001, unpaged) notes:

> because culture-bound syndromes are so varied, there can be no single type of diagnostic or therapeutic approach. For some patients, even the idea of therapy [psychological] seems ill-considered. In some cases, their behaviors are eccentricities that do not need treatment, and, for some people, the therapeutic approach that has nothing to do with any medical system may be most helpful and least disruptive. . . . [For example], sometimes the best therapy is a shamanistic healing ceremony, sometimes it is an antidepressant or antipsychotic, and sometimes it is an antibiotic. . . . The best therapy is that which deals with the problematic factor in the specific case.

COMPLEMENTARY AND ALTERNATIVE MEDICINE (CAM)

The National Center for Complementary and Alternative Medicine (NCCAM), located at the National Institutes of Health, is the leading agency for the U.S. government on scientific research into CAM (Spector, 2009). "CAM is a group of diverse medical and health care systems, practices, and products that are not presently considered to be part of conventional medicine" (National Center for Complementary and Alternative Medicine, 2007, p. 1). **Conventional medicine** consists of allopathy practiced by medical doctors (MDs), osteopathy practiced by doctors of osteopathy (DOs), and medicine practiced by their allied health professionals, such as athletic trainers, physical therapists, psychologists, and registered nurses. **Allopathic medicine** is based on proven, scientific methodology to determine value in the treatment of disease (Spector, 2009). **Osteopathic medicine** is "the art of curing without the use of surgery or drugs . . . and take[s] into account the relationship between body structure and organ functioning" (Spector, 2009, p. 97) when determining a diagnosis. **Complementary medicine** is used in conjunction with or in addition to conventional medicine; for example, aromatherapy may be used in addition to other medicines to help decrease a patient's discomfort following surgery. On the other hand, **alternative medicine** is used *in place of* or as a substitute for conventional medicine. An example of an alternative therapy is treating cancer by using a special diet or herbal medicine instead of undergoing radiation or chemotherapy (both of which are conventional approaches) recommended by a medical or osteopathic doctor. **Integrative medicine** "combines conventional and CAM treatments for which there is evidence of safety and effectiveness" (National Center for Complementary and Alternative Medicine, 2007, 2009a; Spector, 2009).

In 2002, a national survey revealed that 36 percent of adults in the United States used a form of CAM. When the definition of CAM included megavitamin therapy and prayer for health reasons, the number rose to 62 percent (Barnes, Powell-Griner, McFann, & Nahin, 2004), and Blacks, followed by Asians, were the most likely to use CAM defined in this way. Asians were also more likely to use CAM when megavitamin therapy and prayer were not included (figure 2.1), and women were more likely users than men (Barnes, Powell-Griner, et al., 2004).

Intercollegiate student athletes have been reported to use CAM at a higher rate than that of U.S. adults generally; specifically, student athletes most commonly used massage (38 percent), followed by chiropractic medicine (29 percent), lomilomi (a type of massage that combines prayer, breathing, and energy; 14 percent), and acupuncture (12 percent) (Nichols & Harrigan, 2006).

By 2007, the number of adults surveyed using CAM had risen to 38 percent, and the number of children using CAM was reported as 12 percent (Barnes, Bloom, & Nahin, 2008). Specifically, 50 percent of American Indian or Alaska Native, 43 percent of White, 40 percent of Asian, 26 percent of Black, and 24 percent of Hispanic adults used CAM. American Indian or Alaska Native and

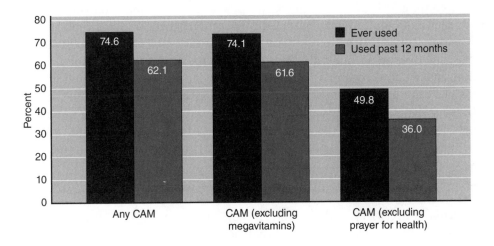

Figure 2.1 CAM usage in the United States (2002).

From P. Barnes, E. Powell-Griner, K. McFann, and R. Nahin, 2004, "Complementary and alternative medicine use among adults: United States, 2002," *CDC Advance Data Report #343*.

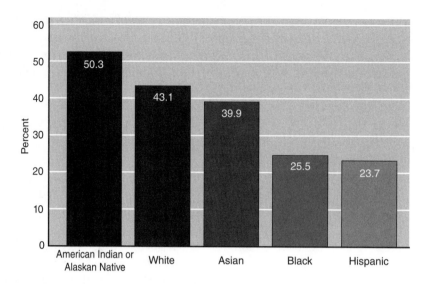

Figure 2.2 CAM usage by race and ethnicity (2007).

From P. Barnes, E. Powell-Griner, K. McFann, and R. Nahin, 2004, "Complementary and alternative medicine use among adults: United States, 2007," *CDC Advance Data Report #12.*

White adults were more likely to use CAM than Asian and Black adults (figure 2.2) (Barnes, Bloom, & Nahin). Women were still more likely to use CAM than were men, and people with higher levels of education and higher income were also more likely users.

According to NCCAM (2007), CAM practices involve four domains (some of which overlap) and several whole medical systems that cut across each of the Asian domains. The four domains are mind–body medicine, biological-based practices, manipulative and body-based practices, and energy medicine. **Whole medical systems**, which are comprehensive health care systems based on theory and practice, include (from Eastern cultures) traditional Chinese medicine (TCM) and the Asian Indian practice of Ayurveda and (from Western culture) homeopathic medicine and naturopathic medicine. What constitutes CAM practices continues to be an evolving definition. As some practices are deemed to be safe and effective by Western medical standards, they may be adopted as conventional medical practices. Likewise, new practices emerge. Some CAM practices, such as acupuncture for knee osteoarthritis (Berman et al., 2004), are supported by some scientific evidence. However, further research is necessary to determine efficacy and safety—as, for example, in the ongoing clinical trials on the use of echinacea for colds (Turner, Bauer, Woelkart, Hulsey, & Gangemi, 2005).

Athletic trainers need to become familiar with the differing CAM practices, determine the extent to which their patients are using such practices, and understand how CAM practices affect patient care and treatment. For example, if a particular CAM practice (e.g., massage) does not interfere with the treatment that the athletic trainer wishes to prescribe, then no cultural conflict arises, and the treatment should be allowed. If, however, the CAM practice is contraindicated, or will interfere with the athletic trainer's treatment plan, then the athletic trainer, the patient, and a CAM practitioner (if involved) should discuss treatment efficacy and determine the best course of action.

Mind–Body Medicine

Mind–body medicine "uses a variety of techniques designed to enhance the mind's capacity to affect bodily function and symptoms" (NCCAM, 2007, p. 2). Intervention strategies such as patient support groups and cognitive behavioral therapy have been adopted into conventional medical practices and are used to promote health. Examples of mind–body medicine include meditation, yoga, tai chi, qigong (pronounced /chee-GUNG/)—which are common in Asia—and prayer (NCCAM, 2007); more specifically, qigong, a practice similar to tai chi, combines movement, meditation, and controlled breathing to enhance the flow of energy in the body (NCCAM, 2009b). When prayer is included in the definition, mind–body medicine is the most commonly used CAM practice in the United States. In fact, in 2002, 53 percent of Americans used mind–body medicine (Barnes, Powell-Griner, et al., 2004). Among adults, the use of several mind–body medicine therapies has increased between 2002 and 2007—deep breathing from 11.6 percent to 12.7 percent, meditation from 7.5 percent to 9.4 percent, and yoga from 5.1 percent to 6.1 percent (Barnes, Bloom, & Nahin, 2008). Among adolescents, prayer was the third most common CAM practice used to treat asthma (Reznik, Ozuah, Franco, Cohen, & Motlow, 2002). In addition, "mind–body therapies have been applied to and studied for various types of pain. Results from clinical trials indicate that mind–body therapies may be effective additions to the treatment and management of arthritis, including rheumatoid arthritis and its pain" (NCCAM, 2005, no page given). However, more research is needed to determine which therapies are effective and how those work.

Biological-Based Practices

When prayer is *not* included, **biological-based practices** are the most commonly used CAM approaches in the United States (used by 27 percent of Americans) (Barnes, Bloom, & Nahin, 2008; Barnes, Powell-Griner, et al., 2004). Biological-based practices consist of herbs, foods, and vitamins found in nature; examples include the use of dietary supplements and herbal products, as well as aromatherapy. Among adults in 2007, the five most commonly used natural products were fish oil (omega-3 fatty acids), glucosamine, echinacea, flaxseed oil or pills, and ginseng (Barnes, Bloom, & Nahin). The most commonly used items among college athletes were creatine products, protein, and amino acids; the use of ephedrine, or herbs containing ephedrine (e.g., ma huang), has declined since 2002, when the National Collegiate Athletic Association began testing for the substance (Hosick, 2005).

Current research on biological-based practices has produced mixed results. For example, the use of echinacea was not found to prevent adult participants from catching a cold or to lessen the severity of a cold. However, critics contend that the dosage used in the study may have been too low and that further research is warranted to determine proper dosing (Turner et al., 2005). Green tea, on the other hand, was found to significantly reduce the severity of arthritis in rats; therefore, researchers recommend further study of green tea as a complement to conventional treatment of rheumatoid arthritis (Kim et al., 2008).

Manipulative and Body-Based Practices

Manipulative and body-based practices "focus on structures and systems of the body," including bones and joints, soft tissues, and the circulation and lymphatic systems. Manipulative and body-based practices are based on manipulation, which involves a passive, quick thrust of one articulating surface on another. The purpose is to realign the body in order to restore health. Practitioners of manipulative and body-based practices believe that the body is self-regulating, that it can heal itself, and that body parts are interdependent. Manipulation may be performed as part of other therapies, such as massage, reflexology, and the Feldenkrais method, which is a movement therapy using "verbal guidance and light touch to teach . . . awareness of how the body moves through space . . . [in order] to improve physical functioning" (Barnes, Bloom, & Nahin, p. 21). Manipulation and body-based practices have been commonly used to treat musculoskeletal injury and dysfunction. As was reported in a 2007 survey, Puerto Rican and Mexican American adults were more likely than Mexican adults to use biological-based and manipulative body-based practices (Barnes, Bloom, & Nahin). Manipulation may also be performed as part of whole medical systems such as chiropractic medicine and naturopathy, or as part of conventional medicine such as osteopathy (NCCAM, 2007). In fact, among all adults surveyed, 8.6 percent were likely to use chiropractic or osteopathic manipulation (Barnes, Bloom, & Nahin).

Energy Medicine

Energy medicine involves the use of two types of energy fields: biofields and bioelectromagnetic fields. Biofield therapies (i.e., putative energy fields where energy cannot be measured) are "intended to affect energy fields that purportedly surround and penetrate the human body" (NCCAM, 2007, p. 2). The existence of biofields has not been proven scientifically by Western standards. Some forms of energy therapy "manipulate biofields by applying pressure and/or manipulating the body by placing the hands in, or through, the fields" (NCCAM, 2007, p. 2). Acupuncture, a type of energy medicine, has been found to relieve chronic low back pain (NCCAM, 2009a). Other energy forms such as Reiki (a Japanese practice of touching) are believed to be channeled through the practitioner to heal the patient's spirit, thus healing the body. In therapeutic touch, the practitioner passes her or his hands over the patient's body with the intent of using the practitioner's "perceived healing energy to identify energy imbalances and promote health" (NCCAM, 2007, p. 4).

Bioelectromagnetic-based therapies (involving veritable energy, which can be measured) entail the unconventional use of electromagnetic fields, such as pulsed fields, magnetic fields (magnet therapy), sound therapy (e.g., the use of music, wind chimes, and tuning forks), and light therapy (NCCAM, 2007).

Whole Medical Systems

Whole medical systems are complete systems based in theory and practice; they use a combination of treatments in a holistic, systematic, theoretical approach in order to heal the patient. Whole medical systems may incorporate individual practices or therapies represented in the various domains of CAM.

Traditional Chinese medicine (TCM), the current term for the ancient system of medical practices that originated in China, is based on the belief that qi (pro- nounced /chee/), or vital energy that flows throughout the body, must remain balanced in order to maintain health. Disease results from a disruption of the flow of qi and an imbalance between yin (negative energy) and yang (positive energy). The objective is to bring yin and yang into harmony, thus restoring the flow of qi. Components of TCM include qigong (energy medicine and mind–body medicine), acupuncture (energy medicine), meditation (mind–body medicine), and herbal therapy (biological-based practice) (NCCAM, 2007).

Ayurveda (pronounced /ah-yur-VAY-dah/), is Hindu holistic medicine that originated in India more than 4,000 years ago. The literal meaning of *Ayurveda* is science or knowledge of life. The system integrates the mind, body, and spirit to prevent and treat disease and is considered a way of life. Ayurvedic medicine is the foundation of Chinese medicine (Spector, 2004) and includes the use of herbs (biological-based practice), nutrition (biological-based practice), yoga (mind–body medicine), and massage (manipulative and body-based practice) (NCCAM, 2007).

Homeopathic medicine originated in Germany. Homeopathy is based on the law of similars; in other words, like cures like. In this practice, patients are given a very small dose of a highly diluted medicinal substance that in larger, more con-centrated doses would cause the symptoms or disease (NCCAM, 2007). The small dosage is believed to provoke a healing response.

Naturopathic medicine also originated in Europe. Naturopathy is predicated on the belief that nature has the power to heal. In other words, it posits that self-healing occurs and that the body can establish, maintain, and restore health. Naturopaths use botanical medicine (biological-based practice), homeopathy (whole medical system), and nutrition (biological-based practice) to prevent and treat illness by identifying and removing the underlying cause of illness rather than by suppressing symptoms. Naturopathy is a licensed medical profession in 11 states and carries the degree of doctor of naturopathic medicine (ND) (Alternative Medicine Foundation,

2006; NCCAM, 2007). The use of naturopathy by adults increased in prevalence between 2002 and 2007 (Barnes, Bloom, & Nahin, 2008).

Complementary and alternative medicine is used by patients for several reasons. The most common reason cited was to improve health when combined with conventional medical treatment rather than as a replacement for conventional medicine (Barnes, Powell-Griner, et al., 2004). "While the use of these therapies [CAM] has increased from 2002 to 2007, scientific research provided only limited evidence of clinical efficacy for these therapies. For instance, the National Library of Medicine journal database, PubMed, identified 40 systematic reviews involving acupuncture, massage therapy, naturopathy, or yoga published between 2002 and 2007. Of these, only 10 (25 percent) of the systematic reviews found sufficient evidence to conclude that a given CAM therapy was effective for a given condition: acupuncture and yoga for back pain, acupuncture for knee pain (including osteoarthritis), acupuncture for insomnia, and acupuncture for nausea or vomiting (including postoperative, chemotherapy-induced, and pregnancy-induced). In addition, a systematic review concluded that both acupuncture and, to a lesser extent, massage therapy should be included among recommended therapies for treating back pain" (Barnes, Bloom, & Nahin, 2008, p.6). Regardless of the scientific evidence of the effectiveness of CAM therapies, if patients believe in a practice's efficacy and experience relief of symptoms, they are likely to use the treatment (Spector, 2009). Therefore, athletic trainers should talk with patients about their use of CAM in order to coordinate care and minimize contraindications.

SUMMARY

Cultural competence involves understanding patients from their perspective. In doing so, athletic trainers need to be aware of a patient's beliefs and practices that influence health care. For example, "many Vietnamese patients think that Western medicines are 'too strong' or 'hot' and upsetting [to] one's internal balance and [thus they] may self-adjust downward or take them [medications] only as needed" (McPhee, 2002, unpaged). They may also use herbal medicines in an effort to restore balance (McPhee). Reznik et al. (2002), found that prevalence of CAM use among their inner city adolescent participants was "twice the national average" (p. 1044) and that 21 percent used CAM instead of prescribed medicines for the treatment of asthma. "In clinical encounters, successful diagnosis and treatment may depend on practitioners [athletic trainers] tailoring care based on salient cultural characteristics of the population" (McPhee). Thus, it is essential to be aware of culture-bound syndromes and complementary and alternative medicine. For greater detail about specific racial and ethnic groups and their health care practices, see chapters 6 through 11.

Learning Aids

What Would You Do If . . . ?

1. What if your patient exhibited signs and symptoms suggestive of a culture-bound syndrome?

2. What if your patient—a baseball player with right shoulder pain who bats right-handed and thus rests his bat on his right shoulder while waiting for the pitch—told you that he believes his shoulder pain is caused by a "hex on the bat" rather than an injury. (Assume that evaluation and MRIs do not suggest an explanation for the injury.)

3. What if your patient was using a CAM practice with which you did not agree?

4. Imagine that a patient walks in complaining of elbow pain (tennis elbow), and upon inspection you notice three large ringlike bruises on the medial elbow. When you ask about the bruising, the patient informs you that she used cupping (a technique of traditional Chinese medicine) to treat the condition. Your patient is from China.

Activities

1. Pick a culture-bound syndrome or CAM practice and write a review of the relevant literature. Discuss the history, identify the culture of origin (if known), and discuss relevance for athletic trainers.

2. Pick a culture-bound syndrome or CAM practice and develop a fact sheet or FAQ (answers to frequently asked questions) that could be used by athletic trainers in a particular work place.

Key Terms

Define the following key terms found in this chapter:

Allopathic medicine	Integrative medicine
Alternative medicine	Manipulative and body-based practices
Ayurveda	Mind–body medicine
Biological-based practices	Naturopathic medicine
Complementary medicine	Osteopathic medicine
Conventional medicine	Traditional Chinese medicine
Energy medicine	Whole medical systems
Homeopathic medicine	

Questions for Review

1. Describe several culture-bound syndromes. Give the country or culture of origin for each and categorize them by similarity rather than by geographic region and culture.
2. What are the four domains of complementary and alternative medicine? Differentiate the domains from each other.
3. What are whole medical systems? How do whole medical systems differ from conventional medicine? Give examples.

Demographics and Health Disparities

Learning Objectives

Upon completing this chapter, students will be able to do the following:

1. Discuss changes in U.S. demographics
2. Provide examples of the relationship between demographic categories and health disparities
3. Describe several cultural competence techniques that might positively affect health disparities

---

Jeremy Marra, MS, ATC

I became a certified athletic trainer in 2006 after graduating with my BS in athletic training and sports medicine from Central Michigan University. After completing an internship at Florida Gulf Coast University, I enrolled at Michigan State University and earned an MS degree in kinesiology and physical medicine and rehabilitation. While at Michigan State, I completed a thesis assessing cultural competence of certified athletic trainers belonging to the National Athletic Trainers' Association.

I have always been drawn to athletics, and I knew that whatever career path I chose I would somehow be involved in sport and would work with physically active people. After sustaining an injury that ended my athletic career during my senior year of high school, I realized that I wanted to dedicate myself to helping others achieve. Athletic training gives me the opportunity to continually challenge myself through evaluation and therapy; it also allows me to be on the sideline again, this time providing professional medical advice.

My sport assignments over the past few years have given me the unique opportunity to work with athletes and colleagues from various countries, including Australia,

Photo courtesy of Joseph Marra.

Cuba, Ecuador, Ireland, Mexico, the Netherlands, Scotland, Spain, Trinidad, and Zimbabwe. Through working with these individuals, I have learned that health care professionals must be able to adapt. The biggest cultural barrier I have had to overcome has been language. For example, I worked with a field hockey team that carried four Dutch athletes on the roster and a Dutch head coach, all of whom spoke English as a second language. One athlete in particular, a first-year student, spoke very little English. After she sustained a serious ankle injury, we spent many hours of therapy together. She struggled to understand what doctors were telling her or how to perform certain exercises—so much so that occasionally one of her Dutch-speaking teammates was called on to translate. One of these teammates taught me certain Dutch words that would help the injured athlete understand what was happening, and this knowledge allowed me to communicate more effectively with her during follow-up appointments and rehab work. Throughout our time together, we became more able to understand each other's cultures, which helped her integrate into an English-speaking college and helped me develop stronger interpersonal skills for working with foreign athletes.

My family shares rich cultural traditions—my father is Italian and my mother Irish and Cherokee—and my experiences have taught me never to close my mind to new ideas and never to make assumptions. Culture and race are not the same thing. I have learned not to pass judgment based on a person's appearance, since cultural traditions vary greatly within most ethnic and racial groups—that's what makes each of our athletes or patients unique. As health care providers, we have the responsibility to these individuals to learn from their experiences and adapt our treatment to accommodate their needs—not expect them to adapt to us. Certified athletic trainers have the unique experience to work with a largely diverse population. As a professional, you must take advantage and grow from these experiences, continually using them while providing high-quality care.

"**Health disparities** are differences in the incidence, prevalence, mortality, burden of disease and other adverse health conditions or outcomes that exist among specific population groups" (Michigan Department of Community Health, 2007, p. 1). These differences can "occur by gender, race or ethnicity, education or income, disability, living in rural localities or sexual orientation" (Carter-Pokras & Baquet, 2002, p. 430). In the coming years, such disparities may be affected by a variety of health care challenges brought about by ongoing demographic changes taking place in the United States. This chapter discusses demographic trends, their relationship with disparities in access to health care, and ways in which the disparities might be resolved.

CHANGING DEMOGRAPHICS

This section discusses changes in racial and ethnic composition, language, income and poverty, and insurance coverage in the United States. Treatment of gender and geographic issues is woven throughout. Athletic trainers should understand that changing demographics may pose challenges rooted in the various linguistic, cultural, and social needs of a diverse populace.

Race and Ethnicity

Recent years have seen a racial and ethnic shift in the United States consisting of an increase in total population growth, higher growth rates for people of color, changes in the status of the largest minority group, and the growth of majority-minority states. According to the U.S. Census Bureau (2007a), from 2000 to 2005 the total U.S. population grew from 281 to 296 million for an increase of 5 percent. The slowest growth rate occurred among White people, while other groups grew as follows: Hispanic, 21 percent; Asian, 20 percent; Pacific Islander, 12 percent; American Indian and Alaskan Native, 7 percent; and Black, 6 percent. The make-up of the total population looked like this: non-Hispanic White, 198.4 million (67 percent); Hispanic (of any race), 42.7 million (14 percent); Black, 37.9 million (about 13 percent); Asian, 12.7 million (about 4 percent); American Indian and Alaskan Native, 2.9 million (1 percent); and Pacific Islander, 517,600 (0.2 percent). Thus, approximately 1 in 3 people in the United States were people of color, and Hispanics surpassed Blacks as the largest minority group. In 2005, Texas joined New Mexico, California, Hawaii, and the District of Columbia in having a majority-minority population. Other states close to having the majority of their population consist of people of color include Arizona, Georgia, Maryland, Mississippi, and New York, in each of which people of color currently make up approximately 40 percent of the population (U.S. Census Bureau, 2005).

In intercollegiate sport, the percentage of Division I minority athletes (men and women) in the National Collegiate Athletic Association (NCAA) increased from 31.5 percent in 1999-2000 to almost 34 percent in 2004-2005 (NCAA, 2006). On the other hand, the percentage of National Athletic Trainers' Association (NATA) members who are certified athletic trainers of color was only 10 percent in 2008, up 1 percentage point from 2005 (NATA, 2008). Thus, the athletic training profession is less diverse than at least one segment of its patient population.

Changes in the racial and ethnic composition of the United States are also affected by the number of immigrants living in the United States. An *immigrant* is a person who was not a U.S. citizen at birth. In 2004, 53 percent of immigrants living in the United States were from Latin America (i.e., the Caribbean, Central America, South America), 25 percent were from Asia, 14 percent were from Europe, and 8 percent were from other regions, including Northern America, Africa, and Oceania (U.S. Census Bureau, 2007a).

"Racial and ethnic minorities carry a disproportionate heavy burden due to health disparities" (Michigan Department of Community Health, 2007, p.1). Therefore, if health disparities are not addressed, an increase in the population, both domestic and through immigration, could exacerbate the problem of health disparities.

Language

From 2000 to 2005, the percentage of people in the United States over the age of 5 who spoke a language in the home other than English rose from 18 to 20 percent. Of those, 12 percent spoke Spanish, 4 percent spoke another Indo-European language, and 3 percent spoke an Asian or Pacific Islander language. Furthermore,

47 percent of those who spoke a language other than English indicated that they spoke English "less than well" (U.S. Census Bureau, 2007b). In 2000, the Asian American ethnic groups with the largest percentage of people who were not proficient in English included Cambodian, Hmong, or Laotian (44 percent); Vietnamese (40 percent); Korean (33 percent); and Chinese (32 percent) (Asian Nation, 2008). Of course, with an increase in the number of people who speak limited English comes an increase in the number of people who may experience a lack of access to health care due to language barriers. However, knowing which languages are more likely to be spoken in a given state or geographic region may help athletic trainers adequately prepare to meet the challenges.

Income and Poverty

In the United States, income varies by race and ethnicity, gender, and geographic region, among other variables. In 2005, **median household income** rose approximately 1 percent from the previous year to $46,300. Blacks had the lowest median household income at $30,900, and Asians had the highest at $61,100 (in 2000, the median family income for Asian Indians was $69,470 [Asian Nation, 2008]). The median household income was $50,800 for non-Hispanic Whites and $36,000 for Hispanics (U.S. Census Bureau, 2007a). Men who worked full-time and year-round in 2005 earned a real median income of $41,400, while women earned $31,900; thus women earned approximately 77 percent of what men did (U.S. Census Bureau, 2007a). Regionally, the median household income for the Northeast was the highest at $50,900. The second and third places were occupied by the West and Midwest, at $50,000 and $46,000 respectively. The lowest regional median household income was found in the South at $42,000 (U.S. Census Bureau, 2007a).

Poverty is said to exist when total family income falls below a particular threshold for money income, which includes income before taxes (e.g., earnings, unemployment, social security, dividends) but excludes capital gains and the value of noncash benefits (e.g., Medicaid, food stamps). The 2005 poverty threshold in the United States, as set by the U. S. Office of Management and Budget, was $19,806 for a family of four including two children. By this standard, the number of people living in poverty was 37 million, the number of families was 7.7 million, and the poverty rate was thus nearly 13 percent (U.S. Census Bureau, 2006, 2007a).

The racial and ethnic poverty rates of those 37 million Americans living in poverty in 2005 were as follows: 25 percent American Indian* and Alaskan Native*, 25 percent Black, 22 percent Hispanic, 12 percent Native Hawaiian*, 11 percent Asian, and 8 percent White (U.S. Census Bureau, 2006; *average over 3 years due to small population size). Although Asians as a group had the highest median household income and a relatively low poverty rate, many Asian American ethnic groups lived in poverty (e.g., 13 percent of Chinese; 14 percent of Vietnamese; 16 percent of Koreans; 17 percent of Pacific Islanders; and 22 of percent Cambodians, Hmong, and Laotians) (Asian Nation, 2008).

Poverty rates also varied by geographic region. The South and West had a higher percentage of people living in poverty (14 percent and 13 percent, respectively). The Midwest poverty rate was 11 percent, and the Northeast rate was 11 percent. Poverty rates were lowest for people living in suburban areas (9 percent) and highest for people living inside principal cities (17 percent). For people living outside metropolitan areas, the poverty rate was 15 percent (U.S. Census Bureau, 2007a).

It is important to understand demographic changes in income and poverty because low income and poverty are major causes of health disparities (Brach & Fraserirector, 2000); they affect health status (Starfield, 1992) and are "correlated with poor access to health care services and poor health outcomes" (Brach & Fraserirector, 2000, p. 188). For example, children who live in poverty are more likely to become ill than those who do not live in poverty. And once they become ill, poor children get sicker and die at higher rates than do children who are not poor (Starfield). Furthermore, people of color are disproportionately represented among those who have low income or are poor. Changes in demographics, then, have the potential to greatly affect health disparities.

Insurance

Between 2004 and 2005, both the number of people with insurance and the number of people without it grew. The number of people with insurance increased from 245.9 million to 247.3 million, while the number of people without insurance increased from 45.3 to 46.6 million. The percentage of people who were uninsured increased from 15.6 to 15.9 percent. "The Hispanic population had the highest uninsured rate" (U.S. Census Bureau, 2007a, p.1) (33 percent), followed by Blacks (20 percent), Asians (18 percent), and non-Hispanic Whites (11 percent). The percentage of children without insurance increased from 10.8 to 11.2 percent, and children between the ages of 12 and 17 years were more likely to be affected (U.S. Census Bureau, 2007a).

People who have insurance are covered by private or government insurance plans, or a combination of the two. Because people can be covered by more than one type of plan during a given year, the following percentages given for each type is not mutually exclusive. The private category includes people who were covered by any private plan (68 percent), whether employment-based (60 percent) or direct-purchase (9 percent). Government plans include people who were covered by any government plan (27 percent), whether Medicare (14 percent), Medicaid (13 percent), or military health care (4 percent). The likelihood of having health insurance rises with income (U.S. Census Bureau, 2007a).

As stated earlier in the chapter, "in the United States, racial and ethnic minority populations carry disproportionately heavy burden due to health disparities" (Michigan Department of Community Health, 2007, p. 1). The burden may be exacerbated by changes in demographic trends involving low income, poverty, and lack of insurance. Likewise, the burden is "manifested in increased risk for disease, delayed diagnosis, inaccessible and inadequate care, poor health outcomes and untimely death" (Michigan Department of Community Health).

RELATIONSHIP BETWEEN DEMOGRAPHICS AND HEALTH DISPARITIES

Healthy People 2010 is an initiative of the U.S. Department of Health and Human Services (DHHS; 2000a, 2000b) to increase the quality and years of healthy life and to eliminate health disparities. The 10 leading health indicators studied to determine health disparities are (1) physical activity, (2) overweight and obesity, (3) tobacco use, (4) substance abuse, (5) responsible sexual behavior, (6) mental health, (7) injury and violence, (8) environmental quality, (9) immunization, and (10) access to health care.

Changes in demographics could affect health disparities—including those associated with access to health care—as they are experienced by a given group. Therefore, this section focuses on access to health care. Some predictors of access to health care include having health insurance, a high income, and a regular primary care provider or other source of ongoing health care (DHHS, 2000b). The three primary obstacles hindering access to health care are financial, structural, and personal barriers.

Financial Barriers

Financial barriers include lacking health insurance, being underinsured, lacking coverage for certain medical services, having clinicians refuse to accept an insurance plan, and lacking income (DHHS, 2000a, 2000b). The increase in uninsured people and the fact that a substantial portion of the population lives below the poverty line lead, of course, to greater health disparity. For example, one of the highest uninsured rates, 40 percent, was found for Mexican Americans. Among "adults under age 65 years, 34 percent of those below the poverty level were uninsured" (DHHS, 2000a, p. 1-9). Furthermore,

> being uninsured has a large negative effect on almost all aspects of health care quality and access. In fact, among adults, the negative effects of being uninsured are typically larger than the effects of race, ethnicity, income, and education. Multivariate analyses suggest that lack of insurance is an important mediator of racial, ethnic, and socioeconomic disparities, although race, ethnicity, and socioeconomic position often have independent effects as well (Agency for Healthcare Research and Quality, 2007, p. 12).

Lack of insurance affects access to health care and whether people have a usual source of care (preventive, primary, and tertiary) or usual primary care provider. For instance, DHHS (2000a) reported that Hispanics (approximately 24 percent, and 28 percent of Mexican Americans), "young adults, and uninsured persons are least likely to have a usual source of care" (p. 1-7–1-8). Similarly, "disparities exist in access to a specific source of ongoing care. An average of 85 percent of adults identified a specific source of ongoing care in 1998, but the rate dropped to 76 percent for Hispanics and 77 percent for those below the poverty level" (DHHS, 2000a, p. 1-9). Likewise,

> uninsured people are less than half as likely as people with health insurance to have a primary care provider; to have received appropriate preventive care, such as recent mammograms or Pap tests; or to have had any recent medical visits. Lack of insurance also affects access to care for relatively serious medical conditions. Evidence suggests that lack of insurance over an extended period significantly increases the risk of premature death and that death rates among hospitalized patients without health insurance are significantly higher than among patients with insurance (DHHS, 2000a, p. 1-14).

Certain racial and ethnic groups in the United States tend to have higher numbers of uninsured people than others, thus reinforcing the fact that there is a relationship between demographics and lack of insurance. As a result, members of some demographic groups have limited access to health care.

Structural Barriers

A second kind of obstacle blocking access to health care involves **structural barriers**, which include lack of facilities and lack of nearby primary care providers or other health care providers (DHHS, 2000a, 2000b). For example, Blacks are less likely than Whites, and 18- to 24-year-olds are less likely than other age groups, to have a primary care provider (DHHS, 2000a). Particularly problematic issues include travel distance to providers, "lack of transportation, and the unavailability of specialists" (DHHS, 2000a, p. 1-23). The problem is magnified for Americans living in rural areas, who make up 20 percent of the population, while only 9 percent of physicians live in rural areas (Agency for Healthcare Research and Quality, 2005).

Another problem is the fact that only 10 percent of members of underrepresented racial and ethnic groups are health professionals. "Whites and Asians are overrepresented in the U.S. physician population. Whites comprise 69 percent of the U.S. population and 74 percent of the physician population; Asians comprise 3.6 percent of the U.S. population and 15 percent of the physician population. Hispanics, Blacks, Native Hawaiians and Other Pacific Islanders (NHOPIs) and AI/ANs [American Indians/Alaskan Natives] are underrepresented in the U.S. physician population, composing 12.6 percent, 12.1 percent, 0.1 percent and 0.7 percent of the U.S. population and 5 percent, 4.5 percent, 0.03 percent, and 0.2 percent of the physician population, respectively" (Agency for Healthcare Research and Quality, 2007 p. 11). People of color are also underrepresented in athletic training (10 percent of certified membership in 2008) and physical therapy (11 percent of membership in 2009) (NATA, 2008; American Physical Therapy Association, 2009). Studies have reported that health professionals of color are more likely to serve in geographic areas with high proportions of people of color and in or around areas with designated shortages (DHHS, 2000a).

Personal Barriers

Personal barriers to health care access include cultural and spiritual differences, language, sexual orientation, and concerns about confidentiality and discrimination (DHHS, 2000a, 2000b). "Provider–patient communication is directly linked to patient satisfaction, adherence, and, subsequently, health outcomes (Betancourt, Green, Carrillo, & Ananeh-Firempong, 2003, p. 297). For example, when physicians have not engaged in participatory and inclusive styles of decision making, African Americans have reported less satisfaction with the care they received (Betancourt et al.). In addition, the increase in people who speak a language other than English or who do not speak English well may create communication problems for patients and athletic trainers alike. Cultural factors have been reported as keeping some people from seeking care promptly at emergency departments, even when they are insured (DHHS, 2000a).

REDUCING HEALTH DISPARITIES

Brach and Fraserirector (2000) suggest eight cultural competence techniques that could help reduce health disparities for racial and ethnic groups. These techniques are as follows: interpreter services, recruitment and retention, cultural competence training, coordination with traditional healers, use of community health workers (including family and community members), culturally competent health promotion, immersion into another culture, and administrative and organizational accommodations. Many of these techniques are discussed in detail in chapters 12 and 14; several are discussed briefly in the following paragraphs.

• **Interpreter services:** As athletic trainers, it is important that we learn to access and use interpreter services. Such services—addressing foreign languages and American Sign Language—can improve communication with patients, which in turn helps the athletic trainer gain information about medical history, make accurate diagnoses, and help patients understand treatment regimens. Improved communication also helps patients navigate a health care system's intake process, referral mechanisms, and continuity of care (Betancourt et al., 2003). Interpreter services can also improve patient education and patients' care-seeking behavior (Brach & Fraserirector, 2000).

• **Recruitment and retention of health care providers of color:** Even more than the language translation provided by interpreters, the presence of athletic trainers from the patient's racial or ethnic group enables shared cultural understanding. Brach and Fraserirector (2000) suggest that shared group membership helps increase the quality of communication, rapport, and understanding of cultural nuances; it also reduces the chance of racial and ethnic discrimination, whether overt or unconscious. Some suggestions for recruitment and retention include the following: (1) establish scholarship, residency, and fellowship programs for people of color, (2) hire search firms owned by people of color, (3) expand affirmative action programs to recruit health care providers [athletic trainers] who match the racial and ethnic demographics of the patient population, (4) create a welcoming environment in which to work, (5) have senior executives mentor employees of color, (6) evaluate and compensate senior executives based on a process established to match hiring to community needs, and (7) assess employee satisfaction by racial and ethnic group (Brach and Fraserirector).

• **Cultural competence training:** Training has been demonstrated to change physicians' behavior and has been included in medical education (Brach & Fraserirector, 2000). It has also been found effective in improving knowledge, attitude, and skill in other health care providers (Beach et al., 2005). As a result, training should be included as a fundamental part of health care curricula and professional certification programs. When included in continuing education, training should be specific to the health care provider and relevant to the patient population (Horner et al., 2004). In athletic training, the National Athletic Trainers' Association has identified cultural competence as a foundational behavior that should permeate the curriculum (2006). However, more research is needed to determine whether cultural competence training affects patient outcomes other than patient satisfaction (Beach et al.).

• **Coordination with traditional healers:** Patients do not often tell their physicians or athletic trainers about their use of traditional healers. Brach and Fraserirector (2000) suggest that by "expressing familiarity with cultural beliefs, folk illnesses, and traditional practices and [by practicing] open nonjudgmental questioning, [practitioners] may be able to overcome [patients'] reluctance" (p. 199) to report their use of alternative or complementary practices. Thus athletic trainers should become aware of traditional healers in the community and, where possible, develop referral networks and direct collaboration opportunities (Brach and Fraserirector).

SUMMARY

Disparities related to race, ethnicity, and socioeconomic status still pervade the American health care system. "Although varying in magnitude by condition and population, disparities are observed in almost all aspects of health care" (Agency for Healthcare Research and Quality, 2007, p.2). Prevention and elimination of health care disparities requires coordinated action at the federal, state, and local levels aimed at extending the benefits of regional and community successes nationwide. Athletic trainers have a unique opportunity to bridge the gap in access to health care services, thus minimizing a key disparity. As health care providers employed in secondary schools, athletic trainers are, along with school nurses, often the first health care provider to render care, and need to understand that changing demographics "magnify the importance of addressing racial/ethnic disparities in health and health care" (Betancourt et al., 2003, p. 299). Certain groups are more likely to disproportionately experience financial, structural, and personal barriers to accessing health care, and the groups currently experiencing poor health status and outcomes are growing in relation to the total population (Betancourt et al.). As hypothesized in the REACH 2010 initiative, "if communities are provided time to plan and adequate resources they will eliminate health disparities" (Giles, 2007). Working together, America's patients, providers, purchasers, and policymakers can make full access to high-quality health care a reality for all people (Agency for Healthcare Research and Quality, 2007, p. 16). Those of us who are athletic trainers should do our part.

Learning Aids

What Would You Do If . . . ?

1. What if you lived in a community characterized by disparities in access to health care?
2. What if a substantial population of high school athletes in your care did not have health insurance?
3. What if you worked in rural America, the nearest hospital was 15 miles away, and there were no sports medicine doctors in your community or in the neighboring communities?

Activities

1. Search for demographic data (www.census.gov) and information about health disparities (www.healthypeople.gov) in your community. Discuss how the data are related to the health disparities. Discuss ways in which athletic trainers might help reduce the disparities.
2. Visit a public clinic or health facility. Observe the interaction between patients and health care workers. Speak with a member of the staff about the demographics of the community served, the health disparities, and the agency's efforts to reduce or eliminate the disparities.

Key Terms

Define the following key terms found in this chapter:

Financial barriers	Personal barriers
Health disparities	Poverty
Median household income	Structural barriers

Questions for Review

1. Describe the changes in U.S. demographics regarding race and ethnicity, language, income and poverty, and insurance.
2. What is a health disparity? How are health disparities related to demographics?
3. How might cultural competence techniques be used to reduce health disparities?

PART

II

Cultural
Awareness

In Campinha-Bacote's model, cultural awareness involves self-examination and exploration of one's cultural background. The purpose of part II of this book is to help you reflect, analyze, and engage in self-exploration. Chapter 4 addresses the concept of social location and how it informs one's views of and experiences in the social world. A case study is used throughout the chapter to help you better understand the relationship between social location and cultural competence. Chapter 5 is geared toward helping you conduct a self-assessment in order to determine your own social location, biases, and prejudices—and to understand that everyone has culture.

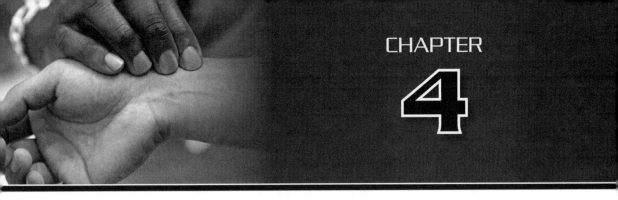

Understanding Difference

Learning Objectives

Upon completing this chapter, students will be able to do the following:

1. Define social location
2. Identify the factors that compose an individual's social location
3. Give examples of how these factors can affect the way in which health care providers view themselves
4. Give examples of how these factors can affect the way in which health care providers view and treat patients
5. Explain the relationship between social location and cultural competence

George Pujalte, MD

I was born on May 2, 1975, in Manila, Philippines. Since the age of 5, I had always wanted to become a doctor in order to follow in the footsteps of my father, who is an orthopedic surgeon. I was educated in the premiere science high school of the Philippines, the Philippine Science High School, then took up pre-med studies in biology at the University of the Philippines in Manila before pursuing the study of medicine at the same institution. I went on to serve as chief resident at Mount Sinai Hospital in Chicago and am currently doing my sports medicine fellowship at the University of Michigan. I have always been involved in medical and surgical missions in the Philippines, and I hope one day to return to the Philippines with the knowledge I have gained in the United States. My goals are to help indigent patients in the Philippines and improve the country's quality of medical care and education, particularly in the fields of primary care, sports medicine, and orthopedics.

Photo courtesy of George Pujalte

As health care providers, athletic trainers spend many hours with their patients (e.g., practice, competitions, performances) and often become confidants or advisors. However, the relationship does not occur in a vacuum. Every interaction is mediated by the **social location** of both the patient and the health care provider. Social location is one's position in, and place relative to, society; it may be based on differences in race, class, gender, sexuality, religion, geography, nationality, ability, or age. This chapter focuses on race, class, gender, sexuality, and religion. Social location informs how one sees, experiences, and understands the world (Shingles, 2001). As an athletic trainer, how does one's social location affect one's view of the athletic training and health care environments? How does one's social location affect the ways in which one interacts with people—namely, patients and colleagues—perceived to be of similar or different social location? In other words, how does it affect one's cultural competence?

As when carrying luggage on a trip, we each carry our social location and particular world view with us wherever we go (see figure 4.1). Thus patients and athletic trainers alike bring their own luggage into the health care environment. The question, then, is what happens when each person begins unpacking and exploring her or his luggage and that of others?

Figure 4.1 The process of developing cultural competence begins with unpacking one's luggage.

UNPACKING THE LUGGAGE

Just as unpacking luggage is a process, so too is developing cultural competence. As stated in chapter 1, the process of developing cultural competence takes time, energy, and commitment; it is an active, conscientious choice. The first step in the process involves engaging in cultural awareness, which entails an in-depth, self-examination. To begin the self-examination, the athletic trainer should identify and understand his or her social location. To help you with the unpacking process, this section discusses various components of social location: race, ethnicity, class, gender, sexuality, religion, and spirituality. In order to illustrate the relationship between social location and cultural competence, the case of a person we call "Jane" is referenced throughout the chapter.

Jane

Jane is an athletic trainer in a midsized, outpatient sports medicine clinic located on the East coast. She grew up in a small Midwestern farming community, where, aside from a few migrant families of Mexican descent, the townsfolk were Caucasian, as is Jane. She is a member of the Christian Reformed Church. She also believes that homosexuality is a sin against God.

Race and Ethnicity

Racial formation in the United States occurred as Europeans left their shores and encountered people who did not look and act as they did (Omi & Winant, 1994). In fact, James Baldwin suggested that "no one is white before he/she came to America. . . . It took generations, and a vast amount of coercion, before this became a white country" (as cited in Johnson, 2001, p. 21). The creation of racial categories is a transformational process. **Race is socially constructed**—its meaning changes over time based on systems of privilege and oppression (Johnson). It functions as a social marker of difference, differentiating treatment based on perceived physical characteristics. **Ethnicity**, which is different from race, involves the cultural heritage of a group. It may be based, for example, on common geographic region, language or dialect, migratory status, food, traditions, music, literature, kinship, race, religious faith, settlement and employment patterns, or internal sense or external perception of distinctiveness (Spector, 2004).

History

Racial groups have been defined differently throughout U. S. history, both socially and legally. In fact, the racial categories used by the U. S. Census have changed in every decade from 1889 to 2000. For example, in 1890, the categories were White, Black, Mulatto, Quadroon, Octoroon, Chinese, Japanese, and Indian. In 2000 and

2010, citizens could check as many categories as they wanted. Some of the categories were White, Black, African American or Negro, American Indian or Alaska Native, Asian Indian, Chinese, Filipino, Japanese, Korean, Vietnamese, Native Hawaiian, Guamanian or Chamorro, and Samoan. Spanish/Hispanic/Latino formed a separate category considered as an ethnic group whose members can be of any race (Davis, 2005; Schaefer, 2007; U. S. Census, 2010).

Just as racial groups overall have been redefined broadly, so too have individual groups, such as Whites and Blacks. At the initial time of immigration to America, the Irish, Italians, Greeks, Jews, and other people from Eastern and Southern European countries were considered "non-White" by Anglo-Saxon Protestants in England and the United States (Barrett & Roediger, 2005; Johnson, 2001). The immigrants were met with prejudice and scorn and were merely tolerated because they provided a source of cheap labor. After World War II, however, in the mid-1940s, the United States had a tremendous need for professional, technical, and managerial workers. The GI Bill of Rights provided veterans with the opportunity to obtain an education and move into the middle class (Brodkin, 2005). Over time, the new immigrants and their descendants acculturated into White culture, which provided additional means for upward social mobility (Diller, 2007). As stated by Rubin (2007),

> "Then, too, the immigrants—no matter how they were labeled, no matter how reviled they may have been—were ultimately assimilable, if for no other reason than that they were white. As they began to lose their alien ways, it became possible for native Americans to see in the white ethnics of yesteryear a reflection of themselves. Once the shift in perception occurred, it was possible for the nation to incorporate them, to take them in, chew them up, digest them, and spit them out as Americans—with subcultural variations not always to the liking of those who hoped to control the manners and mores of the day, to be sure, but still recognizably white Americans" (p. 192).

On the other hand, historically, African Americans were classified according to their amount of African Black ancestry, regardless of their White ancestry. For example, using historical terminology and phrasing, an offspring of a "pure" White and a "pure" African Negro (i.e., Black) was labeled a Mulatto, which means hybrid in Spanish. The offspring of a Mulatto and a White was labeled a Quadroon—the second-generation result of "mixing with Whites," who had three White grandparents and one Black grandparent. The third generation of mixing with Whites—the offspring of a Quadroon and a White—was called an Octoroon. Such a person usually looked White and had seven White great-grandparents and one Black great-grandparent. Neither Mulatto, Quadroon, nor Octoroon was considered White, because "any person with *any* known African black ancestry" (Davis, 2005, p. 5) was considered Black. This definition of who is Black developed out of American slavery, was sustained through Jim Crow segregation, and is maintained even today as the "one-drop rule," which holds that a single drop of "Black blood" makes you Black (Davis). The twist of the one-drop rule is that it applies only to American Blacks—no other groups. Likewise, it is applied only in the United States; it is not found in any other nation in the world (Davis). For a complete discussion of the one-drop rule and the definition of Blackness, see *Who is Black?* by James Davis.

Implications of Racial and Ethnic Differences

How does race affect the ability to provide culturally appropriate care? For example, for Jane (see case study on page 49) who is White, how does her social location shape her reality? How might she view patients and colleagues who are White and those who are not? How might her views affect how she treats them? Jane might say, "I don't see color. Mine or theirs, color is not important to me when treating patients." In a study of female certified athletic trainers from a variety of cultures (Asian/Asian American/Pacific Islander, American Indian/Native American, Hispanic, and Caucasian/White), Shingles (2001) found that race was not perceived by the athletic trainers to be important in the relationships they developed with their athletes or in how they treated their athletes. The majority of women studied were more likely than not to say that they "treated all athletes the same" regardless of race/ethnicity. However, African American women also tended to say that they shared a cultural connection with their African American athletes in particular, especially when working in a predominately White environment. The athletic trainers indicated that the athletes perceived them as someone with shared cultural values whom they could look up to as a role model and talk to about almost everything, including family issues and adapting to the classroom. American Indian or Native American, Asian and Pacific Islander, and Hispanic women athletic trainers rarely worked with athletes of their racial or ethnic group. However, when they did, they expressed a similar cultural connection. White or Caucasian female athletic trainers routinely worked with athletes in their racial group. Although their relationships were predominately positive, they did not overtly express having a cultural connection with their athletes (Shingles).

The notion of "color-blindness"—which may be taught in athletic training and health care curricula and constructed in society as politically correct behavior—is problematic. So too is the notion of "treating all athletes or patients the same." When athletic trainers are taught to treat injury and illness without regard to who is being treated, the assumption is that the injury (and subsequent treatment) occurred within a vacuum and not within a sociocultural context. For example, one might say that an ankle injury is an ankle injury, regardless of whose body the ankle is part of. But to assume that an ankle injury is disconnected from the person to whom the ankle is attached suggests a fragmentation of mind and body (Shingles, 2001). Such an assumption denies the patient's social reality and presupposes that racial, ethnic, and cultural differences are insignificant (Burton, 1995).

Social Class

Since **class** is socially constructed, it involves more than the amount of money one has amassed. Social class affects the way in which people dress, speak, and compose ideas; it affects where one works and lives, the type of car one drives (and whether a person owns a car at all), and the type of health care (if any) that one receives (Langston, 2007). Ehrenreich (1995) and Langston contend that the lasting myth of the United States as a classless society allows the ruling class to maintain the status quo. In fact, "the richest 10 percent of the U.S. population holds more than two-thirds of all the wealth, including almost 90 percent of cash, almost half the land, more than 90 percent of business assets, and almost all stocks and bonds" (Johnson, 2001, p. 45). On the other hand, in 2005, 37 million people (13 percent of the population) and 7.7 million families lived in poverty (U.S. Census Bureau, 2006). Of those 37 million, about 25 percent were American Indian* or Alaskan Native,* 25 percent Black, 22 percent Hispanic, 12 percent Native Hawaiian,* 11 percent Asian, and 8 percent White (U.S. Census Bureau; *average over three years due to small population size). U.S. Census data suggest that social class is linked to race, because many racial and ethnic minority groups are disproportionately represented at or below the poverty level (Sue & Sue, 2008).

In health care, classism is manifested through lack of access, lack of opportunity, and socioeconomic conditions. For example, poor people (those with total family income below 100 percent of the federal poverty level) received lower-quality care and less access to care than did high-income people (those having family income above 400 percent of the federal poverty level) (Agency for Healthcare Research and Quality, 2007). The disparity in health care is associated with the poor lacking a source of ongoing care, lacking a usual primary care provider, and experiencing an inability to access care or a delay in receiving care (Agency for Healthcare Research and Quality). Furthermore, as of the most recent census data, one of every six people in the United States is uninsured—specifically, one in three American Indians,* Alaskan Natives,* and Hispanics; one in four Native Hawaiians*; one in five Asians and Blacks; and one in nine Whites. Likewise, one of every nine children is uninsured (U.S. Census Bureau, 2006; *average over three years due to small population size). Lack of health insurance produces a large negative impact; it decreases access to and opportunity for high-quality health care (Agency for Healthcare Research and Quality, 2007). When provided, however, the services of an athletic trainer are typically free of charge to athletes at the high school, collegiate, and professional sport levels. Salaries of athletic trainers are paid by the employer, and services are not typically reimbursed by the athlete or third-party payers, such as insurance companies.

How might Jane's social class shape the ways in which she views and treats patients? Here is one example—an excerpt from an athletic training student's reflective journal entry on how people from a different class are viewed:

> One question in particular that sticks out in my mind asked what ethnic group makes me the most uncomfortable and why. I knew right away my answer but it took me a few moments to explain my reasoning. I came to the conclusion that it was not any one ethnic group in particular that made me the most uncomfortable to be around, but rather a certain social class. Throughout my life I have found myself to instinctively put up my guard or avoid eye contact with those from lower class societies, regardless of their ethnicity or culture. My realization of this bothered me because I have never been one to judge a person's character based on their social status or income. . . . I thought more about my answer and found that my upbringing and way of life is very different from people living on welfare and in lower class, therefore there is a difference in culture. I was

raised in a comfortable suburban neighborhood, ranked in the top five safest cities in America, and those in poverty grow up around crime everyday [sic]. My little cousins who are in fifth grade, first grade, and kindergarten live in poverty, and already I notice how their daily living situations are influencing their personalities and culture. For Christmas my cousins all received a copy of the Soulja Boy cd, whereas if I were their age, I probably would have gotten the Hannah Montana album. I can already see how my culture varies vastly from my cousins', even at their tender ages. These kids will grow up learning to be tough in order to survive, and it is this "toughness" that makes me the most uncomfortable.

In the journal excerpt, the athletic training student wrote about being uncomfortable around people "from lower class societies, regardless of their ethnicity or culture" and noted "instinctively put[ting] up my guard or avoid[ing] eye contact." The student also wrote about feeling uncomfortable when confronted with the "toughness" associated with surviving in harsh circumstances. As a future athletic trainer, the student might create barriers between self and patient due to this lack of comfort and the associated body language ("putting up my guard"). This kind of nonverbal communication might be perceived by patients as a lack of respect (Robert Wood Johnson Foundation, 2007), and such barriers could render the athletic trainer ineffective. At the extreme, the athletic trainer might even choose not to treat patients perceived to be from a lower class in order to avoid feeling uncomfortable.

It is important for athletic trainers to "understand how poverty affects the lives of people who lack financial resources" (Sue & Sue, 2008, p. 151). Unintended class bias or classism affects an athletic trainer's ability to deliver appropriate services, from accurate assessment through to diagnosis and treatment (Sue & Sue).

Gender

As with race and social class, the social construction of gender has evolved from biological theory to a view of gender as differentiated and hierarchical, and from there to a conception of gender as a social institution (Lorber, 1994). **Gender** is different from biological sex in that gender refers to social practices, rituals, and learned behaviors (Shingles, 2001). Such differences were historically posited in Western society as being binary—that is, either one or the other (man or woman). Some societies posit a third gender or alternate genders, such as two-spirits (berdaches), hijras, or xaniths, who are biologically male but dress, behave, and are treated as women. Some African and American Indian societies include "manly hearted" women, who are biologically female but work and marry as men, due to their economic status (Lorber). For a continued discussion of berdaches, read *The Zuni Man-Woman* by Will Roscoe (1992).

Another gender category is transgender. As a term, transgender is usually associated with "people whose appearance and/or behaviors do not conform" (Crooks & Baur, 2008, p. 62) to the historical gender roles of man and woman and who do not want to change their biological sex. Transgendered identities include transvestitism (usually cross-dressing to achieve sexual arousal); assuming the role of a drag queen or drag king (usually cross-dressing to achieve psychosocial gratification or to entertain [Crooks & Baur, 2008]); gender bending (as done by radical faeries, tranny bois, and tranny girlz); and questioning (questioning one's gender identity) (DeMark, 2007). The term transsexual, different from transgender, is usually associated with people who want to change their biological sex. However, someone who is transsexual may cross-dress to conform to one's sense of self by wearing clothing that is deemed as normal and congruent with self-identity (Denny, Green, & Cole, 2007).

Biological sex is determined by sex chromosomes and refers to differences in external genitalia and reproductive organs, which are ascribed as female or male. Historically, biological theories purported that men were naturally superior to women. In this paradigm, men were born to be strong and aggressive, and women were born to nurture (Crooks & Baur, 2008). Women were also considered too weak to engage in physical activity, because to do so would damage the uterus, thus endangering procreation (Coakley, 2004). Once the biological myth of the male/female (strong/weak) binary and associated gender roles was dispelled, other theories evolved.

Based on ideology, gender was then reconstructed as society redefined femininity and masculinity and ascribed different behaviors to each gender. For example, men were to work outside the home, while women were to work within it. "Making men and women *different* from one another is the essence of gender. It is also the basis of men's power and domination" (Baca Zinn, Hondagneu-Sotelo, & Messner, 2005, p. 2). Theorizing gender in terms of differences between women and men thus served to treat each as a homogenous category in conflict with the other.

Among others, Lorber (1994) argued that gender as a social institution was used to "construct women as a group to be subordinate to men as a group" (p. 35). Connell (1992), while not denying that male authority was evident and socially constructed, nonetheless argued that there was a "gender order" within masculinities—that is to say, masculinity was not fixed. Rather, masculinities are expressed differently depending on one's social location. Therefore, subordination is relative (i.e., changes with circumstances) and relational to race, social class, and sexuality.

How might Jane's gender affect the ways in which she treats her patients? She might treat women differently than she treats men because of her gender, the gender of a given patient, and each person's notions of gender roles. For example, in a study of female athletic trainers, the women interviewed expressed that their relationships with female athletes were more informal or comfortable than were their relationships with male athletes. "Women athletes wanted the athletic trainers to get to know them" and were more likely to "divulge more things." One female athletic trainer indicated that she "could gossip with the girls." On the other hand, the interaction with men athletes was considered "professional" by some women. In other words, the women had to watch what they said around the men, because their words and actions might be misinterpreted as sexual (Shingles, 2001).

Jane might also believe racialized stereotypes about women and thus respond inappropriately and treat the patient ineffectively. For example, Retha Powers (1989), an overweight Black woman, struggled with compulsive overeating and dieting. When she divulged her struggles to a white female high school counselor, the counselor said, "You don't have to worry about feeling attractive or sexy because Black women aren't seen as sex objects, but as women. . . . Also, fat is more acceptable in the Black community—that's another reason you don't have to worry about it [battle with compulsive overeating]" (Powers, 1989, pp. 78, 134). The counselor's "presumption of Black women's strength and physical deviance completely overshadows and rejects Powers' reality of having an eating problem" (Beauboeuf-Lafontant, 2005, p. 87).

Regardless of gender, athletic trainers need to be careful not to assume gender roles or make sexist assumptions. If a patient identifies as a man or as male, refer to the patient as *him* and *he*. Likewise, if the patient self-identifies as a woman or as female, use *her* and *she*. If an athletic trainer is unsure of a patient's gender or sexual identity, one should ask, keeping in mind that such information is privileged and confidential (Crooks & Baur, 2008).

Sexuality

The more progressive discourses on **sexuality** have shifted from deviance to lifestyle to social construction (Baca Zinn et al., 2005). In the social construction paradigm, sexuality is no longer thought of as dualistic or universal, such as homosexuality versus heterosexuality. Rather, sexualities are viewed on a continuum based on behaviors, identities, and ideologies. They include gay, lesbian, bisexual, transsexual, down-low (in which men have sex with men and women but do not consider themselves gay or bisexual), straight, and questioning (DeMark, 2007). Sexual experiences and attitudes are shaped by gender, race, age, culture, and nationality (Baca Zinn et al.). Sexualities provide a "potential source of both pleasure *and* danger, both empowerment *and* oppression" (Baca Zinn et al., p. 159)—for example loving relationships (pleasure), rape (danger), sexual freedom (empowerment), and prostitution (oppression).

Heterosexism, consisting of "the institutionalized structures and beliefs that define and enforce heterosexual behavior as the only natural and permissible form of sexual expression" (Andersen & Collins, 1995, p. 6), can be seen as a system of oppression that affects everyone. In a society where heterosexuality is privileged, valued, and rewarded while all other sexualities are stigmatized and punished (Griffin, 1998), how might Jane's sexuality affect the ways in which she treats patients? If Jane is heterosexual, she might erroneously assume that a patient is also heterosexual and thus ignore the patient's actual needs. For example, if a female patient indicates that she is sexually active, Jane might ask if she is using a contraceptive method. If the patient says no, then Jane might ask, "Are you trying to become pregnant?" The patient again says no, and Jane discusses issues of preventing unwanted pregnancy and provides information about several forms of contraceptive. By failing to realize that the patient is sexually active with another female, Jane provides inappropriate advice. Therefore, Jane should directly ask about sexuality in order to provide appropriate counsel and treatment, but then keep the information confidential. As with gender and sexual identity, information about a patient's or athlete's sexuality is privileged and confidential.

Religion and Spirituality

"Religion and social class play a huge role in my eyes with a person's desire to know their identity. For me, I choose to seek judgment of how to treat others in the Bible through my identity with Christ" (excerpt from an athletic training student's reflective journal entry).

Religion can be defined as an organized set of beliefs, practices, and ethical values focused on a "divine or superhuman power or powers to be obeyed and worshiped as the creator(s) and ruler(s) of the universe" (Abramson, as cited in Spector, 2000, p. 81). As distinct from religion, **spirituality** may be viewed "as primarily relational—a transcendent relationship with that which is sacred in life (Walsh, 2000) or with something divine beyond the self (Emmons, 1999)" (as cited in Miller & Thoresen, 2003, p. 27). The U. S. Census Bureau does not collect demographic data about religious affiliation (doing so is prohibited by law). However, in 2001, there were an estimated 160 million self-identified Christian adults in America. Of those who identified as Christian, the top five religious groups were Catholic (about 51 million), Baptist (34 million), Methodist/Wesleyan (14 million), Lutheran (9.5 million), and Presbyterian (6 million). Americans who identified with other religions totaled about 8 million, and the top groups in this category were Jewish (about 3 million), Muslim/Islamic (1 million), and Buddhist (1 million) (Info Please, 2007). In 2007, about three-quarters of Americans identified as Christian (51 percent Protestant, 24 percent Catholic, 1.7 percent Mormon), and about 5 percent identified as being in other religions, which included Judaism (1.7 percent), Buddhism (0.7 percent), and Muslim/Islam (0.6 percent). About 16 percent of Americans were unaffiliated with a religion (PEW Forum on Religion and Public Life, 2008).

Churches, mosques, temples, and other places of worship are agencies of socialization that teach their members how to behave. As religious organizations, they provide a frame of reference and meaning, based on doctrine, for why health and illness occur, and how to treat others. For example, some occupational therapists who considered themselves to be religious were more likely to pray for a client and use spiritual language with a client (Taylor, Mitchell, Kenan, & Tacker, 2000). They were also more likely to have a positive view of spirituality in the practice of occupational therapy. Similarly, in a nationwide study of 2000 physicians, 55 percent indicated that "their religious beliefs influence[d] their practice of medicine" (Curlin, Lantos, Roach, Sellergren, & Chin, 2005).

Given that Jane is religious, how might her religious beliefs affect the ways in which she views and treats patients? Jane might believe that religious teachings "are related to health in that adherence to a religious code is conducive to spiritual harmony and health. [In this light, Jane might view illness as] punishment for the violation of religious codes and morals" (Spector, 2000, p. 82). Thus it is possible that Jane might believe that an injured or ill patient is suffering justly; as a result, Jane might not be sympathetic or treat the patient positively. She might push or impose her personal religious beliefs onto the patient. On the other hand, Jane might find through her religious beliefs that it is incumbent on her to help others in need. She might also feel comfortable helping patients deal with religious questions and issues (Egan & Swedersky, 2003) or choose to refer the patient to appropriate spiritual or religious leaders.

REPACKING THE LUGGAGE
Intersection of Race, Class, Gender, Sexuality, and Religion

One cannot always separate pieces of one's cultural luggage. To do so would be akin to disassembling a piece of travel luggage. For example, during the 2008 U.S. presidential campaign season, many pundits argued that African Americans would support Barack Obama, whereas women, particularly those older than 35, would support Hillary Clinton. If this were so, then one of the authors of this text, who happens to be an African American woman over the age of 35, would, if voting for a Democrat, be left in an impossible quandary! It raises the question, "Which part of me do they want—my African American half or my woman half?" In reality, of course, the two cannot be separated. Similarly, Jane cannot be torn apart from her conservative Christian upbringing as a straight White person in a farming community. Her "class and race privilege may blind her to issues of race and class, or her experience of gender inequality may foster the illusion that this automatically prepares her to know everything she needs to know about other forms of privilege and oppression" (Johnson, 2001, p. 52). Thus fragmentation ignores the complexities, social realities, and experiences of people at different social locations that intersect race, ethnicity, class, gender, sexuality, and religion. Fragmentation also presupposes that social categories are dichotomous or dualistic—that is, it hinges on "either/or" thinking (Andersen & Collins, 1995; Collins, 1991), in which gender means either woman or man and sexuality means either straight or gay. When forced into a dichotomy, social locations become dependent on their polar opposites. The assumption is that one side of the dichotomy is superior to the other, which does not recognize the interlocking dimensions of social inequality (Baca Zinn & Dill, 2005).

In health care, for example, social locations intersect in such a way that men may have different realities. Men may be both privileged and disempowered simultaneously, rather than either privileged or disempowered. Working-class White men, gay Chicano men, and middle-class African men may all enjoy gender privilege, but the privileges may or may not be fully realized, experienced, or perceived when they intersect with class, sexuality, ethnicity, and race (Messner & Sabo, 1990). In the movie *Crash*, the White male police officer played by Matt Dillon is empowered by race and gender when he sexually assaults an African American woman (played by Thandie Newton) during a traffic stop. However, his race and gender do not empower him in his interactions with a different African American woman (played by Loretta Devine) who prevents him from obtaining health care for his sick, working-class father. Nor did race and gender privilege prevent Lindsy McLean—the real-life, longtime head athletic trainer for the San Francisco 49ers football team—from being abused because of his sexuality. McClean is a member of the National Athletic Trainers' Association Hall of Fame, yet he was victimized because he is gay, "starting in the early '90s, when a 350-pound lineman would chase him around, grab him from behind, push him against a locker and simulate rape" (Bull, 2004, p. 93).

SUMMARY

Class (Ehrenreich, 1995; Langston, 2007), race (Omi & Winant, 1994), gender (Connell, 1992; Lorber, 1994), and sexuality (Jordan, 1995) are socially constructed. The meaning of social locations such as race, gender, and sexuality have evolved and changed throughout history in relation to differing social contexts, as well as religious and scientific movements. "The dominant categories are the hegemonic ideals, taken so for granted as the way things should be that white is not ordinarily thought of as a race, middle class as a class, or men as a gender" (Lorber, 1994, p. 33). However, gender, race, ethnicity, class, and sexuality should be examined relationally and juxtaposed with power relations in order to better understand the unique experiences within context (Smith, 1992). Athletic trainers and their patients may view health, fitness, and illness differently based on social location, and they may construct different types of meanings in life and career experiences. Therefore, the athletic trainer must understand how one's social location affects one's view of the social world and one's treatment of patients. As a graduate athletic training student wrote, "It makes a big difference knowing your athlete and their social status. . . . It makes a big difference with how the athlete deals with serious injuries and their attitude toward rehabilitation. You want to be able to talk to the athlete [patient] and understand their concerns and questions" (as cited in Biddington, 2007, p. 72).

Learning Aids

What Would You Do If . . . ?

1. What if a cross country runner in her first year of high school confides in you, the athletic trainer, that she thinks she might be gay? You are a closeted lesbian.

2. What if you were Korean American and learned from your grandfather that when Japanese forces invaded Korea they decimated your family? You are now an athletic trainer with Japanese American patients.

3. What if during a meeting with colleagues one of the men in the group responds to a comment by saying, "That's so gay"?

4. What if you were the only female traveling with the male basketball team to a game and several team members began telling derogatory stories and jokes about Asian and Pacific Islander women. You are Filipino American.

5. What if a man applies for the position of head strength and conditioning coach at your college? You are an athletic trainer whose religious beliefs are such that you believe homosexuality is a sin, you are on the search committee, and you happen to know that the man is gay.

Activities

1. Define your social location.
2. Observe your athletic training environment for 2 weeks, then answer the following question: How might your social location affect your practice as an athletic trainer and your ability to provide culturally competent care?

Key Terms

Define the following key terms found in this chapter:

Class	Race	Social location
Ethnicity	Religion	Socially constructed
Gender	Sexuality	Spirituality
Heterosexism		

Questions for Review

1. What is social location?
2. What factors make up an individual's social location?
3. Describe what it means for race, class, gender, and sexuality to be socially constructed.
4. Give several examples of how social locations can affect the treatment of patients in athletic training or other health care situations.
5. Discuss the concepts unpacking and repacking cultural luggage.

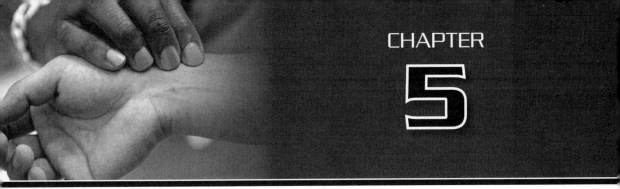

Understanding Self

Learning Objectives

Upon completing this chapter, students will be able to do the following:

1. Conduct a self-assessment
2. Define *culture* and discuss it relative to feeling cultureless
3. Define *generalization*, *stereotype*, and *prejudice* and give examples of each
4. Define *advantage*, *disadvantage*, and *privilege* and give examples of each

Veronica Ampey MS, ATC

I am a BOC-certified athletic trainer with an undergraduate degree in health fitness in corporate and hospital settings from Central Michigan University and a master's degree in sport science from the United States Sports Academy. I have been employed as an athletic trainer for the past 20 years in both collegiate and secondary school settings.

Like many, I began my undergraduate experience as a pre-med major. As I began to seriously contemplate a career in health care, I initially considered traditional medicine and physical therapy. Further research introduced me to able-bodied rehabilitation as an allied health field. I have appreciated the ability to intertwine my love of sport and health to build not just a job but also a career. Athletic training, regardless of the setting, is an exciting and highly challenging career that I am glad I discovered.

I don't feel that I've experienced blatant racism as a health care professional. Nonetheless, as an African American female, many cultural experiences have affected me. Several years ago, for example, a White faculty member visited my athletic training room. During the course of our conversation, she digressed and commented on a small, well-known photograph of Malcolm X that was pinned to a corkboard near my desk: "Doesn't that picture of that scowling Black man disturb you?" Though I can no longer recollect the reason for the visit, I clearly recall the ensuing dialogue that I used as a convenient teachable moment! I've also been faced

Photo courtesy of NATA.

with the challenge of promoting treatment compliance in athletes accustomed to nontraditional or alternative approaches and the dilemma of addressing religious practices that seem contradictory to participation in competitive athletics. In these instances, I've learned about such varied subjects as arnica (an herb), traditional Chinese medicine, and Ramadan.

The United States has increasingly become a melting pot of—among other things—diverse races, religions, and cultures. Thus an inability to keep an open mind will likely be detrimental to anyone working with an individual or a population who differs from what is reflected in one's own mirror. On the other hand, the ability to step outside of your comfort zone, and the willingness to learn and experience new and different things, will prove to be of great advantage to anyone in a health care profession.

Before one can understand others, one must understand oneself. As one nursing student wrote in a journal:

I feel as if I have been asleep my whole life. I didn't realize who I was, what I believed, or where I was going. I now know what I value about myself and my profession and what I need to do to practice from a culturally sensitive and competent perspective (St. Clair & McKenry, 1999, p. 233).

In order to understand themselves, athletic trainers should engage in active cultural awareness and self-assessment. They should examine their culture, beliefs, and values and work to understand the nature of generalizations, stereotypes, and prejudices—and their effect on people. Finally, athletic trainers should understand their social location (as discussed in chapter 4) and their advantages, disadvantages, and privileges relative to their patients and the social world. The purpose of understanding oneself is to learn the effect of one's values on interactions with others in order to minimize the risk of imposing one's values, beliefs, and behaviors on others (Campinha-Bacote, 2007).

CULTURAL AWARENESS AND SELF-ASSESSMENT

Cultural awareness is defined as "self-examination and in-depth exploration of one's own cultural background" (Campinha-Bacote, 2003, p. 18). Before one can gain cultural knowledge about others and understand the effect of culture on their lives, it is important to understand oneself. In doing so, it is important to determine how one's lived (embodied) experiences (or lack thereof), social location, culture, and family traditions might help or hinder one's efforts to provide culturally competent care. For specific questions to ask, see the self-assessment example in the sidebar.

Culture is important in athletic training because it influences decision making. It influences whether a person seeks preventive services, and it influences an athletic trainer's expectations for patients' behavior with each other, with the athletic trainer, and with the health care system (Salimbene, 2001).

Self-Assessment

When conducting a self-assessment, athletic trainers should consider the following questions:

- Who am I? What is my social location (as discussed in chapter 4)?
  - What are my racial, ethnic, and cultural groups?
  - What are my class, religion, gender, sexuality, and age?
  - How is who I am now influenced by who I was before (Tatum, 1997)?
  - Who do my parents, peers, and society say I am (Tatum)?
- How does my social location affect how I think about, and behave around, people whose social location is different than mine?
  - What perceptions and stereotypes do I have regarding individuals or groups who are different from me?
  - What biases and prejudices do I hold toward individuals or groups who are different from me?
  - Do I believe that my way of thinking, believing, or being is the right or proper way (Lattanzi & Purnell, 2006; Purnell & Paulanka, 2003)?
- Has there ever been a time when I was "cast into a minority status" (Welch, 2003, p. 72)?
  - If yes, how did I feel?
  - If yes, how might the experience help me better understand other people who are "cast into a minority status"?
  - If no, how do I think I might feel if I were "cast into a minority status"?
- Which aspects of social location (e.g., race, ethnicity, class, gender, sexuality, religion) do I feel most comfortable with and why? Which do I feel least comfortable with and why?
- Who will I become (Tatum)?

EVERYONE HAS CULTURE

Culture may be defined as "the sum total of socially inherited characteristics of a human group that comprises everything which one generation can tell, convey, or hand down to the next" (Fejos, as cited in Spector, 1996, p. 68). Culture may also be defined as the "sum of beliefs, practices, habits, likes, dislikes, norms, customs, rituals . . . that we learn from our families [friends, schoolmates, religious institutions, or pop culture, among other things] during the socialization years" (Spector, p. 68) and is largely unconscious (Purnell & Paulanka, 2003).

Students in a class about cultural competence, athletic training, and health sciences were asked, "What is your **culture**?" The varied responses included the following: "American," "Christian," "middle-class," and "I do not have culture." The students who said they had no culture were always White. Why might they have felt cultureless? Ruth Frankenberg (2008) has provided some insight. She interviewed 30 White women of different ages, sexual orientations, regions of origin, political orientations, and social classes, and asked them about their identities. She found that the women presented discourses (i.e., intellectual conversations) on Whiteness as dualistic. From a dualistic perspective, life is viewed philosophically as consisting of two oppositional elements, such as good and evil, Black and White, or gay and straight (Ferber, 2007). In this case, the women characterized and conceptualized Whiteness as a polar opposite to "Other" cultural forms. For example, when one woman contrasted being White with being a "New Yorker" or "Midwestern girl," she spoke of "the formlessness of being white" (Frankenberg, 2008, p. 82). She went on to say, "If I had a regional identity that was something palpable, then I'd be a white New Yorker, no doubt, but I'd still be a New Yorker'" (Frankenberg, 2008, p.82). The White "Other"—that is, the White "New Yorker" as compared with "Whiteness"—was marked by region. It could also have been marked by class or ethnicity, as in, for example, White "working class" or "Italian American." Each would be contrasted with the normative (dominant) White cultural group. In other words, because the women were White and a part of the cultural norm, they did not think of "White" by itself as constituting an identity.

Another example of the dualistic "White versus Other" notion was demonstrated by some women who contrasted Whiteness with people of color. Here, people of color and their culture were cast as the polar opposite—the "Other." For example, two women spoke of "Mexican" music versus "regular" music, where "regular" meant "White." Similarly, the Jamaican daughter-in-law of one participant was viewed as "coming with diversity," meaning that because she was Jamaican she was diverse, as opposed to being White and thus not diverse. People of color, then, along with their culture, were viewed as the embodiment of difference, whereas "whites stood for sameness" (Frankenberg, 2008, p. 83). In these examples, White was implicitly posited as the unmarked neutral category, and other cultures were specifically marked cultural. As unmarked and neutral, Whiteness remained the normative standard with which Others were compared.

This unmarked or normative status of Whiteness demonstrates the "power of white culture" (Frankenberg, 2008, p. 83) and its privilege (Frankenberg, 2008; McIntosh, 2007; Oglesby, 1993). This point was well illustrated by Chris Patterson, who was interviewed by Frankenberg,: "'Well what *does* white mean?' One thing is, it's taken for granted. . . . [To be White means to] have some sort of advantage or privilege" (Frankenberg, 2008, p. 83). Not only does membership in a normative (or dominant) group grant one a privileged status; it is also institutionalized in such a way that its members are taught not to see the privilege of group membership (McIntosh, 2007) or to have "little awareness of group membership" (Oglesby, 1993, p.253). As such, "White people don't have to see themselves as white, we have the luxury of seeing ourselves as individuals" (Katz, as cited in Oglesby, 1993, p. 253).

Oglesby (1993) and Frankenberg (2008) suggested that White racial identity be examined and that Whites move toward higher levels of consciousness in order to "develop a clearer sense of where and who we are" (Frankenberg, 2008, p. 87) and to participate consciously in a diverse culture. "Rather than feeling 'cultureless,' white women [people] need to become conscious of the histories and specificities of our cultural positions, and of the political, economic, and creative fusions that form all cultures" (Frankenberg, 2008, p. 87). By engaging in such cultural awareness in order to understand oneself, an athletic trainer can lay the foundation for understanding his or her patients.

GENERALIZATIONS, STEREOTYPES, AND PREJUDICES

A **generalization** is "a statement presented as a general truth but based on limited or incomplete evidence" (Encarta Dictionary: English [North America], 2008). Welch (2003) suggests that generalizations are used to process and simplify large amounts of information. However, when the information is not verified for accuracy and becomes standardized over time as the perceived characteristics for all people in a given group (Sue & Sue, 2008), the generalization becomes a stereotype.

A **stereotype** is "an undifferentiated, simplistic attribution that involves a judgment of habits, traits, abilities, or expectations . . . assigned as a characteristic of all members of a group" (Weinstein and Mellen, as cited in Diller, 2007, p. 35). Some stereotypes are perceived as positive, while others are perceived as negative. In one example of a positive stereotype, Asian Americans are considered the "model minority" (Lai, 1995; Schaefer, 2007; Takaki, 2007; Tatum, 1997) thanks to high income (Schaefer, 2007), academic achievement (Ligutom-Kimura, 1995; Schaefer, 2007), a perception of Asian American women as submissive and demure (Ligutom-Kimura, 1995), and an expectation that Asian Americans will be trouble free. Asian American men are privileged by gender and perceived to be privileged by class and education (Abrums & Leppa, 2001). Athletic trainers who believe and act upon the model minority stereotype of Asian Americans would expect the patient to comply with treatment recommendations without complaint. If the patient does complain or fail to comply, the athletic trainer may be surprised and unsure of how to respond.

If, on the other hand, the patient conforms to the stereotype, his or her needs may go unrecognized and overlooked (Schaefer, 2007). Stereotyping a person (Asian American or otherwise) denies his or her cultural and social realities and dismisses real problems that he or she may face (Lai, 1995; Shingles, 2001). Although some Asian American families earn $75,000 or more a year, just as many earn less than $10,000 a year (Schaefer, 2007); moreover, Asian American families are often multigenerational and include 4 to 6 members who contribute to the income, thus meaning that the reported amount must support more people than one might expect (Asian Nation, 2008). In addition, many Asian American ethnic groups include a large percentage of members who live in poverty: 13.1 percent of Chinese Americans; 13.8 percent of Vietnamese Americans; 15.5 percent of Korean Americans; 16.7 percent of Pacific Islander Americans; and 22 percent of Cambodian, Hmong, and Laotian Americans (Asian Nation). Thus the model minority is a myth (Asian Nation) that athletic trainers should not use as a basis for understanding Asian Americans.

Most stereotypes are perceived as negative. For example, female athletes and coaches who are not married or dating men are stereotyped, with negative associations in the stereotyper's mind, as lesbians—particularly those who participate in basketball and softball (Griffin, 1998). The threat of being labeled a lesbian in sport or athletic training has far-reaching consequences; it has caused coaches and athletic trainers alike to lose or be denied a job (Anderson, 1991; Griffin, 1998). As one woman indicated, the assumption that she might be a lesbian was brought up when she discussed issues about getting a pay raise (Shingles, 2001). Unfortunately, stereotyping "leads to oversimplification in thinking about ethnic [and other] group members...[and] provides justification for the exploitation and ill treatment of those who are racially and culturally different" (Diller, 2007, p. 35).

When negative thought and feeling become attached to a stereotype, the stereotype becomes a **prejudice**. For example, stating that "all Mexicans are lazy" is a stereotype. The statement, "I do not like Mexicans because they are lazy" is a prejudicial statement based on a negative stereotype. A "prejudice is a preconceived judgment or opinion, usually based on limited information" (Tatum, 1997, p. 5). Prejudice includes negative feelings toward others and constitutes "a powerful force that provides fuel for discriminatory behavior and a rationale for justifying it [discrimination]" (Johnson, 2001, p. 58). All humans are capable of prejudices; however, some groups have sufficient power to enact their prejudices over other groups in the form of discriminatory practices.

Thus it is important for athletic trainers to become aware of, learn to recognize, and develop understanding of the stereotypes and prejudices they hold—and how prejudices can lead to discrimination. When athletic trainers develop awareness, they create opportunities to challenge stereotypes and prejudices by gaining accurate knowledge about individuals or groups in order to unlearn the assumptions which initially created the stereotypes or prejudices. They can then change their behavior and eliminate discriminatory practices.

ADVANTAGES, DISADVANTAGES, AND PRIVILEGES

To have an **advantage** means to occupy a superior position, to enjoy a benefit, or to gain something. Being at a **disadvantage**, on the other hand, means experiencing an inferior or prejudicial condition or suffering a loss or some sort of damage, particularly to one's reputation or finances. A **privilege** involves "a right or immunity granted as . . . an advantage, or favor," especially to some and not to others (*Merriam Webster's Collegiate Dictionary*) because of group membership rather than because of what one has done or failed to do (McIntosh, 2007).

Johnson (2006) writes about privilege as a paradox. He states that individuals experience privilege or the lack thereof, but that individuals themselves are not what is actually privileged. In his opinion, social groups are privileged or oppressed, relative to group membership or perceived group membership. Baca Zinn and Dill (2005) would argue that social groups are privileged *and* oppressed. For example, as discussed in chapter 4, gender privileges may or may not be fully realized, experienced, or perceived when they intersect with social class, sexuality, and race. In this vein, a gay middle-class man would be privileged by his social class and gender group membership even as he is oppressed by his sexuality group membership. As Johnson further argues, privilege is "a social arrangement that depends on which category we happen to be sorted into by other people and how they treat us as a result" (p. 35) and that conscious or unconscious discrimination has the effect of maintaining the structure of privilege.

In seeking to further understand oneself, it is important to explore how systems of advantage, disadvantage, and privilege affect one's life and work as an athletic trainer. To delve deeper, answer the following questions:

- How am I advantaged by my social location (e.g., race, ethnicity, class, gender, sexuality, religion)?
- How am I disadvantaged by my social location?
- How am I privileged by my social location?

When asked these questions, female athletic trainers responded in different ways (Shingles, 2001). Some African American women felt privileged when working with African American athletes but initially disadvantaged due to gender when working with male African American coaches. The following excerpt serves as an example of privilege as paradox, wherein race provided an advantage in bridging the cultural gap even as gender served as a means for oppression through sexism.

> *As a graduate student [athletic trainer], my coaches that I dealt with specifically at the high school were resistant [to my working there], simply because I was a female and not so much because I was Black. Because, again, dealing with all Black [male] coaches at the high school, I think some of them were, initially, not sure about my ability to help them (Shingles, 2001, p. 148).*

Some female Asian American and Pacific Islander American athletic trainers used their heritage to their advantage by allowing racial and gender stereotypes about Asian women as exotic, quiet, or unassuming to progress unchallenged (Hossfeld, 1997). For example, one woman talked about how the stereotype was used to make athletes perform their rehabilitation because it was difficult for the athletes to say no to her. The athletes' perception of her as quiet magnified the effect when she did demonstrate displeasure with them, and they tended then to react positively and do what she wanted them to do. She indicated that the athletes did not talk back to her or complain when she asked them to perform their exercises. On the other hand, racial privilege was not perceived by female athletic trainers who were Caucasian, or "non-ethnic looking" Hispanic/Latina, or "non-ethnic looking" American Indian. One Caucasian woman indicated, "I just feel like I belong" (Shingles, 2001). Similarly an American Indian woman said, "I don't think it [race or ethnicity] ever really advantaged me or disadvantaged me. From looking at me, no one would even know I was American Indian" (p.168).

These Caucasian women, like those studied by McIntosh (2007), may not have perceived racial privilege because "whites are carefully taught not to recognize white privilege, as males are taught not to recognize male privilege" (p. 76). Similarly, the Hispanic/Latina and American Indian women who had lighter skin may have benefited from skin color and perceived group membership as White, thus avoiding disadvantages due to race and ethnicity (Shingles, 2001) and perhaps missing advantages, as when African American women athletic trainers said their race helped them interact with African American athletes. McIntosh (2007) provides a myriad of examples of White (pp. 79-81) and heterosexual privileges (pp. 85-86) that she observed. Some include:

- I can avoid spending time with people whom I was trained to mistrust and who have learned to mistrust my kind or me.
- I can go shopping alone most of the time, fairly well assured that I will not be followed or harassed by store detectives.
- I can turn on the television or open the front page of the paper and see people of my race widely and positively represented.
- I can be fairly sure of having my voice heard in a group in which I am the only member of my race.
- I can go . . . into a supermarket and find the staple foods that fit with my cultural traditions, [or] into a hairdresser's shop and find someone who can deal with my hair.
- I am never asked to speak for all the people of my racial group.
- I can be late to a meeting without having the lateness reflect my race.
- I can choose blemish covers or bandages in "flesh" color and have them more or less match my skin.
- My children do not have to answer questions about why I live with my partner (my husband).
- Our children are given texts and classes that implicitly support our kind of family unit and do not turn them against my choice of domestic partnership.
- I can talk about the social events of a weekend without fearing most listeners' reactions.

For a more detailed discussion of White privilege, see McIntosh's essay "White Privilege and Male Privilege: A Personal Account of Coming to See Correspondences Through Work in Women's Studies" (2007).

Examples of *gender*-normative privilege include the following (Lambda 10 Project, n.d.):

- Strangers do not assume they can ask me what my genitals look like and how I have sex.
- My validity as a man/woman/human is not based on how much surgery I have had or how well I "pass" as a non-transperson. . . .
- I am not expected to constantly defend my medical decisions.
- Strangers do not ask me what my "real name" [birth name] is and then assume that they have a right to call me by that name.
- People do not disrespect me by using incorrect pronouns even after they have been corrected. . . .
- I do not have to worry about whether I will experience harassment or violence for using a bathroom or whether I will be safe changing in a locker room. . . .
- I do not have to defend my right to be a part of "queer," and gays and lesbians will not try to exclude me from *our* movement in order to gain political legitimacy for themselves. . . .
- If I end up in the emergency room, I do not have to worry that my gender will keep me from receiving appropriate treatment, or that all of my medical issues will be seen as a result of my gender. ("Your nose is running and your throat hurts? Must be due to the hormones!").
- My health insurance provider (or public health system) does not specifically exclude me from receiving benefits or treatments available to others because of my gender.
- My identity is not considered "mentally ill" by the medical establishment.
- I am not required to undergo an extensive psychological evaluation in order to receive basic medical care.
- The medical establishment does not serve as a "gatekeeper," determining what happens to my body.

In everyday life, privilege happens in little ways—in the things we say and do. Johnson (2006, pp. 55–56) provided several examples:

- Looking at people as if to ask, "What are *you* doing here?"
- Talking about things associated with the "in-group"
- Whether we choose to acknowledge diversity and make room for it
- Whether we acknowledge people's presence (Do we touch them? If so how? If not, why?)
- Choosing not to share information (informal rules) with new colleagues
- Choosing not to invite people to our home, out for a drink, to play golf or cards (social spaces where informal rules are shared)
- Telling people, "You are so articulate." (The statement is not a compliment. The underlying assumption is that the speaker was not expected to be articulate.)
- Using images of darkness/blackness as negative and whiteness as positive (racial privilege)

- Using "queer," "that's so gay" as negative or insults (heterosexual privilege)
- Using the phrase "having balls" (but not having ovaries) as a sign of courage (gender/sexual privilege)

As with stereotypes and prejudices, athletic trainers must acknowledge that advantages, disadvantages, and privileges exist and that both athletic trainers and their patients are affected by social location. In relation to their patients, athletic trainers are privileged by their position in the health care environment and by their specialized knowledge and skills. Because of these privileges, athletic trainers have the power to share or withhold vital information and services. At the same time, athletic trainers may be disadvantaged or oppressed in relation to patients, colleagues, or the health care system because of aspects of their social location (e.g., race, gender, sexuality). By acknowledging and understanding how they are advantaged, disadvantaged, and privileged, athletic trainers can learn to change the ways in which they participate in the privileges in their lives and challenge the structure of privileges. For an in-depth discussion of privilege, read Allan G. Johnson's *Privilege, Power, and Difference* (2006).

SUMMARY

According to Campinha-Bacote, "unfortunately, healthcare professionals often reflect the attitudes and discriminatory practices of their society. A healthcare professional's culture and ethnic background [i.e., social location] can affect interpreting, assigning meaning to, and creating value judgments about their patients. In addition, the lack of awareness of one's [own] biases [prejudices, advantages, disadvantages, and privileges] can result in the lack of diagnostic clarity" (2007, p. 35). Therefore, in order to appropriately care for patients, athletic trainers need to first understand who they are, what they believe, what their comfort levels are, and how to go beyond their current levels of comfort. As one graduate student in athletic training wrote in an assignment:

> At times as humans, we are drawn to those we feel most comfortable with and may tend to provide care for those individuals first. We must make sure that we provide equal care to all athletes in need. Care should be given first to those whose health needs are most critical (Biddington, 2007, p. 72).

Athletic trainers must understand themselves: "The process of gaining cultural awareness [i.e., understanding self] is an important first step. . . . However, solely becoming aware of isms and one's biases . . . does not insure the rendering of culturally competent care. The healthcare professional's journey towards cultural competence must move beyond cultural awareness and include insights into other components of cultural competence" (Campinha-Bacote, 2007, p. 35). These components—which include cultural knowledge, cultural skill, cultural encounters, and cultural desire—are discussed in subsequent chapters.

Learning Aids

What Would You Do If . . . ?

1. What if someone assumed—based on their perception of the way you looked—that you were a recent immigrant, then asked where you came from and expressed surprise at how well you spoke English?
2. What if, after doing your self-assessment, you determine that you are prejudiced toward a particular group or groups?

Activities

1. Answer the self-assessment questions. With a partner or in a small group, discuss your answers and compare each other's responses.
2. Read McIntosh's essay about White privilege and male privilege (2007), then return to the section addressing advantages, disadvantages, and privileges in this chapter and answer the three questions provided there for enhancing self-understanding. With a partner or in a small group, discuss your answers and compare each other's responses.

Key Terms

Define the following key terms found in this chapter:

Advantage   Generalization   Privilege
Culture   Prejudice   Stereotype
Disadvantage

Questions for Review

1. What is cultural awareness? What types of questions should be asked during a self-assessment?
2. What is culture? Describe the concept of Whiteness as an unmarked cultural norm.
3. Differentiate the following terms: generalization, stereotype, prejudice. Give examples.
4. Differentiate the following terms: advantage, disadvantage, privilege. Give examples.

PART

III

Cultural Knowledge

Part III of the text addresses cultural knowledge, which in Campinha-Bacote's model involves three components. The first component entails learning about cultural values and health-related beliefs that differ from your own. The second involves learning about health disparities and disease incidence between and among groups and how best to address the disparities. The third issue addresses treatment efficacy or effectiveness. After reading the material in part III, you will have cultural knowledge about various racial and ethnic groups found in the United States.

Cultural beliefs and behaviors vary depending on ethnicity. The following chapters alert you to cultural differences and familiarize you with ways to provide better care. The examples given in these chapters may apply to some, but not all, people within a culture. Generally speaking, elders and first generations adhere to the practices and beliefs of their country of origin, whereas second and third generations acculturate more fully to the new dominant culture. We hope that athletic trainers will attempt to immerse themselves into the culture of the athlete and view the world from that perspective.

Chapters 6 through 11 discuss the following aspects of each culture addressed: demographic and cultural background, brief history of country of origin and immigration, primary languages and communication styles, family structure, daily living and food practices, spiritual or religious orientation, health care, biocultural assessment, common sensitivities and conditions, beliefs about illness, preventive healing practices, symptom management, and treatments. The specific cultures are as follows: Native American (American Indian and Native Alaskan [Eskimo and Aleut]) in chapter 6; Asian American and Pacific Islander American (Chinese, Filipino, and Vietnamese) in chapter 7; Black (African American, sub-Saharan African, and Haitian) in chapter 8; Latino (Mexican, Puerto Rican, and Cuban) in chapter 9; White European (German, Irish, and English) in chapter 10; and Middle Eastern (Arab-collective [Lebanese, Syrian, and Egyptian] and Iranian) in chapter 11.

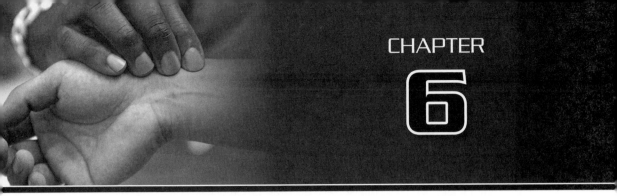

Native American

Learning Objectives

Upon completing this chapter, students will be able to do the following:

1. Define the term Native American
2. Explain concerns that a Native American might have when working with an athletic trainer who is not a Native American
3. Describe the types of illnesses most often experienced by American Indians
4. Describe the types of illnesses most often experienced by Native Alaskans
5. Identify who typically makes the decisions in a Native American family
6. Identify effective and culturally competent forms of communication with Native American athletes
7. Describe religious beliefs associated with specific groups of Native Americans
8. Describe healing ceremonies

Jan Perkins

I am a physical therapist. I grew up in a "company town" in Newfoundland, Canada. The town was literally owned by an American company that ran a mining and milling operation there. Consequently, nobody was allowed to own their own house or build within 5 miles (8 kilometers) of town, and all those who lost their job or retired had to leave town. Thus I knew growing up that leaving my hometown after school was not an option but a requirement. Perhaps that background left me with a sense of impermanence that resulted in my living in more than a dozen places on three continents during the first 15 years after my high school graduation.

Robert Brown; Central Michigan University.

I entered the field of health care on the recommendation of a relative. I visited a department, talked to a therapist, and liked what he said. I also saw physical therapy as a field that would let me move around, something I knew even then that

I wanted to do. I ended up choosing to go to England for my initial physical therapy education—I selected the school by sticking a pin into a map while blindfolded—and then completed my physical therapy degree in Canada. I went on to work in a variety of places, including both large urban centers and small one-therapist towns located in isolated areas; I also did fly-in clinics in remote towns in the Canadian north. I gradually moved into teaching and have now been a faculty member in physical therapy at a state university in a rural region for several years.

At one point in my career, I worked with military veterans in a long-term care setting. I remember one man who had spent several years as a prisoner of war in the Pacific theater. He was receiving long-term care because of dementia and behavioral problems, which included resisting personal hygiene care, stealing and hiding food, and rummaging through others' belongings. Sleep problems meant that he wandered around and disturbed residents at night. He stole and hid uniforms donated by a sports team for a lounge display. Many of his behaviors were upsetting and frustrating for both staff members and veterans. A crisis occurred when, in response to complaints by roommates, the staff decided to move him to a new room. His reactions were extreme, and he became very upset and agitated. Eventually, when it was clear that his belongings were being moved despite his objections, he left the room. When finally found, he had gone to the ward storage area and constructed a cave from wheelchairs and other pieces of equipment. Then he crawled his way back into his refuge and tried to both hide and keep watch. Only letting him keep his old room and moving the others instead restored peace on the unit.

What does the irrational behavior of this elderly man with dementia have to do with culture? He had been a prisoner of war in a particularly notorious setting, and his horrific experiences shaped the rest of his life. The one belonging he consistently wore was the badge of his POW association; membership in that group had become his main cultural identification, and the camp experience shaped his dementia as it had done with his earlier postwar life. He usually believed that he was back in the prison camp, and he could not be convinced otherwise. Viewed from this perspective, all of his problem behaviors were remnants of the strategies that had allowed him to survive for years in the camp—hiding food, scavenging other resources, and trying to avoid being selected for what could turn out to be fatal moves to work camps or forced marches. Once staff members recognized his cultural identification, it became easier to care for him. For example, his food hiding posed an unacceptable health and hygiene problem, but confronting him directly and reclaiming it did not help; to the contrary, he would get upset and become more creative and secretive in his hiding places. Instead, staff members simply identified favorite hiding places, checked them regularly, and removed food when he was not in the area. He never missed the food, as evidenced by the fact that he continued to use the same hiding places. In my work with him, I found that while I could not convince him that the ward was not his old prison camp, I could distract him by having him reminisce about his life before the camp. This practice transported him to an earlier cultural identity that was safe and allowed him to relax and cooperate during therapy. We both enjoyed our interactions much more.

Culture is dynamic, and an individual's culture can evolve over time as she or he integrates new experiences into personal identity. To learn about culture, I suggest that you talk to people, read about cultures, travel when you can, and, above all, listen to other people's perspectives. Be flexible in your own views and open to the idea that interacting with others will shape you. My patient who had been a POW could not tell me of his prison camp culture, but I could research and read what others had written. That led me to reading and talking with experts about how extreme stress can affect people. In health care, we often deal with people who have undergone trauma and stress. I have never treated another person like the former prisoner of war, but the lessons that his care taught me about stress and coping gave me insights that helped me work with others at difficult times in their lives. Learning about differing perspectives and beliefs is never a waste. My own perpetual traveling wound down after an interaction with another veteran. But that is a different story.

Knowledge of Native American culture can help an athletic trainer avoid stereotypes and understand the reasons for a patient's decisions and behaviors. Each section in this chapter includes several subsections: communication, family structure, spiritual orientation, biocultural assessment, common conditions, beliefs about illness, symptom management, and treatment. Other features include lists of dos and don'ts, as well as identification of characteristics that are distinctive in a given culture. Readers are also reminded that not all people in a group will adhere to each of the listed items.

The term **Native American** refers to peoples who are indigenous to America, and two groups fit this description: American Indians and Native Alaskans.

AMERICAN INDIAN

American Indians have a unique culture of their own. It is important for the athletic trainer to understand the similarities and the differences of this culture to one's own, avoid the generalization that everyone adheres to the same beliefs that are part of this culture, and keep an open mind when working with athletes whose culture may be different than their own.

Demographic and Cultural Background Information

To help you develop understanding of American Indian people, this chapter provides a brief history of country of origin and immigration, primary languages and communication, family structure, daily living and food practices, and spiritual or religious orientation.

Country of Origin and Immigration

The term **American Indian** refers to indigenous peoples and their predecessors from the area referred to today as the continental United States (see figure 6.1). It is necessary to use the term American Indian to differentiate these peoples from the other group of original inhabitants in North America—the Native Alaskans.

Figure 6.1 Native American map of the United States.

The term American Indian should not be confused with people from the country of India. Many American Indian elders prefer the term American Indian over the alternative term Native American (Lipson, Dibble, & Minarik, 1996).

European explorers brought a large number of European settlers to the United States. As more Europeans arrived, more American Indians were displaced from their lands. Treaties were signed as a way for American Indians to define areas for Europeans to inhabit, but the Europeans never truly limited their land use. In fact, Europeans seldom adhered to the treaties, and, eventually, American Indians were forced onto reservations, mostly in the western portion of North America. During their forced emigration to the new land, usually west of the Mississippi River, many American Indians died, including chiefs, medicine men, and elders. With the loss of so many people, some important cultural information, such as traditional medical remedies and history, was lost.

As one might imagine, American Indians often feel distrustful of Europeans and Americans due to their failure to abide by treaties. In addition, Europeans brought communicable diseases (e.g., measles, smallpox, influenza) that caused numerous deaths among American Indians (Downes, 1997).

The Europeans felt it was best to educate American Indians in their ways, and they forced American Indian children into schools where they were not allowed to speak their native language, dress in traditional clothing, practice their religion, or carry on their culture. Europeans devalued everything about American Indians, causing anger and resentment (Diller, 2007). To keep from losing the traditions of their culture, American Indians told stories and passed them on through the generations within the confines of their own homes.

Groups of American Indians who are related by blood are referred to as **tribes**. Today, more than 500 American Indian tribes are present in the United States

(Lipson et al., 1996; U.S. Census Bureau, 2000; Yehieli & Grey, 2005). To be a member of a certain tribe, one must have a certain amount of ancestry in that tribe. Each tribe has its own standard, or "blood quantum" requirement; most often, the minimum requirement for membership in a tribe is one-fourth tribal ancestry (Yehieli & Grey). A person who meets a tribe's blood quantum requirement can receive health care, vote in tribal elections, own land within tribe's national boundaries, use eagle feathers, and get educational expenses paid (Livesay, 2002).

Each tribe has its own culture, traditions, language, beliefs, and customs drawn from the tribe's unique history and signifying specific events of importance. The largest tribe in the United States is the Cherokee (U.S. Census Bureau, 2000; Spector, 2004).

Most health-related information written about American Indians concerns the Navajo, Cherokee, Hopi, Shoshone, and New England tribes (Spector, 2004) because they have been more receptive to having their cultures researched; the vast majority of this material addresses the Navajos. Because of the partial nature of this research, readers may find that some characteristics discussed in this chapter vary somewhat in practice. Athletic trainers should become familiar with the health practices of the tribes with which they work.

Primary Languages and Communication Styles

- The primary language of American Indians is English.
- Some tribe members still speak their native language.
- Older generations speak the native language of their tribe, and younger generations have to learn the native language in cultural classes (Yehieli & Grey, 2005).
- Native languages are primarily spoken in the home (Purnell & Paulanka, 2005).

DOS AND DON'TS

- Don't refer to an American Indian as a squaw or warrior.
- Do shake hands; a weak handshake is a symbol of humility.
- Don't say "How" as a greeting.
- Do say "Good morning. How are you?"
- Don't ask for a person's American Indian name.
- Don't point using your fingers.
- Do purse your lips and move them to indicate a direction.
- Do allow an American Indian to reflect on questions.
- Do use patience.
- Don't take notes while communicating with an American Indian.

DISTINCTIVE TO THIS CULTURE

- Eye contact is avoided as the eyes are thought to form an entryway to the soul and a way to steal it.
- This culture is respectful of those deemed superior in status.
- Personal space should be at what is considered distant (Yehieli and Grey, 2005) (5 to 12 feet, or about 1.5 to 3.5 meters).
- Storytelling is a way to answer a question, even one about an illness.

Family Structure

In some tribes, the entire family lives together, including recently married children. The head of household varies depending on the tribe. In some instances, the oldest person is the head; in others, it may be the mother.

DISTINCTIVE TO THIS CULTURE

Some American Indian tribes recognize berdaches—individuals who play a cross-gendered role within the family (Scott, 2005). Berdaches do work usually associated with the opposite sex; their dress, lifestyle, and role are recognized as that of the opposite sex; and they have sexual and emotional attachment to individuals of the same sex (Scott). Their lifestyle is said to have resulted from supernatural intervention, and American Indian societies typically view berdaches as occupying a position of honor and as signs of luck and good fortune (Scott). Those outside of American Indian culture may view berdaches negatively as homosexuals, and it has been felt by some that renaming berdaches as "two-spirits" would remove the negative stereotype.

- "Two-spirit" is a term used to describe gay, lesbian, bisexual, and transgendered Native Americans (Oropeza, 2002). The term was coined to distinguish Native American gays and lesbians from mainstream gays and lesbians (Oropeza).
- The Lakota tribe uses the term *wintke*, the Navajo tribe uses *nadleeh*, and the Cheyenne tribe uses *hee-man-eh* (Spectrum Center, 2009).

Daily Living and Food Practices

- American Indians live in present time, meaning that what is happening right now is most important; they typically do not follow calendars or become overly concerned with time (Yehieli & Grey, 2005). For example, an athlete living in present time might not take medication as prescribed because he or she does not feel ill at that time; as a result, the illness might fester. Thus an athletic trainer may face challenges in getting an athlete to arrive on time for appointments or take medication at proper times during the day.
- Haircutting can signify shame (Native Languages of the Americas, 2007). If there is a need to cut or shave hair—for example, to tape a body part for a wrestler or to meet competition requirements for hair—the reason should be explained and permission should be obtained. The cut hair should be given to the person.
- The eldest female adult is usually the person who must give consent for medical procedures (Salimbene, 2005). Thus, if consent is needed, check with the eldest female and show respect for her decision.
- An American Indian patient may distrust paperwork (Lipson et al., 1996; Yehieli & Grey, 2005) due to the history of failed treaties in the United States. Explain the need for a signed document and how it will be used. You may have to return the documents and all copies at the end of the patient's participation in care.

- Diet often consists of high-fat food, which places greater stress on one's heart and contributes to obesity, high blood pressure, and high cholesterol. Thus athletic trainers need to monitor American Indian athletes in these areas and be prepared to suggest diet modification or refer them to a nutritionist.
- American Indians are known to be lactose intolerant and may choose to avoid milk products. However, avoiding lactose-containing products (e.g., whey) may lead to a deficiency of vitamin D and contribute to health issues including rickets, osteoporosis, muscular weakness, and psoriasis (Purnell & Paulanka, 2003). An athletic trainer can recommend the enzyme lactase to help break down lactose, and calcium supplements can help prevent some illnesses brought about by lack of lactose-containing foods.
- Some American Indian ceremonies require restriction of certain foods as a way of ensuring that the ritual will work; one example is a no-salt diet (Purnell & Paulanka, 2003). An athletic trainer should inquire about any food restriction and monitor the need for supplementary nutrition.

Spiritual or Religious Orientation

- American Indian spirituality is based on bringing life in balance with nature (Purnell & Paulanka, 2003). It is believed that harming nature, or not taking care of oneself, will only cause an American Indian to become ill. When an American Indian does become ill, spiritual ceremonies may be used. One such practice includes the use of cornmeal around one's bed as a ritual to improve health or to support treatment (Salimbene, 2005). Outside of American Indian tribal spirituality, some American Indians follow the beliefs of traditional Christian or of the Jehovah's Witnesses. An athletic trainer may have to ask how an illness occurred from the athlete's perspective, then work within the athlete's spiritual context to support healing—for example, by allowing the practice of spiritual healing ceremonies while using ice and compression for ankle swelling.
- The narcotic peyote is used by American Indians as part of religious rituals. An athletic trainer should investigate with the National Collegiate Athletic Association whether the use of peyote by an American Indian athlete will be viewed as a violation of athletic participation rules.

Health Care Information

This section addresses biocultural assessment, common sensitivities and conditions, beliefs about illness, preventive health practices, symptom management, and treatments.

Biocultural Assessment

- Actual skin color is brown, varying light to dark brown. An athletic trainer who must evaluate pallor or jaundice should use the nail beds, the inside of the lip, or the sclera.

- According to Schrefer (1994), 12 percent of American Indians have 25 vertebrae instead of the more common total of 24, and this condition can lead to lower back pain and lordosis. Thus it is prudent to check for this possible anomaly during a physical examination.
- Schrefer (1994) indicates that the peroneus tertius muscle is absent in 3 to 10 percent of the American Indian population. The absence of peroneus tertius means that the athlete may have difficulty dorsiflexing and everting the ankles.
- Schrefer (1994) indicates that there is an absence of palmaris longus muscle of 2 to 12 percent, which means that the athlete would not be able to forcefully flex the wrist.
- Navajo Indians are known for having a larger than normal number of ear anomalies. During a physical examination, such anomalies should be documented so that the athletic trainer has recorded knowledge of the preexisting condition, which may be especially helpful when determining the extent of a cauliflower ear.

Common Sensitivities and Conditions

- American Indians are more likely than average afflicted with diabetes, alcoholism, ear anomalies, and heart disease (Yehieli & Grey, 2005). Athletic trainers should watch for the signs and symptoms associated with these conditions when working with American Indians.
- Ghost sickness is a culture-bound syndrome among American Indians. It is believed to occur in one of two ways: (a) when a person has contributed to another's death or impending death (e.g., driving a car in an accident) or (b) when a dead person is unsettled in the afterlife and his or her spirit goes into a living person.
- Several conditions found more often among American Indians may be unfamiliar to an athletic trainer: Navajo neuropathy, Salmonella, Shigella, and tuberculosis. Any athlete who might have one of these conditions should be referred to a physician for care. An explanation of signs and symptoms of these conditions is available in the appendix.

Beliefs About Illness

American Indians believe that mind, body, and spirit must be in harmony in order to prevent illness. If a person becomes ill, it is thought that one of the three components is out of harmony. Animals and plants are thought to be part of the spirit world, so they must be in harmony as well (Salimbene, 2005). Thus one's relationship with the earth and others plays a role in health: If the earth is harmed, so will its people be harmed, and vice versa (Spector, 2004, p. 189). Those who most strongly believe in the relationship between harmony and illness often live on reservations (Salimbene, 2005). Some American Indians do look to conventional germ theory or a mechanism of injury as the cause of a problem or illness. Those who believe germ theory and seek assistance from a physician first are likely to be highly educated, live in cities, and economically stable. About 56 percent of American Indians fit this category (Salimbene, 2005).

- When an American Indian becomes ill, the sickness is thought of as an opportunity to cleanse oneself. Illness is thought to be brought about by disharmony of events in the past or the future, by the loss of one's soul, by the breaching of a taboo, or by evil spirits or witchcraft (Spector, 2004, p. 189; Salimbene, 2005). An athletic trainer should inquire into the patient's belief in order to support and work toward resolution of the illness.

- Some American Indians believe that seizures result from breaking the taboo on incest (Salimbene, 2005). As a result, working with the family of an athlete who experiences a seizure can pose challenges; for example, family members may not want to discuss the situation and may disassociate themselves from the athlete.

- If a person faints or falls unconscious, he or she is considered to have been touched by witchcraft (Salimbene, 2005). For an athletic trainer, an American Indian's belief about the cause of illness can certainly challenge one's ability to treat or even give basic care. Keep in mind the goal of determining the cause of the fainting or unconsciousness.

- Some bodily fluids are believed to be used by sorcerers to cause illness (Gropper, 1996). Thus an athletic trainer must use care to destroy bodily fluids of American Indians so they do not fall into the hands of a person who wishes ill will. The athletic trainer can ask the athlete if he or she would like to be present when bodily fluids are destroyed.

Preventive Health Practices

Many American Indians live in poverty, and it can be a struggle for them to pay for a physician's services. Moreover, many American Indians who live on reservations adhere to the culture of the past, and they are likely to seek the assistance from healers and traditional healing rituals of their culture and avoid seeking care from a physician or following Western preventive measures. Medicine men are the healers of choice and are considered to be all-knowing. Medicine men are thought to be able to tell their patients what is wrong with them without having to ask questions.

Given that American Indians are more than average afflicted with alcoholism, diabetes, and heart disease, treatment programs should include preventive measures in these areas. There is an enormous amount of alcoholism among American Indians. As a result, alcohol is forbidden on reservations, and preventive programs have been put in place to educate American Indians about alcoholism. To reduce the incidence of diabetes, heart disease, and stroke, athletic trainers can also recommend a low-fat diet, and avoiding simple sugars and increasing fiber intake can reduce obesity and the incidence of diabetes. It may also be helpful to recommend other healthy habits, such as monitoring cholesterol levels, seeking regular physical examinations, reducing salt intake, increasing exercise, and keeping one's blood pressure down.

Many generic medications contain a lactose filler. To avoid gas and constipation associated with lactose intolerance, encourage patients to consult with their physician or pharmacist.

Symptom Management

- Pain is generally met with a stoic demeanor, as if the athlete is supposed to live with this pain (Purnell & Paulanka, 2005).
- An American Indian athlete may not be able to share the feeling of malaise and may even maintain his or her level of activity, which can create confusion for an athletic trainer (Lipson et al., 1996).
- Because vomiting and diarrhea are viewed as sources of embarrassment, an American Indian athlete may hide them from the athletic trainer (Lipson et al., 1996).
- Depression may be described as a physical ailment, which can puzzle an athletic trainer and challenge him or her to accurately diagnose and help the athlete (Lipson et al., 1996).
- Once symptoms are found and classified, it may be easier for athletic trainers to assist in the treatment process. Medicine men are thought to be capable of determining an illness without touching an athlete, and if a medicine man makes a diagnosis the athlete may then be more inclined to seek treatment from an athletic trainer.

Treatments

American Indians have been known for their ability to resolve illness through the use of traditional medicinal or spiritual practices (Yehieli & Grey, 2005). American Indians may use traditional practices even when they accept Western medicine as valid because traditional practices may make them feel comfortable. Western medicine will be sought by those who are acculturated and when a disease or illness, such as diabetes, is believed to have been introduced by Europeans (Yehieli & Grey). An American Indian who has been prescribed medication may stop taking it once symptoms subside, either to save it for another episode of illness or because it costs a lot of money that an athlete may not have in the future (Hendrix, 2002). Thus, an athletic trainer needs to encourage American Indian athletes to take medication as prescribed in order to ensure that the illness or injury is resolved.

Once the illness or injury has been determined, American Indians may perform ceremonies to begin the return to harmony. This type of ceremonial process is referred to as purification. The process of purification may involve total body immersion in water, sweat lodges, and other rituals (Spector, 2004, p. 193). Healing ceremonies may last as long as a week and involve a great number of people, the use of herbs, stargazing, or chants. The athletic trainer needs to know if a sweat lodge has been used, since it may cause dehydration, elevated body temperature, heat exhaustion, and malaise.

Shamans

A medicine man or woman, also known as a **shaman**, is consulted to determine what has caused an illness or injury. The shaman is able to visualize things in the spirit world and will make a diagnosis through stargazing, crystal gazing, or hand trembling.

A shaman **stargazer** is a diagnostician who uses stargazing to determine the illness and type of treatment needed. The stargazer goes to the home of the ill person and while there asks for silence. He then covers all the lights and fires and takes the ill person outside. While they are outside, those in the home are asked to close their eyes and wait for a vision to come. The home must be silent, and the people within must concentrate on the illness. The stargazer and athlete stand outside in the dark. The stargazer holds a crystal in his hand and points it toward the sky. A prayer is said by the stargazer asking for guidance about the illness. The light of a star is reflected by the crystal and gives the stargazer answers to how the illness occurred and how to treat the person (Walter, & Fridman, 2004) on the ground. When the stargazer and the patient return to the home, lights are turned on and each person tells the story of what he or she saw during the stargazing. The stargazer then determines what the next treatment will be and who will perform it.

Crystal gazing is the practice of looking into a crystalline gem or crystal ball. The staring causes a trance for the one who is looking at the crystal, and the trance allows the shaman gazer to make contact with the supernatural spirit, who identifies the problem. The crystal gazer then shares the diagnosis.

A shaman diagnostician can also be a **hand trembler**. In this practice, the shaman places cornmeal in the hand of the ill person and waves his own hand over the patient. As he does so, his hand begins to tremble, and he then determines the cause of the illness and prescribes a treatment.

Once the shaman has made the diagnosis, he will share a course of action. Treatments can include chanting, prayer, herbal medicines, laying on of hands, salves, sweat lodges, drums, singing, sand painting, purgatives, or referral to Western medicine. If the athlete is not acculturated, he or she may be hesitant to work with a Western practitioner. The athletic trainer should work with the shaman to support the care of the athlete. A combination of Western medicine and traditional American Indian practices can lead to improved health without exacerbating the reservations the athlete may have. The athletic trainer needs to ask questions of the shaman to ensure that any herbals used do not conflict with prescribed medication or drug rules for athletes. Healing practices vary among tribes, but the ultimate goal is to restore harmony between the athlete and nature (Downes, 1997). Marbella, Harris, Diehr, Ignace, & Ignace (1998) indicate that 86 percent of American Indians would consider using a healer in the future, whereas only 15 percent shared that they were using both healers and physicians at the same time.

Herbals

Salicin, a chemical found in willow, is used in aspirin in Western medicine and is used by American Indians for the same effect; coca is also used as a pain killer

(Perrone, Stockel, & Krueger, 1989). Spector (2004) has listed some herbal remedies used by Oneida Indians for various illnesses:

- Witch hazel for a cold
- Comfrey for a sore throat
- Elderberry flowers for diarrhea
- Tansy and sage for a headache
- Dried raspberry leaves for an ear infection
- Blueberries for diabetes
- Lettuce eaten daily for insomnia

Kennett (1976) has shared the following remedies used by various American Indian tribes:

- Boneset plant for fever (Menominee, Iroquois, and Mohegan)
- Boneset plant for diuretic (Iroquois)
- Sunflower root for drawing blisters (Ojibwa)
- American elder bark and root for headache or phlegm removal (Meskwaki)
- Hops for insomnia (Meskwaki)
- Willow bark tea for stiff joints (many tribes)
- Spikenard root tea for backaches (Cherokee)
- Witch hazel for backaches and to ease legs for runners (Menominee)

Many of today's medicines have come from herbs used over the years by American Indians, and many holistic or alternative medicine practitioners consider American Indian medicine as their primary source of information for health. Athletic trainers need to familiarize themselves with how herbals and modern medicines may interact; in some combinations, these treatments may negatively affect each other.

Chanting, Drumming, and Sand Painting

Chants for health can be divided into general categories depending on their purpose; here are several: (a) for good health, (b) to counteract offenses against the Holy People believed to cause colds, pain, upset stomach, skin disorders, and back problems; and (c) to counteract injuries such as sprains, strains, and fractures (Anthro4n6, 2004a)

Drumming, singing, and rattles are sometimes used to treat an ill person by creating noise that interferes with the negative messages being sent by evil spirits. When the spirits are unable to pass their message, the illness can be cured (Spector, 2004).

Navajo medicine men do **sand painting** in the home and on the floor of the ill person (Anthro4n6, 2004b). The sand painting is made with cornmeal, sand, charcoal, and gypsum. Holy People are depicted in the sand painting for the purpose of drawing the illness out of the sick person. When the painting is completed, the sick person sits on it to begin the drawing-out process (Spector, 2004).

Protection

Corn or cornmeal may be spread around the ill person for healing of minor ailments (Perrone et al., 1989). Beliefs about this practice differ according to the tribe.

The bear is the symbol of health and physical strength (Kiva Trading, 2007), and the bear symbol may be placed in a sacred spot in the home or worn as an amulet.

An ill person may wear a medicine bag around his or her neck. The bag contains healing herbs such as sawgrass. The bag should not be removed without explaining why it is necessary to do so. If the bag is removed, it should remain close to the athlete (Yehieli & Grey, 2005; Lipson et al., 1996).

NATIVE ALASKAN

Native Alaskans have a unique culture of their own. It is important for the athletic trainer to understand the similarities and the differences of this culture to one's own, avoid the generalization that everyone adheres to the same beliefs that are part of this culture, and keep an open mind when working with athletes whose culture may be different than their own.

Demographic and Cultural Background Information

To help you develop understanding of Native Alaskan people, this chapter provides a brief history of country of origin and immigration, primary languages and communication, family structure, daily living and food practices, and spiritual or religious orientation.

Brief History of Country of Origin and Immigration

Native Alaskans are members of a group of people who live in Alaska. They can be subdivided into two main categories: **Eskimos** and Aleuts. Eskimos live in four main areas—the former Soviet Union, United States, Canada, and Greenland (*Encyclopedia Britannica*, 2009). Native Alaskans do not use the term Eskimo to describe themselves. Instead they use Inupiat or Yupik, which are tribal names. The term **Aleuts** describes people of the Aleutian Islands in Alaska (Black & Liapunova, 2004).

According to historians (Griffin, 2010), Native Alaskans arrived in Alaska by crossing a land bridge from Asia that no longer exists. It is also believed that Native Alaskans are closely related to Asians.

Inupiats live in the coldest regions, which most people would consider uninhabitable. It is extremely cold during the vast majority of the year, and the sun is not seen from the fall into the early spring. On summer days, the sun never sets completely. Inupiats were a **nomadic** population, meaning that they moved based on the availability of food, which was affected by weather and seasonal change. Inupiats no longer need to be nomadic since they no longer need to hunt for food and are able to purchase food locally.

The Aleuts were primarily hunters of seals and otter for furs. Aleuts do not have to hunt because food is available within their community. Over time and under the influence of oversight by Russians and Americans, much of the Aleut language, tradition, and religion were lost (Downes, 1997).

Currently 58 percent of Native Alaskans live in urban areas ("American Indians and Alaska Natives and Immunizations," 2006), and many Native Alaskans transition regularly between their urban homes and reservations or rural areas (Oropeza, 2002). Approximately 7.5 percent of Native Alaskan homes do not have a safe water supply or sewer facilities (Indian Health Service, 2002).

Primary Languages and Communication Styles

- Most Inupiats and Aleuts speak English, but both groups have their own native language.
- Dialects vary based on where the people live ("Eskimo-Aleut," 2007).
- English is spoken by members of younger generations who have become acculturated.

DOS AND DON'TS

- Do speak English and shake hands.
- Do refer to Native Alaskans as Inupiat or Yupik.
- Do refer to Native Aleutians as Aleuts.
- Don't rub noses with Native Alaskans.

DISTINCTIVE TO THIS CULTURE

Personal space should be at what is considered social distance (5 to 12 feet, or about 1.5 to 3.5 meters) (Hendrix, 2002).

Family Structure

At one time, the family structure involved three generations living in the same house. Once married, a man was expected to live at his parents' home with his wife. Today, the family structure follows a more European style, in which elders live apart from their children. Married couples live on their own, though often within the same community in which they were born. Males are the head of household.

Daily Living and Food Practices

- Males are the hunters and gatherers for food that must last throughout the winter.
- Females in the household are childbearers, cleaners, and food preparers.
- Some areas of Alaska still do not have conveniences (e.g., grocery stores, churches, drugstores) often associated with urban society.
- Food is often made from scratch based on what is available at the time.
- The hunting once necessary for survival is now limited based on increased ability to transport food to distant rural areas.
- Children are taught the traditional aspects of their culture.
- Consent for any sort of procedure will come from the parents of a child.
- If an adult is to have a procedure, he or she may give permission.

- Native Alaskans function in present time.
- The majority of food comes from sea mammals, such as seals and whales. Other primary foods include fish, fox, polar bear, and caribou (Downes, 1997). Some meat is eaten raw in order to conserve cooking fuel.
- Fruits and vegetables are hard to come by due to the short growing season.

Spiritual or Religious Orientation

Native Alaskans have little time for a religion that requires church attendance, readings, and baptism. A people who must live in cold and hunt to eat had to create a religion that could accommodate their need to work constantly. As a result, spiritual ceremonies take place in the home.

Native Alaskans have their own traditional religion. Religions in traditional cultures tend to expect their people to maintain harmony in their life—a balance between mental, emotional, and physical states.

Native Alaskans feel a connection to the land and to the animals that feed them. All animals are thought to have souls, and when an animal is killed a ritual is performed to allow the animal spirit to return and continue to live again ("Eskimo-Aleut Religion," 2010).

Inupiats and Aleuts tend to believe in a few deities—Sedna, Aningaaq, and Sila. Sedna has the power to provide food from sea animals—or not, if Native Alaskans violate her wishes. Aningaaq is the god of sunlight, warmth, and life. The god of air is Sila. Animals are critical to the life of Native Alaskans, providing food, clothing, and weapons. Every part of the animal is used to the benefit of the people, who perform ceremonies before, during, and after a hunt. If at any time a Native Alaskan violates the rituals and causes imbalance in the environment, the person's spirit may wander off.

The three spirits of Native Alaskans are future life, current life, and evil. It is believed that if the second spirit leaves a person, then he or she will die. The athletic trainer may hear about concerns of the spirit depending on the illness. If the athlete believes that somehow the illness is life-threatening, he may express concern. The athletic trainer must address the concern to provide relief and comfort for the athlete.

Health Care Information

To truly understand a culture's beliefs about health, one must understand various aspects: biocultural assessment, common sensitivities and conditions, beliefs about illness, preventive health practices, symptom management, and treatments.

Biocultural Assessment and Sensitivities

- Schrefer (1994) indicated that 12 percent of Inupiats have 25 vertebrae (instead of the more common number of 24). The increased number can add to lordosis and back pain, and it is prudent to check for this anomaly during a physical examination.
- Torus protuberances are larger in Native Alaskans, which may cause difficulty in using mouth guards. As many as 50% of the people have this condition (Schrefer, 1994).

- The long bones in Inupiats are less dense than in Whites (Schrefer, 1994), which may leave Inupiats more prone to fractures.
- Because Inupiats are descendents of Asian peoples, their facial features resemble those of Asians.
- Skin tone in Inupiats is light brown, hair is black, eyes are dark, and high cheekbones are common.
- No specific biocultural differences have been noted between Inupiats and Aleuts in published materials.

Common Sensitivities and Conditions

- Illnesses associated with Native Alaskans include alcoholism, cirrhosis of the liver, type 2 diabetes, suicide, heart disease, and lactose intolerance (McCabe, 2001; U.S. Department of Health and Human Services, 2000).
- Some conditions found among Native Alaskans may be unfamiliar to an athletic trainer—for example, pibloktoq and methemoglobinemia (McCabe, 2001; Penn State Life Sciences Library, 2007; U.S. Department of Health and Human Services, 2000). Any athlete who might have one of these conditions should be referred to a physician for care. More information about these conditions is in the appendix.

Beliefs About Illness

Native Alaskans believe that failure to be in harmony with animals causes illness and possibly requires relocation to another community.

- Those who adhere to traditional beliefs also believe that the family—not just the athlete—feels the illness.
- The entire family has to be treated holistically (Salimbene, 2005).
- Those who live within cities do adhere to belief in germ theory.

DISTINCTIVE TO THIS CULTURE

- Stories may be used to express symptoms.
- Native Alaskans who accept germ theory may seek assistance from an athletic trainer. Most others will seek traditional methods, such as a shaman, hot springs, or massage.

Preventive Health Practices

Programs have been started to help prevent alcoholism, diabetes, and suicide among Native Alaskans as part of a U.S. government effort to provide culturally competent health care at 12 regional sites throughout Alaska. The programs' strength resides in the competency and knowledge of the individuals who run them. Such preventive programs can be challenging because so many Native Alaskans live in isolated rural areas.

- Athletic trainers face a challenge in trying to convince Native Alaskans to do preventative self-examinations.
- Native Alaskans may fare better with same-sex athletic trainers because of issues with modesty (Glanz, 2003).
- The athletic trainer needs to learn how to discuss private matters in a non-offensive way (Oropeza, 2002). One successful strategy is to have the athlete conduct personal physical self-examinations in the shower, since touching oneself in that setting is allowed in Native Alaskan culture (Oropeza, 2002). Native Alaskans are modest about their bodies, so they feel less comfortable doing self-examinations (Oropeza, 2002).
- To avoid gas and constipation associated with lactose intolerance, encourage patients to consult with their physician or pharmacist to determine whether their medications contain lactose filler.

Symptom Management

- Native Alaskans are stoic about their pain. They may believe it is a necessary part of the healing process. It is important for an athletic trainer to determine whether the patient is experiencing pain, how bad it is, and whether the athlete needs care. To be able to determine the level of pain, the athletic trainer needs to earn the respect of the athlete. It is important to listen to the athlete rather than talk, so ask a question and wait for an answer. One simple solution to pain is application of ice.
- To be successful when working with a Native Alaskan, an athletic trainer must take a holistic approach by caring for the physical, emotional, mental, and spiritual aspects of the athlete (Oropeza, 2002). This kind of approach fits with the traditional medicine practices of Native Alaskans.

Treatment

- There are approximately 90 physicians per 100,000 Native Americans (Intercultural Cancer Council, 2001), which means that even those Native Alaskans who would prefer Western medicine often find it easier and more convenient to use their community healers.
- The healing of an athlete, especially elder athletes, may have to be done spiritually because of their personal beliefs and respect for traditional healers (Management Sciences for Health, 2003).
- The athlete may believe that problems created by White people's illnesses require treatment by means of Western medicine (Hendrix, 2002).
- The spiritual healer in the Native Alaskan tradition is the shaman or angakut; hot springs may be used in conjunction with a healer.

Shamans (Angakut)

Native Alaskans turn to shamans, or angakut, for their health care. One can only guess at the number of people who use shamans. Shamans are thought to be able to travel between the real world and the spirit world; the shaman can travel to the sky and into the depths of the sea to speak with the spirits. Shamans perform ceremonial rituals to keep a person healthy; they use eagle feathers, incense, chants, music, and ceremonies to enter a trancelike state and talk with spirits (Robinson, 2002).

Hot Springs

Native Alaskans use hot springs to resolve arthritis pain, joint pain, headaches, and muscle aches (Downes, 1997). Healers also provide treatment through massage in conjunction with the hot springs (Downes). The heat and minerals of the hot springs are thought to have the greatest effect on the healing process. Hot springs are not readily available in every area and may require travel to another community.

SUMMARY

Native Americans were indigenous to North America. Two cultures thought of as Native American: American Indians and Native Alaskans. Native Americans learned how to care for themselves by using natural substances such as roots, leaves, barks, fruits, seeds, and flowers. Among these peoples, belief in spirits and being one with nature are vital to staying healthy.

Understanding the lack of trustworthiness by Caucasians perpetuated by Native Americans may help an athletic trainer understand why Native Americans act in certain ways or refuse certain things. Athletic trainers who learn to take a holistic approach that treats the patient's physical, mental, emotional, and spiritual aspects may be able to serve as better caregivers. It is also helpful to improve one's communication skills. Communication skills that are helpful include taking time to listen, not being in a hurry, and using terminology that is easily understood. Since Native American peoples believe in community and family, an athletic trainer may need to incorporate these parties into his or her planning and treatment considerations. Athletic trainers will be more successful in working with Native Americans when they do so in a way that makes the patient feel comfortable.

Learning Aids

What Would You Do If . . . ?

1. What if a Native American athlete indicated that seeing a shaman has to be part of the healing process for an injury?

2. What if it came to your attention that one of your soon-to-be athletes regularly uses peyote for religious reasons? Drug testing is a mandated program for athletes.

3. What if you have set up an appointment for a Native American but he fails to show up for it? The next day you ask him, "What happened?" He responds by saying, "I did not feel like it was necessary to go that day. Could you set another appointment?"

4. What if a student athlete refuses to remove a medicine bag that is on a necklace? The referee will not allow the student to participate unless the bag is removed.

5. What if a parent will not allow you the opportunity to work with her son's injury unless you lay out your holistic approach? What is your response?
6. Public institutions such as schools have an obligation to uphold a separation between church and state. Therefore, discussion about God can be offensive to those the athletic trainer may work with. How would you as the athletic trainer be able to work with the spiritual side that Native Americans may have without violating the separation of church and state?

Activities

1. Investigate the following items and determine their relationship to maintaining or regaining health in Native American culture: sweet grass, clay medicine bowl, and medicine bag.
2. Animals have varying meanings to each tribe. Make a list of animals that may cause illness or help one maintain or regain health in Native American belief, and explain the process by which this is believed to happen.
3. Investigate through the National Collegiate Athletic Association how peyote can be used for religious ceremonies without violating drug rules for athletes.
4. Investigate various ceremonies and rituals performed by shamans and examine how they may overlap with your own beliefs about health care.
5. What alternative explanations can the athletic trainer use if an athlete believes in witchcraft as a cause of illness?

Key Terms

Define the following key terms found in this chapter:

Aleut	Hand trembler	Sand painting
American Indian	Native Alaskans	Shaman
Chant	Native American	Stargazer
Crystal gazing	Nomadic	Tribe
Eskimo		

Questions for Review

1. What groups are included under the umbrella term Native American?
2. In light of history, what concerns might a Native American have when dealing with a Caucasian athletic trainer?
3. What types of illnesses are most often associated with American Indians and Native Alaskans?
4. Who is the decision maker in Native American households?
5. Identify effective and culturally competent forms of communication to use with Native American athletes.
6. Describe the religious beliefs of each main group of Native Americans.
7. Describe healing ceremonies and how each supports improved health.

Asian American and Pacific Islander American

Learning Objectives

Upon completing this chapter, students will be able to do the following:

1. Describe religious and health beliefs commonly held by Asian Americans and Pacific Islander Americans
2. Describe the spiritual aspects of culture that some Asian Americans and Pacific Islander Americans share
3. Explain some Asian American and Pacific Islander American cultural sensitivities regarding medications
4. Describe how an Asian American or Pacific Islander American family might influence the care of an athlete
5. Be prepared to care for an athlete while supporting his or her cultural needs
6. Explain the evolution of Asian American and Pacific Islander American health care
7. Explain how home remedies affect health care among Asian Americans and Pacific Islander Americans
8. Understand how origins and history have played a role in Asian American and Pacific Islander American health care practices

Marianne Chung, MPH, CHES

I am the associate director of a multiservice community center that provides comprehensive social and health services for Georgia's Asian American and Pacific Islander American communities. I serve on several boards promoting Asian and Pacific Islander communities and the prevention of breast cancer and domestic violence. Prior to joining the Center for Pan Asian Community Services, I conducted educational research and taught English in Taiwan as a Fulbright Junior Scholar. I have also worked as a research fellow at the National Center for Injury Prevention and Control. I have a BA degree in

Photo courtesy of The Center for Pan Asian Community Services, Inc.

sociology and a master of public health degree in health education from Emory University.

I am a third-generation Asian American, and my interest in community service and cultural diversity is rooted in my gratitude toward my family and my strong belief in human rights. I believe that promoting understanding and unity helps us work and live together peacefully. When we act in the spirit of service, we can change the world.

This chapter explores the mores of various Asian American and Pacific Islander American cultures—specifically, Chinese, Filipino, and Vietnamese. The goal is to help you prepare to support and provide the best possible heath care for Asian American and Pacific Islander American athletes.

Athletic trainers may not always be aware of the cultural factors that affect their athletes; in addition, each athletic trainer brings his or her own cultural influences into the health care setting. This chapter addresses cultural differences that may create misunderstandings, even conflicts, and thus interfere with health care. The chapter can help you prepare yourself to approach, communicate with, and work effectively with Asian American and Pacific Islander American athletes to improve health care outcomes. The chapter is divided into several categories: communication, family structure, spiritual orientation, biocultural assessment, common conditions, beliefs about illness, symptom management, and treatment. Other features include lists of dos and don'ts, as well as identification of characteristics that are unique to a given culture. Readers are also reminded that not all people in a group will adhere to each of the listed items.

The term Asian American and Pacific Islander American refers to a diverse community that includes more than 43 sub-ethnic groups and more than 100 languages. The Asian American and Pacific Islander American grouping includes South Asians (e.g., Nepalis, Indians), Southeast Asians (e.g., Laotians, Thais, Malaysians), Central and West Asians (e.g., Afghans, Pakistanis), and East Asians (e.g., Koreans, Japanese). The term Asian American and Pacific Islander American is broad, and athletic trainers should not assume that the information presented here is applicable to all Asians and Pacific Islanders. The three Asian and Pacific Islander cultures discussed in this chapter (Chinese, Filipino, and Vietnamese) were selected because they produce the largest number of immigrants in the United States (U.S. Census Bureau, 2000). Athletic trainers should understand that each Asian or Pacific Islander culture involves unique beliefs and needs; in addition, many of the beliefs and superstitions discussed here vary by age—that is, members of older generations may believe one thing, while younger people adhere to other cultural beliefs.

CHINESE

 Chinese have a unique culture of their own. It is important for the athletic trainer to understand the similarities and the differences of this culture to one's own, avoid the generalization that everyone adheres to the same beliefs that are part of this culture, and keep an open mind when working with athletes whose culture may be different than their own.

Demographic and Cultural Background Information

This section covers the following areas: history, language, family structure, daily living and food practices, and spiritual or religious orientation.

Brief History of Country of Origin and Immigration

There are more Chinese than there are of any other Asian group in the world. China is composed of Mainland China, or the People's Republic of China (see figure 7.1). China also includes Hong Kong, Macau, and Taiwan (Central Intelligence Agency, 2009) China has a number of regions or countries that it supports. Taiwan, which after World War II came under the political rule of China. Taiwan established its own constitution and democratic way of life. Hong Kong is part of China due to a special agreement with the United Kingdom that allows Hong Kong to have its own economy, education, religion, and politics and extends for a term of 50 years starting in 1997. Macau became part of China after an agreement with Portugal in 1987 (Central Intelligence Agency, 2009). There is great debate as to whether Tibet is part of China. The debate hinges on the question of whether the incorporation of Tibet into China was done under the guidelines of international law (Friends of Tibet [NZ], 2008; Rangzen, 1995; Rastogi, 2008).

The early Chinese immigrants came to the United States to labor in gold mines and on railroads. Most of the immigrants were men who were helping to support their families back in China. In 1882, the United States suspended immigration from China for 40 years. A quota was then established that would only allow 105 Chinese immigrants per year (Lipson, Dibble, & Minarik, 1996), and discrimination was a common practice, preventing Chinese from entering places of business or

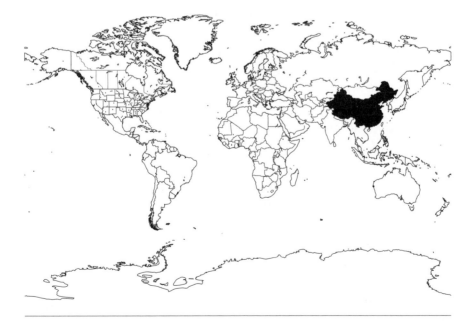

Figure 7.1 Map of China.

gaining employment in higher-paying jobs. During World War II, the United States virtually halted immigration from Asian countries. After the war, the immigration bar was lifted, and the resultant immigration, along with the fact that the United States and China had been allies during the war, led to an improved relationship between the two countries (Spector, 2004; Lowell, 1996).

Urban areas populated by Chinese people in the United States came to be called "Chinatown," though today Chinatowns are not exclusively Chinese but are culturally diverse communities. Those who live within a Chinatown area may be less inclined to use Western medicine. Lipson et al. (1996) indicate that health practices vary based on the length of time one has spent in the United States. Those who immigrated more than 40 years ago are most inclined to use Chinese folk medicine. Those who immigrated 25 years ago may combine Chinese folk medicine and Western medicine.

The majority of Chinese immigrants in the United States live in the major cities in New York, Texas, Hawaii, and California. Many of the most recent Chinese immigrants came to the United States for a college education and chose to stay; many Chinese immigrants maintain close ties with family members who remain in China. The second largest group of immigrants to the United States is Chinese (Purnell & Paulanka, 2003).

Primary Languages and Communication Styles

Mandarin is the written language of China. Dialects of the Chinese language include Mandarin, Cantonese, Wu, Min, Yue, and Hakka (Accredited Language Services, 2010; Lipson, Dibble, and Minarik, 1996).

DOS AND DON'TS

- Do use Mr., Mrs., or Ms. and the last name.
- Do greet the oldest male first in a group setting.
- Don't take a position of higher authority, such as standing, when the eldest family member may be shorter or even seated.
- Do sit side by side.
- Don't use a hand gesture with the palm up and fingers curled to call someone; doing so is considered disrespectful (it is how animals are traditionally called).
- Don't expose the bottom of your shoe toward a person who is Chinese; doing so is a sign of disrespect.
- Do try to pair Chinese women with female athletic trainers; physical touch by the opposite sex is considered taboo (Lipson et al., 1996).
- Do take your time when working with a Chinese athlete; Americans are viewed as always being in a hurry.

DISTINCTIVE TO THIS CULTURE

- Waving goodbye is considered disrespectful, since the palm is up (Rundle et al., 1999).
- Leaning on a table at any time conveys disrespect.

- In China, the family name is said before the given name.

- Discussing a private matter is considered disrespectful to the family; as a result, athletic trainers may face a challenge in obtaining information needed to treat an athlete.

- Eye contact is avoided when a person is in a position of authority, such as a physician.

- Looking down, or showing no facial expression, may be a sign of respect or concentration.

- Clenching the teeth and breathing loudly and heavily is a sign of displeasure (Seligman, 1999).

- Laughing during a tense situation may seem unusual to most, but it is the way the Chinese deal with such situations until they determine a proper response (Seligman).

- The space between people should be at least 2 feet (0.6 meter), which is known as personal distance; only when one's comfort level has reached a certain point will the distance be narrowed.

- Conversations tend to be soft and may appear to a Caucasian to be abrupt. From a Chinese perspective, Americans tend to be loud.

- Silence can be a sign of either respect or anger; an athletic trainer should not assume that silence means the person has no questions, or even understands.

- Open displays of emotion occur among family and friends. It is unlikely that emotion or private issues will be shared until the athlete is comfortable with the athletic trainer.

- Chinese people favor sequential thinking, so when working with an athlete and explaining an injury, start with how the injury occurred instead of with the diagnosis

- The concept of "saving face" can cause a Chinese athlete to be noncompliant. Saving face, or maintaining family honor and harmony, is known as **mien**. It can affect health when, for example, a Chinese athlete outwardly agrees with the course of care while he or she is with the athletic trainer but ultimately does not follow the plan because he or she disagreed yet did not verbalize this disagreement to the trainer (Salimbene, 2005). The athlete thus creates the appearance of harmony even though he or she actually disagrees with the trainer.

- The word "no" is avoided in Chinese culture because it is considered disrespectful.

- It is disrespectful for an athlete to ask questions of the person in authority. Thus an athlete may nod during the conversation, but this does not mean that he or she agrees or understands. According to Rundle et al. (1999), a person may say yes when really meaning no. This can, of course, create a huge problem for an athletic trainer, who may need to rephrase the statement to ensure clear understanding.

- Chinese women do not take their husband's name upon marriage; rather, a married woman uses her family name followed by her given name.
- According to Purnell and Paulanka (2003), the color white signifies death in Chinese culture. Thus, wearing a white medical jacket, considered professional attire in the United States, may cause concern for a Chinese athlete. The athletic trainer can remove the jacket, or at the very least explain why wearing a white jacket is necessary in the profession.

Family Structure

Generally, three generations live together in a Chinese home. It is believed that every person plays an integral role in society and within the family, and the elders in a family are highly regarded. Chinese families are patriarchal; decisions are made by the eldest male in the family. If he is not present when a decision needs to be made, it may be put off.

Once married, a woman is expected to become part of her husband's family and live with them in order to support the family and reduce bills. A mother-in-law's relationship with her daughter-in-law can be tenuous, as the daughter-in-law is to be submissive. (Purnell & Paulanka, 2003).

DISTINCTIVE TO THIS CULTURE

- When one refers to their family in Chinese culture, the discussion includes ancestors, immediate family, and those who may have been adopted.
- Men are expected to provide financial support.
- Women are expected to take care of the home, make meals, and provide caregiving during illness.
- Children are expected to take care of their parents and grandparents.
- Traditional belief posits quiet and respect as the characteristics of a successful person. Obedience to superiors is expected without questioning of authority.
- Only one child is allowed by law in China. A male child is more valued than a female child because he can carry on the family name and care for the parents in their old age. One of the benefits to living in the United States is the ability to have as many children as desired of either gender.
- Males are given preferential treatment as they grow up. In some cases, a female baby may be put up for adoption, abandoned, or even killed.
- When making a choice between an education and a job, education will be the priority. In the United States, Chinese children are expected to attend Saturday school for Chinese education.
- At birth, a child is considered one year old (Spector, 2004).
- In Chinese culture, homosexuality is viewed as a mental health issue and considered taboo (Chinese Society for Study of Sexual Minorities, 2003). In many parts of China, homosexuality is punishable by death, so it is hidden. Homosexual persons tend to have a close circle of friends and generally do not share their sexuality openly. They refer to one another as comrades.

Daily Living and Food Practices

- Chinese people live very much in the present and may not consider being on time to be as important as what is currently happening. Thus if it is important for an athlete to be on time for a medical appointment, this fact must be emphasized (Lipson et al., 1996).
- Chinese people eat three meals a day; the largest one is eaten in the evening.
- In Chinese culture, food is placed into two categories: hot or warm **(yang)** and cold or cool **(yin).** Chinese people believe that balancing yin and yang is necessary for staying healthy. Yin foods include fruits, cold liquids, crab, duck, tofu, watercress, and some vegetables (cabbage, bean sprouts, carrots, cucumber) (Parkinson, 2010). If yin foods are heated, they can become yang foods. Yang foods include hot liquids, beef, chicken, eggs, ginger, sesame oil, wine, bamboo, mushrooms, broccoli, liver, peanuts, and soups (Parkinson, 2010; Downes, 1997). Illnesses caused by an excess of yang foods are treated with yin, and vice versa.
- According to Ji (2007), vegetables and grains make up 80 percent of the Chinese diet; meats and fruits are eaten as supporting foods.
- Fruits are generally peeled before being eaten, because in China the skin is contaminated by unsanitary conditions (Purnell & Paulanka, 2003).
- Some Chinese persons prefer no ice in their drinks; heated drinks are often preferred. Again, this probably results from the fact of unsanitary conditions, which necessitates boiling of water in China.
- Desserts typically consist of fruits.
- Food preparation utilizes oil and salt, which can contribute to cardiovascular problems, cancers, and hypertension.
- Food falls into five categories based on taste—sweet, sour, bitter, salty, and pungent—and each taste is considered to relate to certain organs. Sweet relates to the spleen and stomach, sour to the liver and gall bladder, bitter to the heart and small intestine, salty to the kidneys and bladder, and pungent to the large intestine and lungs (Ji, 2007).
- When food is consumed, it needs to be balanced across the five categories in order to balance yin and yang and thus lead to harmony in health.
- A person who is ill will drink plenty of hot fluids in the belief that yin (cool liquids) would shock the body and keep one ill (Lipson et al., 1999). It is also believed that, if an athlete's organ is not strong, he should eat that organ from an animal in order to strengthen the athlete's own organ (Erickson D'Avanzo & Geissler, 2003). The athletic trainer might talk with the family member responsible for nutrition to address the ways in which diet might affect the athlete's health. For example, an athletic trainer might recommend serving beef to an athlete who is anemic or avoiding oil-fried foods for an athlete who has a heart condition (Salimbene, 2005).

Spiritual or Religious Orientation

- Those who practice religion do so within the privacy of their own homes and generally adhere to one of three religions: Buddhism, Catholicism, and Protestantism (Purnell and Paulanka, 2003). Buddhism teaches self-control even during illness, and the resulting stoicism may make it difficult for an athletic trainer to determine a patient's pain level (Salimbene). Two other traditions, Confucianism and Taoism, are considered to be religions by some and philosophies by others. Confucianism promotes moderation, since excess is believed to bring about illness (Salimbene, 2005). Taoism emphasizes being in tune with all things—both on earth and in heaven—and in being one in spirit and in mind. All things are dependent upon each other. If one thing goes awry, the person will have to adjust to bring about harmony once again. Factors such as stress, fighting, or riots will cause disharmony that will bring about illness.
- Additional forms of spirituality include massage, creation of artworks, meditation, and prayer (Spector, 2004).
- Chinese people tend toward strong belief in the ability of ancestors to prevent or cure illness.
- Yin and yang must be in harmony or illness will occur.
- The body must be intact to ensure that the spirit goes to heaven, according to Confucianism (Salimbene, 2005). As a result, Chinese people are not likely to donate organs (Salimbene, 2005).

Health Care Information

This section addresses the unique beliefs, sensitivities, conditions, illnesses, and treatments associated with Chinese culture. It provides you with specifics about how to best care for Chinese athletes and their families using both Western and traditional treatments.

Biocultural Assessment

- The skin color of Chinese people ranges from yellow to a dark tone.
- Body and facial hair is limited; hair is usually straight and black.
- Chinese people are most likely to have an ulna that is longer than their radius (Schrefer, 1994; Purnell & Paulanka, 2003).
- The long bones in the body of Chinese people are less dense than those of whites (Schrefer, 1994). About half of all Chinese adults have a bony protuberance of the hard palate of the mouth; it is problematic only if there is constant irritation of the area, possibly by a mouth guard or dentures.
- Hip measurements are generally about 1.6 inches (4 centimeters) smaller in Chinese females and 2.8 inches (7 centimeters) smaller in Chinese males than in Westerners (Purnell & Paulanka, 2003, 2005).

Common Sensitivities and Conditions

- Some Chinese persons are sensitive to certain medications, including beta-blockers, antidepressants (e.g., propranolol), antipsychotics (e.g., haloperidol), atropine, and recreational drugs such as alcohol (Purnell & Paulanka, 2005).

- An upset stomach is common with use of analgesics (Purnell & Paulanka, 2005).

- Codeine has a significantly weaker effect on Chinese people (Wood, 1997).

- Illnesses and conditions that commonly afflict Chinese people include hepatitis B, hypertension, lactose intolerance, osteoporosis, and tuberculosis (Purnell & Paulanka 2003, 2005; Schrefer, 1994; Erickson D'Avanzo & Geissler, 2003).

- Several other conditions found more often among Chinese persons may be unfamiliar to an athletic trainer: coccidioidomycosis, glucose-6-phosphate dehydrogenase deficiency, shenkui, qi-gong psychotic reaction, shenjing shuairuo, and thalassemia. Any athlete who might have one of these conditions should be referred to a physician for care. The appendix provides the signs and symptoms of these conditions in greater detail.

Beliefs About Illness

It is believed by the Chinese that two opposing energy forces—yin and yang—control health and life. These forces do not work against each other; rather, they create balance. A body that is in balance is referred to as **dao**. Illness is caused by an imbalance between yin and yang.

Chi or **qi** is the natural life force or energy that exists in all living things. Chi also means to have the body in harmony with the world. It can be inherited at birth, and additional chi comes from a person's surroundings and food. Trouble within the person, the local environment, or the world can bring disharmony and illness. Other causes of illness are spirits and inappropriate behaviors.

Chinese belief also holds that in every person are **meridians** or pathways along which energy (chi or qi) flows through the body. Meridians are known as electrical pathways. There are 12 meridians—6 yin and 6 yang. The meridians are important during the diagnosis and treatment of a Chinese athlete. It is believed that a blockage of a meridian prevents energy from flowing properly, thus necessitating treatment. More information about meridians is given in the treatments section included later in this discussion.

DISTINCTIVE TO THIS CULTURE

- Everything fits into either the yin or yang categories. For example, the sun is yang, and the moon is yin. The symbol used to describe yin and yang is a circle with a white comma-like side and a black comma-like side. When bandages are applied, the yin-yang symbol may be placed on the bandage (Lucas, 1987).

- Yin characteristics of an illness include coldness, cold sweats, cramping pain, swelling, weight loss, illness inside the body, slow onset, lack of thirst, lots of clear urine, and tiredness (Chmelik, 1999; McCabe, 2005; Adler & Mukherji, 1995; Kaptchuk, 2000; Leininger & McFarland, 2002). Some yin illnesses or perceived illnesses include inability to deal with winter, impotence, low blood sugar, arthritis, and backache. An athlete with a yin illness requires the body to be warmed and dried.

- Characteristics of yang illnesses include fever, anger, irritation, red face, quick temper, green sinus discharge, indigestion, thirst, dryness, sudden onset of symptoms, burning pain, convulsions, dry mouth, sore mouth, constipation, lack of perspiration, panting, and locus in the upper part of the body. Heat makes the symptoms worse. The back of the body, skin, and hair are primary areas for location of yang illnesses. Illnesses associated with yang include heat stroke, rash, headache, indigestion after alcohol use, sinus infection, and high blood pressure (Chmelik, 1999; McCabe, 2005; Adler & Mukherji, 1995; Kaptchuk, 2000; Leininger & McFarland, 2002).

- An athletic trainer needs to be conscious of the fact that some treatments, medications, and surgeries fall into yin and yang categories. For example, Leininger and McFarland (2002) described chemotherapy as a hot treatment. In such instances, yin foods would have to be prescribed to balance the treatment. Thus the athletic trainer should ask the athlete which category a given treatment falls into.

- Mental illness is believed to be caused by an imbalance of emotions, an ancestor's displeasure, or possession by an evil spirit.

- Birth defects are thought to be caused by something the mother did during pregnancy. For example, Lipson et al. (1996) indicate that going to a zoo during pregnancy is thought to cause the child to look like an animal.

- The head is considered the most important part of the body. The soul of the person is said to live in the head, and touching the person's head may cause the soul to leave the body, resulting in illness. If the athletic trainer has to examine a patient's head, he or she should first explain the reason and obtain permission to do so (Rundle et al., 1999).

Preventive Health Practices

- The primary focus of Chinese physicians is to prevent illness by ensuring that the body and mind are in harmony. Thus the best physicians are considered to be those whose clients rarely get sick.

- Given the lower bone density and common lactose intolerance among Chinese persons, it may be prudent to consider calcium replacement and bone density testing for osteoporosis (Purnell & Paulanka, 2005).

- Chinese people accept the process of immunization and may have practiced a form of it early on in their culture.

- One hindrance to prevention among Chinese people is the need for modesty, which may cause avoidance of preventive examinations such as mammograms, breast self-examinations, and prostate exams. Encourage preventive health care and promote the notion that a person can take charge of his or her own well-being. Proactive ways to take part in maintaining one's health include breast self-examinations for female athletes and testicular self-examinations for male athletes; both can be done privately.

- Asians who may not have health care benefits or who are financially strapped are less likely to seek care. This, of course, can cause problems since some illnesses or conditions will worsen and become much more challenging for both the athletic trainer and the athlete.

- Advise a Chinese athlete to avoid the lactose fillers often found in generic medications. To avoid gas and constipation associated with lactose intolerance, encourage patients to consult with their physician or pharmacist.

Symptom Management

- Displays of pain are considered a weakness in Chinese culture, and Chinese persons have a high pain tolerance. Thus they may not make the athletic trainer aware of their degree of pain. Pain is treated with acupuncture, massage, application of warmth over the area, or acupressure. One clue to the presence of pain is loud inhalation of air through pursed lips (Axtell, 1993).

- Vomiting, fatigue, and nausea are considered to be signs of too much yin and are treated accordingly (Lipson et al., 1996). The athletic trainer will have to ask about symptoms, especially since Chinese persons may choose to treat themselves without sharing the information.

Treatments

Chinese belief holds that all body structures are interrelated. If one part of the body is ill, all parts of the body have been affected in some way. As a result, athletic trainers must ensure that care is integrated with all other systems in order for a cure to occur. For example, in treating a sprained ankle that involves swelling, the athletic trainer would have to deal with the lymphatic system to decrease swelling and help the circulatory system bring repair materials to the site. The athletic trainer might use massage to decrease spasm, and a Chinese healer might use acupuncture to control pain.

It is believed that minor illnesses can be treated without a physician by using yin and yang. Unfortunately, a major illness may be ignored or treated by yin and yang, thus delaying necessary care. Chinese healers rely on their knowledge of signs and symptoms of past illness to treat a current illness. They keep a written log of recipes for healing, so that there is a record for future generations as they take on the role as healers (Lucas, 1987).

The Chinese people are well known for their contributions to the world of medicine. Chinese physicians are known for their ability to prevent illness, and it is becoming more common now in Western medicine to treat the body as a whole, rather than addressing only a single system or body part.

A Chinese physician makes a diagnosis by using observation, listening, smelling, questioning, and touching (A World of Chinese Medicine, 2006). During **observation**, the physician examines skin tone, eyes, nails, and tongue; a Chinese physician can diagnose 100 conditions by looking at the tongue (Spector, 2004). The person's energy level also helps the Chinese physician determine the illness. The Chinese physician listens to the patient's breathing and smells his or her breath, coughing, or other body odors. The tone of the person's voice can also help determine the type of illness. Questioning explores the history of the illness and previous illnesses. Questions may involve yin and yang behaviors that could be considered hot or cold, such as stress, food, work, exercise, emotional well-being, and signs and symptoms.

Palpation, or touching of the body, is used to determine pulse, pain, and body temperature. A Chinese physician may take six different pulses on the hands to help determine the cause of illness or identify the organ that is primarily affected (Spector, 2004). Three fingers (index, middle, and ring) are used to take a pulse. There are also 12 pulses that can be felt—one for each of the 12 meridians (A World of Chinese Medicine, 2006).

If an athlete uses Western medicine to resolve an illness, the treatment must coincide with the athlete's cultural beliefs. For example, if being out of balance causes the person's illness, the care must bring back the balance. If an athlete perceives that Western medicine may not bring about balance, he or she may refuse the care that is offered (Purnell & Paulanka, 2003). Indeed, some Chinese people believe that it is a waste of time and money to seek the assistance of a Western physician. In addition, it is thought that if a treatment hurts, it will likely put the body out of balance and contribute to the illness (Purnell & Paulanka, 2003). Once the athlete begins to feel better, he or she is likely to stop treatment and may not keep appointments for follow-up care. Traditional Chinese medicine (TCM) is widely used by Chinese athletes, especially those who are poor, since TCM is less expensive (Purnell & Paulanka, 2003).

Each illness has a number of associated treatments. Traditional Chinese treatments include cupping, moxibustion, acupuncture, and acupressure. Each method is used as a way to bring about health and support qi. The athletic trainer should be aware of traditional Chinese treatments and of the fact that some of them may leave distinctive markings on the skin. Traditional Chinese medicine treatments are listed below to help you understand how each practice may affect the treatment that you provide.

Acupressure

This therapy uses the hand, fingers, elbow, or small implements to place pressure on sensitive points. The pressure is held on the point until the sensitivity of the point decreases—usually for 10 to 12 seconds. Pressure placed on a point can refer pain to another area. When pain is referred, that area has to receive acupressure. The pathway that connects pressure point areas is a meridian.

Acupressure is used to relieve headache, stress, digestive trouble, muscle ache, menstrual cramps, and sinus problems; it is also used to improve circulation and stimulate the immune system (Reed, 1990).

Acupuncture

This medical practice supports qi. It involves placing needles into one of the 365 points on the qi meridian that greatly influence the success of treatment (Spector, 2004). Acupuncture is used to improve the flow of qi though the meridians by unblocking them. Various types of needles are used for a variety of problems, including stress, flu, asthma, headache, other pain, fatigue, and muscle issues. In China, and now in the United States, surgery can sometimes be done without anesthesia by simply using acupuncture (Purnell & Paulanka, 2003; Spector, 2004).

The twelve meridians are as follows: bladder, gallbladder, heart, kidney, large intestine, liver, lung, small intestine, spleen, stomach, paracardium, and triple heater (also known as the triple warmer or triple burner [Anisman-Reiner, 2007]). Acupuncture works with these 12 organs to bring about dao. There are six yin organs and six yang organs. Yin organs include the heart, pericardium, lungs, spleen, liver, and kidney. Yang organs include the small intestine, triple heater, stomach, large intestine, gallbladder, and bladder.

Moxibustion

Moxibustion is a heat therapy that can be used alone or in conjunction with acupuncture. It is used to stimulate the flow of qi and can take two forms: direct and indirect. Moxibustion can also be divided into scarring and nonscarring forms.

This therapy uses the mugwort plant (Acupuncture Today, 2007). The leaves are crushed and rolled or powdered. If rolled, it is then burned and placed close to an acupuncture needle inserted into a muscle. The heat travels down the needle into the muscle to increase circulation in the area. The athlete indicates his or her comfort level with the amount of heat. The indirect moxibustion occurs by lighting the rolled leaves and placing them close to the skin until they heat the area.

In powdered form, the mugwort is shaped into a cone and burned on ointment directly over an acupuncture point. This type of burning is known as direct moxibustion. Scarring moxibustion occurs when the preparation is placed directly on the skin until it burns itself out. This form of treatment can leave permanent scars, as well as blisters. Nonscarring moxibustion occurs when the preparation is not placed on the skin.

Bonesetting

In Western medicine, a person with a fracture or dislocation goes through X ray, manipulation, and casting. Bonesetters in China do not believe that surgery is necessary to fix bones; instead, they feel a bone fracture or dislocation to determine what needs to be done, then manipulate it back into place. The aligned bones are placed in wooden splints for about 6 weeks to complete the healing. Bonesetters also use herbal medicines in plaster that is applied to the fracture or dislocation (Radhika, 2000).

Cupping (Fire Cupping)

Cupping is a Chinese therapy that causes the skin and tissue to be drawn upward, in a vacuum, thus stimulating circulation in the area underneath the cup. This is a form of acupressure. The practitioner creates suction with the cup, then places it on the skin. Cupping takes two forms—one with heat and one without.

Fire cupping is done by lighting an alcohol-laden cotton ball on fire underneath the cup. The heat creates suction, and the cup is then placed on the body. Cups are placed in a series and left in place for approximately 20 minutes. They leave a distinctive pattern that remains for several days. An athletic trainer who is unfamiliar with cupping may be confused upon seeing this pattern on an athlete's body; in such cases, it may be prudent to ask the athlete if cupping was involved.

Cupping is intended to open the qi meridians of the body. It is use to support the lymph system, improve circulation, and release toxins from the body. Traditional issues that respond best to this form of treatment include respiratory problems, menstrual pain, digestive problems, and general soreness. Cupping is avoided when a person has a fever, bleeding disorders, inflamed areas, convulsions, cramping, or skin disorders (Dharmananda, 1999).

Gua Sha

Gua sha is a home remedy used to relieve a person who has a fever, food poisoning, fatigue, muscle or tendon injury, poor circulation, or indigestion (Nielsen, 2001). The technique is done by placing oil on the skin in the area of work, then using the edge of a spoon, dish, or coin (coining) to scrape the skin. Each scraping is about 4 inches (10 centimeters) long (Nielsen; Pich, 2005). As a result of the scraping, capillaries break, which causes bruising that can run the length of the treatment area and thus can be very large. An athletic trainer may be very concerned about such an injury based on its appearance. One should remember that this is a culture-specific treatment, not physical abuse (Nielsen, 2001). Gua sha is used before cupping in some instances, but never afterward.

Massage

Massage is a hands-on technique of rubbing, tapping, friction, vibration, and rolling of the skin to improve circulation to the muscles, joints, and soft tissues. Massage helps relieve stress, tension, muscle soreness, and pain. It brings about relaxation and supports the circulatory, nervous, and lymphatic systems.

Aromatherapy

Aromatherapy is thought to have been passed on from the Chinese to other cultures. It uses oils made from plant leaves, stems, bark, and petals that are heated or crushed to release the oils. The type of oil is determined by the illness or condition.

The oils are placed on the skin via massage performed on the areas that hold stress—typically, the back, shoulders, neck, legs, and face. The oils can also be inhaled through use of a special burner. Aromatherapy is used most often for sleeplessness, headache, and depression (Complementary Healthcare Information Service—UK, 2007).

Herbal Remedies

These remedies have been passed down from generation to generation. They use roots, bark, stones, insects, bones, shells, fruits, seeds, and leaves. The crushed ingredients are placed together to help heal the ill. Some are made into teas. Lipson et al. (1996) and Spector (2004) identify the following herbal remedies:

- Antlers—bone strength and impotence
- Ginseng—anemia, colic, depression, indigestion, impotence, and rheumatism
- Snake flesh—eye health and vision
- Turtle shells—kidneys and gallstones

Kennett (1976) shares the following remedies:

- Camphor and blue copperas applied to a pork shinbone, then applied externally—hemorrhoids
- Ephedra plant—fever
- Sphagnum moss—wounds
- Brine-soaked lemons—wounds

Spector (2004) shares the following remedies:

- Ground seahorse—gout
- Heated tienchi flowers—remedy nausea, dizziness, and hot-tempered person
- Urine from young boys—wound healing, ease a sore throat, and resolve lung diseases

When an athletic trainer asks what medicines a Chinese athlete is taking, he or she may not report herbals being used. The athletic trainer should pursue this line of questioning to ensure that there is no complication or interaction with other medicines. A Chinese person may refer to herbals as tonics. In Chinatown, to obtain herbals one must have a prescription from a Chinese physician. An herbalist makes the tonic.

Qigong

Qigong therapy involves breathing, exercise, and meditation to improve one's qi. Thousands of qigong practices exist, the most common one being t'ai chi. The theory behind qigong is that maintaining one's health is of the utmost importance. *Qi* means breath, and *gong* means work. Since breath is an extension of life, controlling it keeps one healthy, as does the physical work. Gong involves controlled physical movements that create strength, stamina, coordination, balance, and flexibility. This is a form of exercise combined with a component of spirituality. Persons of any age can do qigong. Movements are choreographed so that a yin movement is followed by a yang movement, and vice versa. Typically, this exercise is performed twice per day.

Protection

Jade is considered a good luck charm and may be worn around the neck; it is thought to protect one from danger and illness. It is believed that if the jade is broken or becomes dull, misfortune will befall the wearer (Spector, 2004). It is also said that if the jade is broken, bad energy is drawn to the jade and bad luck or illness will befall the person (Spector, 2004).

A rope worn around the waist is meant for good luck and good health. Some people write a Chinese character on a piece of paper and hang it on a doorway or wall or place it on the body for good health. They may burn the paper and pour the ashes into a tea and drink it for good health (Spector, 2004). An athletic trainer needs to obtain permission to remove any good luck charms or amulets from an athlete.

FILIPINO

Filipinos have a unique culture of their own. It is important for the athletic trainer to understand the similarities and the differences of this culture to one's own, avoid the generalization that everyone adheres to the same beliefs that are part of this culture, and keep an open mind when working with athletes whose culture may be different than their own.

Demographic and Cultural Background Information

Filipinos have developed a unique culture because they live on so many islands. It is hard enough for one who lives there to know what is occurring on each of the islands—and all the more challenging for an athletic trainer who may have lived solely in the United States. To better prepare you to work with Filipino athletes, this section addresses the following aspects of Filipino culture: history, language, family structure, daily living and food practices, and spiritual orientation. It also provides information about biocultural assessment, common conditions, beliefs about illness, prevention, symptom management, and treatments.

Brief History of Country of Origin and Immigration

The Philippines is a group of 7,107 islands in the South Pacific (see figure 7.2). The islands are largely volcanic in origin and lie in the Pacific Ring of Fire, which means they are prone to eruptions, earthquakes, and the corresponding devastation (Purnell & Paulanka, 2003).

At various times, the Philippine islands were governed by Spain, then the United States, and lastly Japan before they finally became an independent nation after World War II. After immigrating, the first group of Filipinos in the United States stayed together in small communities because of discrimination (Downes, 1997). The second group of immigrants came to the United States to work in agricultural fields, specifically in Hawaii. The majority made their home in Hawaii and in the western continental states. Many Filipino immigrants were granted citizenship for joining the military to fight in World War II. More recent immigrants came to the United States as white-collar workers. Today, many Filipinos live in New York, New Jersey, Washington, Hawaii, Texas, and Illinois (Purnell & Paulanka, 2003).

Primary Languages and Communication Styles

The major ethnic groups within the Philippines are Tagalog, Cebuano, and Ilocano. The Philippines is home to 11 languages and 87 dialects (Erickson D'Avanzo &

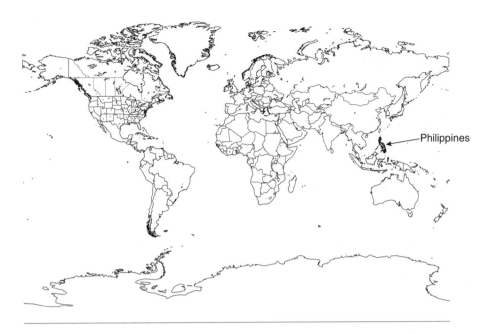

Figure 7.2 Map of the Philippines.

Geissler, 2003); the primary language is Filipino, and Tagalog is the main dialect (Purnell & Paulanka, 2003). English is the predominant language for business, trade, and education.

DOS AND DON'TS

- Do greet a person for the first time by using Mr., Mrs., or Ms. and the person's last name.
- Don't attempt to shake hands; doing so is considered unusual.
- Do greet by using a hand raised, as in a casual "Hi."
- Do allow trust to develop before asking for personal information.

DISTINCTIVE TO THIS CULTURE

- In Filipino culture, children assume their mother's maiden surname as their middle names, and their father's surname as their own.
- When a young woman marries, her mother's maiden surname no longer appears as her middle name. Instead, her father's surname becomes her middle name and then she adopts her husband's surname as her own.
- In the less traditional parts of Filipino society, hyphenation (i.e., combining the wife's and husband's last names, in that order) is fast becoming the practice.
- Filipinos generally find physical proximity to nonfamily members uncomfortable. Thus athletic trainers may need to keep some physical distance—initially, say between 5 and 12 feet (about 1.5 to 3.5 meters).

- The practice of females walking hand in hand is not associated with lesbianism. However, it is extremely rare to find two grown men holding hands, even gay men, because machismo is a very strong concept in Filipino culture.
- Americans tend to speak louder than Filipinos and thus may be considered abrasive (Purnell & Paulanka, 2003).
- Most Filipinos speak English, but proficiency varies. Speaking slowly may help a Filipino listener understand. An athletic trainer may need to ask a Filipino athlete often whether he or she understands what is being said. Ask questions periodically to determine understanding. Filipino athletes may nod their head while listening, thus leading one to think that they understand, when in fact they do not.
- Filipino culture is typically very private, but a Filipino athlete will share information necessary for proper treatment. Topics considered to be sensitive family issues are often kept private until an athletic trainer can be trusted. Issues that might be considered private include sex, separation or divorce, mental illness, and sexually transmitted disease (Erickson D'Avanzo & Geissler, 2003). To obtain information regarding private matters, an athletic trainer may need to let the athlete know that it is necessary for proper care.
- Filipinos respect authority, and athletic trainers may be viewed as respected authoritative figures.
- Women are often submissive to men (Erickson D'Avanzo & Geissler).

Pakikisama is a Filipino concept that can be translated approximately as "going along with whatever is the prevailing opinion or sentiment" (Downes, 1997). Pakikisama is similar to "saving face" in Chinese culture, and an athletic trainer needs to be aware that a Filipino may agree with what is being said when in reality he or she is disagreeing internally. If there is a disagreement, a third party who is Filipino and joins the encounter will often take one side of the argument instead of helping to find common ground.

After describing a course of treatment, an athletic trainer might ask the athlete to repeat it in order to ensure the athlete's comprehension. If a Filipino athlete is comfortable with an athletic trainer, he or she may touch the trainer on the hand or shoulder (Francia, 1997).

Family Structure

To most Filipinos, family is the utmost priority, and the individual is often considered to be secondary. Many Filipinos feel a strong connection with their ancestors and to future generations. Familial stories are passed on from generation to generation, and three generations may be found in the same home.

DISTINCTIVE TO THIS CULTURE

- The oldest father often speaks for the family. Decisions are made after all options are considered, and input is received from most if not all family members. If there is no father, the eldest son fills the role of the father.

- In a traditional Filipino household, women are expected to care for the ill and run family finances (Erickson D'Avanzo & Geissler, 2003). If no mother is present, the eldest daughter assumes this role. The mother often has a say in decisions made within the household (Erickson D'Avanzo & Geissler; Downes, 1997).
- **Hiya** is a Filipino concept that roughly translates to embarrassment, and it moves Filipinos into avoiding any action that may result in "losing face." For many, it is important to lead a life of avoiding hiya in order to avoid embarrassing oneself or one's family. As in most cultures, proper behavior is expected in Filipino culture, and hiya is a primary determinant of what is deemed proper or improper. In some instances, an athlete may be concerned about the athletic trainer's opinion of them, especially if an illness or disease is embarrassing (e.g., a sexually transmitted disease) (Downes). Thus an athletic trainer may have to develop a relationship of trust before symptoms of a hiya illness will be shared by the athlete.
- Homosexuality, particularly among males, is often viewed with ridicule.

Daily Living and Food Practices

- The Filipino concept of "being on time" depends largely on one's perception of an event's importance. For family or social events, many Filipinos think it is okay to be late. Interruptions to such events are often expected and are viewed as acceptable. However, if one risks punitive consequences for being late, as with reporting to work, a Filipino will almost always be on time (Purnell & Paulanka, 2003).
- **Bahala na** is the Filipino outlook on life—the belief that God controls all things. Unexpected changes in plans are taken in stride, as are illness and death (Lipson et al., 1996).
- Keeping clean is of paramount importance in Filipino culture. It is considered highly embarrassing for anyone to smell bad (Lipson et al.). Thus if your athlete's hygiene declines, this could be an indication of health care issues, and it should be explored.
- Filipinos, especially those who can afford to, tend to eat three major meals a day, with several snacks in between. The typical diet includes rice, fish, and vegetables. Meals are often high in salt, sugar, and protein.
- Water is the preferred drink—preferably cold due to the hot climate of the Philippines.
- Most Filipinos are Catholic, and as a result fish is often eaten instead of meat on Fridays and on certain religious holidays as a form of abstinence.
- Lugaw, a type of rice porridge also referred to as congee, is often cooked as a traditional restorative meal for a person who is ill.
- Cold fluids and ice are often avoided during illness.
- Cold foods and acidic foods are avoided in the morning because of Filipino belief that they cause indigestion (Lipson et al.).

- Coconut is a favorite food among Filipinos. Because of its high fat content, it may contribute to the high rate of hypercholesterolemia among Filipinos.
- Being overweight is often viewed by Filipinos as a sign of having money, and there may be no expectation that weight loss is necessary for good health. If a sport requires an athlete to maintain a certain weight class, the athletic trainer may need to educate the coach about this Filipino belief.

Spiritual or Religious Orientation

Most Filipinos are Roman Catholic, though some practice Islam, Buddhism, or a Protestant faith.

The Filipino concept "bahala na" may be considered by Westerners as fatalism. It translates, approximately, as a belief that events in life are beyond one's individual control and thus should be left to God or other supernatural forces. Life and death are often viewed by Filipinos as determined by God: God decides what happens in life and when death should occur. Filipinos believe that leading a Godly life will result in going to heaven in the afterlife (Downes, 1997), and intervention may be viewed as an attempt to control life, or the length of one's lifetime, beyond God's determination or will. Thus Filipino athletes may comment that they are willing to accept God's decision on their medical fate instead of allowing athletic trainers or physicians to help them. This stance may pose a challenge for athletic trainers when an athlete's refusal of treatment increases the length of time that the athlete has to be away from competition.

With all this in mind, an athletic trainer may need to work to gain an athlete's trust in order to be able to treat an injury or illness. An athletic trainer might try to convince the athlete that God gave the trainer skills in order to help with such problems.

Health Care Information

The following sections address specifics of health care as it relates to Filipinos. An athletic trainer who takes an active role in learning this information is likely to establish better cultural relations with his or her athletes. The material covered here includes biocultural assessment, common sensitivities and conditions, beliefs about illness, preventive health practices, symptom management, and treatments.

Biocultural Assessment

- Filipino skin tone is dark brown. It may cause difficulties for an athletic trainer as it may be challenging to determine skin color changes. The conjunctiva may be most reliable in determining skin color changes (Erickson D'Avanzo & Geissler, 2003). Athletic trainers should also view the nail beds and the inside of the lips.
- Hair is black or brown.
- Filipinos tend to have a broad bridge of the nose, and opticians should attend to this fact when fitting them for glasses (Purnell & Paulanka, 2003).

- The eyes of Filipinos are commonly almond-shaped and dark brown. The assessment of papillary reaction may be a challenge because of the darkness of the eyes (Purnell & Paulanka, 2003).

Common Sensitivities and Conditions

- Filipinos may have sensitivities to central nervous system drugs.
- Medication in the Philippines is given over-the-counter (i.e., without prescription). Thus a prescription from an American physician may be confusing for Filipinos who are not acculturated, and it is likely that some infections will have adapted to an antibiotic as a result of the overuse of antibiotics.
- Asians have a lower tolerance for alcohol and more adverse reactions to it (Purnell & Paulanka, 2003).
- People of Filipino heritage are at risk for several major cancers: breast, liver, cervical, lung, and prostate (Erickson D'Avanzo & Geissler, 2003).
- Individuals of Filipino descent have a high rate of heart disease.
- Typical illnesses and conditions include arthritis, coronary artery disease, type 1 diabetes, lactose intolerance, wheat intolerance, gout, hepatitis B, hypertension, vitamin A deficiency, and tuberculosis.
- Athletic trainers should be aware that Filipinos tend to let illnesses become advanced before seeking care (Purnell & Paulanka; Anderson, 1983).
- Several other conditions found more often among Filipinos may be unfamiliar to an athletic trainer: kidney stones, glucose-6-phosphate dehydrogenase deficiency, mali mali, schistosomiasis, malaria, thalassemia, thyroid cancer, hypercholesterolemia, and hyperuricemia. Any athlete who might have one of these conditions should be referred to a physician for care. See the appendix for further information on signs and symptoms of these conditions.

Beliefs About Illness

Filipinos believe they become ill because of either natural or supernatural causes (Downes, 1997). Many of them believe that a healthy person is one who has balance in his or her life and that a person without balance becomes ill. Once ill, a person may regain health by determining where the imbalance occurred and attaining balance again. For example, to a Filipino, a laceration that causes large blood loss could put their system out of balance (Lipson et al., 1996).

- Some Filipinos believe that if a person does bad things he will become sick. Some also believe that bad thoughts lead to illness.
- Some Filipinos believe that abrupt changes in ambient temperature—for example, going outdoors in the winter without a coat—can lead to illness.
- If a person believes in supernatural causes of illness, he or she is more likely to have a fatalistic view of life. Some Filipinos believe that spirits, witchcraft, and ghosts may cause illness.

- Some Filipinos believe in the concept that the "evil eye" can cause illness. It is often believed to be received through the mouth or eyes, which provides another reason to avoid eye contact. Some believe that the evil eye can be removed by placing saliva across the ill person's forehead.
- Some Filipinos believe that having a handicapped child is God's way of teaching a family how to deal with adversity. Some also believe that an evil spirit has consumed the child, or that the disability constitutes payback for a sin or previous improper behavior (Erickson D'Avanzo & Geissler, 2003).
- **Kulam** means witchcraft on some of the Philippine islands. Kulam may mean that a hex has been placed on a person to make him or her ill. In some instances, a doll may be pierced with needles with the intention of causing corresponding areas of the body of the hexed person to experience the sensations.
- Mental illness is sometimes thought by Filipinos to be hereditary or caused by witchcraft (Erickson D'Avanzo & Geissler).
- An **amok**, in Filipino terms, is a person who suddenly turns violent. The outcome of this behavior is often death or incarceration. It is often thought to occur as the result of a loss or insult (Downes, 1997). In Western medicine, this behavior is thought to result from mental illness.
- Western medicine's adherence to germ theory may conflict with a Filipino's belief in the supernatural. Alternately, athletes may use both cultural healers and Western healers at the same time. Cultural healers may prescribe herbals that can interact with medications. An athletic trainer might ask if the athlete is working with a cultural healer and then work in conjunction with the healer to treat the athlete.
- Filipinos believe that treatment should provide immediate relief; if it does, the athlete may seek another healer (Downes).

Preventive Health Practices

Many Filipinos believe in the concept of balance for good health. Thus they may emphasize eating right, living a stress-free life, and participating in many activities.

- Lactose filler can be avoided by consulting with a physician or pharmacist regarding medications.
- It is also believed that to prevent illness a person should eat pigeon soup, avoid too much sun and rain, and soak one's feet in salt water after working in the fields (Spector, 1996).
- Use of religious adornments, statues, or prayer is believed by some Filipinos to protect against illness.
- Filipinos may avoid the preventive practices of mammograms and pap smears because of a belief in modesty.
- Modesty among Filipino women makes it difficult for them to be examined by male physicians.

Symptom Management

Filipinos often allow an illness to flourish before deciding to do anything about it; this of course leads to more complicated cases for athletic trainers. If an athletic trainer establishes a good relationship with an athlete before he or she becomes ill, the athlete may have the confidence and the conviction to be more proactive with prevention.

- Pain is often not verbalized, and evaluating facial expressions may be a more reliable way of checking for pain. Some Filipinos believe that God gave them the pain and that remaining silent about it will make them stronger (Lipson et al., 1996).
- Many Filipinos avoid therapeutic medications for fear of becoming dependent (Lipson et al.). An athletic trainer may need to explain the fact that a given medication is either not the type that poses a risk of dependency or will not be taken long enough to cause dependency.
- Any condition leading to breathing difficulty may result in anxiety, which can compound the preexisting shortness of breath. Offering oxygen may cause a Filipino athlete to become more anxious, resulting in greater difficulty breathing and a refusal to take the oxygen (Lipson et al.). The athletic trainer needs to give an explanation to the athlete to ease his or her concern.
- Depression may not be acknowledged because of the stigma associated with mental health issues in Filipino culture (Lipson et al.). An athletic trainer may need to reassure the athlete or find a way to define the illness as something not associated with mental health.
- When an athlete vomits, he or she may inform the athletic trainer but possibly not until he or she has cleaned it up (Lipson et al.).

Treatments

Filipinos believe in home remedies, and an athletic trainer needs to ask what home remedies a Filipino athlete may have used. The following sections discuss some traditional Filipino treatments, such as exorcism, flushing, heating, use of healers, and home remedies.

Exorcism

If a person is believed to have been taken over by a demon or a hex, then an exorcism may be done to remove it. The exorcist, most often a Roman Catholic priest, says prayers that appeal to God and angels to remove a hex or a demon. Holy water may be used to support the exorcism.

Flushing

Flushing involves efforts to remove toxins from the body by promoting the excretion of bodily fluids. Flushing methods include vomiting, perspiration, and menstrual bleeding (Downes, 1997). The resulting loss of bodily fluid may cause fatigue and dehydration. An inquiry by the athletic trainer may help determine if flushing is being used.

Heating

Heating is believed by many Filipinos to help cure an illness believed to have been brought about by the body getting cold in the first place. It is believed that once the body is brought back "into balance," the illness will resolve itself.

Hilot Healers

The art of **hilot** healing is passed down from generation to generation in the Philippines; no formal educational training is involved (Erickson D'Avanzo & Geissler, 2003). Some believe that a "breech baby" will ultimately become a hilot. These healers use massage, manipulation, and herbs to treat muscles, joints, and ligaments. A healer may relocate a dislocation or massage a muscle in order to bring relief. Hilot healers also use prayers to support healing.

Hilot healers who use herbs and plants in their practice are known as **arbularyos**. The word *arbularyo* roughly translates as herbalist, but arbularyos rely not only on herbs but also on a strong faith-based approach. Arbularyos may test the believed healing properties of a plant on an athlete and record the various illnesses or injuries that each preparation was used to treat. Individuals who do not have money or insurance to pay for a physician may often look for alternatives for their care, and arbularyos are almost always less expensive.

Home Remedies

According to Erickson D'Avanzo and Geissler (2003), traditional home remedies include the following:

- Garlic—high blood pressure
- Ginger root—indigestion, sore throat
- Malunggay leaves—fatigue
- Ampalaya (bitter melon)—diabetes and fatigue (ampalaya has been recommended by the Department of Health in the Philippines to support liver health and management of diabetes and HIV [Ampalaya.com, 2004].)

VIETNAMESE

 Vietnamese have a unique culture of their own. It is important for the athletic trainer to understand the similarities and the differences of this culture to one's own, avoid the generalization that everyone adheres to the same beliefs that are part of this culture, and keep an open mind when working with athletes whose culture may be different than their own.

Demographic and Cultural Background Information

This section covers the following areas: a brief history of country of origin and immigration, primary languages and communication, family structure, daily living and food practices, and spiritual or religious orientation.

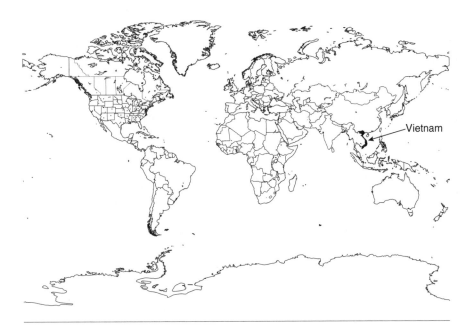

Figure 7.3 Map of Vietnam.

Brief History of Country of Origin and Immigration

Vietnam, located in the South Pacific, is part of Southeast Asia (see figure 7.3). Situated between China and Cambodia, it has been ruled by China, France, and Japan. The United States became involved in the Vietnam War in the 1950s for fear that the small Asian country would fall into communist rule. After the United States left Vietnam in 1973, refugees were allowed to come to America. They left their country under the stress of war, economic failure, and lack of infrastructure, and that stress most certainly would have an impact on a person's health. Another example of a health-related effect can be found in the birth defects caused by the chemical Agent Orange, which was used to defoliate areas of Vietnam during the war (Erickson D'Avanzo & Geissler, 2003).

Vietnamese who have come to the United States are known as Viet Kieu. In Vietnam, they are viewed as having abandoned their home country, and they are not trusted there (Curry & Nguyen, 1997). Since 1975, the majority of Vietnamese immigrants coming to the United States have made their homes in California and Texas (Purnell & Paulanka, 2003). There are approximately 1.2 million Vietnamese living in the United States (Purnell & Paulanka, 2003).

Primary Languages and Communication Styles

The official language is Vietnamese. Those who speak Chinese, French, or English were likely influenced by the military occupations in the country (Lipson et al., 1996). Vietnamese who have been acculturated to the United States tend to speak English.

DOS AND DON'TS

- Do greet a person by shaking hands. A double handshake is a sign of extreme respect. (However, a male should not shake the hand of a female.)
- Do bow, with eyes away from the person you are greeting; this is a sign of respect for a person of authority or an elder.
- Do use Mr., Mrs., or Ms. followed by the given name of the person. In Vietnam the family name is listed first and the given name is last (Purnell & Paulanka, 2005).

DISTINCTIVE TO THIS CULTURE

- A person's name is listed in reverse order—last, middle, first.
- The last name of more than half of the population in Vietnam is Nguyen (Curry & Nguyen, 1997).
- When addressing an athletic trainer, a Vietnamese athlete may use a title, such as Mr. Athletic Trainer. The athlete is likely to continue to use Mr., Mrs., or Ms., along with the person's first name, long after permission is given to use the first name only.
- Women may need female athletic trainers when discussing sex or birth control.
- Males who have been friends for a long time may walk arm in arm.
- Female friends may walk hand in hand. The athletic trainer should not assume that this means touch is acceptable.
- When speaking, most Vietnamese will stand as a sign of respect (Erickson D'Avanzo & Geissler, 2003).
- Vietnamese people are soft spoken, and Westerners who speak loudly may be viewed as disrespectful.
- When an athlete's eyes blink in proximity to a verbal message, it means the person is understanding (Erickson D'Avanzo & Geissler).
- The athlete may nod and smile, which would lead the athletic trainer to believe that he or she is accepting what is being discussed. However, sparing a person's feelings is a Vietnamese cultural norm, so the athlete may nod and smile even when he or she internally disagrees. Thus an athletic trainer needs to remember that smiling, avoiding eye contact, and nodding do not necessarily mean consent. They may mean anger or unhappiness.
- As with most Southeast Asians, one should summon a person only with the palm down. Using the hand with the palm up is the way in which animals are summoned.
- Always sit upright. Do not slouch—it is a sign of disrespect.
- Taboo behaviors include taking a photo with only three people in it or placing one's feet on the furniture (Erickson D'Avanzo & Geissler). In an athletic training facility, one may find the athlete is unwilling to place his or her feet on the examination table. It may be helpful to explain that this is not a sign of disrespect.

Family Structure

Typically, three generations live together in one household. The family is very close, and family is considered more important than the individual. Men are expected to provide financially for the family. The male will also do heavy-duty household chores that require physical labor. Women handle cleaning, child care, meal preparation, and care of ill family members.

DISTINCTIVE TO THIS CULTURE

- The father is the decision maker for the family. In the absence of a father, the eldest male will make the decisions. The lunar calendar is used to make decisions (Erickson D'Avanzo & Geissler, 2003). Each day in the calendar indicates what kinds of decisions should be made. For example, if an athlete is to have surgery, the calendar will indicate which days will be of good fortune for both the physician and the athlete (LifeEvents, 2001). Thus the family will need to know the birth date of the physician to ensure the best outcome.
- Women stay behind the scenes but play a critical role in influencing the decision-making process by sharing their thoughts with their husbands or fathers.
- Women are expected to change their last name to their husband's upon marriage.
- Children are highly prized and encouraged to succeed in all aspects of their lives.
- Children are expected to care for parents and grandparents when they can no longer care for themselves.
- Grandparents take care of small children who are not in school.
- A person's age is calculated starting at the time of conception (Purnell & Paulanka, 2005). Birthdays are celebrated at the lunar new year, and everyone celebrates on the same day (Purnell & Paulanka, 2005). Since there is a challenge (based on the differences in the belief of what a birth date should be) determining birth dates, many list January 1 as their date of birth.

Daily Living and Food Practices

- Time may not be considered important. Socially, Vietnamese are frequently late. Athletic trainers may need to emphasize the point if they believe it is important for an athlete to be on time; they may also need to stress the importance of taking medication on time.
- The present is valued more than the future.
- White attire is worn after death by mourners. Thus an athletic trainer should avoid wearing white clothing, because it might be perceived as a sign that death is coming.
- Sending flowers at a time of illness should be avoided; flowers are sent in the Vietnamese culture only after death (Purnell & Paulanka, 2005).
- Vietnamese people eat three meals a day; the primary meals are lunch and dinner.

- Vietnamese belief about food holds that it is important to maintain balance between hot (duong) and cold (am) foods in order to stay healthy (Purnell & Paulanka, 2005). Duong foods include spices, coffee, chicken, peppers, candy, and onions. Am foods include rice, water, tea, duck, fish, fruits, and vegetables.
- Meals typically consist of rice, fish, green leafy vegetables, tea, water, and pork. Other common items include noodle soup, baguettes, bean sprouts, pâté, and coffee.
- Food is typically eaten with salt, soy sauce, and fish sauce.
- Fruit is the common dessert.
- Food is eaten with chopsticks.
- Icy beverages and dairy products are avoided (many Vietnamese are lactose intolerant, and issues of bone density should be considered) (Purnell & Paulanka, 2005).
- When a Vietnamese person is ill, the food of choice is rice porridge with warm tea (Lipson et al., 1996). An athletic trainer making recommendations for dietary changes needs to be aware of Vietnamese food practices.

Spiritual or Religious Orientation

- The four primary religions of Vietnam are Buddhism, Confucianism, Taoism, and Catholicism; the most common are Buddhism and Catholicism (Lipson et al., 1996).
- Buddhists believe in doing good deeds, which improve their spiritual standing (Lipson et al., 1996). They also believe in reincarnation.
- Catholics pray and recite the rosary; a priest is the leader in the church. Catholics believe in purgatory—a place where souls go for purification before entering heaven.
- Taoism focuses on being in tune with all things, both on earth and in heaven, and on being one in spirit and in mind. All things are dependent on each other. If one thing goes awry, the person will have to adjust to bring about harmony once again. Stress, fighting, and riots bring disharmony, which in turn brings about illness.
- People who adhere to Confucianism practice moderation in their daily lives. Ming, or fate, guides a person's life. Confucian belief says that a person who has lived a life of Confucianism will be revered (Spector, 2004).

Health Care Information

Topics covered here include biocultural assessment, common sensitivities and conditions, beliefs about illness, preventive health practices, symptom management, and treatments.

Biocultural Assessment

- Skin tone ranges from off-white to dark brown. Some people chew betel leaves, which color the lips a deeper red pigmentation from contact (Purnell

& Paulanka, 2003). Skin pigmentation may pose a challenge in determining cyanosis; the best way to do so is to check the nail beds, conjunctiva, or lips.

- Hair is black and coarse on the head; body hair is sparse.
- Eyes are almond shaped.
- Average height is 5 feet to 5 feet 8 inches (1.5 to 1.7 meters), and average weight is about 130 pounds (59 kilograms). Teeth are larger than Whites' teeth, and, in a profile view, the mouth protrudes significantly.
- About 40 percent of Vietnamese people have torus protuberances in their lower jaw (Purnell & Paulanka, 2003, 2005), which may pose a problem for athletes who wear a mouth guard.
- Vietnamese people have fewer sweat glands and thus less body odor than average (Purnell & Paulanka, 2005). This characteristic may have implications for heat stress, and it is important to emphasize hydration.

Common Sensitivities and Conditions

- Vietnamese people metabolize alcohol more slowly than average (Purnell & Paulanka, 2005).
- According to Purnell and Paulanka (2005), Vietnamese people are more sensitive than average to the effects of beta-blockers, atropine, tranquilizers, and sedatives.
- Vietnamese people are less sensitive than average to side effects of analgesics, except for the gastrointestinal side effects (Purnell & Paulanka, 2005).
- Lower doses of antidepressants can be used by Vietnamese people to get the same effect that Whites receive from higher doses (Purnell & Paulanka, 2003).
- Vietnamese people are prone to anemia, cervical cancer, hepatitis B, lactose intolerance, and malnutrition.
- Several other conditions found more often among Vietnamese may be unfamiliar to an athletic trainer: Japanese encephalitis, typhoid fever, malaria, cholera, choriocarcinoma, dengue, dysentery, and tuberculosis. Any athlete who might have one of these conditions should be referred to a physician for care. Check the appendix for an explanation of signs and symptoms of each of the conditions listed.

Beliefs About Illness

One's beliefs about illness are influenced by past lives. It is thought that past lives determine current life and that present life determines future lives; this is especially true for those who believe in Buddhism (Purnell & Paulanka, 2003).

Those who have lived in the city believe in yin and yang and in germ theory. Rural dwellers are more likely to believe that illness results from sins.

- The primary belief is that there are two opposing energy forces—yin and yang, or, in most communities in Vietnam, am and duong. **Am** is considered to be dark, female, and cold or cool; **duong** is light, male, and hot or warm. Everything fits into of these categories. These forces do not work against each other; rather, they create balance, and it is believed that imbalance can lead to illness.

- Many Vietnamese believe that going to bed with wet hair causes headaches (Spector, 1996). Water is am, and showers, baths, and swimming are avoided during times of illness. The athletic trainer must understand that hot and cold are not about temperature but about balance. Vietnamese belief holds that the body must stay in balance or life will be shortened (Purnell and Paulanka, 2005).

- Some Vietnamese believe that illness is brought on by one's sins, which are also thought to bring about mental illness. It is believed that ancestors who are upset with a person's behavior will impose a mental illness based on the person's sinful behavior. Mental illness may manifest itself as physical ailments to avoid the stigma and embarrassment that mental illness would bring to the family. This phenomenon can be tricky for an athletic trainer, since signs and symptoms may be masked, thus making it difficult to determine the true concern.

- Vietnamese people describe some illnesses as weaknesses. For example, a weak heart may indicate dizziness, weak nerves may indicate headache, and a weak stomach may indicate indigestion (Purnell & Paulanka, 2005).

- Blood is thought to be finite, so the loss of it creates great concern. It is thought that if a person loses enough blood over time, that person's life will be shortened.

- Genetic defects are thought to be caused by God as punishment for bad behavior (Spector, 1996). The family cares for individuals with genetic health issues. After the Vietnam War, more genetic defects occurred—most likely as a result of exposure to chemicals used during the war (Erickson D'Avanzo & Geissler, 2003).

- Some Vietnamese may refuse to seek treatment because it is believed that life and its passage have been predetermined. The resultant delay can allow an illness to advance beyond the ability of a physician to cure it or slow its progression. This same holds true for athletic injuries, and an athletic trainer may need to explain the value of early intervention.

- The head is the most sacred of body parts, and only elders are allowed to touch the head. Thus an athletic trainer needs to seek permission and explain the importance before touching an athlete's head.

Preventive Health Practices

The best preventative health practice is to ensure that the person stays in harmony. Best practice for a balanced life includes eating properly, getting enough sleep, and exercising. It is also essential to maintain good emotional health.

- Exercise is promoted but not expected.
- Vaccinations and physicals are not considered necessary.
- Cervical cancer can be prevented through pap smears, but Vietnamese women fail to have them, because they believe that nothing can be done to treat it (Purnell & Paulanka, 2005).

- Women are not accustomed to preventive mammograms.
- Preventive measures used by Vietnamese people include massage and steam baths (Spector, 1996).
- Dental hygiene is often poor. Some women put lacquer on their teeth in the belief that it strengthens them. Regular dental health practices needs to be encouraged (Purnell & Paulanka, 2003).
- Vietnamese who are lactose intolerant should avoid products that contain whey. Cereals and generic medications typically contain lactose fillers.

Symptom Management

- A Vietnamese person may attempt to keep pain hidden; in some cases, facial expressions will be very telling (Lipson et al., 1996). To control pain, some Vietnamese chew betel leaves for the narcotic effect (Purnell & Paulanka, 2005). Hot compresses are also welcomed (Lipson et al., 1996).
- Tiger Balm is a home remedy used for a number of complaints. It originated in China and comes in two forms: red and white. The red form is used for muscular complaints, the white form for congestion, upset stomach, rash, and headache. The balm's main ingredient is camphor, which creates its aroma.
- An athlete may exhibit anxiousness when having difficulty breathing. It is common for an athlete to breathe more rapidly in this situation, so caution should be used to treat the athlete properly rather than assuming hyperventilation.
- Vomiting may be hidden due to embarrassment. Once an athletic trainer becomes aware of vomiting, the next step should be to determine the seriousness and whether medication is necessary. In this instance, Tiger Balm is often placed under the nose as the remedy.
- The remedy for diarrhea is to increase fluids.
- Constipation is resolved by eating vegetables.

Treatments

Treatment typically consists of self-care first. Over-the-counter medication, acupuncture, massage, and home remedies are used before Western medicine. Information about acupuncture, aromatherapy, cupping (giac), coining (**cao gio**), and massage can be found in the Chinese treatment section of this chapter.

- Western medicine is thought to be extremely strong and thus may not be accepted by a Vietnamese athlete. Another strategy used by Vietnamese is to cut a dosage to fit within their belief system; this action might, of course, render the medication ineffective.
- The Vietnamese family will provide round-the-clock health care for the ill person. A family member may sleep on a straw mat or bed next to the ill person. Food may be cooked on a hot stove near the athlete.

Home Remedies

In many instances, a Vietnamese athlete will use home remedies before seeking the assistance of an athletic trainer. Typical remedies include certain foods, Tiger Balm, plants, and herbs. The remedy will be based on the type of illness. Extra fluids may be used for diarrhea, Tiger Balm for muscular problems and basic illnesses, and rice porridge for all illnesses.

Xong

Xong is a mixture of herbs or oils that are boiled, then inhaled in the belief that doing so will resolve the illness.

Protection

Catholic athletes may use crosses, prayer, and rosary beads to support their health. A priest may listen to the confession of sins as additional spiritual support of the athlete. A Buddhist may use chanting and incense, which is thought to have protective qualities. A Buddhist monk may also be present in support of the ill person.

Ancestors are believed to provide protection from illness, and **am duc** is the accumulation of good deeds by ancestors (Downes, 1997). It is believed that these good deeds protect a person, and ancestors are frequently worshipped.

SUMMARY

This chapter helps you understand the cultures of Asian Americans and Pacific Islander Americans and their health care needs. It is important for athletic trainers to understand that those who are first-generation immigrants will have more beliefs and behaviors rooted in their home country and cultural history. Those who are second- and third-generation residents in the United States are generally more inclined to accept Western medicine or at least be open to trying it.

Asian Americans and Pacific Islander Americans believe in being respectful and may not say no even if they disagree. An athletic trainer needs to be aware of the need for Asian Americans and Pacific Islander Americans to save face. You can help establish a functional comfort level by taking time to work with an Asian American or Pacific Islander American athlete, keeping your tone of voice low, and speaking slowly. Westerners tend to fill silence, but in Asian American and Pacific Islander American culture, it provides time for thinking.

The family is more important than the individual in these cultures, and the priority is to deal with what is happening in the present rather than be concerned with the future. There is a strong belief that God controls everything, and in some instances this belief causes an athlete to put off seeking treatment, which can be devastating to the athlete's health.

The skin color of Asian Americans and Pacific Islander Americans is such that it can be hard to determine cyanosis. Asian Americans and Pacific Islander Americans may also have larger tori protuberances in their mouths, and they are generally more sensitive to the effects of beta-blockers, atropine, tranquilizers, alcohol, and sedatives.

First-generation Asian Americans and Pacific Islander Americans are more inclined to suffer conditions that are common in their home country. Examples include cholera, dengue, dysentery, hepatitis B, Japanese encephalitis, malaria, and typhoid fever. Political strife in the country of origin can contribute to health care issues, as seen following the Vietnam War among Vietnamese people, who suffered birth defects caused by chemicals used in the war and posttraumatic stress disorder.

Asian Americans and Pacific Islander Americans believe in the opposing forces of yin and yang, or hot and cold. In Asian American and Pacific Islander American cultures, these forces are seen at work in illnesses, foods, and the body. It is important that the body stay in balance in order to be well, and an athletic trainer may have to ask if a treatment will coincide with yin and yang expectations of the culture.

Involving Asian Americans and Pacific Islander Americans in their own health care is the most effective way to show respect for the individual. Women may need to be seen by female athletic trainers, especially if modesty or sexually sensitive situations are involved. This is particularly true for preventive mammograms and pap tests.

These cultures are stoic when it comes to tolerance of pain. The thought is that since God is in charge and gave the pain, it should be endured. The athletic trainer needs to anticipate this stance in order to treat for pain effectively. Vomiting is another symptom that may be hidden due to embarrassment, and athletic trainers may need to be proactive in exploring this issue.

Finally, treatment of Asian illnesses or conditions will be based on the beliefs of the athlete. The athlete may use the traditional Asian treatments of acupuncture, aromatherapy, fire cupping, coining, bonesetting, massage, and herbal remedies. Since these treatments are unusual to Western athletic trainers, they must become familiar with each of them. In particular, coining and cupping leave distinctive marks that could lead an athletic trainer to assume that the athlete has suffered abuse or become confused about the treatment. Asian athletes are also likely to use home remedies that could affect the effectiveness of an athletic trainer's treatment. The athletic trainer needs to ask about home remedies and use of herbals to assess for possible effect on treatment and healing.

Understanding the information presented in this chapter can make an athletic trainer more culturally competent, which in turn can lead to greater understanding and a more productive relationship between the athletic trainer and the athlete.

Learning Aids

What Would You Do If . . . ?

1. What if the athlete will follow your treatment plan only if you accept his or her herbalist's remedy in conjunction with your care?
2. What if a superstition is preventing your athlete from following necessary care instructions?
3. What if a parent refuses to believe that there is anything called mental illness, which prevents you from getting proper medication or making a referral to a physician?

4. What if an athlete is using coining to treat a bruise? It is creating more swelling and causing the problem to become worse.

5. What if an athlete believes that witchcraft has caused the illness of his or her child? No cultural healer is available to break the spell.

6. What if your team physician says he would like the mother of a Vietnamese student-athlete who just had surgery to go home? She makes breakfast, lunch, and dinner for her son with a Crockpot in the room. She also sleeps in a chair and never leaves the room.

Activities

1. Obtain a book of translations and learn the greetings for the cultures discussed in this chapter.

2. Using the cultural information presented in this chapter, write a set of athlete history questions to elicit information about treatments that the athlete may have used for resolving an injury or illness.

3. Find a Web site that lists herbal remedies and create a chart addressing possible interactions with prescription drugs.

4. How might an athletic trainer incorporate Asian therapies with Western therapies to treat the following ailments: swelling, muscle soreness, sprain, tendonitis?

5. Examine Asian therapies and determine which ones an athletic trainer might be willing to incorporate into one's repertoire and why.

Key Terms

Define the following key terms found in this chapter.

Am	Dao	Mien
Am duc	Duong	Observation
Amok	Hilot	Pakikisama
Arbularyo	Hiya	Qigong
Bahala na	Kulam	Yang
Cao gio	Meridian	Yin
Chi or qi		

Questions for Review

1. What religious and health beliefs affect health care for Asian Americans and Pacific Islander Americans?

2. What are some spiritual beliefs that Asian Americans and Pacific Islander Americans may share?

3. What medications are Asian Americans and Pacific Islander Americans more sensitive to?

4. How might the family of an Asian American or Pacific Islander American influence his or her care?

5. How can an athletic trainer support an Asian American or Pacific Islander American athlete's health care while also supporting his or her cultural needs?
6. How has health care evolved in Asian American and Pacific Islander American culture?
7. How might Asian American and Pacific Islander American home remedies affect a patient's health care?
8. How have origins and history played a role in Asian American and Pacific Islander American health care practices?

Black

Learning Objectives

Upon completing this chapter, students will be able to do the following:

1. Describe various health care beliefs common among people who are African American, sub-Saharan African, or Haitian
2. Describe various spiritual beliefs of African American, sub-Saharan African, and Haitian people
3. Describe various cultural influences on African Americans, sub-Saharan Africans, and Haitians that affect how an athletic trainer should care for athletes from these cultures
4. Care for a Black athlete while accommodating his or her cultural needs
5. Explain how health care has evolved over time within Black cultures
6. Explain origins of these Black cultures and how members of them may respond to health care situations as a result of their cultural health care history

Sheila Smallwood, RN

I am a registered nurse with a master's degree in nursing education and a focus in adult health. I am also an adjunct faculty member in the nursing department at Winston-Salem State University, a historically black institution. I got into health care because I wanted to help people. I had always thought I wanted to be a nurse, and when I took a career placement survey in high school the results identified nursing as a career fit for me.

When I worked in dialysis, I took care of an adult Jehovah's Witnesses patient with kidney disease. A brief explanation of the role of the kidneys will help crystallize my story. One of the responsibilities of the kidneys is to assist and control the production of red blood cells (RBCs), which carry oxygen to the cells. Without enough of them, a person will eventually die.

stevedavisphoto.com

My patient was a middle-aged female who had been on peritoneal dialysis for several years without needing any blood transfusions; however, her hemoglobin (which carries oxygen to the cells) was always a little low. At that time, no medications were available to stimulate production of hemoglobin, and the only method for increasing the amount was blood transfusion. There came the day when my patient's hemoglobin dropped to critically low values and she was presented with the only option to save her life—a blood transfusion. I will never forget her stating that she would not receive a blood transfusion and would continue her dialysis treatments until she was no longer able to do so. She and I talked about her decision, and it was a simple matter for her. She chose to follow her religious beliefs.

The nursing profession teaches us to respect a person's beliefs, but when I was faced with having to respect and honor the wishes of someone who made a decision that inevitably caused her death, it was hard. As a nurse and a blood donor, I found it difficult not attempting to sway her from her course of action but letting her make a decision very different from the one I would have made. She did in fact die due to complications of low RBCs; however, I feel good about honoring her wishes.

The advice I would give others is to honor each person's belief even when it is not the same as yours. Do not use your personal yardstick to judge others; they have their own.

The United States Declaration of Independence states "that all men are created equal, that they are endowed by their Creator with certain unalienable Rights, that among these are life, liberty and the pursuit of happiness." It seems only fitting, then, that each culture should be appreciated. Since all people are created equal, all should have access to culturally competent health care. Irrespective of ethnicity, each life is equally important, and athletic trainers can play a significant role in putting this declaration into practice.

This chapter presents information about the background of Blacks, where they live, and some of their beliefs. The chapter focuses on the three Black cultures with the largest populations in the United States: African Americans, sub-Saharan Africans, and Haitians (U.S. Census Bureau, 2000).

The term Black refers to a person who has dark-colored skin, especially one of African or Australian Aboriginal ancestry (Apple, Inc, 2005-2007). The term does not distinguish what country a person may be from—just ancestry and biocultural features (*World Book Dictionary*, 2005).

The chapter presents dos and don'ts for interacting with members of each culture, as well as sections discussing characteristics that are distinctive in each culture. At the same time, we must remember that not all people in a culture adhere to each of the listed items. For example, first-generation immigrants often adhere to beliefs and traditions that may not be carried on by members of the next generation.

AFRICAN AMERICAN

African Americans have a unique culture of their own. It is important for the
athletic trainer to understand the similarities and the differences of this culture to
one's own, avoid the generalization that everyone adheres to the same beliefs that
are part of this culture, and keep an open mind when working with athletes whose
culture may be different than their own.

Demographic and Cultural Background Information

Each section of this chapter addresses the U.S. immigration history of the cultural
group, its primary languages and communication practices, family structure, daily
living and food practices, and spiritual or religious orientation. It is essential for
an athletic trainer to work with each athlete as an individual and to ask relevant
questions about culture in order to give the best care possible.

Brief History of Country of Origin and Immigration

The term African American is used to describe a person whose predecessors were
originally from Africa (see figure 8.1). Purnell and Paulanka, 2003 describe other
terms that have been used to refer to this group include "colored," "Negro," "Afro-
American," and "people of color." According to Purnell and Paulanka (2003a),
members of younger generations prefer the term African American, whereas elderly

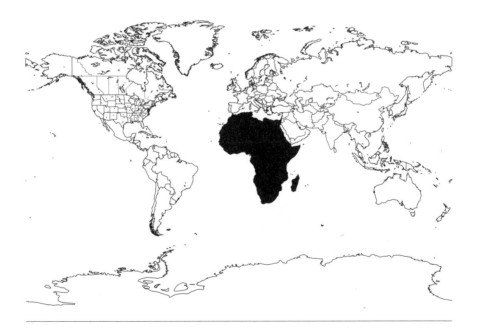

Figure 8.1 Map of Africa.

African Americans may prefer the term Negro or Colored, and middle-aged African Americans prefer the term Black.

African Americans are mostly the descendants of Africans who were forcibly brought to this country and forced into slavery from 1619 to 1860. It is unknown how many slaves came to the United States during that time, but they certainly numbered in the millions (Lipson, Dibble, & Minarik, 1996; Purnell & Paulanka, 2003a). Many African tribes were invaded to supply slaves for the slave trade. The slaves were kidnapped and taken from their families, never to see them again. Most were brought to the South to labor in fields. It should be understood that slavery is not immigration.

Slavery legally ended when the Civil War came to a close. The Emancipation Proclamation of 1862 had freed the slaves, but little changed for them at that time. It was felt among slave owners that unless the U.S. Constitution was amended to address the issue, slaves would never be free, and the Thirteenth Amendment abolished slavery in 1865. The state of Texas, however, did not change its treatment of slaves, and Union troops invaded Texas, took over Galveston, and enforced the law of the land, thus freeing the slaves on June 19, 1865. As a result, in recent years, many African Americans have begun celebrating the freeing of slaves during an event known as **Juneteenth** (Juneteenth Newsletter, 2007).

Once slavery ended, many African Americans moved north in search of better opportunities for their families. Even so, African Americans continued to face problems posed by racism, poverty, and segregation. From this struggle, the Civil Rights Movement was launched to secure rights for African Americans, and this work continues today.

Today, half of African Americans live in Southern states such as Texas. There are, however, large populations living in and around large cities such as Chicago, New York, Detroit, Memphis, and Houston (Spector, 2004). The greatest migration of African Americans to the Northern states came between 1940 and 1970 (Rundle, Carvalho, & Robinson, 1999).

There is a history of medical experimentation on African Americans. In 1932, the Tuskegee Institute studied syphilis in African American men to determine a treatment program. The 600 men in the program were not given sufficient information to understand the risks or the program itself. Even when, in 1945, penicillin was determined as the course of treatment, these men did not receive that care, and they went on to suffer the progressive effects of the disease, including death (Centers for Disease Control and Prevention, 2007). The experiment was stopped in 1972 when a reporter wrote an article blowing the whistle.

Primary Languages and Communication Styles

During slavery, African Americans had to establish a new way to communicate because slaves came from various regions and spoke various languages. In addition, the White slave owners did not want slaves speaking English, so they could keep the slaves from acculturating into society. Thus slaves developed a new language.

Doing so—that is, creating a language for the purpose of communication that is not the primary language for either person involved—is known as **pidgin** communication. If a pidgin language is spoken and passed on to the next generation as its primary language, it is then called a **Creole language.** A number of Creole languages can be found in the United States and the Caribbean (Turbitt, 2008).

The dominant language among African Americans is English. Many African Americans speak standard English in settings dominated by Whites but use a dialect when speaking with other African Americans. This dialect is referred to as **Ebonics**, a name derived from the words *ebony* and *phonics*. Ebonics allows a person to drop certain letters from a word—for example, dropping letter "l" in the word help. Thus the Ebonics word "hep" means "help" in English. Also referred to as African American vernacular, Ebonics is considered a dialect of standard English.

DOS AND DON'TS

- Do greet an African American using his or her title and last name.
- Do expect that some African Americans will be animated and loud and appear confrontational when speaking with family and friends or when they are impassioned.
- Do expect that facial expressions and body movements may be quite pronounced and may seem exaggerated to members of other cultures, which may lead some athletic trainers to feel concerned that a serious conflict is imminent. This is not necessarily the case.
- Don't stare; this is considered to be aggressive behavior with an unfamiliar person.

DISTINCTIVE TO THIS CULTURE

- Personal space is close with friends, but physical proximity is considered confrontational with nonfriends (Purnell & Paulanka, 2003a, 2005). With friends, it is acceptable to have less than 4 feet (1.2 meters) of distance.
- An athletic trainer must take time to explain procedures in detail. African Americans may feel great distrust of the medical community due to the number of times in history when African Americans were unknowingly made part of medical research (Infoplease, 2007). Sharing information openly is crucial to building trust and credibility with the athlete.

Family Structure

Family structure for African Americans was altered during the times of slavery, a slave owners sold adult males and older children to other plantation owners (Purnell & Paulanka, 2005). This phenomenon changed how African Americans viewed their family structure. Single-parent households arose, older children became caretakers, and it became the norm for a home to be without an adult male. Thus the extended family is important in the upbringing of an African American family, and it is not unusual to find three generations living together.

DISTINCTIVE TO THIS CULTURE

- The head of household for African Americans is the father.
- In the absence of a father, however, many households are run by the mother.
- Close friends may be considered family and may be referred to as cousins, aunts, uncles, parents, brothers, or sisters.
- Females serve as the caregivers (Lipson et al., 1996).
- Children are expected to watch over their brothers and sisters.
- It is not unusual for grandparents to serve as guardians of their grandchildren (Purnell & Paulanka, 2003a, 2005; Rundle, Carvalho, and Robinson, 1999); as a result, the athletic trainer may need to clarify who serves as legal guardian for an athlete.
- Purnell and Paulanka (2005) indicate that it is important to include the mother and extended family when providing health information about an athlete.

Daily Living and Food Practices

- African Americans are oriented toward present time and will give precedence to family concerns and needs and to what is currently happening. For example, a person's focus on present time may entail a lack of concern for the future and thus an avoidance of preventive health care.
- Older African Americans tend to be on time for appointments and events (Lipson et al., 1996).
- Males serve as the decision makers after consulting with family members (Lipson et al.).
- The African American diet most typically consists of few fruits, fibers, and vegetables and a large quantity of meat.
- Fruits and vegetables are eaten to improve circulation when a person believes that it is somehow impaired.
- Foods are heavily salted, which can be problematic for a person with high blood pressure.
- If the person is Muslim, he or she follows religious dietary practice and thus avoids pork.
- Being overweight is not uncommon, and it may be thought that a person who is thin does not have the ability to remain healthy in the event of an illness. If an athlete participates in a sport where weight is a key factor, the athletic trainer may be challenged to get him or her to lose weight. The athletic trainer may need to find a way to work with the athlete to support a healthier lifestyle.
- Three meals a day are preferred, and the largest meal is dinner.
- An African American meal may include chitterlings, pig's tail, and pig's feet. These eating practices stem from the days of slavery when slaves were fed only the leftover body parts that slave owners did not eat (Downes, 1997).
- If an African American believes in Voodoo, he or she will tend not to eat out but will prefer to eat at home, where the preparation of food can be controlled.

It is thought that a spell or hex can be placed on someone if spiders, toads, snakes, or lizards are introduced into a person's food or drink (Salimbene, 2005) and that the only way to remove the hex is to work with a Voodoo healer. It is thought that about 3.2 million people worldwide practice Voodoo (Adherents. com, 2007). An athletic trainer must learn the religious beliefs of each athlete to know the types of foods that he or she is not likely to eat; when working with a Voodoo believer, a trainer might suggest that he or she bring food that has been personally prepared and packaged for competitions.

Spiritual or Religious Orientation

Most African Americans are Baptists, Protestants, Jehovah's Witnesses, Methodists, or Muslims (see the Middle East chapter for more detailed information about Islam); some practice Voodoo as a religion.

- The power of prayer is highly regarded.
- It is common for minister to visit the home.
- Outward expression is commonplace at church.
- The **laying on of hands** is thought to give strength to one who is ill. It involves having persons place their hands on an ill person and pray for him or her. The laying on of hands is guided by the spiritual healer of the church. If a person does not have less pain after the laying on of hands, it may be thought that he or she has little or no faith in God (Purnell & Paulanka, 2003a).
- African American women report that they turn to religion most often for help with serious health conditions. African American women who use religion are also more likely than those who were not religious to use alternative medicine (Dessio et al., 2004).

Health Care Information

When healing the body, it is important for an athletic trainer to understand physical features that are specific to African Americans. This section presents information about biocultural assessment, common sensitivities and conditions, beliefs about illness, preventive health practices, symptom management, and treatment. By using this information along with that provided in the previous section, an athletic trainer should be able to care for an African American athlete completely.

When working with athletes from African American culture, an athletic trainer needs to (1) let the athlete do the talking; (2) listen carefully without passing judgment; (3) where necessary, avoid using medical terminology; (4) take time with the athlete; and (5) ask questions about religion, home remedies, beliefs about illness, and healers typically used.

Biocultural Assessment

- African American skin tone ranges from white to very dark brown; in fact, there are so many tones that it is difficult to describe them all effectively. The darkest skin tones may challenge an athletic trainer's ability to determine pallor, jaundice, or cyanosis. Examining the skin in indirect sunlight may enable a more accurate assessment (Salimbene, 2005). Skin conditions may also be determined by examining the sclera of the eye, the inside of the lip, and the nail beds.

- Eye color is most often brown, but some African Americans have blue eyes.
- Hair is generally black and curly; hair and skin tend to be dry, and lotion and oils may be applied daily.
- 11% of African American women are more commonly known to have 23 vertebrae instead of 24 (Schrefer, 1994). Schrefer does not indicate any other race as having fewer vertebrae than African American women. The athletic trainer who is evaluating a back with one less vertebrae may be confused by the lack of that vertebrae.
- According to Schrefer, the second metatarsal is longer than the first toe in about 10 percent of African Americans. The long second toe may make the athlete more prone to ankle sprains.
- The long bones are slightly longer and denser than in Caucasians (Schrefer). The density of a bone may make African Americans less prone to fractures and osteoporosis (Purnell & Paulanka, 2003).
- The peroneus tertius muscle is missing in approximately 13 percent of African Americans (Schrefer). The lack of the peroneous tertius muscle may mean that the athelete has more difficulty dorsiflexing the foot.
- African Americans have greater bone density than Whites, Latinos, and Asians (Purnell & Paulanka 2005), which means that they are less likely to have osteoporosis.

Common Sensitivities and Conditions

- According to Purnell and Paulanka (2003a), due to varying metabolism, African Americans respond differently to alcohol, antihypertensives, beta-blockers, psychotropics, and caffeine. Until more clinical trials are done on African Americans men and women the differences between their responses and Europeans will not fully be know (Purnell & Paulanka, 2003a)
- African Americans experience a higher incidence of cancer, type 2 diabetes, Blount's disease, chemical dependency, pseudofolliculitis, sickle-cell anemia, HIV/AIDS, keloid formation, lactose intolerance, and cardiovascular disease (Purnell & Paulanka, 2003a).
- African Americans are more inclined to vitiligo, a skin condition where pigmentation is absent (Purnell & Paulanka, 2005). Athletes with vitiligo should use sunscreen during outdoor activity, as this skin is more prone to sunburn.
- Here are several other conditions that are found more often among African Americans but that athletic trainers may not typically work with: birthmarks, coccidioidomycosis, epilepsy, falling out, glucose-6-phosphate dehydrogenase deficiency, leukoedema, cirrhosis, and systemic lupus erythematosus (Purnell & Paulanka, 2005). The appendix provides more information regarding these conditions.

Beliefs About Illness

African Americans believe that in order to be healthy a person has to be in harmony with the environment, specifically nature. If a person is out of balance with nature, he or she will experience illness. Illness can enter the body through the action of Voodoo, evil spirits, or demons (Purnell & Paulanka, 2005).

- Prayer is considered important to prevent illness from entering the body, especially if a person lacks harmony with the environment.
- It is believed that being dirty can cause illness, so bathing is done regularly.
- Illness is also believed to result from exposure to cold, rain, wind, or a pathogen. It is expected that a person will be bundled up when going outside in bad weather.
- It is believed that God may punish a person through illness for sinful behavior (Downes, 1997).

DISTINCTIVE TO THIS CULTURE

- The term **dirt** in this culture refers to something similar to germs. It is believed that dirt in this sense travels in the bloodstream and can end up anywhere; it can show up in skin rashes or fever. It is believed that diarrhea and menstruation are ways that dirt leaves the body; as a result, laxatives are commonly used by African Americans. It is also thought that dirt can result from being unclean (Downes, 1997; Salimbene, 2005). Since laxatives can cause dehydration, an athletic trainer may have to be watchful of athletes who practice that form of dirt removal.
- Because contraceptive use is thought to stop the menstrual cycle and menstruation is viewed as a way in which the body gets rid of bad things, African Americans may not used contraceptives (Downes).
- **High blood** is a term used to describe a belief that there is too much blood in the body. High blood is thought to be caused by eating too many rich, red foods, such as beets and red meat. High blood reportedly results in dizziness, headaches, and falling out. When **falling out** occurs, the person collapses with his or her eyes open and is unable to see or respond to anyone (Downes). It is thought that high blood can be reduced by eating "white" foods, which include lemon juice, pickle juice, and garlic (Downes).
- **Low blood**, on the other hand, is associated with anemia and is corrected by eating red foods and taking iron pills. A person with low blood is tired and weak.
- If a child has seizures or a birth defect, some may believe that the parents did something improper, something against God's wishes. It is thought that the only way to heal the child is to have faith and repent to God (Purnell & Paulanka, 2005). An athletic trainer may be able to change this belief by explaining the actual cause of a seizure or birth defect.
- Salimbene indicates that if a physician gives medication to an African American who has a life-long chronic condition (e.g., diabetes), it is likely that the person will seek the opinion of another physician in the belief that

the first physician lacks the necessary knowledge to cure the problem. This is likely the result of distrust of the medical community. Thus an athletic trainer needs to be able share how a diagnosis was made and why a given medication is necessary.

Preventive Health Practices

African Americans are fully aware and accepting of preventive health care information. Some may be aware but unable to use the health care system because they lack medical insurance or financial means. Many may also be reluctant to seek medical care due to past medical experimentation on African Americans; this distrust may be exacerbated by the relatively small number of health care providers who are African American (Purnell & Paulanka, 2003a).

- Some older African Americans may use the *Farmers' Almanac* to determine when health and dental care should be done (Purnell & Paulanka, 2003a, 2005; Salimbene, 2005).
- African Americans are more accepting of being overweight than are White people, and this tendency may increase susceptibility to cancer, heart disease, and stroke. Athletic trainers need to encourage African American athletes to get annual physical examinations and seek assistance at the first sign of an illness.
- Heavily salted food poses a problem for athletes who have high blood pressure. An athletic trainer can work with the athlete to reduce the use of salted foods to support better health.
- A diet high in meats but low in fruits, fibers, and vegetable may make an African American athlete prone to high cholesterol and heart disease. Depending on an individual athlete's health condition, an athletic trainer may have to suggest an alteration in diet.
- Lactose-intolerant individuals should avoid the lactose filler known as whey, which can be found in medications and cereal products.

Symptom Management

- Pain may be expressed both verbally and facially, and resolution of pain is expected. Those who continue to experience pain after receiving prayers and spiritual support are thought by other African Americans to have little religious connection (Purnell & Paulanka, 2005).
- Oxygen is readily accepted when an athlete is having difficulty breathing (Lipson et al., 1996).
- It is preferred that nausea is cured by natural means first, as in the use of ginger ale (Lipson et al.).
- African Americans may use prunes or other fiber-containing foods to control constipation (Lipson et al.).

Treatments

Slavery forced African Americans to develop treatment options. Since slaves did not have access to health care, they had to find ways to take care of themselves, and they did so both through exposure to Native American healing methods and through their own use of trial and error. Treatments that worked well were passed on from generation to generation.

The mother or grandmother typically serves as the primary caregiver when someone is sick. The caregiver decides how to help the ill person without having to go to a doctor. African Americans are accepting of medication and fruits and vegetables as ways to resolve illness

Some African American men and women prefer athletic trainers of the same sex, especially if the concern involves gynecological or urological care (Purnell & Paulanka, 2003a, 2005). For most African Americans, however, a physician or nurse of either sex can give medical care.

Home Remedies

African American culture is accepting of home remedies. African Americans may use roots as well as medications from African American healers. Cotton balls may be placed in one's ears to prevent cold air from entering, and a warm compress may be placed on the chest to help recover from a cold (Lipson et al., 1996). Here is a list of some other home remedies (Spector, 2004, pp. 237–238):

- Cod liver oil—to prevent colds
- Sugar and turpentine—to get rid of worms by consumption and ease back pain by applying to the painful area
- Potato poultice placed on infection site—to cure
- Poultice of cornmeal and peach leaves—to kill bacteria
- Onion poultice—to heal after infection
- Flaxseed poultice—to resolve ear infection
- Goldenrod root tea—to decrease pain
- Sassafras tea—to treat a cold
- Bluestone powder—to decrease inflammation of open wounds and treat poison ivy; applied topically
- Silverware crossed over the area—to treat a sore neck
- Sour or soiled milk on bread—to treat wounds topically
- Salt pork—to treat wounds topically
- Clay placed in a dark leaf—to treat a sprained ankle by wrapping it onto the ankle
- Hot camphorated oil—to relieve congestion and coughing by applying it to the chest covered with flannel cloth
- Garlic, onion, parsley, and water blended—to act as expectorant for colds once consumed

- Hot tea with lemon, honey, peppermint, and brandy—to treat a cold or congestion
- Raw onions wrapped on the feet—to treat fever
- White skin of a raw egg applied topically—to bring a boil to a head
- Garlic applied topically on an ill person or just in the room—to remove evil spirits

Pica is the practice of eating a nonfood substance, such as laundry starch, clay, dirt, paint, or ice. It is most often done as a way to increase iron or to treat illness. It can lead to poisoning, constipation, diarrhea, or bowel obstruction. Pica is most common among women and children, and children who engage in pica usually have a mother who did so as a child (Wiener & Dulcan, 2004).

Protection

African Americans who use home remedies sometimes wear amulets. Asafetida (a smelly plant in the parsley family) is worn to protect against contagious disease. A silver dime may be used to warn the wearer of physical harm if it turns black. If one wears a silver or copper bracelet and the skin underneath it turns black, this is viewed as an indication of illness (Salimbene, 2005).

Voodoo Healers

Voodoo healers are viewed as the most prominent healers. Voodoo healers read animal bones arranged by the person who seeks to be healed (Salimbene, 2005, p. 17). Some voodoo serves good purposes, such as love or good fortune. On the other hand, if it is believed that a hex is the cause of illness, a voodoo healer will need to intervene.

Rootwork

African Americans may also use a diagnostic system called **rootwork** to determine and cure illness. The rootwork system combines belief in supernatural causes of illness and in cures derived from herbs and roots. Root doctors are involved in making charms and casting of spells (McQuillar, 2003). In her book *Rootwork*, McQuillar shares her spell for improving or maintaining health: A person soaks in warm Florida water, rose water, seeds from red apples, and petals from red flowers for half an hour; after soaking, the person must burn an orange 7-day candle. Rootwork was used mostly during the days of slavery due to the lack of conventional health care.

SUB-SAHARAN AFRICAN

 Sub-Saharan Africans have a unique culture of their own. It is important for the athletic trainer to understand the similarities and the differences of this culture to one's own, avoid the generalization that everyone adheres to the same beliefs that are part of this culture, and keep an open mind when working with athletes whose culture may be different than their own.

Demographic and Cultural Background Information

Sub-Saharan Africa includes the following countries: Angola, Benin, Botswana, Burkina Faso, Burundi, Cameroon, Cape Verde, Central African Republic, Chad, Comoros, Congo, Côte d'Ivoire, Djibouti, Equatorial Guinea, Ethiopia, Gabon, Gambia, Ghana, Guinea, Guinea-Bissau, Kenya, Lesotho, Liberia, Madagascar, Malawi, Mali, Mauritius, Mozambique, Namibia, Niger, Nigeria, Rwanda, São Tomé and Príncipe, Senegal, Seychelles, Sierra Leone, Somalia, South Africa, Sudan, Swaziland, Tanzania, Togo, Uganda, Zambia, and Zimbabwe (see figure 8.2).

Athletic trainers should understand that each of these countries and its people have their own practices. One should not generalize the information on the assumption that it applies to all the countries or peoples.

This first section includes a brief history of the country of origin and immigration, then covers primary languages and communication, family structure, daily living and food practices, and spiritual or religious orientation. It also discusses verbal and nonverbal communication in order to help athletic trainers understand how to greet athletes and learn about gestures that may or may not be appropriate for these cultures.

Another important factor is family structure. Athletic trainers need to understand who makes health care decisions, what form of support is provided within the family, and what expectations of family members will help ensure that appropriate care is given. Other topics addressed here include food-related practices that can affect an athlete's health, culturally specific views of time (which can vary considerably).

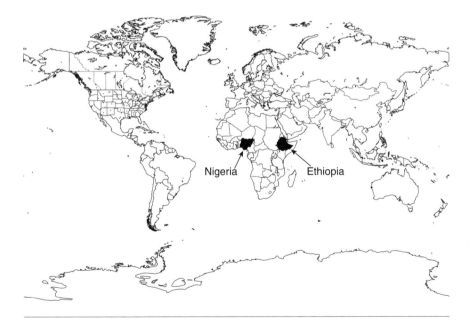

Figure 8.2 Map of Ethiopia and Nigeria.

Brief History of Country of Origin and Immigration

This section focuses on the sub-Saharan African countries of Nigeria and Ethiopia because they produce the highest number of immigrants to the United States (U.S. Census Bureau, 2000). As a result, for the content of this chapter, the term sub-Saharan will be used to refer only to Nigerian and Ethiopian people. When a fact is specific to one country, it will be clearly defined.

Ethiopian immigrants were affected by the National Origin Immigration Quota of 1924, which allowed for only 100 Ethiopians per year to enter the United States (Miller, 2003). As a result of the National Origin Immigration Quota, the majority of people came to the United States as college students or for job opportunities.

During the mid-1970s, Ethiopia had a change in the government, which caused a civil war and tremendous upheaval. Many people were killed, and many escaped the country by becoming political refugees. The majority of those who came to the United States now live in the major metropolitan areas of Washington DC, San Francisco, Seattle, Chicago, Dallas, Houston, Boston, and New York City (Lipson et al., 1996). The majority of Ethiopian refugees were under the age of 40 when they came to the United States (Lipson et al.).

The majority of Nigerians came to the United States for the purpose of education or to avoid political unrest (Rundle et al., 1999). According to the U.S. Census Bureau (2000), Nigerians are the largest group of people to have migrated to the United States from the sub-Saharan countries.

Primary Languages and Communication Styles

- Many languages and even more dialects are spoken in Ethiopia. The primary language is Amharic; other major languages are Oromo, Arabic, English, and Tigrinya (Rundle et al., 1999; Erickson D'Avanzo & Geissler, 2003).
- Nigerians speak English or broken English (Rundle et al., 1999). English is, in fact, regarded as the national language of Nigeria, but Rundle et al. (1999) share that less than half of Nigerians actually speak it. Other languages include Hausa, Yoruba, Ibo, and Fulani (Erickson D'Avanzo & Geissler, 2003).

DOS AND DON'TS

- Do use a handshake to greet Nigerian and Ethiopian people.
- Do expect greetings between family and friends to consist of handshakes, hugs, or kissing on the cheeks three or four times.
- Do expect bowing as part of the greeting process.
- Don't touch the opposite gender in public.
- Do expect that same-gendered friends may hold one another's face with the hands; this is considered an acceptable form of touch and should not be misinterpreted by an athletic trainer as a sign of an intimate or romantic relationship.
- Do expect sub-Saharans to be polite people.

- Do expect sub-Saharans to speak quietly and be reserved.
- Don't make eye contact; it is considered disrespectful, especially with an authority figure.

DISTINCTIVE TO THIS CULTURE

- When sitting in front of the athlete, avoid sitting with the sole of your shoe facing outward; it is considered unclean (Yehieli & Grey, 2005).
- It is considered disrespectful to point a finger in an attempt to call a person over; this is how animals are called (Yehieli & Grey).
- It is considered disrespectful to have the palm up with fingers spread out (Rundle et al., 1999).
- The athletic trainer should do everything with his or her right hand; the left hand is considered unclean. An athletic trainer who is left-handed could learn to use his or her right hand or find a right-handed athletic trainer to care for the athlete.
- Sub-Saharan people are very private and unlikely to reveal personal information. An athletic trainer may need to reassure the athlete that personal information will be kept private.
- An athletic trainer should work hard to create good rapport. It is important for the athletic trainer to be friendly and outgoing.
- Raising one's voice is considered unacceptable.
- Those in authority are very well respected (Foster, 2002); as a result, an athlete is not likely to question medical authority.

Family Structure

Families are close knit. In the United States, however, sub-Saharans have many one-person households. Because of resettlement in the United States, not all members of the family immigrated (Yehieli & Grey, 2005). As a result, friends are viewed as family and may be introduced as relatives (Yehieli & Grey, 2005). Families are large, and family members live close to one another.

DISTINCTIVE TO THIS CULTURE

- The father is the head of the household (Erickson D'Avanzo & Geissler, 2003; Rundle et al., 1999).
- Men are expected to have jobs, make financial decisions, and serve as spokespersons (Lipson et al., 1996).
- Since an athletic trainer is viewed as the person with the most knowledge regarding an illness or injury, he or she may be allowed to dictate treatment. It is important to inform the athlete about procedures, but too much information can lead to unnecessary stress or lack of understanding.
- Women are expected to serve as caregivers. If an injured or ill person lives in a one-person household, friends are expected to fill the role of caregivers.

- The ill person is cared for to the point that he or she does not have to do anything, and an athletic trainer may need to push the athlete to take a more active role in his or her care (e.g., walking, applying hot or cold packs, strengthening muscles, taking medication).

Daily Living and Food Practices

Members of this culture are oriented toward present time, and sub-Saharan people are traditionally late for appointments. According to Erickson D'Avanzo and Geissler (2003), sub-Saharans act as if each hour has 500 minutes, and it may be a challenge to get a person to come to an appointment or take medication as scheduled. An athletic trainer needs to take his or her time when working with such an athlete. It is considered disrespectful to hurry, even if the athlete showed up late.

- If a decision has to be made and the father is not acculturated, then the most acculturated family member will make the decision (Lipson et al., 1996). A household led by a female single parent does not follow the traditional decision-making process; instead, the female head of household will make the decision (Erickson D'Avanzo & Geissler, 2003).
- A sub-Saharan may not know his or her birth date, since it is not considered important. In fact, birth records are generally not kept (Yehieli & Grey, 2005), and an estimate of age may have been given upon the person's immigration to the United States (Yehieli & Grey).
- Though not practiced in the United States, female circumcision (also referred to as genital mutilation) is a common practice in Ethiopia (Rundle et al., 1999). Lipson et al. state that those who are educated do not follow the practice of female circumcision. For those who do, it is believed that the clitoris is a source of illness (Rundle et al.). Circumcision is also thought by cultures who believe in it, to keep a woman from straying sexually and is viewed as a guarantee that when she marries she is a virgin. The process of circumcision may prevent the woman from having orgasms. It is supposed to be performed before a girl reaches puberty, and it is usually done by family members in unsanitary conditions. The prepuce, clitoris, and labia minora may be removed. The labia majora are then sewn shut, and a small opening is left through which urine and menstrual fluids can leave the body. The circumcision may cause the girl to suffer infection or bleed to death. Since female circumcision is illegal in the United States, young sub-Saharan girls living in the States may have the procedure done while vacationing in their homeland. Some women view circumcision as socioeconomic security, meaning she is considered the marrying type (Rundle et al.).
- Being heavy or fat is a status symbol (Rundle et al.) because it means that you can afford good food in large amounts.
- Spicy food is the norm. When a person becomes ill, cold foods are avoided, and warm foods such as soup and hot tea are preferred.

- The traditional diet of Ethiopians consists of legumes and bread with meat. The bread, **injera**, is made of grains with high iron levels (Erickson D'Avanzo & Geissler, 2003). Food is eaten on top of the injera without use of silverware.
- Fruits are not commonly eaten.
- Nigerians' main food sources are yams, beans, fish, meat, chicken, and rice (Rundle et al.).
- Females of the family care for an ill member. In many East African hospitals, food is not provided, so sub-Saharan women who are not acculturated will provide the ill athlete with food. Thus an athletic trainer should not be surprised if the family brings food for the athlete (Yehieli & Grey). This practice can become an issue, however, if the athlete has dietary restrictions. The athletic trainer will have to work with the decision maker of the household to ensure that acceptable foods are provided.

Spiritual or Religious Orientation

The majority of sub-Saharan people are either Muslim or Coptic Orthodox Christian; some practice Catholicism or Protestantism. The term Coptic means Egyptian, and the fundamental practices were derived from Egypt. St. Mark founded the Coptic Church about 55 AD and was martyred in 68 AD (Lipson et al., 1996; Rundle et al., 1999).

- Muslims avoid eating some meats; animals that are carnivorous are considered unacceptable to eat. Fish with scales are acceptable, but those without are not to be eaten. Shellfish are acceptable. It is believed that certain animals are unclean, since they roll around in mud or live at the bottom of the food chain. Animals viewed as unclean include dogs, rats, crows, clams, worms, catfish, and turtles (Essortment, 2002). Foods that are prohibited are known as **haram**.
- A person who practices Coptic Orthodox Christianity may fast 210 days per year. In this case, fasting means that no animal products are eaten; there is also a restriction on all food and drink from sunrise to sunset. A priest can allow a variance in the fasting practice if a person is ill. The period of greatest fasting lasts for the 40 days of Lent, as well as the week prior to it; it ends with Easter. Many members of the Coptic church also avoid eating eggs, meat, or milk on Wednesdays and Fridays (Rundle et al., 1999).

Health Care Information

This section addresses the areas of biocultural assessment, common sensitivities and conditions, beliefs about illness, preventive health practices, symptom management, and treatments.

The athletic trainer should keep an open mind; no two cultures are alike. Some factors to consider when working with a sub-Saharan athlete include acculturation, social status, economic status, education, age, and identity within the culture. The athletic trainer should be able to understand how each factor affects an athlete's health.

Biocultural Assessment

- Sub-Saharan African skin tone ranges from light brown to very dark brown.
- There is no current information on any distinguishable features, disease incidence, or anomalies for Sub-Saharans.

Common Sensitivities and Conditions

- Many illnesses common to sub-Saharan people are seldom seen in the United States because of the more sanitary conditions that prevail here. Some illnesses that an athletic trainer does not typically deal with but that are associated with sub-Saharans include the following: brain fag, bouffée delirante, dysentery, malaria, malnutrition, onchocerciasis, schistosomiasis, trachoma, trypanosomiasis, typhoid fever, yellow fever, and Zar. The appendix provides a comprehensive list of signs and symptoms.
- Some illnesses an athletic trainer works with and may be familiar with include hepatitis B, HIV/AIDS, keloid formations, scabies, and tuberculosis.

Beliefs About Illness

An athletic trainer may face challenges deriving from the fact that many sub-Saharan people do not understand the concepts of disease causes and transmission (Molaligne, 1996). The athletic trainer may have to share information about how to prevent transmission (e.g., washing one's hands; covering one's mouth during a cough or a sneeze; avoiding use of someone else's razor, comb, or clothing).

DISTINCTIVE TO THIS CULTURE

- Some sub-Saharans accept that outside factors (e.g., spoiled food, stress, virus, or bacteria) cause illness.
- Some believe that illness means God is punishing them for inappropriate behavior (sins).
- It is thought that a person who has epilepsy lacks connection with God.
- Mental illness is thought to result from not being close enough to God, thus allowing evil spirits to take action.
- It is believed that fresh air may cause **mitch** (mental illness) (Erickson D'Avanzo & Geissler, 2003).
- Mental illness is thought by Nigerians to be inherited, so it is hidden from others and treated by healers (Erickson D'Avanzo & Geissler).
- Once cured, a person who has been mentally ill may find it difficult to marry and have children due to fear of genetic transfer of the mental illness (Erickson D'Avanzo & Geissler).
- A person who has power may also create an illness upon another using the "evil eye" (Erickson D'Avanzo & Geissler), which is given by looking into another's eyes. It is also believed that the evil eye can be given by praising another person, either purposely or inadvertently ("Common Beliefs and Cultural Practices," 2007).

Preventive Health Practices

- To stay healthy, it is imperative to balance mental and physical health. To balance mental and physical health, it is important to stay physically active and to remain as stress free as possible.
- A person may be put out of equilibrium and thus become ill through exposure to cold, having wet feet, or experiencing increased stress.
- To maintain good health, one must eat correctly, take baths or showers in warm water, and avoid excessive stress.
- Vaccinations are the primary preventive health care practice.
- Uvulectomy is used as a sore throat preventive.
- It is believed that removal of the lower incisors prevents diarrhea (Erickson D'Avanzo & Geissler, 2003).

Symptom Management

- Sub-Saharan people are known for their high pain tolerance and may not complain. As a result, controlling pain can pose a challenge, especially because the athlete may fear addiction to drugs. The athletic trainer needs to anticipate this concern and determine what care is necessary. Some pain medications are not addictive in nature, and sharing this information may comfort the athlete and thus allow him her to control the pain. Ice may also be recommended to control pain without drugs.
- Lipson et al. (1996) indicate that sub-Saharans deal with fatigue by sleeping; use of sleeping aids is avoided due to fear of dependence.
- Lipson et al. report use of lemon peel, ginger root, or fennel to control nausea.

Treatments

Treatments for sub-Saharans depend on the beliefs of the person who is ill. Most often, the treatments of choice involve home remedies and religion. When Western medicine is sought, medication is expected, and failure to receive it, even if it is not necessary, leads the patient to believe that the visit was a waste of time (Molaligne, 1996). Ethiopians may believe that pills do nothing and thus prefer injections (Erickson D'Avanzo & Geissler, 2003). An athletic trainer should anticipate that any medication given may be shared among family members (Yehieli & Grey, 2005) and that once a person feels better he or she may stop taking the medication. Thus the athletic trainer should express the importance of taking the medication even after the patient feels better in order to prevent the illness or condition from flaring up again; the trainer should also express concern that sharing medication with others can be dangerous because of allergies and possible overdose.

Home Remedies

Home remedies for illness include seeds, plants, and grains. If the athlete has an upset stomach, for example, he or she may use fennel, ginger, and lemon peel. Some sub-Saharans may believe that a folk healer is necessary and return to their homeland for care. Epilepsy is treated with herbs and readings from the **Quran**, which is the holy book of Islam (Rundle et al., 1999). Diarrhea is typically treated by drinking rice water—that is, water in which rice has been boiled—and constipation is addressed by taking castor oil, Epsom salts, or herbs (Lipson et al., 1996).

Ethiopian men practice various treatments for illness, one of which is **fire burning**—the practice of heating a stick, then applying it to the skin (Rundle et al., 1999). There is a delicate balance when an athletic trainer views a cultural treatment as harmful and shares that view with the athlete. Sub-Saharan athletes are unaccustomed to the direct approach of Western athletic trainers, and being told about negative outcomes discourages them (Molaligne, 1996). Thus Molaligne has suggested that a family member be given any information that might cause the athlete anxiety. With this in mind, an athletic trainer may achieve best results by working with a family member to suggest that the athlete stop using contraindicated remedies.

Protection

The two main religions support those who are ill through their belief in God. Coptic Orthodox Christians use prayer, confession of sins, and holy water rubbed on the forehead and body; they will also wear crosses or have a rosary. Those who are Muslim (i.e., followers of the Islamic faith) use prayer to **Allah** (supreme deity) and wear jewelry that includes parts of the Quran or a small version of the Quran as an amulet. An athletic trainer should try to understand each form of treatment and be aware that athletes may use one or more to resolve an illness or condition. An athlete may choose to use prayer or amulets instead of seeking the assistance of the athletic trainer.

A rope or leather strap is believed to protect a person from the "evil eye" (Rundle et al., 1999), and tattoos and amulets are thought to keep illness away (Erickson D'Avanzo & Geissler, 2003). Removing amulets or other protective items without permission may cause the athlete to distrust the athletic trainer.

HAITIAN

 Haitians have a unique culture of their own. It is important for the athletic trainer to understand the similarities and the differences of this culture to one's own, avoid the generalization that everyone adheres to the same beliefs that are part of this culture, and keep an open mind when working with athletes whose culture may be different than their own.

Demographic and Cultural Background Information

Welcome to the part of the chapter introducing Haitian culture. It begins by addressing the country of origin (see figure 8.3), how and why Haitians immigrated to the United States, and, once here, where they chose to live. It also addresses communication issues, including primary language, gestures, facial expressions, and body language.

The section on family structure provides information about how a family functions, who is considered part of the family, and who makes the important decisions.

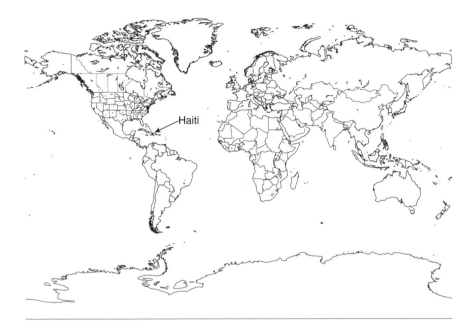

Haiti

Figure 8.3 Map of Haiti.

The section on daily living and food practices provides insight into Haitian views of time, food and the lack of food, and how the type of food affects individual health. Finally, spiritual or religious orientation is discussed in terms of how it plays a role in health care.

Brief History of Country of Origin and Immigration

Haiti is located southeast of Cuba. It became a French colony in 1697 and was named Saint Dominique. The main source of the economy was sugarcane, and African slaves were brought to Saint Dominique to harvest it. Saint Dominique became the leading producer in the sugarcane business.

In 1791, the slave population, which constituted the majority, revolted against the minority White owners and government. After 13 years of unrest, the revolt was successful, and the country was renamed Haiti and became the first independent Black country (Haiti, 2007). In the 1920s, the United States took over Haiti, and the first Haitian immigrations to the United States came during this occupation (Purnell & Paulanka, 2003b).

Haitians also came to the United States during the presidency of Francois Duvalier, also known as "Papa Doc," who ruled with brutality, especially against his political opponents (Purnell & Paulanka, 2003b). The economy collapsed and never recovered, and many fled due to the politics and hard economic times. Haitian refugees were also known as "boat people" because they would try to immigrate illegally on boats into the Florida Keys. Boat people are known to have been poverty-stricken individuals who could not pay for their travel out of Haiti (Purnell

& Paulanka, 2003b), and leaving their home country as a boat person was likely very stressful, especially if one had to leave family or friends behind, not knowing if they would live through the experience.

The U.S. Census Bureau (2000) reports that half a million Haitians live in the United States, but it is believed that in fact as many as 1.5 million live in here, the majority of whom are illegal aliens (Purnell & Paulanka, 2003b). The states with the greatest number of Haitians include Florida, New York, Massachusetts, Illinois, and California (Purnell & Paulanka, 2003b).

Haitians who have immigrated to the United States have moved into communities together with their families and neighbors from the home country (Purnell & Paulanka, 2003b). Living together in neighborhoods helps provide a feeling of comfort and aids them in acclimating to their new country, though Purnell and Paulanka (2003b) indicated that living in a homogeneous neighborhood may slow the acculturation process.

Many Haitians live in poverty and are unemployed in the United States (Purnell & Paulanka, 2003b). Haitians who are educated generally have no problem finding a job and contributing to society.

Primary Languages and Communication Styles

The major language is Creole. French is the secondary language. Creole is spoken by people in the middle and lower classes, who constitute the majority, and French is spoken by those in the elite or upper class.

DOS AND DON'TS

- Do shake the hand of a Haitian when meeting for the first time.
- Do use a title such as Mr., Mrs., Ms., Dr., or Miss when addressing a Haitian (Purnell & Paulanka, 2005).
- Do expect that friends will greet each other with a hug and a kiss, but not in public.
- Do expect to be continually touched on the shoulder or arm when a Haitian is speaking. It is useful to verbally acknowledge what the person is saying.
- Do expect that Haitians may be reserved and quiet.

DISTINCTIVE TO THIS CULTURE

- A person who is in authority may not be confronted.
- Much of the time, a Haitian will seem to concur with a statement by nodding. As a result, an athletic trainer may assume that the person accepts or understands, but this may not be the case.
- Eye contact is often avoided by first-generation Haitian immigrants to the United States, especially when interacting with a person in authority (Purnell & Paulanka, 2003b; Rundle et al., 1999).
- Acculturated Haitians tend to make eye contact, looking directly at the person with whom they are talking (Purnell & Paulanka, 2003b).

- Private information is revealed only if the Haitian person feels comfortable with the athletic trainer. If the private information is considered a disgrace to the person or the family, it is not likely to be shared. The athletic trainer must give assurance that information about a condition will not be shared with anyone else.

Family Structure

Frequently, three generations live under the same roof. The mother, or eldest female in the family, runs the household, and females make most of the decisions, though males are given the appearance of running the family and making all the decisions.

DISTINCTIVE TO THIS CULTURE

- Males are expected to support the family financially. They are also expected to be married. Having a mistress is not uncommon (Purnell & Paulanka, 2005).
- Machismo is prominent in Haitian culture and means being self-assured and virile.
- Anything a family member does is viewed as a reflection on the family. Thus, in a situation where a disease or condition could bring shame to the family, a Haitian may avoid being seen by an athletic trainer. Such a delay in receiving care can allow a condition to worsen, thus complicating treatment. As a result, an athletic trainer may need to reassure an athlete of confidentiality; an athlete who is of legal age and asks for confidentially is entitled to receive it. An under-aged athlete may need to receive support and encouragement in order to talk with his or her parent about a condition that must be made known. One technique is to role-play the scenario with the athlete.

Daily Living and Food Practices

It is not unusual for a Haitian to be late for an appointment, because time is not viewed as important in this culture. However, if the athletic trainer emphasizes that it is important to be on time, then the Haitian athlete may make the effort to arrive in a timely fashion.

The past is appreciated because of its historic perspective. The future, however, is not something that Haitians concern themselves with; they view it as predetermined by God (Purnell & Paulanka, 2005). The present is this culture's main orientation (Rundle et al., 1999).

- The physician is considered the authority in a medical situation.
- Medical consent for procedures may be given as long as the reason is clearly explained.
- Family members will be actively involved in the care of the ill or injured person.
- In the Haitian belief system, the body becomes ill when exposed to too much cold (**fret**) or too much heat (**cho**) (Lipson et al., 1996). If a person exercises and is hot and sweaty, hot fluids or foods may be eaten, whereas cold foods

would be thought to shock the system and cause the person to become ill (one example of a cold food is pineapple). Chofret is an illness believed to be caused by an imbalance of hot and cold, so the term chofret is combined to become a description of that imbalance (Lipson et al., 1996; Purnell & Paulanka, 2005).

- Haitians also believe their diet contains light and heavy foods. Heavy foods are eaten at lunch, the largest meal of the day. They include potatoes, cooked plantains, and cornmeal mush. Light foods include uncooked plantains, bread, and soup.

- Foods not eaten include yogurt, runny egg yolks, and cottage cheese (Lipson et al., 1996).

- The preferred drinks are water, fruit juice, tea, and soda (Lipson et al.).

- Men are given the bulk of the meat, resulting in normal values of protein in their system. Women and children, however, may have low protein values, and an athletic trainer may have to work with a female Haitian athlete to supplement her diet with protein foods that are not meat (e.g., nuts).

- Foods that stimulate a healthy appetite are part of the daily diet. This is important because Haitians view weight loss as a sign of illness. One example of an appetite-stimulating food is **Akasan**, made of evaporated milk, cream, cinnamon, vanilla extract, salt, cornmeal, and sugar.

Spiritual or Religious Orientation

- Many Haitians adhere to a Catholic or Protestant religion while also practicing Voodoo (Purnell & Paulanka, 2003b).

- Practicing Catholics may follow the dietary practice of not eating red meat, pork, or chicken on Fridays.

- Those who practice the Catholic religion may wear religious medals depicting a saint or have rosary beads.

- Voodooism is a religious practice in which a person goes into a trancelike state and communicates with spirits of ancestors known as Loa (Purnell & Paulanka, 2003b). It is believed that Loa can provide the believer with health, protection, and wealth (Purnell & Paulanka, 2003b).

- The saints of the Catholic religion are the same saints in Voodoo but may have a different function (Lipson et al., 1996).

Health Care Information

Haitians are considered relatively new immigrants in the United States, and they have their own cultural beliefs, practices, forms of symptom management, and treatments, which may be hard for the athletic trainer to understand.

Biocultural Assessment

- Haitian skin tone ranges from light brown to very dark brown. The darkest skin tones may challenge an athletic trainer's ability to determine pallor, jaundice, or cyanosis. An athletic trainer may achieve best results by using the sclera of the eye, the inside of the lip, the palms, and the nail beds to determine any medical skin conditions.

- Eye color is most often brown.
- Hair is generally black.

Common Sensitivities and Conditions

- There is no current information on any common sensitivities or anomalies for Haitians.
- Common illnesses and conditions among Haitians that athletic trainers do not typically deal with include boufée delirante, cholera, dengue, and malaria. The appendix provides a more comprehensive list of signs and symptoms.
- Athletic trainers are probably familiar with the following conditions that may affect Haitian athletes: type 1 diabetes, hepatitis B, HIV/AIDS, hypertension, sexually transmitted diseases, and tuberculosis.

Beliefs About Illness

Illness is believed to have three levels: brief illness (goes away in a short time), illness (puts the person in bed), and finally death. It is thought that illness is sent from God or caused by hot or cold air or by foods. It is also believed that an evil spirit can take over the body, and this kind of illness is thought to be more serious, because it will tend to become more serious than an illness sent by God. Prayer is believed to help the healing process and resolve illness.

DISTINCTIVE TO THIS CULTURE

- Haitians believe that in order to maintain health a person must be clean and must exercise, stay warm, eat right, and obtain good sleep; whenever there is an imbalance, a person is likely to become ill. Haitians also believe that a person can become ill as the result of a hex placed on him or her, and they try to avoid giving reason for another to cast such a spell.
- It is also believed that foods can cause illnesses or troubling conditions; for example, acne is thought to be caused by drinking fruit juices (Lipson et al., 1996).
- Tiredness is viewed as a blood disorder, which may be thought of as anemia. An athletic trainer should not confuse this with the clinical diagnosis of anemia. The tiredness could be a result of multiple health items.
- When a person is given bad news, it may cause a fright or **sezisman**. The belief is that the person will have a headache, higher blood pressure, and loss of vision (Lipson et al.). To resolve it, one may use a cold compress on the head and drink tea.
- In the minds of many Haitians, physicians should be male and nurses should be female (Lipson et al.). This expectation may create a problem for a female athletic trainer, who may have to earn the trust of a Haitian athlete. If the athlete cannot cope with a female athletic trainer, it is best to have a male athletic trainer work with that athlete. The male athletic trainer can then convey the

confidence that he has in the females on the staff as a way of supporting the female athletic trainers.

Preventive Health Practices

- Being balanced in one's daily life is critical to remaining healthy. Features of good health include proper diet, balance between hot and cold, exercise, rest, and spirituality.
- Walking is the most common form of exercise.
- Enemas are given to children to ensure healthy bowels, prevent acne, and invigorate the body (Lipson et al., 1996). Children are also given **lok**—a mixture of tea leaves, juice, syrup, and oil that acts as a laxative—to maintain a healthy state (Lipson et al.).
- Women are not allowed to physically touch their bodies except for bathing. Thus some simple measures such as self-breast examinations will not be done, which places Haitian women at risk for illness that progresses needlessly. An athletic trainer should provide literature about the need to perform breast self-examinations, and it may be necessary to request that women see their physician more than once a year for preventive examinations.
- It is more common that Haitian men have both a wife and a mistress (Purnell & Paulanka, 2005). An athletic trainer may need to discuss methods for prevention of sexually transmitted disease. This topic can make for a delicate and challenging conversation, because Haitians are modest about their private lives. It is important that the athletic trainer be factual and avoid making judgments of the beliefs and behaviors of the athlete.

Symptom Management

- Some Haitians use each other's signs and symptoms to diagnose their own illness or injury. Self-diagnosis is the first line of treatment for Haitians.
- Haitians may use hot tea, roots, broth, and hot and cold foods before seeking the advice of a Western medical practitioner. If Western medicine is used, injections are preferred over pills (Lipson et al., 1996).
- Haitians may have a low pain tolerance, and the athletic trainer may find that it is a challenge to determine the source of the pain. The person may describe the pain as being all over, making it difficult for the athletic trainer to assess or treat it (Lipson et al.).
- When faced with breathing difficulty, some Haitian athletes may describe it as asthma. It may in fact be asthma or hyperventilation (Lipson et al.), and the athletic trainer needs to make sure that the signs and symptoms are ones associated with the condition being treated.
- Constipation is treated with tea or laxatives.
- Diarrhea is most often a concern for children, as it is believed that the suffering child may have had a hex placed on him or her (Lipson et al.). The family may seek assistance from a Voodoo healer. The athletic trainer should be sure to assess for dehydration brought about by the diarrhea.

- Fatigue is viewed by Haitians as a sign of weakness, and the Haitian treatment for fatigue is to eat red meat, vitamins, bouillon, and liver (Lipson et al.). The athletic trainer should investigate the cause of the fatigue.

Treatments

Haitians who do not believe in Western medicine are generally first-generation immigrants, who are most likely to use alternatives such as voodoo, home remedies, and certain foods.

Home Remedies

Haitians living in the United States ask family members in Haiti to send them ingredients (e.g., roots and leaves) for home remedies (Purnell & Paulanka, 2005). The combination of home remedies and Western medicine can cause complications, and the athletic trainer must ask what home remedies are being used.

When a person has a high temperature or a cold, warm fresh castor oil is rubbed onto one side of the body. The next day, the other side of the body gets the warm castor oil (Erickson D'Avanzo & Geissler, 2003). This process continues until the person returns to health. The family will take care of the needs of the ill person.

Some use the term "cold" to refer to any respiratory issue (e.g., pneumonia, asthma, flu) (Lipson et al., 1996). In Haitian culture, a respiratory ailment is known as "oppression," and the home cure for it is to open a coconut; fill it with sugarcane syrup, honey, and nutmeg; and bury it for one month (Purnell & Paulanka, 2005). The coconut mixture is given, after it is dug up, to the person in doses of 1 tablespoon twice per day until it is gone.

Voodoo

Voodoo belief holds that disease is brought about naturally or by the supernatural. It is thought that illness created by natural causes is brief in duration. Supernatural illness is thought to be caused by angry spirits, and to cure it the athlete and his or her family offer feasts to the spirits. Should an athlete or family choose to not offer feasts, it is feared that great misfortune may follow (Purnell & Paulanka, 2005). Each person has a spirit that protects him or her, and illness occurs when there is a failure between the person and spirit.

Food

Food can play an important role in the resolution of illness. When a person is ill, hot tea is the fluid of choice. Foods for times of illness include pumpkin soup, bouillon, and a soup made with meat, dumplings, yams, and green vegetables. Other favorites include oatmeal, milk, cornmeal, sugar, and porridge (Lipson et al., 1996). Many Haitians are becoming more conscious about their diets and reducing their consumption of fat and salt.

Gas is believed to cause pain in the head (headache), stomach (stomachache), and extremities (rheumatism). The thinking is that gas enters the body through the ears, mouth, and stomach and is able to travel through the bloodstream to various parts of the body. To prevent gas from entering the body, Haitians avoid eating leftovers. Foods used to eliminate gas include tea made from garlic, cloves and mint, plantains, and corn (Purnell & Paulanka, 2005).

SUMMARY

Blacks are defined not by country but by skin color and ancestry. One should understand that each generation of Blacks may have a preference as to how they are addressed as a group. Some of the preferences are *African American, Negro, colored, sub-Saharan,* and *Black.*

Blacks who came to the United States brought with them their beliefs, family traditions, religions, foods, and languages. Some members of these cultures migrated to the United States; others were kidnapped from their families and brought forcibly for the purpose of slavery. Being forced into slavery had implications in many areas of life, including language, health care beliefs and treatment, religion, and food practices. The families of African Americans are close, and even those who are friends are considered brothers and sisters.

In some instances, people of the United States forced Blacks to create new languages or abused their power in ways that have caused a lack of trust in the health care system among Blacks even today. For the most part, Blacks are verbal, and they may share information regarding pain, difficulty breathing, and most illnesses. The athletic trainer may find Blacks' speaking volume to be louder than that of some groups.

The skin color of Blacks can make it hard for an athletic trainer to determine cyanosis or jaundice. Blacks are more prone than average to some illnesses and conditions; these include high blood pressure, heart disease, HIV/AIDS, keloid formation, lactose intolerance, leukoedema, pseudofolliculitis, sickle-cell anemia, systemic lupus erythematosus, and vitiligo.

Preventive health care may be avoided if the Black person lacks health insurance and the means to pay for treatment. Some may also avoid preventive practices because of modesty issues; this is something the athletic trainer can work on via education.

Treatment for various conditions may be sought in a variety of ways: home remedies, protection, spiritual orientation, use of certain foods, showers, heat, cold, Voodoo, and Western medicine.

An athletic trainer will need to understand the nuances of the Black culture to work effectively with Black athletes. Understanding the scope of Black culture will make it easier for the athletic trainer to be respected within this community.

Learning Aids

What Would You Do If . . . ?

1. What if an athlete you are working with smells awful, and when you inquire he says that he has rubbed turpentine on his fractured clavicle?
2. What if an athlete seems constantly fatigued but blood work does not indicate an illness?
3. What if an athlete wants you to work with his folk healer? You are skeptical that any good would come from doing so.
4. What if you are left-handed and a Muslim athlete is leery of having you treat him?

5. What if a loud discussion, which seems very similar to an argument, arises in your facility? You notice that the discussion is among Black athletes.

6. What if an athlete who has been given pills returns to you and is still sick? The bottle is empty, and the athletic trainer asks "Who took the pills?" The athlete responds that "I did." He has a brother who is sick with a similar illness.

7. What if you need to examine an athlete who refuses your care because he or she needs a practitioner of the same sex? No such person is immediately available.

8. What if a Black athlete has what appears to be a "falling out" experience in a crowd of people on the sideline at a game? What would your response be as people stare at you and wonder why you are not doing anything?

Activities

1. Design a program for each group discussed in this chapter that would support prevention of illnesses common in the United States but not in the culture's home country.

2. Using the home remedies listed within this text, determine if there is any merit beyond psychological support for the use of each. Consult several textbooks written about Black home remedies (see the references).

3. If you had to design a diet to promote health among African Americans, what would it look like?

4. How will your care of Blacks need to change to make them more comfortable?

5. Examine your beliefs regarding HIV and how they may affect your care of an athlete who is HIV-positive.

6. Write your personal beliefs and stereotypes about Black culture. Explain how these beliefs may affect your care of Black athletes.

7. How can trust be established between a Black athlete and a White athletic trainer?

Key Terms

Define the following key terms found in this chapter:

Allah	Fire burning	Lok
Akasan	Fret	Low blood
Cho	Haram	Mitch
Creole language	High blood	Pidgin
Dirt	Injera	Quran
Ebonics	Juneteenth	Rootwork
Falling out	Laying on of hands	Sezisman

Questions for Review

1. What are the primary differences between the Black groups discussed in this chapter?
2. What are the primary similarities between the Black groups discussed in this chapter?
3. How might religious or spiritual beliefs affect health care among Blacks?
4. What is the purpose of laxatives in Black culture? What should an athletic trainer be concerned with when an athlete uses laxatives?
5. Why is mental illness often hidden in Black culture?
6. Explain the evolution of health care among Blacks.
7. How can an athletic trainer incorporate present-day health care while accommodating the needs of a Black athlete?
8. Why might some Blacks be fearful of athletic trainers, physicians, or other health care providers?
9. Why do some people in Black culture appreciate being slightly overweight?

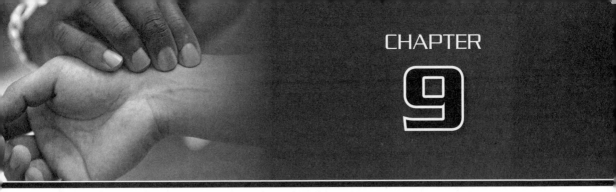
Latino

Learning Objectives

Upon completing this chapter, students will be able to do the following:

1. Describe the type of athletic trainer preferred by members of the Latino cultures discussed in this chapter
2. Explain how past health care experiences of members of this culture can affect health care beliefs for Latinos in the present day
3. Discuss differences between the three Latino cultures described in this chapter regarding treatments, religions, decision making, and common illnesses
4. Explain how religion plays a role in health care
5. Describe the various cultural influences that affect care of an athlete
6. Discuss how an athletic trainer can support a Latino athlete's culture without hindering care
7. Explain how home remedies affect health care

Luzita Vela, PhD, ATC, LAT

I grew up in the Rio Grande Valley in the city of Pharr, Texas where I graduated from PSJA North High School. I am a third generation Mexican-American who grew up in a border town with a large Hispanic population. I was instantly attracted to a health care profession at a young age because of my interest in biology, anatomy, and physical activity. I also felt that a career in patient care would be fulfilling and meaningful. I have a bachelor of science in kinesiology from Texas Woman's University in Denton. I earned my masters of science degree in athletic training from Barry University in Miami, Florida, and a PhD in kinesiology with an emphasis in athletic training from the Pennsylvania State University.

Photo courtesy of Texas State University-San Marcos

I am currently an assistant professor and clinical education director at Texas State University in San Marcos, Texas. Prior to that (2005-2007), I was an assistant professor in the Department of Sports Medicine at West Chester University in West Chester, Pennsylvania. I also served as the head athletic trainer for West Chester's women's field hockey and lacrosse teams during my tenure. Prior to West Chester, I was an assistant athletic trainer and assistant professor at Hope College in Holland, Michigan. I am an active member in the profession and serve on the NATA Professional Education Committee and review manuscripts for the *Journal of Athletic Training*, the *Athletic Training Education Journal,* and *Athletic Training and Sports Health Care*. My research interests include evidence-based practice, disablement, clinical outcomes assessment, and clinical education.

My cultural background has given me some interesting insights into the role of faith and family in the health care process. I have personally witnessed the comfort with modern, western health care grow from generation to generation within my own family, from my grandparents to my nephews and nieces. Whereas my grandma's solution for an ailment was primarily based in religion and herbal remedies, my siblings and I learned to straddle the world of the old and new when seeking treatment.

Athletic trainers are in a unique position because they are afforded the element of time to understand each patient's culture and health care needs. My advice to any athletic training student is to remember that patient values are an integral part of employing evidence-based practice. Therefore, we as health care providers are charged with the responsibility of fully understanding our patient to provide the best quality health care possible.

The term Latino refers to any individual born in a Latin American country or descended from a person born in such a country. Latinos originated in South America, Central America, Mexico, Cuba, Puerto Rico, the Dominican Republic, and the West Indies. The term Hispanic is not used in this chapter, because it refers to all individuals who speak Spanish, including those in Europe. The term Latino refers to both men and women when speaking of the culture in general. When speaking specifically of females, the term Latina is most specific.

This chapter focuses on three cultures that were the source of the great immigration from Latino countries to the United States: Mexico, Puerto Rico, and Cuba (U.S. Census Bureau, 2000; Yehieli and Grey, 2005; Chong, 2002). Each of these Latino populations is discussed in detail, from the country of origin through the acculturation of the culture's members to the United States. This chapter is intended to give the reader an opportunity to learn customs and practices of Latino culture. For each culture, the chapter includes special features that address dos and don'ts, as well as distinctive characteristics of the culture.

We should remember that not all members of a given culture adhere to each of the characteristics discussed and that first-generation immigrants often adhere to beliefs and traditions that may not be carried on by members of the next generation.

MEXICAN

Mexicans have a unique culture of their own. It is important for the athletic trainer to understand the similarities and the differences of this culture to one's own, avoid the generalization that everyone adheres to the same beliefs that are part of this culture, and keep an open mind when working with athletes whose culture may be different than their own.

Demographic and Cultural Background Information

The acculturation process varies for each person and culture. This section addresses the history of the country of origin and immigration, primary languages and communication, family structure, daily living and food practices, and spiritual or religious orientation.

Brief History of Country of Origin and Immigration

Mexicans are descendents of Central American Indians, Native Americans, Spanish, Africans, and Europeans. Spanish people came to Mexico (see figure 9.1) as explorers, looted gold and riches from the Aztec Indians, and claimed it for Spain. Other tribes supported the Spanish in conquering the Aztecs.

First-generation Mexican immigrants were able to freely move back and forth between the United States and Mexico until the mid-1940s (Ngai, 2004; Lipson, Dibble, & Minarik, 1996; Downes, 1997). Once it became illegal to cross the border, many Mexicans stayed in the United States but maintained their culture and values.

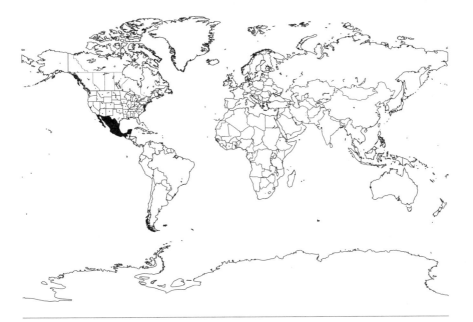

Figure 9.1 Map of Mexico.

Immigrants who try to cross the border illegally are under stress of getting caught, being deported, or dying.

Mexicans have come to the United States to be with family members who immigrated previously and for employment opportunities, health care, and education. First-generation immigrants have often found only temporary work in fields, doing physical labor, or taking on jobs that Americans refuse to do (Lipson et al., 1996; Downes, 1997). Second- and third-generation immigrants have been able to find white-collar jobs that require college education.

Today the majority of Mexican immigrants to the United States live in Arizona, California, Colorado, Illinois, Florida, New Mexico, and Texas (Purnell & Paulanka, 2003). The majority of Mexicans live in cities, and many fail to complete a high school education; Los Angeles is the U.S. city with the largest Mexican population (Spector, 2004).

Primary Languages and Communication Styles

Mexicans speak a variety of languages, including Spanish, English, and an indigenous Indian language (e.g., Nahuatl and Maya) (Purnell & Paulanka, 2005; Erickson D'Avanzo & Geissler, 2003; Lipson et al., 1996). There are several dialects of Spanish and of the Indian language.

DOS AND DON'TS

- Don't address a person by his or her first name unless you have received permission to do so.
- Do greet with Señor (male), Señora (married female), or Señorita (unmarried female).
- If you must wave, do so with the palm down so as to not offend the person.
- Don't point at a person; doing so is considered disrespectful (Rundle, Carvalho, & Robinson, 1999).
- Do shake hands, and always start with the oldest person first (Malat, 2003).

DISTINCTIVE TO THIS CULTURE

- Mexican people are soft spoken.
- A raised voice is thought to indicate anger; staying calm is a respected virtue (Malat, 2003).
- Silence tends to be a part of the evaluation of words that have been said (Malat).
- Mexican people may seem to agree when they really do not; nodding may mean nothing more than respect for the athletic trainer (Malat).
- The mother's and father's surnames will be the surname of the child; the father's name will come first (Malat).
- Personal distance is close (1.5 to 4 feet, or 0.5 to 1.2 meters).
- Women may greet each other with a kiss or cheek-to-cheek hug even if it is their first meeting (Malat).

Family Structure

It is not uncommon to see three generations living under the same roof. Everyone is expected to contribute, including the youngest and oldest members. The needs of the family are deemed more important than the needs of the individual (Downes, 1997).

DISTINCTIVE TO THIS CULTURE

- Machismo is a stereotype for Mexican males, so keep an open mind not to stereotype each person with this attitude (Purnell & Paulanka, 2005).
- A large family is thought to be a sign of machismo because the man of the house has sexual prowess (Purnell & Paulanka, 2003).
- Adults are respected for their knowledge.
- Members of an extended family may live close to one another as a way to maintain cultural identity.
- The extended family can also give support in times of health care needs (Purnell & Paulanka, 2005).
- The Mexican male is expected to provide for his family financially, whereas women are expected to take care of the children and run the home, but in many households both adults work.
- Decision making is primarily the responsibility of the adult male, but all close adults may be consulted.
- An athletic trainer may find her- or himself in a small group of family members while sharing medical information (Purnell & Paulanka, 2005; Lipson et al., 1996).

Daily Living and Food Practices

Mexicans are oriented toward present time; they are focused on "right now" rather than on the past or on future events or outcomes. Thus a Mexican athlete who completes a questionnaire regarding health may not share past medical conditions or illnesses if they are thought to have no bearing on how the athlete feels now. This tendency may make it more challenging for an athletic trainer to treat an illness or condition.

- Foods most common in the Mexican diet include rice, beans, onions, fruits, potatoes, fish, meats, tortillas, and plantains.
- Prepackaged food is not viewed favorably; tortillas, for example, are not store bought but made from scratch.
- Many Mexicans are lactose intolerant.
- Malnutrition is prevalent among Mexicans who are poor (Erickson D'Avanzo & Geissler, 2003).
- Foods are classified as hot or cold, depending not on temperature but on how each reacts within the body.

- Foods considered hot include peppers, cereal, oils, liquor, coffee, tea, ice, and some fruits (Downes, 1997).
- Foods considered cold include water, vegetables, dairy, meats, citrus fruits, and tropical fruits. Some foods can be either hot or cold depending on how they are prepared (Downes, 1997).
- First-generation immigrants believe that an illness considered cold should be treated by hot foods and vice versa.

Spiritual or Religious Orientation

About 90 percent of Mexicans are Catholic (Erickson D'Avanzo & Geissler, 2003); the secondary religion is Protestantism. Less than five percent of people also adhere to **espiritism**, a form of belief in God and spirits. Adherents communicate with spirits via a séance while in a trance or channeling (Kardec, 2007). People involved in espiritism believe that they are supported and enriched through prayer and belief.

Health Care Information

This section presents the particulars of Mexican health culture in the following categories: biocultural assessment, common sensitivities and conditions, beliefs about illness, preventive health practices, symptom management, and treatments. We would do well to remember, however, that all cultures have their own variations, whether in skin color, health beliefs, sensitivities, conditions, or health threats.

Biocultural Assessment

- Mexicans have a rich, blended genetic history that includes Central Americans, Native Americans, Spanish, Africans, and various Indian tribes.
- Skin tone ranges from very light to a dark brown. Dark skin tones may pose a challenge for the athletic trainer examining for cyanosis or jaundice. It may be easiest to do so by using the palms, soles of the feet, inside of the lip, nail beds, or sclera of the eyes.
- Depending on the genetic history, eye color can be blue or brown.
- Depending upon genetic history, hair may be straight and black or blond. Those with black hair have genetics that may be more closely related to indigenous Indians (Purnell and Paulanka, 2005). Blond hair may have resulted from Spanish background (Purnell and Paulanka, 2005).

Common Sensitivities and Conditions

- Mexico's mixed heritage makes it difficult to determine therapeutic doses of certain drugs (Purnell & Paulanka, 2003).
- Mexicans are more sensitive to antidepressants than are members of most cultures (Purnell & Paulanka, 2005).
- Antihypertensive drugs may not work as well in Mexican people.
- Mexicans have high rates of cancer, heart disease, and alcohol and drug abuse.

- Illnesses and conditions common among Mexicans that athletic trainers are familiar with include hypertension, type 1 diabetes, HIV/AIDS, and lactose intolerance.
- The following conditions affecting Mexicans may be less familiar to some athletic trainers: amoebic dysentery, intestinal parasites, malaria, dengue (Purnell & Paulanka, 2003, 2005; Downes, 1997; Spector, 2004) The appendix provides a more comprehensive list of signs and symptoms.

Beliefs About Illness

In traditional Mexican culture, it is believed that illness results from three causes: sin, imbalance, and witchcraft. Acculturated immigrants are accepting of Western medicine.

DISTINCTIVE TO THIS CULTURE

- It is thought that physical and mental illness is God's way of conveying unhappiness with a person; this view posits a strong external locus of control over illness.
- A person with an emotional illness may then cause a physical illness in their body from too much stress.
- Life is about balance, and imbalance may make a person sick.
- Each person is responsible for maintaining his or her balance.
- Mexicans believe that illness can result from an imbalance of hot and cold; this belief is tied to the four body humors (blood, yellow bile, phlegm, and black bile). An imbalance in the humors is thought to cause either physical or emotional illness.
- Other illnesses include **espanto** (shock), **susto** (fright), **mal de ojo** (the "evil eye"), and **mal aire** (bad air caused by exposure to drafts).
- There is a belief in Mexican culture in the supernatural or witchcraft (Lipson et al., 1996).
- **Envidia** refers to envy (Spector, 2004). When a person is successful, it is kept quiet because others may envy him or her, thus resulting in illness due to good fortune. A spiritual healer (espiritualista) is used to resolve these forms of witchcraft illness.
- Touching a child's head is believed to cause an illness called **caida de la mollera**, which involves dehydration and vomiting and results in a fallen fontanel (Downes, 1997). In reality, the dehydration of the child can cause serious illness and death, but the dehydration is more often caused by diarrhea. Thus an athletic trainer must be careful to explain when touching of the head is necessary.

Preventive Health Practices

Mexicans who believe that being healthy or unhealthy depends on God's will may not focus on preventive practices (Yehieli & Grey, 2005). The athletic trainer should investigate an athlete's beliefs in order to determine whether additional family support is needed to ensure that the athlete takes needed preventive measures.

Obesity is common among Mexicans and is usually associated with dietary issues. A good preventive is to teach the athlete how to eat a diet that is low in fat and high in fruits and vegetables. Dental disease is also a common problem among Mexican people, and it is important to stress the need to brush one's teeth, to floss daily, and to have one's teeth cleaned professionally twice a year.

The sexually transmitted conditions of cervical cancer and HIV among women are believed to be transmitted unnecessarily by their partners in Mexican culture. The strong Catholic religious belief that condoms should not be used may be the common link to transmission of sexually transmitted diseases in this culture. Women may also believe that if their partner uses a condom, this means that he thinks she is unclean (Purnell & Paulanka, 2005). Thus athletic trainers need to encourage abstinence or condom use (Downes, 1997).

The athletic trainer should understand that the Latino population has the worst record of using the health care system and that Mexican men use the health care system the least of all (Downes, 1997). Mexicans who are illegal in the United States may not go to a dentist, doctor, or athletic trainer for fear of being sent back to Mexico.

Preventive screening for pesticides should be mandatory for athletes who are migrant workers. The athlete is more likely to comply if the athletic trainer involves the entire family in preventive plans (Purnell & Paulanka, 2005). It is important to stress preventive health care and put each person on a regular screening schedule.

It may be necessary to provide free clinics for those who are in the country illegally and have no health care insurance. Also, clinic hours need to be extended beyond 6 p.m. so that those who work can attend without worrying about lost pay. Avoidance of the health care system has to become a primary focus of Western medicine if we are to provide Mexican people with care that is respectful and supportive.

Those who are lactose intolerant should be counseled to prevent problems by avoiding lactose products. Some products do not list lactose on the label but may be identifiable by asking a pharmacist about lactose in medications and by looking for whey on food labels.

Symptom Management

- Males tend to prove their masculinity by hiding their pain, and the athletic trainer may have to watch for facial expressions to determine whether pain exists; women are more inclined to express pain (Lipson et al., 1996).

- Exhaustion could be a symptom of illness or of the person's inability to adapt to the American work culture. Feelings of exhaustion may result from not having a long period of rest or **siesta** during the middle part of the day (Lipson et al.).

- Many members of Mexican culture believe that diarrhea is a way of ridding the body of illness (Lipson et al.). The accepted method for rehydrating after diarrhea is to drink tea.

- Mexicans respect pharmacists so much that they might not visit a physician. A Mexican person may visit the pharmacy and get advice on how to manage symptoms (Lipson et al.).
- In Mexico, a prescription is not required to obtain medication; this difference may cause adjustment pains for Mexican immigrants in the United States.

Treatments

Those who believe that God causes illness may use prayer and spiritual protection as a form of treatment. If one believes that an illness is caused by imbalance, then he or she may use foods and faith healers. Witchcraft and supernatural illnesses are treated by curanderos, espiritualistas, and protective methods.

Curanderos and Curanderas

A **curandero** (male) or **curandera** (female) is a healer who is believed to use natural remedies and supernatural ways to treat illnesses. The belief is that evil spirits cause illness and that the curandero or curandera can contact the spirits in an attempt to bring about a cure. Athletic trainers may not view this practice as useful, but it is best not to express one's opinion about this practice as the athlete may lose respect for the athletic trainer. Keep your feelings under control.

A curandero or curandera may work in a religious direction or through cleanings (Spector, 2004). Religious rituals include prayers, candles, money offerings, confessions, and placing the hands on the body (laying on of hands). For example, some Mexicans believe that abdominal pain is caused by **empacho**—a ball of food stuck in the lining of the stomach—and the treatment of choice is massage of the spine (Spector, 2004).

Cleaning done by the curandero or curandera is done by waving an unbroken egg or herbs over the ill person. It is believed that the neck is a vulnerable area (Spector, 2004).

The curandero or curandera comes to the home of the ill person and engages in social conversation. Curanderos and curanderas tend to be very informal, and in contrast, physicians may seem to be very straight laced and impersonal. The curandero or curandera views the body and its surroundings as one; thus the entire setting must be considered for the solution.

If a professional curandero or curandera is not available, a grandmother or other family member may perform a healing ceremony that involves brushing the palms over the ill person's body while repeating Catholic prayers over and over to release evil spirits (Vela, 2008). The athletic trainer may need to ask about healers and learn to work with them.

Folk Remedies and Cures

Purnell and Paulanka (2005) state that "almost all" Mexicans use herbal medicines and teas. Thus an athletic trainer must ask what herbals are being used so that any harmful interactions can be prevented. Herbals for various illnesses are sold by herbalists. First-generation Mexican immigrants may use herbs to maintain or improve health. For example, teas may be used to keep a person hydrated during vomiting and diarrhea (Lipson et al., 1996).

Kennett (1976) lists the following folk remedies and cures (many involve chemicals found in traditional Western medicine):

- Oil of turpentine, herbal artemisia, and datura stramonium (jimson weed)—for hemorrhoids
- Pulverized avocado seed, plantain water, and powdered charcoal—for diarrhea (used as an enema)
- Taking medicine with the left hand—for curing kidneys
- Taking medicine with the right hand—for curing the liver
- Steeped willow leaves made into a tea—for colds
- Papaya fruit—applied to heal skin conditions
- Mexican magnolia brewed into a tea—for heart complaints
- Consumption of young alligators, washing of the skin with urine—for scabies
- Brewed tea with yam root—for arthritis
- Pushing hands deep into an anthill—for arthritis

Food

The athletic trainer will need to determine if the illness is viewed as hot or cold, then prescribe food that opposes the illness. The athletic trainer can show respect for this belief by simply asking about the illness. Mexican people do not have a list of hot or cold illnesses. Each person may believe differently. The athletic trainer may be able to prescribe additional care from Western beliefs that can resolve the illness.

Some medications are considered hot or cold. Asking the ill person which medications are hot or cold will help the athletic trainer determine the hot or cold foods to suggest for balance. The treatment that an athletic trainer uses could also fit within the cultural belief of hot and cold so as to show sensitivity to the athlete's beliefs.

Protection and Religious Practices

Mexican babies are protected from the evil eye through the use of a deer's eye bean pinned onto the clothing of the baby. The deer's eye bean may have the image of a saint on it. It is also believed that one can receive protection from the evil eye by wearing a pendant called the miraculous hand (more commonly known as the hand of God) or through placing the rosa y cruz (pink cross) over the door of a home to bring the occupants good fortune and health (Spector, 2004).

There is a tremendous belief in prayer in Mexican culture. Guided by the religion of choice, prayer is used to support a person and prevent illness or free him or her from it. Some may burn candles while praying. The candle of El Niño Fidencio, named for a famous healer in Mexico, is used for protection (Spector, 2004).

Visiting religious shrines is also commonplace to protect someone against illness. The visit to the shrine may involve lighting candles, giving gifts of money, and praying. Many homes have places of prayer, as well as candles and religious statues to offer protection from illness. When an illness is successfully treated, prayers of thanks are offered to God or to the saint who helped resolve it (Spector, 2004).

PUERTO RICAN

Puerto Ricans have a unique culture of their own. It is important for the athletic trainer to understand the similarities and the differences of this culture to one's own, avoid the generalization that everyone adheres to the same beliefs that are part of this culture, and keep an open mind when working with athletes whose culture may be different than their own.

Demographic and Cultural Background Information

To really understand a culture, the athletic trainer needs to understand the variables that make it unique. The section gives a brief history of country of origin and immigration, primary languages and communication, family structure, daily living and food practices, and spiritual or religious orientation.

Brief History of Country of Origin and Immigration

Puerto Rico is an island in the Caribbean (see figure 9.2). The first inhabitants were the Taíno Indians (Purnell & Paulanka, 2003). Later, Spanish explorers claimed the island and called it home, as did African slaves. Interracial marriages took place between the three primary peoples—the Spanish, the Africans, and the native Puerto Ricans (Purnell & Paulanka, 2003).

The United States has had control of Puerto Rico since the end of the Spanish–American War. The Jones-Shafroth Act of 1917 gave Puerto Ricans citizenship in the United States, designated the type of government Puerto Rico would have, and established the ability of the United States to control all governmental matters (Library

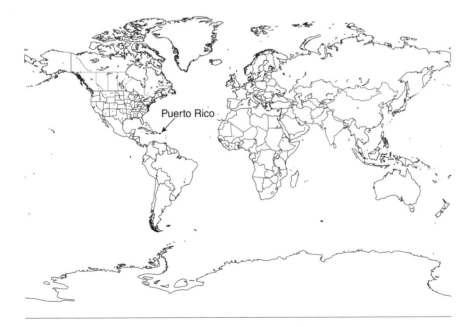

Figure 9.2 Map of Puerto Rico.

of Congress, 1998). Some Puerto Ricans are offended by their lack of sovereignty, and efforts by some to make Puerto Rico the 51st state have stirred controversy.

Puerto Ricans have settled in the United States in the Northeastern and Northwestern states. The largest population of Puerto Ricans lives in the cities of New York and metropolitan New Jersey (Spector, 1996). Most came to the States because of the need for employment, and many travel between the two countries to visit relatives (Purnell & Paulanka, 2003).

Primary Languages and Communication Styles

Puerto Rico's main languages are Spanish and English.

DOS AND DON'TS

- Don't attempt to mimic the accent.
- Do expect to be interrupted frequently.
- Do expect Puerto Ricans to speak rapidly and in a high-pitched tone of voice.
- Do shake hands with the eldest male.
- Don't discuss sex, or anything to do with sex, until trust has been established.

DISTINCTIVE TO THIS CULTURE

- Puerto Rican males greet each other with a handshake and a pat on the shoulder (Purnell & Paulanka, 2003; Axtell, 1993).
- Puerto Rican women greet each other with hugs and brushing of the cheeks (Purnell & Paulanka, 2003; Axtell).
- According to Axtell (1993), when a Puerto Rican person wiggles his or her nose, it means, "What's going on here?"
- When a Puerto Rican wants to point out a direction, he or she uses puckered lips to point in the direction desired (Axtell).
- When calling someone, the fingers are pointed downward and curled under in a waving movement (Axtell).
- It is a sign of respect to make eye contact, except with someone who is older.
- It is considered very inappropriate for a woman to stare at a man (Axtell).
- The personal space between the athlete and athletic trainer should start at 5 to 12 feet (about 1.5 to 3.5 meters). Those who are acculturated tend to feel comfortable when physically closer right from the beginning (Lipson et al., 1996).
- The athletic trainer may be able to create an atmosphere of trust by explaining things and going slowly.

Family Structure

Family is important in Puerto Rican culture. Children live at home until married, and once married they are expected to live close by.

DISTINCTIVE TO THIS CULTURE

- The male is the head of the household.
- Macho behavior is encouraged.
- Men are encouraged to be sexually promiscuous.

- Females are expected to remain sexually conservative.
- Women are to take care of the home, prepare meals, care for children, and provide discipline.
- Women are expected to care for injured or ill family members, including grandparents.
- Family support is provided during illness, financial problems, and stressful situations.
- The eldest male is the decision maker in the family and should be consulted when determining a course of action.

Daily Living and Food Practices

- Puerto Ricans are oriented toward present time, and being on time is considered to be of little consequence. For example, if a physician asks about a diabetic condition and the athlete is not exhibiting signs or symptoms at the moment, he or she may deny having the condition.
- Puerto Ricans eat three meals—breakfast, lunch, and dinner—and two snacks on a daily basis.
- Primary foods include beans, coffee, fish, fruits, malta, meats, rice, potatoes, plantains, and tea. Malta is a carbonated drink that is dark brown and sweet.
- Foods are believed to be either hot or cold, but not based on temperature or spiciness. The belief is that hot and cold environments cause illness or injury. Hot foods are used to treat cold illnesses, and vice versa. Hot conditions include fever, infection, and sore throat; they may be treated by means of foods such as eggs, peas, oils, and chili peppers (Schrefer, 1994). Cold illnesses and conditions include joint pain, colds, and headache; they are treated by foods such as fruits, vegetables, fish, honey, and raisins (Schrefer).
- Being overweight is acceptable and considered as proof of healthiness.
- Being overweight is also viewed as a sign of wealth, and some people may desire to be heavy.

Spiritual or Religious Orientation

- The majority of Puerto Ricans are Catholic. Others adhere to a variety of spiritual and religious orientations; they include Baptists, followers of Espiritism, Jehovah's Witnesses, Pentecostalists, Santerians, and Seventh Day Adventists.
- The practice of Espiritism is a blend of Catholicism and Taíno Indian and African beliefs (Lipson et al., 1996). Followers believe in evil and good spirits (Lipson et al.). Even though Espiritism is no longer widely used, it is respected by Puerto Ricans (Lipson et al.).
- Santeria is an African Voodoo religion that uses animal sacrifice and magic spells. Believers in Santeria wear protective symbols and use rituals to address particular illnesses. The priest may use items during a ritual to ensure the effectiveness of the ceremony; for example, a priest may use dirt from a child's grave to impart the value of kindness as part of the ritual (Bird, 2004).

Purnell & Paulanka (2005) have described how the following herbs are used to support health and good luck:

- Apostoteb, yerba bruja, and zarzaparilla (sarsaparilla)—used to get rid of evil
- Manzanilla, mejorana (marjoram), and verbena—used for good luck

An athlete's spiritual orientation should be respected by the athletic trainer; failure to do so could result in distrust.

Health Care Information

Puerto Ricans have the poorest health among the Latino cultures discussed in this chapter (Downes, 1997). This is based on having the highest death rates based on all causes of death (Downes, 1997). Thus an athletic trainer should take particular interest in Puerto Rican culture in order to help members of this culture improve their overall health. This section covers the following topics: biocultural assessment, common sensitivities and conditions, beliefs about illness, preventive health practices, symptom management, and treatments.

Biocultural Assessment

- Skin color ranges from light to dark. Dark skin may challenge the athletic trainer in determining cyanosis or jaundice.
- Hair is generally black and either straight or curly.
- Puerto Ricans tend to be shorter than most other groups in the United States.

Common Sensitivities and Conditions

- No drug sensitivities have been noted.
- Puerto Ricans are more prone to asthma, type 1 diabetes, cancer, hypertension, and HIV.
- Two conditions found among Puerto Ricans that may be unfamiliar to some athletic trainers are coccidioidomycosis and dengue. The appendix provides a more comprehensive list of signs and symptoms.

Beliefs About Illness

In traditional Puerto Rican culture, it is believed that illness results from hereditary, sin, evil, negative environmental forces, or lack of personal attention to one's own health (Lipson, et al.).

DISTINCTIVE TO THIS CULTURE

- Puerto Ricans tend toward belief in hot and cold foods and conditions.
- Many first-generation Puerto Ricans believe that illness is caused by evil spirits (Schrefer, 1994), and it is likely that they will use a curandero or espiritista to resolve supernatural forms of illness.
- Puerto Ricans believe that a person who is mentally ill is weak and that it is hereditary (Lipson, et al.).

Preventive Health Practices

- Sex education is important because it is typically avoided by Puerto Ricans.
- Puerto Ricans tend to use emergency room services for acute conditions (Purnell & Paulanka, 2005).
- To improve preventive practices, incorporate and familiarize the Puerto Rican community and families with the health care system that is available.
- Some problems affecting Puerto Ricans could be reduced with preventive care, including breast cancer, pelvic cancer, and use of illicit drugs (Purnell & Paulanka, 2003).
- Puerto Ricans consume alcohol at a greater rate than do Mexicans and Cubans (Purnell & Paulanka, 2003); it may be helpful to implement a preventive educational program.
- Puerto Rican women believe that being overweight is good (Purnell & Paulanka, 2005), and athletic trainers need to make sure to emphasize consumption of a low-fat diet that is high in fiber, fruits, and vegetables.
- Preventive education should be conducted during convenient times for members of the community.
- It may be very helpful to offer free preventive screenings.

Symptom Management

Puerto Ricans may endeavor to control symptoms by using teas mixed with a variety of other contents (Lipson et al., 1996), such as botanicals (e.g., seeds, plant leaves) and animal parts (e.g., skin).

- Warm tea with lemon or mint may be used to care for stomach upset.
- Natural foods such as prunes are used to resolve constipation.
- Pain is controlled by using heat and drinking tea.
- It is believed that asthma can be resolved by drinking a tea made from snails, alligator's nail, or Savila plant leaf (Lipson et al., 1996).
- Nausea may be controlled by smelling *alcoholado* (isopropyl alcohol-like substance) or applying it to the forehead (Lipson et al.).
- Difficulty breathing is handled by fanning or blowing into the face (Lipson et al.).

Treatments

Treatment may depend on the athlete's belief about the cause of the illness. Some may seek the assistance of a curandero, some may use herbal remedies, and others may seek the assistance of a physician. Puerto Rican culture is very oriented toward spirituality, and prayer and confession of sins are deemed important (Lipson et al., 1996).

Curandero

A curandero is a spiritual healer. These healers are more common in rural areas where physicians and athletic trainers are not plentiful. A curandero gets to be a healer by means of being anointed in a vision. The curandero may do an apprenticeship or may be born into the profession. Healers use rituals, herbs, prayer, religious symbols, and candles.

A botanica is a store where herbs and other "medicines" can be purchased. The medicines in this instance are not prescribed medicines. A curandero may recommend an herb or candle, for example, that can be purchased from the bontanica.

Folk Remedies

Some Puerto Ricans may use home remedies before seeking the assistance of a physician. Here are some folk remedies (Lipson et al., 1996):

- Mint, camphor, eucalyptus oil—aches and colds
- Fresh urine—eye problems or insect bites
- Baking soda—heartburn, diarrhea
- Warm milk and sugar—ulcers
- Laxatives—parasites
- Olive oil—earaches
- Maravilla lotion—cuts and bruises

Spector (2004) lists the following remedies:

- Pinching the spine or massaging the stomach—empacho
- Massage—paralysis of limbs or face
- Relaxation—susto

Food Remedies

Puerto Ricans may believe that food will help resolve an illness. One traditional food remedy is hot tea with rum and lemon. Alcohol is thought to pep up an ill or older person, and it may be added to coffee. Hot and cold foods are used to resolve hot and cold illnesses (Spector, 2004; Purnell & Paulanka, 2003, 2005).

Protection

A small black fist worn as a necklace is believed to protect the wearer from illness and misfortune. An athlete may also use holy water, candles, and rosary beads for protection. Those who follow Santeria are likely to seek the assistance of a santero (priest).

CUBAN

 Cubans have a unique culture of their own. It is important for the athletic trainer to understand the similarities and the differences of this culture to one's own, avoid the generalization that everyone adheres to the same beliefs that are part of this culture, and keep an open mind when working with athletes whose culture may be different than their own.

Demographic and Cultural Background Information

Cubans have their own unique culture. This portion of the chapter provides a brief history of country of origin and immigration, primary languages and communication, family structure, daily living and food practices, and spiritual or religious orientation.

Brief History of Country of Origin and Immigration

Cuba is an island south of Florida (see figure 9.3). From the arrival of Christopher Columbus until 1899, the island was controlled by the Spanish (Purnell & Paulanka, 2003), who used it as a stopover on the way to Mexico. Cubans have also been influenced by other cultures from the Soviet Union, the United States, and Africa (Purnell & Paulanka, 2003). The Monroe Doctrine, a United States policy, was aimed at deterring European influence and acted as a major influence on Cuba until 1902, at which point Cuba became an independent country (Purnell & Paulanka, 2003).

Cuba was a democratic country until 1959, when Fidel Castro overthrew the government and created a socialist state (Purnell & Paulanka, 2003), which prompted many Cubans to immigrate to the United States. Cubans in the United States live in areas where many previous Cuban immigrants took up residence—primarily in Miami and the Florida Keys. These close-knit communities help Cubans maintain their culture. In 1980, the Mariel boatlift brought 120,000 Cubans to the United States who were used to communist rule and thus were socially different from those

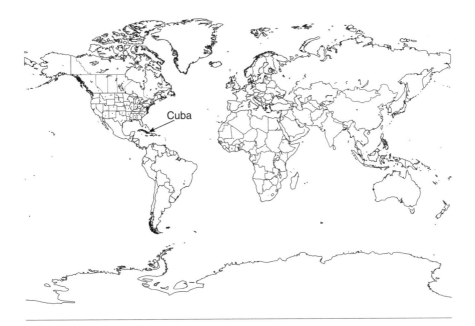

Figure 9.3 Map of Cuba.

who had immigrated previously (Lipson et al.). During the Mariel boatlift, Castro let prisoners out of jail and allowed them to go to the United States (Lipson et al.).

Today, the majority of Cubans in the United States live in Florida (Purnell & Paulanka, 2003); other states with large Cuban populations include New Jersey, New York, California, and Illinois (Lipson et al., 1996). Most Cubans attempt to come to the United States by escaping in boats that are overflowing with people. If they are able to touch ground in the United States, they can stay; if they are caught in the offshore waters, however, they are sent back to Cuba. Many die during the attempt.

Primary Languages and Communication Styles

The primary language is Spanish (Erickson D'Avanzo & Geissler, 2003). The secondary language is English (Lipson et al., 1996). Many Cubans combine Spanish and English into a new language form known as Spanglish.

Cubans gesture with their hands and may speak loudly; this should not be interpreted as anger (Lipson et al., 1996).

DOS AND DON'TS
- Do shake hands.
- Don't use the person's first name without permission.
- Do use the person's title and full last name when meeting him or her for the first time.
- Do greet the oldest person first.
- Do make eye contact (Lipson et al., 1996).

DISTINCTIVE TO THIS CULTURE
- Athletes will have their father's and mother's last names (the father's name is usually listed first and the mother's name is listed second).
- Silence means that a person does not understand or may be uncomfortable.
- Touching and kissing are common among family members.
- Women prefer to be cared for by female athletic trainers.

Family Structure

Three generations of family members may live in the same home or within the same community. Grandparents are expected to care for grandchildren, and adult children are expected to care for their parents until death.

DISTINCTIVE TO THIS CULTURE
- Females are expected to take care of the family and the household.
- Males are responsible for the safekeeping of all family members.
- The father is responsible for providing financial support.
- Female family members are the primary caregivers when someone is ill.
- Family friends are expected to visit when a person is ill.
- Women have consciousness of how the family looks in the eyes of the community. This concern is known as verguenza (Purnell & Paulanka, 2005).

- Men are expected to express their machismo and strength in the community.
- Same-sex male relations may be viewed as part of virility and power, rather than homosexuality (Purnell & Paulanka, 2005). Homosexuality is not accepted in Cuban culture (Purnell & Paulanka, 2005).

Daily Living and Food Practices

Cubans are oriented toward present time; whatever is happening right now is most important. If a person is from the upper class, he or she may show up late as a way to demonstrate personal importance. Athletes who are older may be oriented toward the past. The past means that one focuses on the past and the hope to return to Cuba (Lipson, et al.)

- Cubans eat three meals per day.
- Acculturated Cubans make dinner their biggest meal.
- Unacculturated Cubans typically make lunch their biggest meal.
- Typical foods include chicken, fish, beef, pork, casseroles, rice, yams, olive oil, garlic, plantains, mangoes, tomatoes, soups, stews, juices, coffee, and sweets.
- Cubans are not partial to vegetables, which they think should be eaten only by animals (Erickson D'Avanzo & Geissler, 2003). Thus, an athletic trainer who is responsible for an athlete's nutrition must consider the individual's culture, and a coach may require an explanation of why an athlete has a personalized dietary plan that is dissimilar from that of fellow team members.

Spiritual or Religious Orientation

- The primary religion for Cubans is Catholicism.
- Santeria is also practiced by those who are unacculturated or who do not believe in Western medicine (Lipson et al., 1996; Erickson D'Avanzo & Geissler, 2003).
- The most recent immigrants have no religious affiliation because of the suppression of religion under the leadership of the communist regime (Vela, 2008).

Health Care Information

A culturally competent athletic trainer understands the health variables that may change how care is given. This section provides information about biocultural assessment, common sensitivities and conditions, beliefs about illness, preventive health practices, symptom management, and treatments.

Biocultural Assessment

- About 80 percent of Cubans are White, and about 5 percent are Black (Purnell & Paulanka, 2003, 2005).
- Those with White features have various skin, eye, and hair colors (Purnell & Paulanka, 2005).
- Those with Black features have various skin tones. They also have the physical features of African Americans (Purnell & Paulanka, 2005).

Common Sensitivities and Conditions

- Cubans are more sensitive than Whites to antidepressants (Purnell & Paulanka, 2005).
- Some illnesses and conditions that are more common among Cubans may be familiar to athletic trainers: gingivitis, heart disease, lactose intolerance, periodontitis, and suicide (Purnell & Paulanka, 2003, 2005; Erickson D'Avanzo & Geissler, 2003; Downes, 1997).
- Other illnesses and conditions that Cubans face may be less familiar to many athletic trainers, such as coccidioidomycosis and mal de pelea (Purnell & Paulanka, 2003, 2005; Erickson D'Avanzo & Geissler, 2003; Downes, 1997). The appendix provides a more comprehensive list of signs and symptoms.

Beliefs About Illness

The Cuban population accepts the Western theory of germs (Lipson et al., 1996). There is also a strong belief that illness can result from being nervous or under stress (Lipson et al.).

Belief in the "evil eye" is prominent; specifically, it is believed that the evil eye can cause illness in another person. Those who adhere to Santeria may also believe that illness is caused by Voodoo evil.

DISTINCTIVE TO THIS CULTURE

- Mental illness is viewed in two ways: either caused by hereditary or stress (Lipson, et al.).
- Mental illness is stigmatized, so it is hidden (Lipson et al.).
- Mental illness may be expressed as a physical ailment. Thus an athletic trainer who cannot find a reason for an athlete's physical ailment should consider evaluating him or her for a mental health issue.
- Birth defects are thought to result from one of three causes: genetics, stress, or seeing a child with a defect during the pregnancy (Lipson et al.).

Preventive Health Practices

The Cuban health care system allows for medical care of all of its people. Given that the U.S. health care system is quite different, some Cubans may be challenged to obtain needed services without insurance. The health care system in Cuba also focuses on prevention, and many illnesses (e.g., tuberculosis) are prevented through vaccination programs and direct access to health care.

- Cubans need to be encouraged to eat healthily and avoid high-fat foods. Cubans believe that being overweight is healthy; being skinny, in contrast, is thought to indicate that one is unhealthy, typically as the result of a disease. The athletic trainer should encourage exercise and preventive check-ups for all family members.

- Women tend to avoid mammograms and pelvic examinations out of embarrassment and because of present-time orientation.
- Those needing to avoid lactose should avoid products that contact whey, as well as generic medications (which typically use lactose as a filler).

Symptom Management

- Cubans will not hide their need for pain medication, oxygen, or medical treatment.
- All family members may discuss vomiting, diarrhea, or constipation in an ill person; the discussion may center on the person's eating habits to determine the cause of the illness (Lipson et al., 1996).
- Nausea is thought to mean that an illness is getting worse (Lipson et al.).
- Depression is viewed as a mental illness and thus may be hidden to avoid shame (Lipson et al.).
- An athlete suffering fatigue may share this fact with the athletic trainer, who can refer the athlete to a physician for appropriate medication (Lipson et al.).

Treatments

Cubans are in tune with Western medicine and will follow their physician's directions. At the same time, some may use a priest before seeking Western medical care, and it is important for the athletic trainer to check all remedies that may have been employed.

Folk Remedies

Folk remedies, which originated in this area from African slaves, are used when one believes that an illness has been caused by evil or Voodoo. Treatment may include the following practices (Spector, 1996; Purnell & Paulanka, 2005):

- Pig skin—to cover cuts
- Drinking olive oil and salt—for sore throat
- Tea with lemon—for sore throat
- Carrots—for eye problems
- Cinnamon—for cough, congestion, menstrual cramps
- Sour orange—for cough, congestion
- Spearmint leaves—for stomach upset, anxiety
- Turpentine—for sore muscles
- Egg white on head—for hair growth
- Butter—for burns

Protection

A small black fist worn as a necklace is believed to protect the wearer from illness and misfortune. It is also believed that a black stone, azabache, will protect the wearer from the evil eye (Purnell & Paulanka, 2005) and that the eye of St. Lucy worn on a necklace or bracelet will protect the wearer from the evil eye and from blindness (Purnell & Paulanka, 2005)

Religion

Santeria is used for supernatural illnesses. If the family believes in Santeria, a priest can work to heal a person who is ill. The priest may read rocks, nuts, or shells to determine the nature of the illness and the course of treatment. Santeria priests treat illnesses caused by spiritual or emotional illnesses (Purnell & Paulanka, 2005). Treatment may include food restrictions or wearing the same color of clothes for a time (Erickson D'Avanzo & Geissler, 2003).

Athletic trainers need to determine whether any of the rituals or folk remedies used by an athlete will interfere with traditional medication. Trainers should ask the athlete what he or she is using, then work with him or her to combine care plans. For example, if an athlete is taking blood thinners, it would be important to know if he or she is using any green vegetables or herbs that also thin the blood. If so, the athletic trainer could adjust the medication or request a reduction in the use of vegetables and herbs. If the athletic trainer cannot convince the athlete to support a combined health care plan, then working with the family may help to gain the athlete's respect for the plan.

SUMMARY

Latino culture has been prominent in the United States for many years. It has been greatly influenced by the Spanish—especially, of course, in terms of language.

Women in these cultures are responsible for caring for the household, and males are the primary financial providers. Families tend to be large, and multiple generations may live in the same home or close to each other. There is a strong belief in machismo—the notion that men must show their virility. Women, on the other hand, are expected to remain modest.

Latino culture values respectful behavior and eye contact, and athletic trainers should know that nodding does not necessarily mean that a Latino agrees with what is being said. The athletic trainer may find that the family is involved in listening to medical information about the athlete. Decisions are made by the father and he is responsible for making the announcement of that choice.

The priority for Latinos is to deal with what is happening in the present rather than be concerned with the future. This present-time orientation may challenge the athletic trainer in that Latinos are not likely to come to appointments on time or to think about preventive behaviors. The athletic trainer may have to emphasize the need for proper health care prevention and the need to take prescribed medications and complete treatments as requested.

There is a strong belief in God, especially through the Catholic religion. Some people also believe in espiritism and Santeria while practicing Catholicism. Another belief involves the evil eye, which is thought usually to enter the body through supernatural means; thus a supernatural healer must be used to resolve it.

Latino skin color can make it hard to determine cyanosis. Mexicans and Cubans are more sensitive to antidepressants than are members of most cultures, and antihypertensive drugs may not work as well in Mexican people.

Mexicans are especially prone to hypertension, diabetes, lactose intolerance, dysentery, parasites, HIV/AIDS, malaria, and dengue. Puerto Ricans are more likely to have asthma, diabetes, cancer, coccidioidomycosis, dengue, hypertension, and HIV. The Puerto Rican family is responsible for caring for the athlete and for handling chores and food preparation. Cubans are more prone to coccidioidomycosis, gingivitis, heart disease, lactose intolerance, mal de pelea, periodontitis, and suicide. Cuban vaccination programs have been successful in preventing some illnesses.

Latinos believe that foods and illnesses can be hot or cold and that foods can be used to help resolve illness if one consumes foods that are opposite (hot or cold) of the illness. Latinos believe that it is important for the body stay in balance in order to be well. The athletic trainer may have to ask if a treatment will be hot or cold so as not to complicate things for the athlete.

Latinos are likely to share their symptoms and expect them to be cared for by the athletic trainer. Puerto Ricans may self diagnose and describe asthma as difficulty breathing and not really have that condition.

Preventive health care practices for Latinos work best when family members are involved. It is important to open clinics at times that are convenient for the population being served—not for the convenience of the athletic trainer.

Treatment of Latino illnesses or conditions will be based on the athlete's beliefs. The athlete may choose traditional Latino treatments such as protection, religion, use of a curandero or curandera, or herbal remedy. The athletic trainer needs to ask about home remedies and herbals and make sure there is no impact on the treatment.

Respecting the Latino culture and understanding some of its specific behaviors may enable the athletic trainer to serve Latinos much more competently. If an athletic trainer accepts and works within the cultural beliefs of the Latino population—and understands how to use Western medicine in conjunction with it—he or she will be better able to build a trusting and successful relationship with a Latino athlete.

Learning Aids

What Would You Do If . . . ?

1. What if a person who is wearing an amulet refuses to remove it before surgery?
2. What if a female athlete seems to be hiding something that may play a role in her illness?
3. What if the athlete smokes and insists on using turpentine for his muscular soreness?
4. What if a family continues to eat a diet high in fat and cholesterol? The family has a history of heart disease and early death, but they believe that being heavy is healthy. The woman who handles food preparation for the family knows how to cook only those foods that she grew up with.
5. What if a Cuban wants a spiritual healer but cannot find one and asks that you, the athletic trainer, use herbals to resolve the illness?

Activities

1. List all the home and folk remedies discussed in this chapter and investigate whether or not there is merit in the use of each.
2. Do a superficial examination of an athlete with dark skin to ensure your ability to determine jaundice or cyanosis.
3. Design a plan to teach preventive health care for illnesses common among members of each Latino group discussed in this chapter.
4. How can the athletic trainer convey information to an athlete who has weak English comprehension skills? How might this be done without the use of an interpreter?

Key Terms

Define the following key terms found in this chapter:

Caida de la mollera	Envidia	Mal de ojo
Curandera	Espanto	Siesta
Curandero	Espiritism	Susto
Empacho	Mal aire	

Questions for Review

1. Define the characteristics that a Latino athlete would most likely prefer in an athletic trainer.
2. How do historical health care practices among Latinos affect care and beliefs in the present day?
3. Explain the differences between the three Latino cultures discussed in this chapter in the areas of treatment, religion, decision making, and common illnesses.
4. Can religion help or harm the care of a Latino athlete? If so, how?
5. What cultural influences on Latino culture may affect the care of Latinos? How?
6. How can an athletic trainer be supportive of a Latino athlete's culture while still giving proper care?
7. How do home remedies affect health care among Latinos?

White European

Learning Objectives

Upon completing this chapter, students will be able to do the following:

1. Describe the commonly held cultural beliefs of those who are White European
2. Describe the various spiritual beliefs that are widely shared among White Europeans
3. Describe the biocultural sensitivities of White Europeans
4. Explain the various cultural influences that may change how an athlete feels about health care
5. Be able to support an athlete who has cultural needs
6. Explain how health care practices have evolved for White Europeans

Jodi Brookins-Fisher, PhD, CHES

Much of my life experience comes from the midwest, as I attended undergraduate and graduate school there. I attended a western university for my doctoral program, where I was exposed to different cultures. However, my home life has most shaped my early days of thinking (or lack thereof) about diversity. I come from the outskirts of an urban area that is divided by a river—it divides city and suburbia and blacks from whites (it is historically one of the top 10 most segregated cities in the U.S.). This really affected the environment in which I was raised.

Attending college was an awakening experience for me. I realized that my family's way of thinking was not that of others and that *everyone* had something to offer our community and society. This realization, along with working as a public health educator in HIV/AIDS, shaped my approach to teaching and life. I chose public health because I think it is important to help individuals and communities acquire the skills to prevent disease and other health crises. Now, in the university setting, I hope that I instill these beliefs in my students. In my doctoral program, I worked with gay youth and realized that I had the power to advocate on others' behalf. Thus began my life mission to improve the lives of others by first improving myself. I hope my experiences, coupled with self-reflecting activities in the classroom, help my students to become better health professionals. I feel that being a person who is open to others is more important than the information that I teach, as only when we understand each other will real change happen. I encourage others in health care professions to experience different cultures while being open to their views. Listening will go far in one's cultural competence.

I am a professor in the School of Health Sciences at Central Michigan University. My research interests include the evaluation of university-community partnerships, programs for underserved populations, and sexuality education curricula. I have been involved in several national and state organizations and have held several leadership positions. I have received the President's Award for GLC-SOPHE (Great Lakes Chapter of the Society for Public Health Education) and the Distinguished Service Award for both GLC-SOPHE and national Eta Sigma Gamma. I also received Central Michigan University's Excellence in Teaching Award, Registered Student Organization Advisor Award, and Outstanding Teacher Award in my department. As a human rights advocate, I have been recognized for contributions to underserved populations, especially GLBTQ (gay, lesbian, bisexual, transgendered, and queer) populations. In my spare time, I like to spend time with my family and friends. I also enjoy running and outdoors activities.

Many people may believe that the term **Caucasian** is synonymous with White European, but it is not. Caucasian includes people who are of White European, North African, and Southwest Asian ancestry (Merriam-Webster Online). The three countries who have produced the greatest immigration of White Europeans into the United States are Germany, Ireland, and England (U.S. Census Bureau, 2000). Other countries considered to be Caucasian nations include Poland, Italy, Greece, France, Norway, Portugal, Scotland, Sweden, Anatolia, Caucasus, Mesopotamia, Kurdistan, Iran, Algeria, Egypt, Libya, Morocco, Sudan, and Tunisia. This chapter features Germany, Ireland, and England because they are the sources of the largest White European populations currently living in the United States.

The largest immigration into the United States by White Europeans occurred in the early 1800s (Leininger & McFarland, 2002). The majority came to the United States for opportunities, and the influx of immigrants went through Ellis Island Immigration Station in New York.

For each culture discussed, the chapter includes dos and don'ts, as well as lists of distinctive cultural characteristics. However, it should be remembered that not all members of a culture are characterized by each of the listed items. For example, first-generation immigrants may adhere to beliefs and traditions that may not be carried on by members of the next generation. The longer a person and his or her family have been in the United States, the more likely they are to have adapted to Western culture.

GERMAN

Germans have a unique culture of their own. It is important for the athletic trainer to understand the similarities and the differences of this culture to one's own, avoid the generalization that everyone adheres to the same beliefs that are part of this culture, and keep an open mind when working with athletes whose culture may be different than their own.

Demographic and Cultural Background Information

To create a better awareness of the German people, this section provides a brief history of country of origin and immigration, primary languages and communication, family structure, daily living and food practices, and spiritual or religious orientation.

Brief History of Country of Origin and Immigration

Historically, the boundaries of Germany changed as control over various surrounding countries changed hands (see figure 10.1). Germans immigrated to what is now the United States for many reasons, but opportunity to own land was a primary influence. When fascism befell the country, many left to avoid the conflict (Purnell & Paulanka, 2005). Many others were drawn to the opportunity to practice religion without persecution (Downes, 1997).

Settling in the United States, Germans formed their own communities, in which they preserved the traditions of German culture. These areas were sometimes referred to as Germantown. Nearly 40 percent of Germans in the United States live in the Northeast (Spector, 2004), but the communities with the greatest number of

Figure 10.1 Map of Germany.

German immigrants can be found in Texas in the cities of Victoria, Cuero, Gonzales, New Braunfels, and Fredericksburg (Spector, 2004).

Primary Languages and Communication Styles

The primary language in Germany is German, and the secondary language is English. Within Germany, a number of dialects are spoken, and even Germans may be challenged in trying to understand them all. Many families continue to speak German regardless of the amount of time they have been in the United States.

DOS AND DON'TS

- Do keep a physical distance of about 3 feet (0.9 meter) (Purnell & Paulanka, 2005).
- Do shake hands.
- Do look a person in the eyes.
- Do use Mr., Mrs., or Miss and the person's last name. Ms. is not a commonly used title (Loveland, 2005). It is also acceptable to call a person by his or her title and professional title (Purnell & Paulanka, 2003 CD). An example of title and professional title is Mr. Supervisor.
- Don't beckon someone by pointing a finger and waving or by calling out his or her name.
- Do beckon someone by nodding the head backwards.
- Don't chew gum in public or talk with your hands in your pockets (Purnell & Paulanka, 2003 CD).
- Don't point your finger to your head as it is an insult (Purnell & Paulanka, 2003 CD).
- Do use the German sign for good luck, which is the thumb between the index and middle fingers (Purnell & Paulanka, 2003 CD).

DISTINCTIVE TO THIS CULTURE

- Eye contact can be expected during conversation (Purnell & Paulanka, 2005).
- Emotions are often kept in control and are not observed or discussed (Purnell & Paulanka, 2005). Thus an athletic trainer may find it challenging to determine whether information given has been understood or accepted. You must ask.
- Privacy is an expectation in German culture; use caution when walking in on an athlete (Purnell & Paulanka, 2005).
- Approval may be given by knocking knuckles on the table.
- When a person touches his or her nose, the motion indicates that what was said is to be kept secret (Foster, 2000).

Family Structure

German families are patriarchal, but acculturated families share leadership equally. Grandparents may live close to the family and may support children and grandchildren. Children are expected to help their elderly parents maintain their independent living (Purnell & Paulanka, 2005).

DISTINCTIVE TO THIS CULTURE

- Decision making is done through consultation between the parents.
- Grandparents will be consulted in the decision-making process, but the advice may not be used (Purnell & Paulanka, 2005).
- Men and women are expected to have jobs.
- Women are responsible for meals and household chores. Men do heavier work.
- It is the mother's duty to ensure that medications are taken as prescribed (Purnell & Paulanka, 2003).
- An athlete who is challenged by having to make a health care decision may be helped by the extended family.
- German families value education, respect, proper behavior, reputation, and politeness (Purnell & Paulanka, 2005).
- The family takes over the responsibilities for a person who is injured or ill (Purnell & Paulanka, 2003 CD).

Daily Living and Food Practices

- Germans are oriented toward the present and future, and preventive health care is important. For example, a German with future orientation might engage in a daily regimen of exercise and set up a home gym to ensure the ability to exercise even in bad weather.
- Being on time is important to the German people; it is considered insulting to be late. Appointments will be kept, and medical recommendations will be followed. It would not be unusual for an athlete to be upset if an appointment does not start on time—the delay may be viewed as disrespect for his or her time.
- Germans eat three meals per day—breakfast, lunch, and dinner.
- Lunch is the largest meal of the day.
- Typical foods include meats, potatoes, butter, vegetables, eggs, fish, cheese, pasta, bread, pickled vegetables, cream, yogurt, and cereal.
- Drinks include water, beer, and mixed drinks.
- German food is high in fat.
- Celebrations generally include food and beer.

Spiritual or Religious Orientation

The primary religion in Germany is Protestantism (38 percent); the second most prevalent religion is Catholicism (34 percent) (Erickson D'Avanzo & Geissler, 2003).

- For Catholics, common spiritual practices include prayer, personal devotions, and giving. It is traditional to confess sins to a priest and ask for forgiveness.
- Confession is thought to be helpful in times of illness, since it gives the ailing person relief from the burden of sin.
- Typical religious objects include rosaries, medals with saints, and crosses. These objects should be removed only with permission.

- A priest may be present at times of illness, and the athletic trainer needs to allow privacy during such a visit.
- It is also common for others to pray for those who are ill.
- The ill maybe anointed with oil to support the healing process.
- The Protestant religion teaches that daily practices must include keeping the mind and body healthy (University of Virginia Health System, 2006).
- For Protestants, it is traditional to wear crosses, pray, read from the Bible, and fast. Privacy should be given during times of prayer.

Health Care Information

This section provides specific information about their health in the following categories: biocultural assessment, common sensitivities and conditions, beliefs about illness, preventive health practices, symptom management, and treatments.

Biocultural Assessment

- Germans are fair-skinned people (Purnell & Paulanka, 2005).
- Eye color can be blue or brown (Purnell & Paulanka, 2005).
- Hair color can be blood or dark (Purnell & Paulanka, 2005).
- White males have a thicker-than-average parietal occiput (Schrefer, 1994). A thicker-than-average parietal occiput may mean that white males are less inclined to fracture than other ethnic groups.
- A longer second tarsal is found in 8 to 24 percent of Whites (Schrefer), and an affected athlete is more prone to ankle sprains.
- The palmaris longus muscle is absent in 12 to 20 percent of Whites (Schrefer), and an affected athlete is unable to forcefully flex his or her wrist.

Common Sensitivities and Conditions

- Fair-skinned people are more vulnerable to skin cancer resulting from overexposure to the sun (Purnell & Paulanka, 2005).
- Germans may require lower dosages of blood pressure medications (Purnell & Paulanka, 2003 CD).
- Some illnesses and conditions common to Germans may be familiar to many athletic trainers: breast cancer, heart disease, skin cancer, and stroke. (Purnell & Paulanka, 2005; Erickson D'Avanzo & Geissler, 2003).
- Other illnesses and conditions faced by German people may be less familiar to many athletic trainers: cystic fibrosis, Dupuytren's disease, hereditary hemochromatosis, Lyme disease, myotonic muscular dystrophy, and sarcoidosis, (Purnell & Paulanka, 2005; Erickson D'Avanzo & Geissler, 2003). The appendix provides a more comprehensive list of signs and symptoms.

Beliefs About Illness

Most Germans believe in Western medicine and the theory that germs cause illness. They will seek the assistance of athletic trainers for illness. They recognize that eating properly and exercising regularly support good health; drinking cod liver oil and cleanliness are also viewed as important to health (Spector, 2004).

DISTINCTIVE TO THIS CULTURE

- Some Germans believe in the "evil eye" as a means by which one person can make another ill subject to evil.
- Others believe that drafts can cause illness (Spector, 2004).
- Mental illness is viewed as an imperfection; thus, counseling is not readily sought out (Purnell & Paulanka, 2005).
- Some Germans believe that they can prevent illness by wearing warm clothes, wearing an asafetida bag, and sleeping with the windows open (Spector, 2004).
- It is also believed that one can keep illness away by practicing one's religion and wearing religious scapulars under one's clothing. A scapular is a cloth that is tied together by a string. The string goes over the back of the neck with cloth hanging over a shoulder.

Preventive Health Practices

- Since Germans are future oriented, they are inclined to accept information about and adhere to preventive practices.
- A diet that is high in fat will cause heart disease, stroke, and breast cancers—all of which are conditions often found within this culture. An athletic trainer should encourage exercise, balanced diet, and avoidance of high-fat foods.
- Many Germans like beer, and alcohol consumption may be of concern. An athletic trainer should discourage driving after drinking, as well as drinking to excess. Athletes may need a reminder of team rules regarding drinking.
- Garlic and onions are eaten to prevent heart disease (Purnell & Paulanka, 2005).
- Being a fair-skinned population, it is important for Germans to stay covered while in the sun. They should use sunscreen at a level of SPF 15 or higher to reduce the risk of sunburn and skin cancer.

Symptom Management

- Germans are a stoic population, and they may show little response to pain.
- It may be believed that pain is part of illness and that one must let pain have its place (Purnell & Paulanka, 2005).
- Nausea is dealt with by ingesting ginger ale (Purnell & Paulanka, 2005).

Treatments

Treatments can be broken down into three categories: Western medicine, home remedies, and, infrequently, powwows. Those who have been acculturated hold physicians in high regard for their educational background and seek the assistance of a physician as the first line of defense when it comes to care.

Home Remedies

Germans commonly use several home remedies for illnesses (Purnell & Paulanka, 2005):

- Upset stomach—ginger ale, then toast and hot tea; if this is retained, then a form of scrambled eggs is given
- Swollen glands—cleavers herb

Spector (2004) shares several other home remedies:

- Constipation—castor oil
- Sore throat—gargling with warm salt water
- Earache—warm oil in ear
- Cough—honey and milk
- Aches and pains—Olbas Oil
- Toothache—clove oil applied to the tooth
- Headache—ice wrapped in cloth on head

Powwowing

Powwowing is a folk healing art also known as hex. It is used to heal adults and children and to protect people and animals. The term *powwowing* was borrowed from Native Americans to describe a healing practice used by Germans. The German practice of powwowing is disappearing, and it is difficult to find proper resources. Most of those who use powwowing are likely in the advanced years of their lives.

Powwowing involves a combination of charms, sayings, and faith in the supernatural. Powwows are performed by a powwow doctor or **braucher.** David Kriebel (2007) finds some examples of powwowing:

The first principle involves "transferring" the disease or condition to another object. For example, it is believed that a potato rubbed on a wart during a certain phase of the moon will cause the wart to be transferred to the potato. A powwow doctor can also lay hands on the ill person and transfer physical healing powers to the person.

The second principal involves **passing through** and is used in the treatment of children. In this practice, a child rotates around the leg of a table. The passing through is done three times or in multiples of three in order to resolve the illness.

A powwowing doctor might also give the ill person a small bag with a German phrase written backwards and thus readable only in a mirror. The bag will also contain a charm, the nature of which is based on the disease, and will be adorned with the abbreviation INRI which means Jesus of Nazareth. The bag is worn around the ill person's neck.

IRISH

The Irish have a unique culture of their own. It is important for the athletic trainer to understand the similarities and the differences of this culture to one's own, avoid the generalization that everyone adheres to the same beliefs that are part of this culture, and keep an open mind when working with athletes whose culture may be different than their own.

Demographic and Cultural Background Information

In order to help the athletic trainer understand Irish culture, this section provides a brief history of country of origin and immigration, primary languages and communication, family structure, daily living and food practices, and spiritual or religious orientation.

Brief History of Country of Origin and Immigration

The Celtic people came to Ireland (see figure 10.2) thousands of years ago; they were known as barbarians and engaged in battles against the Roman Empire. One subculture of the Celts was made up of the Gales, who included people from France, Scotland, England, and Germany.

The Irish came to what is now the United States because of the potato famine (potatoes formed a primary source of food and income) and because of discrimination by English Protestants (Purnell & Paulanka, 2005), who, through the Protestant governing body in Ireland, forced Irish Catholics to abandon their Gaelic language and speak English. Immigrating to the United States, the Irish settled in neighborhoods in Illinois, Maryland, Michigan, New York, Pennsylvania, South

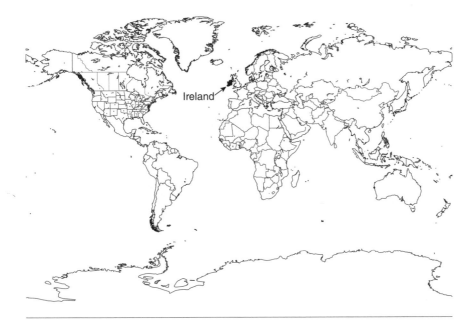

Figure 10.2 Map of Ireland.

Carolina, and Virginia (Purnell & Paulanka, 2003, 2005). Irish immigrants would send money back to their families in Ireland to support them; once enough money was available, the rest of the family could come to the States. The Irish worked long hours on farms and the railroads to support their families.

Irish neighborhoods gave these immigrants a way to maintain their culture in the United States, where they were subjected to prejudice from other White Europeans because of their accents (Purnell & Paulanka, 2003, 2005). They were able to find sanctity within their neighborhoods and in the Catholic Church. The Irish value their families, religion, and education. Because the Irish look like Europeans, it has in the end been relatively easy for them to blend into American culture (Foster, 2000; Purnell & Paulanka, 2005).

Primary Languages and Communication Styles

The national language of Ireland is Gaelic (also known as Irish). English, spoken with an Irish accent, is also a primary language; the accent places emphasis on the first part of each word.

DOS AND DON'TS

- Do greet an athlete by using Mr., Mrs., Miss, or Ms. and his or her last name.
- Do take the initiative to introduce yourself.

DISTINCTIVE TO THIS CULTURE

- The "Mac" that precedes many Irish last names means "son of"; "O" means "descended from" (Purnell & Paulanka, 2005).
- Personal space should be greater than 4 feet (1.2 meters); the athletic trainer may need to request to move into the personal space of an Irish athlete, so be sure to explain the need for doing so.
- Lack of eye contact may imply that a person is untrustworthy (Purnell & Paulanka, 2005); thus, when discussing a health condition, be sure to make eye contact.
- Facial expression is a common way of showing emotion, even in difficult situations (Purnell & Paulanka, 2005).
- Hand and body gestures are limited among the Irish.

Family Structure

Irish families are patriarchal but moving toward a paradigm wherein women stand on an even footing with men; nearly one-quarter of all Irish women function as the head of the household (Erickson D'Avanzo & Geissler, 2003).

An Irish father is responsible for the financial support of the family. Sons often follow their father's line of work and help support the family. Mothers are expected to manage the household and oversee the education of the children. The father is responsible for in-home chores, such as washing the dishes (Purnell & Paulanka, 2005). The extended family often lives nearby—perhaps in another city but maintaining contact (Purnell & Paulanka, 2005).

DISTINCTIVE TO THIS CULTURE

- Irish families tend to be large.
- Adult children are expected to care for elderly parents.
- Children live at home until married.
- Children are expected to marry within the same religion.
- Irish people tend to hold a strong religious view against premarital sex.
- Grandparents are expected to help with grandchildren.
- If a decision has to be made, the eldest family members will be consulted (Purnell & Paulanka, 2005). Athletic trainers may need to speak with all the potential decision makers (Purnell & Paulanka, 2005).

Daily Living and Food Practices

The Irish are oriented toward the past, present, and future. The past constitutes a major focus because it is viewed as the basis for what is currently happening; this focus is evidenced through the storytelling that is commonplace among the Irish. Irish people are also concerned with the present, and living in the moment is considered the most important thing; as a result, athletic trainers must emphasize the importance of showing up on time for appointments. Finally, the Irish are also concerned with the future (Purnell & Paulanka, 2005), as evidenced by the value they place on education and saving money. An Irish person will arrive on time for work, but may be 20 to 30 minutes late for a social event (Erickson D'Avanzo & Geissler, 2003).

The Irish prefer to identify themselves as a group rather than as individuals. This orientation results in strong family relationships and connections within the Irish community (Purnell & Paulanka, 2005).

- Irish people eat three meals a day; lunch is the largest meal of the day, though when one is entertaining guests dinner may be the main meal and stretch into the later hours of the evening.
- It is common to eat snacks between meals.
- The typical Irish diet consists of eggs, fish, meat, cake, vegetables, butter, bread, broth, tomatoes, seafood, and pudding.
- Typical drinks include tea, milk, coffee, beer, soda, and water.
- Fast food is not considered part of an Irish balanced diet (Spector, 2004). Eating high-quality food is considered to be more important than saving time.

Spiritual or Religious Orientation

- The vast majority (93 percent) of Irish people are Catholic (Erickson D'Avanzo & Geissler, 2003); Protestants form the second most prominent religious group.
- Catholicism places importance on prayer and forgiveness of sin; when an athlete is praying, do not interrupt.
- A priest will provide the Holy Sacrament (a wafer and a sip of wine), which will be used to seek forgiveness of sins (Purnell & Paulanka, 2005).

- During times of illness, an athlete is allowed to avoid the practice of not eating red meat on Fridays during Lent (Purnell & Paulanka, 2005).

Health Care Information

This section addresses Irish culture in the areas of biocultural assessment, common sensitivities and conditions, beliefs about illness, preventive health practices, symptom management, and treatments.

Biocultural Assessment

- The Irish are taller than the average European American (Purnell & Paulanka, 2003, 2005).
- Irish people are typically fair-skinned and dark- or red-haired.
- No adverse drug reactions or hypersensitivities to drugs are reported for this population (Purnell & Paulanka, 2003, 2005).
- White males have a thicker-than-average parietal occiput (Schrefer, 1994).
- A longer second tarsal is found in 8 to 24 percent of Whites (Schrefer), and an affected athlete is more prone to ankle sprains.
- The palmaris longus muscle is absent in 12 to 20 percent of Whites (Schrefer), and an affected athlete is unable to forcefully flex his or her wrist.

Common Sensitivities and Conditions

- The Irish are prone to sarcoidosis, which may not be familiar to athletic trainers. The appendix provides a more comprehensive list of signs and symptoms.
- Athletic trainers should be familiar with the conditions that most often affect Irish people; these include alcoholism, heart disease, lung cancer, skin cancer, and osteoporosis.
- Irish children are prone to phenylketonuria and neural tube defects (Schrefer, 1994).

Beliefs About Illness

- The Irish also believe in keeping one's feet warm and dry, dressing warmly, and getting adequate sleep to stay healthy (Purnell & Paulanka, 2003).
- The Irish believe in eating a balanced diet, sleeping with the window slightly open for fresh air, and exercising, and these practices can certainly support good health (Spector, 1996). The athletic trainer may encounter difficulty when trying to change a behavior that is contrary to the Irish belief of a healthy diet. An athlete needs to be ready to change an existing habit.

DISTINCTIVE TO THIS CULTURE

- Irish confidence in having a healthy constitution may deter them from seeking medical attention until late in a disease process (Purnell & Paulanka, 2005).
- There is a belief among the Irish that sometimes one must suffer; it is God's way or a dictate, and illness or injury is thought to result from doing something morally wrong (Purnell & Paulanka, 2003, 2005).

Preventive Health Practices

- Since heart disease is a primary cause of death among the Irish, it is helpful to recommend a diet low in fat and cholesterol.
- Sunscreen can be helpful in reducing the incidence of skin cancers; other protective measures include wearing long-sleeved shirts, long pants, and a wide-brimmed hat.
- Changing the Irish belief that there is a need to drink can reduce the likeliness of dependence on alcohol.
- Many Irish people are heavy smokers. If an athlete smokes, recommend a smoking-cessation program.

Symptom Management

- The Irish value good health and usually speak up when they are ill or injured.
- Pain and other symptoms will be readily reported.

Treatments

Non-Western treatments practiced by Irish people fall into three categories: folk remedies, protection, and spirituality. Some may be considered more as preventive measures than as treatments or cures.

Folk Remedies

Folk remedies are practices passed down from generation to generation to resolve an illness. The Irish use whiskey and honey to suppress a cough, honey and lemon for a sore throat, hot tea for nausea, tea and whiskey for a cold, and a damp cloth for a headache (Purnell & Paulanka, 2003).

Preventive folk remedies include the following: boiling nettles and drinking the result, avoiding going to bed with wet hair, wearing a camphor-laden cloth around one's neck, and eating porridge before going to bed (Spector, 1996).

Spector (1996, 2004) lists the following practices for improving health:

- Cold—eating a whole onion and drinking a shot of whiskey
- Fever reduction—tying onions on the wrist and a dirty sock on the neck, or taking cover under blankets in order to sweat
- Skin wounds—wrapping warm bread, sugar, and soap in linen onto the wound to prevent infection
- Flu—applying poultices and molasses
- Health restoration—drinking plenty of tea and ale
- Toothache—applying whiskey to the tooth
- Stomachache—adding camilla and maloa (herbs) to boiling water
- Muscle pain—applying carbon leaves in a hot cloth

Kennett (1976) shares these remedies:

- Gas—½ pint of milk and 4 teaspoons of soot
- Cold—hot milk and rum; pat of butter rolled in sugar

- Sore throat—cabbage leaf tied around the neck
- Hoarseness—cabbage juice and honey
- Shingles—zinc ointment, 10 Our Fathers, and 10 Hail Marys
- Boil—poultice of comfrey root
- Warts—applying the milky sap of dandelion
- Rheumatism—touching a dead man's limbs

Protection

The Irish may wear religious medals to help them in times of illness. There are patron saints for nurses, hospitals, sick people, and hospitals—for example, St. Bernadette for sick people and St. Dymphna for epileptics and those with mental disorders.

Spector (2004) identifies the following practices thought by the Irish to protect a person from illness: being goal oriented, having strong faith and close family ties, eating lots of oily food, placing onions under the bed, not looking in the mirror at night and closing closet doors to prevent evil spirits, and wearing a bag of camphor during flu season.

Spirituality

The Irish people's strong belief in God leads them to leave matters of illness in God's hands. Prayer allows those who believe to let go of their fears. If a person is ill, a priest may come and give communion and pray with the person. Some Irish people believe in the power of God more than in medicine to cure their illness. This belief may lead them to let an illness or injury be until it advances to a stage that makes it more challenging for the athletic trainer to resolve. The result, of course, is a longer recovery time for the athlete.

ENGLISH

The English are the source of the dominant culture in the United States. As a result, readers may notice that the information provided here is not as broad as in the discussion of other cultures addressed in this book. The English have a unique culture of their own. It is important for the athletic trainer to understand the similarities and the differences of this culture to one's own, avoid the generalization that everyone adheres to the same beliefs that are part of this culture, and keep an open mind when working with athletes whose culture may be different than their own.

Demographic and Cultural Background Information

This section provides a brief history of country of origin and immigration, primary languages and communication, family structure, daily living and food practices, and spiritual or religious orientation.

Brief History of Country of Origin and Immigration

The English immigrated to what is now the United States and established colonies. The greatest immigration from England took place between 1600 and 1775; it occurred for many reasons, including adventure, flight from religious persecution,

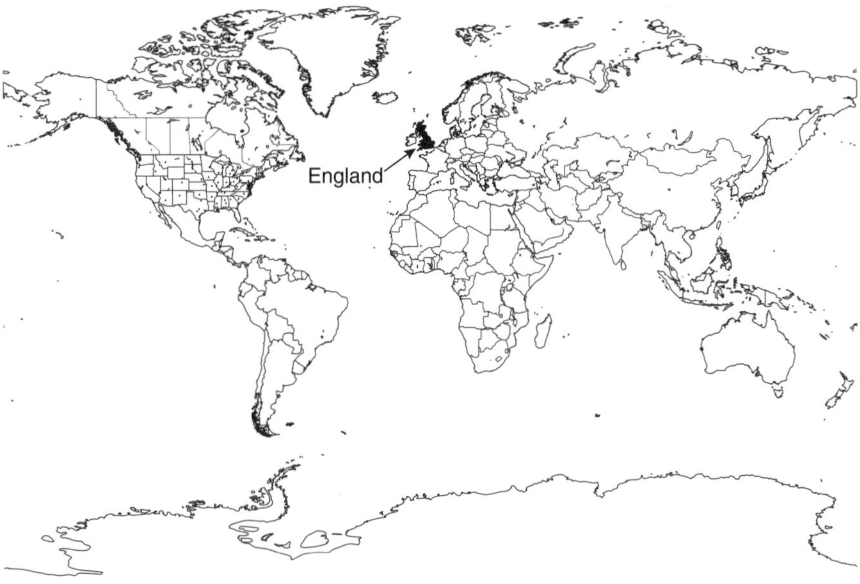

England

Figure 10.3 Map of England.

seeking of economic opportunity, and, in the case of convicts, forced departure from England (Bryant, 1999) (see figure 10.3).

The early settlements were established along the east coast, specifically in Virginia and Massachusetts (Chao & Spencer, 2008). Over time, many English settlers were killed by disease, harsh winters, and American Indians. Those who remained continued their western migration to settle more land. Immigration into what is now the United States from England slowed as death, disease, and harsh winters increased. In the 1700s, more immigrants came from other European countries than from England. The traditions and culture brought by the English eventually formed the foundations on which the United States was created. The states with the greatest percentage of English among their population are Maine, Utah, and Idaho (U.S. Census Bureau, 2000); of course, a great number of English people live in each state throughout the nation.

Primary Languages and Communication Styles

The primary language of the English is, naturally, English. The English sometimes use the same words as acculturated citizens but with different definitions; for example, where the word "elevator" is used by acculturated citizens, English immigrants may say "lift." The speech of the English is slow and deliberate, and the volume may be low, making their speech hard to hear.

DOS AND DON'TS

- Do greet a person for the first time using Mr., Mrs., Ms., or Miss and the person's last name (Foster, 2000).

- Do shake the person's hand.
- Do make eye contact when speaking with someone.
- Do keep your hands at your sides when speaking (Foster, 2000).
- Don't point directions with your finger. Instead, use the head or chin to indicate a particular direction.
- Don't hug or pat a person on the back (Foster).

DISTINCTIVE TO THIS CULTURE

- Facial expressions are kept to a minimum, which can make it difficult for an athletic trainer to read the face of an English person (Foster, 2000).
- The interpersonal distance between the athletic trainer and the athlete can be close—about 4 feet, or 1.2 meters (Foster).
- It is considered impersonal to use small talk or ask questions as conversation starters.
- It is proper to keep one's feet flat on the floor (Foster, 2000).
- Crossing one's legs is usually done only by women and at the ankles (Foster).

Family Structure

Children live with their family until age 18 and are then expected to move out and start their own lives. The goal of elderly English persons is to live independently, so they may live close enough to get help from family members yet not within the same home. Males and females are on equal footing in terms of who is in charge, but the reality is that males still get paid more than females do for the same jobs.

DISTINCTIVE TO THIS CULTURE

- Decisions are made after consultation with a number of family members.
- The father may announce the final decision.

Daily Living and Food Practices

- The English are future oriented, and one is expected to take care of one's health and to be educated.
- The English believe in being on time and expect others to do the same.
- Due to their sense of time, it is important to them to meet expectations and take medication when prescribed (Erickson D'Avanzo & Geissler, 2003).
- The English eat three meals per day.
- Breakfast is usually large and eaten before 9 a.m. (Foster, 2000).
- Lunch is usually eaten between 1 p.m. and 2 p.m. and typically consists of a sandwich or salad (Foster, 2000). Dinner is eaten at 8 p.m. and is often preceded by an alcoholic beverage and an appetizer (Foster, 2000).
- Typical foods include meats, sausages, custards, fruits, jams, crumpets, potatoes, and custard. Customary drinks include tea, beer, and water; tea is the preferred beverage.

- Many English people do enjoy eating the stereotypical fish and chips (Erickson D'Avanzo & Geissler, 2003).
- English enjoy deep-fried Mars candy bars (Erickson D'Avanzo & Geissler, 2003).

Spiritual or Religious Orientation

The religious beliefs of those from England include primarily the faiths of Anglicanism, Catholicism, and Judaism; many other religions are also represented, but these three are dominant.

Catholics honor the holidays of Lent, Ash Wednesday, Easter, and Christmas. Meat is avoided on Ash Wednesday, on Fridays during Lent, and, for some Catholics, on every Friday. Catholics believe in God and view the Bible as the book of God's readings. Prayer, personal devotions, and giving are common practices. It is traditional to confess one's sins to a priest and ask for forgiveness. Confession is thought to be helpful in times of illness because it gives the sick person a relief from the burden of sin.

Typical religious objects include rosaries, medals with saints, and crosses. Removal of any of these objects should be done only with permission. A priest may be present during times of illness. The health care provider needs to allow privacy during such visits. It is also common for others to say prayers for the ill person. The ill are anointed with oil to support the healing process.

- Anglican beliefs include the idea that life begins at conception, that marriage is between a man and woman, that sex is for procreation and should occur only after marriage, that people need to be of high character, and that God's word is truth.
- The Torah, given to Moses for Jews to abide by, regulates how Jewish people are to live their lives. Some men and boys wear a cap called a yarmulke.
- Eating kosher foods is important to many Jewish people. Kosher foods are chosen and prepared in accordance with Jewish law; some examples are chickens, fish, cows, sheep, and goats. The blood from animals must be drained before the meat is eaten. Meat cannot be eaten with dairy, and pork and shellfish are forbidden. Utensils must also be handled in a kosher manner. Vegetables and fruits are permitted (Rich, 2007).
- Followers of Judaism may avoid surgery from sundown on Friday through sundown on Saturday.

Health Care Information

This section provides information about biocultural assessment, common sensitivities and conditions, beliefs about illness, preventive health practices, symptom management, and treatments.

Biocultural Assessment

- White males have a thicker-than-average parietal occiput (Schrefer, 1994). A thicker than average parietal occiput may mean that white males are less inclined to experience fractures than other ethnic groups.

- A longer second tarsal is found in 8 to 24 percent of Whites (Schrefer), and an affected athlete is more prone to ankle sprains.
- The palmaris longus muscle is absent in 12 to 20 percent of Whites (Schrefer), and an affected athlete is unable to forcefully flex his or her wrist.

Common Sensitivities and Conditions

- Illnesses and conditions most common among the English that athletic trainers are likely to be familiar with include heart disease, stroke, and tooth decay.
- Though less familiar to many athletic trainers, cystic fibrosis is also common among the English. The appendix provides a more comprehensive list of signs and symptoms.

Beliefs About Illness

The English accept germ theory and modern Western medicine. About 20 percent of the English population uses massage, herbal remedies, and alternative methods (Erickson D'Avanzo & Geissler, 2003). Most English continue to use Western medicine when they use alternative therapies.

Spector (2004) shares the following health maintenance beliefs based upon the respective religion:

- Baptist: Eat well, walk daily, read, and stay warm.
- Catholic: Exercise, sleep, take lots of walks, avoid drinking and smoking, work hard, leave the bedroom window open at night, rest, keep the house clean, avoid wearing dirty clothes, take baths, and clean up immediately after meals. In addition, keep the kitchen at 90 degrees in the winter and eat a good diet that includes lots of fish and vegetables but minimal red meat and no fried food.
- Episcopal: Take cod liver oil, get good rest, eat a good diet, and use vitamins.

Anglicanism is thought to be the religion that is closest to Catholicism. It is thought to be the religion that links the Catholic to the Protestant. Anglicans believe that the Bible consists of the writings of God himself. Anglican beliefs include the idea that life begins at conception, that marriage is between a man and woman, that sex is for procreation and is to be done only during marriage, that people need to be of high character, and that God's word is truth.

Jews believe in God. They do not believe that Jesus came to earth from heaven or that he died for their sins. The Torah is the document that regulates how people are to live their lives; it was given to Moses for Jews to abide by. Some men and boys wear a cap called a yarmulke. During times of prayer, a prayer shawl will be worn by all. An amulet showing the Star of David may be worn to indicate belief in Judaism.

Preventive Health Practices

- Most English understand the need for preventive health care but fail to behave proactively (Erickson D'Avanzo & Geissler, 2003).

- Sex is a private matter in most English families. If the athletic trainer deems it necessary based on an illness, sex may have to be discussed privately.
- Changing the diet of English people is important in order to reduce obesity; a diet low in fat and fried food helps prevent heart disease and obesity.
- The athletic trainer can support preventive dental care by encouraging the athlete to regularly brush, clean, and floss the teeth.

Symptom Management

- It is important that everyone is able to act at ease around the injured or ill English athlete.
- The sick person may not share that he or she is in pain or in need of medication when others are around (Erickson D'Avanzo & Geissler, 2003). Thus the athletic trainer may need to isolate the athlete from family and friends in order to determine the level of pain.

Treatments

There is a strong belief in making use of physicians and allowing the medical community to care for an injured or ill person. The family can give some minimal home care, but the preference is for a physician.

Spector (1996) discusses the following practices for restoration of health among the English:

- Fever—drinking chamomile tea
- Cough or congestion—placing formaldehyde crystals in a bag on the chest
- General illness—feeding the person warm, sweet milk with bread cubes

Frances Kennett (1976) discusses the following English folk remedies:

- Stomach disorders—yellow bark in ale or wine
- Diuretic—dandelion tea
- Diarrhea—fig, senna leaves, and treacle
- Liver ailments—boiled dandelion roots
- Colds—elder leaves or flowers in a tea
- Colds—onions boiled in molasses
- Coughs—licorice boiled in water
- Itching—inner bark of elder tree boiled in vinegar
- Boils—dock tea
- Bleeding—application of a cobweb
- Warts—daily rubbing with raw meat
- Rheumatism—carrying a raw potato in a pocket
- Sprain—tying a red thread around the joint
- Epilepsy—dried frog body worn in a bag around the neck

SUMMARY

White Europeans are not always considered as immigrants because they are the majority population in the United States, and they may be thought of as the creators of Western medicine, but it was Hippocrates. Upon immigrating to the United States, White Europeans generally settled in areas where people from their country of heritage had settled before them. Thus it became easy for them to maintain the culture of their homeland. Acculturation to the United States may have been easier for members of this group because most of them already spoke the English language.

The White Europeans discussed in this chapter speak three languages, depending on one's homeland of origin: German, Gaelic, and English. Eye contact is important to show respect and gain trust. When greeting a person for the first time, it should be done formally with a handshake and the use of a title before the last name. The physical distance between the athletic trainer and the athlete may be relatively close. Before touching an athlete, provide an explanation of the need to do so.

Facial and head gestures are preferred over the use of hands (as in pointing). Athletic trainers should keep their hands out of their pockets and avoid pointing with a finger or crossing their legs.

Most family members live close to one another. Medical decisions are made after consultation with the adults in the family.

Orientation to time is very important to Whites, and most are future oriented. As a result, they value education and the prevention of illness.

Eating three meals a day is common for Whites. For some, the diet is high in fat and fried foods. An athletic trainer can share that an improved diet means decreasing one's consumption of red meat and fried foods.

The vast majority of White Europeans have an affiliation with the Catholic church. Judaism, Anglicanism, and Protestantism are discussed in terms of beliefs and implications for an individual's health care.

Bioculturally, White Europeans have light skin, which makes it is easy to determine if there is a change in skin color due to a health problem. For example, cyanosis and jaundice are easily distinguishable due to color change.

Diseases and conditions that affect White Europeans include alcoholism, breast cancer, cystic fibrosis, Dupuytren's disease, heart disease, hereditary hemochromatosis, lung cancer, Lyme disease, myotonic muscular dystrophy, osteoporosis, sarcoidosis, skin cancer, and stroke. Athletic trainers can look for signs of these conditions and recommendations for preventive measures as possible.

Pain relief may be a challenge for the athletic trainer working with this population, because White Europeans tend to be stoic. The athlete may feel concern that others will be uncomfortable if he or she is in pain and thus may hide the experience. The athletic trainer may have to anticipate pain and be proactive in treating it.

Other values vary by culture but include working hard, exercising, and leaving the window open when sleeping. Getting an adequate amount of rest is viewed as essential to staying healthy.

Treatments vary by culture and belief. Most White Europeans believe in home remedies and may use them while also taking medication as prescribed by a Western medicine physician. Some believe that wearing a medal may help prevent illness. Still others believe that God will protect them from ill health.

Learning Aids

What Would You Do If . . . ?

1. You are working with an athlete who has been determined to be mentally ill with depression. You overhear other athletes talking about the illness as incurable. How do you deal with this?
2. You have been asked by the head athletic trainer to provide information about how religion among the Caucasian population will impact the health care of these athletes. What will you write?
3. You have a desire to work with athletes with Irish ancestry. Please share how you would find areas where a large Irish community lives.
4. An English athlete believes in being stoic in the presence of pain. Based on the injury, it is obvious that the athlete has to be in pain. The athlete's family is there to support. What are your thoughts about controlling the pain?

Activities

1. How might home remedies affect a patient's health care? Build a chart that indicates home remedies and the impact on the athlete's health.
2. What preventive measures can be taken in each of the cultures discussed here to improve one's health based on the listed common illnesses or conditions?
3. Interview an athletic trainer whose primary culture is German, Irish, or English and ask how his or her culture affects his or her work with athletes from other cultures.
4. Investigate whether belief in something—even if there is no scientific basis for it—can improve a person's health.

Key Terms

Define the following key terms found in this chapter:

Braucher	Caucasian	Passing through

Questions for Review

1. What cultural beliefs of White Europeans might affect your treatment of an injured athlete?
2. How does religion play a role in the health of White Europeans?
3. What particular biocultural aspects are particular to White Europeans?
4. What are some cultural influences that may change how an athletic trainer deals with a White European athlete?
5. How can an athletic trainer support the cultural needs of a White European athlete while providing effective care?
6. Explain the evolution of health care practices among White Europeans.

Middle Eastern

Learning Objectives

Upon completing this chapter, students will be able to do the following:

1. Describe the health beliefs of those from the Middle East who have now immigrated to the United States
2. Describe the health practices of men and women from the Middle East who have immigrated to the United States
3. Describe the spiritual cultures of Middle Eastern people
4. Explain the various cultural influences that affect care of a patient
5. Describe how to care for a patient while accommodating cultural needs
6. Explain how health care has evolved for people who have emigrated from the Middle East

Dr. Mahmoud Tarsin, MD

© Amjad Tarsin 2009.
http://www.amjadtarsin.com

I am a urologist at Detroit Medical Center. I was born in Tripoli, Libya and graduated from Cairo University School of Medicine in Egypt. I completed my training in Adult and Pediatric Urology and Renal Transplant Surgery. I have practiced medicine in Cairo, Libya, Saudi Arabia, Bahrain, England, and the United States. One of my proudest achievements was my involvement in the participation in the setting of the standards for international law for humanitarian concerns in Geneva (1971-1973).

I choose health care because when I was a teenager, my mother was severely sick and needed to have a surgery. My deep attachment to my mother made me wish I was a doctor to cure her from her illness. At that moment I decided to study medicine so I could help the needy and my loved ones.

In my practice in Saudi Arabia, due to the cultural barrier in separating men and women, I came across a female patient who greatly needed my help. However, she refused my care because I was a male doctor. There were no female doctors that were qualified to provide her with the proper care. Only after a lengthy discussion with her husband did she decide to receive my care.

I recommend all health professionals try to understand and respect the cultural differences and be patient with cultures they are unfamiliar with. Try to communicate with other members of the patient's family when needed. I find all cultures have a common bond and similar support structure within families.

Opinions vary as to which countries are part of the Middle East. Having lived and practiced in the region, M. Tarsin (personal conversation, 2008) offered the following description: The Middle East can be divided into four areas—African, European, Asian, and Near Eastern. The African countries include Morocco, Algeria, Tunisia, Somalia, Libya, Egypt, and Sudan. The European Middle East includes Turkey and Cyprus. The Asian countries include Saudi Arabia, the United Arab Emirates, Oman, Iraq, Bahrain, Jordan, Lebanon, Syria, Palestine, Qatar, and Yemen. The Near Eastern Middle East includes Pakistan, Iran, and Afghanistan. The Middle East as a whole is home to a variety of cultural groups within each of the countries: Arabs, Armenians, Assyrians, Azeris, Berbers, Chaldeans, the Druze, Greeks, Jews, Kurds, Maronites, Persians, and Turks (Erickson D'Avanzo & Geissler, 2003).

This chapter addresses two Middle Eastern populations: Arab-collective nations (Lebanon, Syria, and Egypt) and Iran. The term Arab-collective is defined by Holes (2000) to mean "an indigenous population which is historically of tribal Arabian origin." Arab-collective also implies adherence to orthodox Sunni Islam (Holes, 2000). The Arab-collective nations and Iran are addressed because they are the sources of the largest immigrant populations from the Middle East to live in the United States (U.S. Census Bureau, 2000).

For each culture, the discussion includes dos and don'ts, as well as lists of items distinctive to that culture. We would do well to remember that not all people within a culture adhere to each of the listed items. For example, first-generation immigrants to the United States may hold to beliefs and traditions that may not be carried on by members of the next generation.

ARAB-COLLECTIVE
(LEBANESE, SYRIAN, EGYPTIAN)

Lebanese, Syrian, and Egyptians have a unique culture of their own. It is important for the athletic trainer to understand the similarities and the differences of these cultures to one's own, avoid the generalization that everyone adheres to the same beliefs that are part of these cultures, and keep an open mind when working with athletes whose culture may be different than their own.

Demographic and Cultural Background Information

The Arab-collective populations have a rich history that, once learned, will help the athletic trainer become more culturally competent in working with them. This section addresses a brief history of country of origin and immigration, primary languages and communication, family structure, daily living and food practices, and spiritual or religious orientation.

Brief History of Country of Origin and Immigration

The region (see figure 11.1) has been involved in territorial wars with each other, and this reality continues today. Much of the fighting results from cultural and religious differences.

Immigration by Arab-collective people to the United States has occurred several times over several hundred years. Reasons include the wish to get away from historical disputes and the desire to attend college, and many students did not return to their countries after finding plentiful job opportunities in the United States. Other groups immigrated because of economic conditions, politics, or the desire for access to higher standards of living (Lipson, Dibble, & Minarik, 1996). In some instances, men would immigrate first, and, once they had saved enough money and established a housing situation, the rest of the family would come.

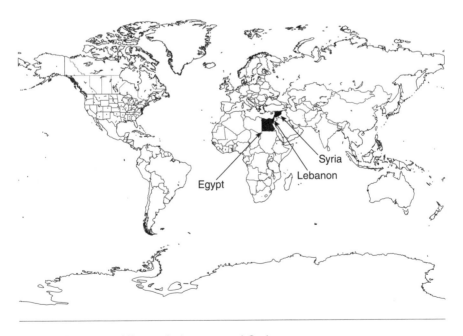

Figure 11.1 Map of Egypt, Lebanon, and Syria.

One of the largest populations of Middle Easterners in the United States is located in Dearborn, Michigan. Other states with the greatest populations of Arab heritage are California, Ohio, and Texas (Purnell & Paulanka, 2003, 2005).

Primary Languages and Communication Styles

The primary language of the Arab population is Arabic. The second language is English, which is taught in Arabic schools, and the tertiary language is French (most commonly spoken in Tunisia and Algeria). There are also various dialects, but most Middle Easterners can understand each other.

DOS AND DON'TS

- Do greet by using Mr., Mrs., or Dr., along with the person's first given name (Purnell & Paulanka, 2003).
- Do use Arabic terminology for mother (Um) or father (Abu) when communicating with the parents of an athlete (Purnell & Paulanka, 2003). This can provide a level of comfort that the health care provider is familiar with the culture.
- Don't be offended if a handshake is refused (Erickson D'Avanzo & Geissler, 2003). A handshake is more likely when there is a comfort level the athletic trainer.
- Don't shake hands with the left hand; this would be considered insulting (since the left hand is used to clean oneself after using the toilet, it is considered unclean).
- Don't be surprised if women hide their hands from view (Erickson D'Avanzo & Geissler).
- Do follow up an initial contact with a phone call to the athlete. The call will reinforce that the athletic trainer is concerned about the athlete.
- Do ask permission to evaluate a body part.
- Do make small talk about one's family and country of origin.
- Do sit or stand at the same level as the athlete.
- Do give details about, and a rationale for, everything you do.

DISTINCTIVE TO THIS CULTURE

- It is not uncommon for an Arab-collective person to address an athletic trainer with his or her professional title followed by first name—for example, Athletic Trainer Tom or Physical Therapist Suzanne.
- Being courteous may help gain the confidence of the athlete (Purnell & Paulanka, 2003).
- Sometimes men greet each other with an open hand, with one person placing both hands over the other's extended hand (Erickson D'Avanzo & Geissler, 2003).
- Hugging is expected among men when there is a close relationship, but not between men and women. Closeness, including touching, is acceptable between women (Purnell & Paulanka, 2005).
- Open affection among couples is not done in public.

- Sometimes when greeting a woman, a man may place his hand on his heart as a sign of respect and nod (Erickson D'Avanzo & Geissler).
- A physician is highly regarded, and Arabs believe that they should not waste the physician's time.
- It is thought to be disrespectful of someone's authority to outwardly disagree (Lipson et al., 1996).
- It may be helpful to engage other family members to elicit compliance from an athlete.
- People in authority, especially physicians (especially male), will receive the utmost respect from Arab men; however, nurses, physical therapists, and athletic trainers may not be viewed with the same respect. This is something that has to be dealt with. If there is a problem when working with an athlete, try to match the sex first (Salimbene, 2005).
- Those who are not acculturated are more likely to have gender or respect issues. Fears of incompatibility may be allayed by matching the sex of the athletic trainer with the sex of the athlete. As with any match that is not working, switch to another athletic trainer.
- Male physicians can care for both male and female athletes, but in issues of sex, birth control, and pregnancy a female must be cared for by a female physician.
- When a female athletic trainer is respected by and has a professional relationship with a male athlete, this is likely due in part to the athlete's being acculturated.
- The athletic trainer should take extra time to talk with the Arab person or family. Jumping into the evaluation, or treatment of the athlete, shows indifference toward the people involved.
- The athletic trainer may need to gain the confidence of an Arab athlete before he or she will share confidential information, even if the information is pertinent to the athlete's care.
- Another person may speak on behalf of the injured or ill party. The spokesperson may insist on going to surgery with the athlete in order to serve as the athlete's voice.
- A family member is likely to be in the room during the examination process, and he or she will answer all of your questions if the athlete does not understand English well.
- If another person speaks for the athlete, especially to interpret from English to Arabic, it is possible that essential information may be left out unintentionally (Purnell & Paulanka, 2003). Thus the athletic trainer may need a medical translator and may have to pursue a line of questions to make sure that everything important is effectively shared and understood. In times of a health crisis, the athletic trainer may need to use the athlete's primary language.
- When interviewing an ill or injured Arab athlete, an athletic trainer must ask very specific questions. Athletes tend to answer questions succinctly, which may necessitate a more thorough questioning process to accurately determine

the extent, origin, or even symptoms of the illness or injury. The athlete may express depression by stating that he or she has pain everywhere (Erickson D'Avanzo & Geissler).

- If an Arab believes that he or she has been wrongly accused or dealt with improperly, he or she may employ the attitude of **maalesh** or "it really doesn't matter." This behavior is projected at the accuser in response to the negative development, in the case of the athletic trainer. Maalesh may occur, for example, when an athlete is not following a prescribed treatment or when complications occur.

Family Structure

The family is of the utmost importance, and multiple generations may live under the same roof. Recent immigrants may maintain close ties to their native homeland, possibly including ties to tribes within their home country. This is a patriarchal culture, and the eldest family members are greatly respected (Lipson et al., 1996).

DISTINCTIVE TO THIS CULTURE

- Women fill the role of maintaining the home, caring for children and injured and ill family members, and making all meals.
- Fathers act as the disciplinarians of the children.
- Respect is expected of children.
- The wife exerts much influence in decision making but may not show it publicly so that her husband appears to be in charge (Purnell & Paulanka, 2003).
- It is expected that the male has a job.
- Consent for care or treatment may come from the oldest male figure in the family or in the form of a group decision (Salimbene, 2005). It may be given orally rather than in writing, and if written consent is necessary the athletic trainer may need to explain the reason (Lipson et al., 1996).
- If an athlete is terminally ill, consent must come from him or her.

Daily Living and Food Practices

- Many Arabic people are oriented toward present time; that is, they live in the present. They do not plan for the future, because it is believed that only Allah's will can make the future occur (Salimbene, 2005). For example, if an Arab athlete taking medication begins to feel better, he or she may stop taking the medication in the belief that it is no longer necessary since Allah has willed him or her to get better. Thus an athletic trainer may have to emphasize that the athlete must take the medication until it is used up and that he or she must keep follow-up appointments.
- Females wear a head covering called a **hijab** and are sometimes also covered head to toe. They are allowed to show only their faces and hands in public. Some men wear a head covering called a **kufi**. Athletic trainers should not attempt to remove the head covering of a female or male without need—and permission.

- Females are not likely to show skin unless it is necessary, and the athletic trainer may have to explain to the athlete why it is necessary to do so.
- Modesty is expected and is part of the lifestyle. It is thought best to emphasize intellect rather than the physical stature ("Muslims," 2006).
- Muslims eat meat only if it has been prepared in the way of **halaal**, which means that the sacrificed animal has to be healthy. The name of Allah must be said, and the animal must then be killed quickly by having its throat slit. An animal must be butchered immediately after being killed. The person who slaughters the animal must be a believer in Islam and say a traditional prayer when doing the slaughtering (Islamic Services of America, 2004).
- Muslims do not consume pork, pork products, alcohol, or food prepared with alcohol (e.g., wine or beer). It is unacceptable to eat animals that are carnivorous.
- Fish with scales are acceptable; those without scales are not to be eaten.
- Shellfish are acceptable.
- Animals that roll around in mud or occupy the bottom of the food chain are deemed unclean and unacceptable for eating. Animals viewed as unclean include dogs, rats, crows, clams, worms, catfish, and turtles (Essortment, 2002).
- Prohibited foods are known as haram.
- Some food is considered **mashbooh**, meaning that there is a question about whether it can be eaten; foods in this category include gelatin, emulsifiers, and enzymes ("Muslims").
- Vegetarian meals are acceptable as an alternative to having to worry if a food is mashbooh.
- It is important to know the origination of medication so as to not violate the dietary code of Islam. Some medications contain gelatin and fillers that would be mashbooh.

Spiritual or Religious Orientation

- The Islamic faith allows for most Western health practices, but the following are not allowed: Cesarean section, organ transplant, blood transfusion, and autopsy.
- Uneducated people believe that a jealous person could wish an illness or injury upon them by means of a practice known as the "evil eye." For protection, they may wear an amulet adorned with a portion of the Quran, which is the holy book for Muslims. The amulet should not be removed unless permission is given.
- Muslims pray five times a day (morning, noon, afternoon, sunset, and evening). Prayer is done while facing toward **Mecca**, to the east, when in the United States. Mecca is the holiest place in the world for Muslims hence the reason to face it while praying. It is not unusual for an athlete to pray while in the hospital; an athlete may also be unable to make certain medical appointments due to the time of prayer.

- A number of religious holidays may affect the health of a Muslim, especially **Ramadan**, which occurs annually on a variable date dependent on the cycle of the moon. Ramadan is a month of fasting. It is a time for Muslims to remember the suffering of the poor and to appreciate the things that Allah has given them. Fasting is done during the day and means no water or food. Food is allowed after dark (iftar) and before sunrise (shurooq). If a person is ill, it is acceptable to eat during the fasting hours. A person using medication that is best taken with food may have an upset stomach while fasting. The athletic trainer may have to explain the need to eat and work with the athlete to convince him or her to eat when ill. The athletic trainer may also have to find a private place for those who are fasting to occupy while the rest of the team eats. Women who are pregnant, menstruating, and all those who are ill at the time of Ramadan will be required to fast at another time of the year (Purnell & Paulanka, 2003; "Ramadan," 1992).
- Muslims are the people who follow the religion of Islam.
- Friday is the holiest of days.
- Allah is the ultimate highest power in Islam; as a result, there is a relaxed attitude about life, since Allah is believed to be in charge.
- The Quran is the religious text; it includes the **Five Pillars of Islam**: profession of faith (shahada), prayer (salat), giving (zakat), fasting (sawm), and pilgrimage (hajj). One professes one's faith to Allah.
- Prayer is used as a way to heal a person who is ill. A large group may be involved in the prayer session.

Health Care Information

A culturally competent athletic trainer understands the health variables that may change how care is provided. Topics covered in this section include biocultural assessment, common sensitivities and conditions, beliefs about illness, preventive health practices, symptom management, and treatments.

Biocultural Assessment

Arabs are known for their olive skin appearance, and their skin color may pose a challenge for an athletic trainer in diagnosing jaundice, pallor, or cyanosis (Purnell & Paulanka, 2003). The athletic trainer can use the nail beds, the whites of the eyes, the inside of the lip, or the palms of the hands to determine skin color changes. Auburn or blond hair is most common (Purnell & Paulanka, 2003).

Common Sensitivities and Conditions

- Arabs do not metabolize the following drugs well: antiarrhythmics, antidepressants, and beta-blockers (Purnell & Paulanka, 2003).
- Arabs cannot metabolize some analgesic drugs, which means that a patient in pain may not get comfort from using them (Purnell & Paulanka, 2003).
- Some Arabs marry their first cousins (Purnell & Paulanka, 2005), and genetic closeness in marriage can contribute to inherited disorders such as familial Mediterranean fever.

- Environmental illnesses more commonly found in Arab countries include malaria, trachoma, and typhoid fever. However, because these illnesses are not generally found in the United States, an athletic trainer is unlikely to see them here.
- Illnesses and conditions that affect Arabs but may be unfamiliar to an athletic trainer include Dubin-Johnson syndrome, Dyggve-Melchior-Clausen syndrome, familial hypercholesterolemia, Mediterranean glucose-6-phosphate dehydrogenase deficiency, schistosomiasis, and thalassemia. The appendix provides a more comprehensive list of signs and symptoms.
- Conditions common among Arabs that an athletic trainer will be familiar with include hepatitis A, hepatitis B, sickle-cell anemia, and tuberculosis.

Beliefs About Illness

Health care is viewed as a hierarchy in which the physician is at the top. Physicians are recognized for being successful at resolving the illness or injury (Purnell & Paulanka, 2005). If the physician fails, then it is attributed to God's will (Purnell & Paulanka, 2005).

DISTINCTIVE TO THIS CULTURE

- Diseases are thought to occur because of a change in environmental temperature, poor diet, grief from the death of a person, germs, or emotional distress (Purnell & Paulanka, 2005; Lipson et al., 1996).
- Mental illness is not understood and is hidden from people outside the family.

Preventive Health Practices

- It is believed that a Muslim must dress properly to prevent illness; if it rains, it is important to keep the feet dry (Spector, 2004).
- Make sure inoculations are done (Spector, 2004).
- Preventive practices should include a reduction in consumption of high-fat foods (especially red meat), as well as genetic counseling, and vaccinations. Keep in mind that Arabs believe Allah is in charge and thus there is no need for prevention. If the athletic trainer is trusted or respected, however, an Arab athlete is more likely to follow recommendations.
- The success of preventive practices increases if the family is involved (Purnell & Paulanka, 2005).

Symptom Management

- Arabs tolerate pain and may not give an accurate answer about how significant the pain is.
- Pain may be communicated to family members and one's circle of friends but usually is not shared beyond those groups (Purnell & Paulanka, 2005). The athletic trainer may have to pursue the question of pain level and may be able to befriend a family member who is willing to share the information.
- If an athlete has difficulty breathing, he or she may then hyperventilate out of fear (Lipson et al., 1996).

- Placing oxygen on an athlete to support breathing may cause him or her to feel anxious; this problem can be reduced by providing an explanation about the need for the support.
- Arab athletes may believe that vomiting can cause physical harm due to loss of nutrients (Lipson et al.); the preferred treatment for vomiting is medication (Lipson et al.).
- Fatigue is described as "low blood" or "inability to open one's eyes" (Lipson et al., 1996). The athletic trainer can explain that this symptom can be addressed by getting rest.
- Constipation may be dealt with through the use of laxatives (Lipson et al.), and athletic trainers need to inquire about an athlete's use of over-the-counter medications for symptom control.

Treatments

It is believed that a person who is ill needs to rest, and the family may be involved in providing care for the person by doing such things as preparing food, distributing medication, changing dressings, and changing bed linens. Importance is placed on getting rid of the illness, and the athlete may therefore select more extreme measures than are medically necessary.

Some may seek the assistance of a healer or **Imam** who recites the words from the Quran for relief. Some people may use herbal medicines to help cure themselves.

Home Remedies

An Arab family may try to solve a family member's illness before seeking professional help. They may do so in a number of ways (Atallah, 1996; Lipson et al., 1996; Tarsin, personal conversation, 2008):

- Using heavy blankets and clothing to keep the body warm and cause sweating
- Drinking a lot of fluids to relieve stomach pain or the flu
- Easing a sore throat with sugar
- Using bloodletting to reduce high blood pressure
- Using cupping massage to resolve bronchitis, high blood pressure, and back pain
- Bandaging the head with a cotton cloth to relieve a headache
- Burning a body part with hot metal to relieve sciatica and stomach pain
- Drinking boiled grain water to relieve kidney stones
- Drinking tea for a sore throat
- Drinking boiled mint or sage once cooled for stomach pain
- Drinking lemonade and juice for the flu
- Fasting to cure illness (Purnell & Paulanka, 2003)

The athletic trainer needs to be familiar with these remedies because they may conflict with or be contradictory to the treatment given by the trainer. If the remedy is not harmful to the process, the athletic trainer may still want to acknowledge it as a sign of respect and competence.

Prayer

Arabs view the body as a vessel that is to be maintained in a healthy way. Allah is the entity in control of life and death and is able to make the person live a good life that is free of pain and stress. When someone is ill, the Quran is used in prayer. Traditional medicine and healing oils are also used (Erickson D'Avanzo & Geissler, 2003). Some body parts may be cauterized in an effort to maintain health, but this treatment is rarely if ever done (Erickson D'Avanzo & Geissler).

IRANIAN

Iranians have a unique culture of their own. It is important for the athletic trainer to understand the similarities and the differences of this culture to one's own, avoid the generalization that everyone adheres to the same beliefs that are part of this culture, and keep an open mind when working with athletes whose culture may be different than their own.

Demographic and Cultural Background Information

This portion of the chapter acquaints you with the demographic and cultural background of Iran. Categories addressed include a brief history of country of origin and immigration, primary languages and communication, family structure, daily living and food practices, and spiritual or religious orientation. The second section about Iran presents health care information.

Brief History of Country of Origin and Immigration

Iran is situated between Turkey and Iraq (see figure 11.2). The majority of the population lives in the northern portion of the country (Purnell & Paulanka, 2005).

Figure 11.2 Map of Iran.

Until the 1930s, Iran was called Persia, and many people with a traditional background call themselves Persians instead of Iranians (Purnell & Paulanka, 2005). The population includes city and rural people, various social classes and ethnic groups, and people living in tribes (Purnell & Paulanka, 2005).

In the mid-20th century, the Shah of Iran implemented an economic policy that provided for national health care and education (Purnell & Paulanka, 2005). The Shah and his regime allowed women to go unveiled in public. The Shah also implemented repression against anyone who did not follow his political beliefs (Purnell & Paulanka, 2005). In 1978, however, martial law was declared after violent protests that would ultimately lead to the fall of the Shah in 1979, when Shiite Muslims took power in Iran and made the government conservative (Purnell & Paulanka, 2003). Education is highly valued in Iran (Purnell & Paulanka, 2005), and Iranian immigration to the United States has typically been geared toward educational purposes. Some people have stayed after receiving their degrees, and many male Iranian immigrants are self-employed (Purnell & Paulanka, 2003). The largest populations of Iranians in the United States are found in California (Purnell & Paulanka, 2003, 2005) and in the Northwest.

Discrimination against Iranians immigrants has occurred whenever tension has risen between the governments of Iran and the United States. During these times of crisis, Iranian immigrants have not been able to find jobs affording the same economic status as Whites; thus it is not uncommon to take a job beneath one's education in order to maintain the family (Purnell & Paulanka, 2005).

Primary Languages and Communication Styles

The major language is Farsi (Lipson et al., 1996), but many Iranians speak more than one language. Other common languages include Turkish, French, English, Kurdish, and Armenian (Purnell & Paulanka, 2003). English is used when conducting business, though many older Iranians do not speak English and thus need an interpreter.

DOS AND DON'TS
- Do shake a hand, bow slightly, and use the person's last name.
- Do address an adult before greeting children.
- Do stand up when someone enters the room (Lipson et al., 1996).
- Do expect men to bow upon greeting and place a hand over their chest (Purnell & Paulanka, 2003). An athletic trainer should take a cue from the athlete as to how he or she wishes to be greeted.
- Do use a handshake with all family members as a sign of respect.
- Do ask an Iranian athlete to come into a room by waving your palm down to call her in.
- Do hand information to an Iranian athlete with your right hand. If you are left-handed, this could pose a problem, because the left hand is considered unclean. Thus a left-handed person should try to use his right hand in the presence of an Iranian; otherwise, prescriptions and important papers may be thrown away as "unclean."

- Do expect women to greet other women—and men to greet other men—with a kiss on the cheek.
- Do sit up straight.
- Don't let the bottom of your foot show toward someone or stretch your leg toward someone (Purnell & Paulanka, 2003, 2005).

DISTINCTIVE TO THIS CULTURE

- One's private thought is known as **baten**. Private thoughts may not be shared unless the athletic trainer is a friend. An example of the intensity of this tendency toward privacy can be seen in the fact that a man may not say his wife's first name around other men.
- Because physicians are perceived as most knowledgeable, it is easier for them to gain access to private information.
- It is thought to be disrespectful to outwardly disagree with someone deemed to be in authority. Thus Iranians are likely to nod or affirm even if they disagree with what has been said; yet even though they may not verbalize their disagreement, they may choose eventually not to follow instructions.
- An athletic trainer who has the best relationship with the athlete may have to share bad news. The news should be shared gradually and in the presence of the family spokesperson (Lipson, et al.).
- Modesty is expected.
- If a medical issue could bring shame or a negative judgment on the athlete, he or she may not share information about it. Thus the athletic trainer may need to take time to gain the athlete's trust before a good working relationship can be developed.
- It is useful to match the sex of the athlete with the physician or athletic trainer, since the athlete may be more likely to share medically sensitive information in that scenario.
- Tilting one's head forward means "yes," tilting it backward means "no," and tilting it to the side means "what?"
- The American thumbs-up signal is considered vulgar.
- If an athletic trainer would like to show or give something to an Iranian, it is appropriate to have both palms facing up.
- The personal space between Iranians tends to be very intimate (1.5 to 4 feet, or 0.5 to 1.2 meters), and Americans may find it intrusive (Purnell & Paulanka, 2005).
- Eye contact is made among close friends and family.
- Eye contact may not be made with one whose social status or age is greater as it is considered disrespectful (Purnell & Paulanka, 2005). Athletic trainers should respect this lack of eye contact when working with an athlete who may be older.

Being able to hide one's true feelings is a prized characteristic, and most conversations with outsiders are superficial. The ability to manipulate people is known as **zeranghi** (cleverness) (Purnell & Paulanka, 2003). Bargaining is commonplace. Rarely is the rule really the rule, or the price really the final price. There is always discussion and bargaining to obtain what one desires.

Another common stance is **ta'arof** (expressed courtesy) or the public persona one puts on with those outside of one's intimate circles (Purnell & Paulanka, 2003). Ta'arof involves the appearance of respect and courtesy, but it should be understood that they are not meant to be sincere. The purpose is to be respectful, but not allow the athletic trainer into the inner circle of the athlete. **Zaher** refers to proper and controlled behavior for the public (Purnell & Paulanka, 2005, pp. 249–250). On the other hand, baten is freely shared among family members and is not judged (Purnell & Paulanka, 2003). For the athletic trainer, then, it is best to get to know the athlete and his or her family. Building a positive relationship—one that is about trust and in the best interest of the athlete—may help the athletic trainer avoid the thicket of superficial courtesy behaviors.

When Iranians speak to each other, they can be very impassioned, loud, opinion-ated, and repetitive. Outsiders may view such a conversation as argumentative or threatening; in reality, however, the conversation is traditional (Purnell & Paulanka, 2003). Once an athletic trainer becomes close with to an athlete, the athletic trainer can behave similarly if needed.

Family Structure

The family is the strongest social unit, and children live at home until they get married. Children are expected to respect the family even when away from home. Multiple generations of the family may be very close and maintain frequent contact with family members and friends. Friendships begin at birth and continue through-out life. Acculturated Iranians, however, are not likely to have a strong network of friends in the United States (Purnell & Paulanka, 2005).

DISTINCTIVE TO THIS CULTURE

- The father is the family leader, and the eldest son is second in line.
- The eldest male is the decision maker in the family.
- The father is expected to have a job and provide for the family.
- The father is also in charge of the family finances (Purnell & Paulanka, 2005).
- If the financial situation is problematic, this fact is kept quiet, even among close family members.
- The father who owns a business is expected to have other family members join him in the business.
- The mother and daughters are expected to take care of the home life (Purnell & Paulanka, 2005).
- Drinking, smoking, and sex are considered inappropriate for teenagers.
- Sex outside of marriage is not acceptable.
- Dating is not accepted among traditional families (Purnell & Paulanka, 2005).
- Having a baby outside of marriage is considered taboo and is not discussed.

- Same-sex relations are forbidden and can result in the death of the individuals by the government (Purnell & Paulanka, 2005). Thus an athletic trainer who is privy to such information should not share it with family members.
- Adults are seen as the voice of knowledge and are held in high regard.
- Men have the right, in this culture, to correct women and are considered superior. In the United States, however, this practice is not common, which may create a feeling of lack of power among men.

Daily Living and Food Practices

- Iranians live with a focus on the present and the future (Lipson et al., 1996). Being on time for appointments and business is a must, but timing is flexible for social events (Lipson et al.).
- Consent for any procedures will be given through the patient's family spokesperson. This person is used to keep stress from the patient (Lipson et al.). The athletic trainer may need to determine who is serving as the family spokesperson; it could be the eldest male or even the eldest female.
- Iranians eat three meals a day.
- Dessert is always served and consists of fresh fruit.
- After each meal, hot tea is served.
- Fresh food is eaten for its nutritional value.
- Food is purchased and eaten on the same day, as opposed to storing it for later use.
- Fast food is not considered fresh or as having any nutritional value; thus, it is not likely to be part of an Iranian's diet.
- Iranians who are Muslims avoid pork and alcohol.
- Foods are considered hot (**garm**) or cold (**sard**) (Purnell & Paulanka, 2005), and an individual's health is thought to depend on balancing hot and cold foods. Examples of hot foods include candy, garlic, fruits, some vegetables (onions), wheat, poultry, and walnuts. Examples of cold foods include beer, beef, plums, rice, grapes, yogurt, dairy, and cucumbers.
- Without a balance of food, a person can become "hot" with sweating and itching (Purnell & Paulanka, 2005).
- It is believed that a person who has eaten an overabundance of cold foods may become ill, vomit, shiver, or become dizzy (Purnell & Paulanka, 2005).
- Ice water is avoided during times of ill health. Warm tea is preferred (Lipson, et al.).

Spiritual or Religious Orientation

The major religions of the Iranians include the Báhá'i Faith, Judaism, Christianity, and Islam (Erickson D'Avanzo & Geissler, 2003). The religion practiced most often by the Iranian population is Islam (Young & Koopsen, 2005).

Health Care Information

A culturally competent athletic trainer understands the health variables that may change how care is provided. This section addresses biocultural assessment, common sensitivities and conditions, beliefs about illness, preventive health practices, symptom management, and treatments.

Biocultural Assessment

- Iranians are known for olive skin but also can be fair in complexion. Darker skin color may pose a challenge for an athletic trainer in diagnosing jaundice, pallor, or cyanosis.
- Black or dark brown hair is most common (Purnell & Paulanka, 2003).
- Eyes can be blue, green, to nearly black eyes (Purnell & Paulanka, 2003).

Common Sensitivities and Conditions

- Iranians are prone to stress-related illnesses due to conditions such as war or cultural shifts related to changes in government.
- The stress-related conditions include anxiety attacks, ulcers, and depression (Purnell & Paulanka, 2003).
- Iranians have a higher-than-average rate of smoking.
- Some conditions with a higher incidence among Iranians may be familiar to many athletic trainers: cardiovascular disease, diabetes, and vitamin B_{12} and folic acid deficiency (Erickson D'Avanzo & Geissler, 2003; Purnell & Paulanka, 2005).
- Primary illnesses and conditions among Iranians that may not be familiar to athletic trainers include cholera, Dubin-Johnson syndrome, hypertension, malaria, Mediterranean glucose-6-phosphate dehydrogenase deficiency, thalassemia, and zar (Purnell & Paulanka, 2005). The appendix provides a more comprehensive list of signs and symptoms.
- Conditions common among new Iranian immigrants include hookworm, dysentery, and meningitis, all of which are caused by unsanitary conditions in Iran (Purnell & Paulanka, 2005).

Beliefs About Illness

Three major forms of medical belief can be found among Iranians: humoral, sacred, and modern (Purnell & Paulanka, 2005).

DISTINCTIVE TO THIS CULTURE

- The four humors of medieval physiology are blood, yellow bile, phlegm, and black bile. Each fluid is thought to give off vapors that affect an athlete by going to his or her brain. If a person becomes ill, the caregiver may examine the balance of the humors to determine the cause of the current illness. The examination of the athlete and the signs associated with the illness will determine the cause. For example, if the athlete is hot and dry, yellow bile is the problem. If the athlete is hot and moist, then blood is the problem. Black bile is the problem if the person is cold and dry, and cold and moist means phlegm is the problem (Gill, 1999). Once the cause of the illness is determined, the diagnostician will prescribe an increase in the opposite humor. For example, if black bile was the issue (cold and dry), then an increase in hot and moist is necessary (blood humor). This could be accomplished by a warm bath. An imbalance in the humors is thought to cause either physical or emotion illness. A person with an emotional illness may then cause a physical illness in himself or herself.

- Sacred medicine derives from the text of the Quran and the wish of Allah. In this approach, illness is created by jinns—evil supernatural entities that give power to those who possess them. A person who possesses a jinn can cast illness on another person (Purnell & Paulanka, 2005). It is believed that holy men can heal all illness caused by jinns (Purnell & Paulanka, 2005).

- Many Iranians also believe that the "evil eye" can cause a person to suffer illness or injury (Spector, 2004). Jinns are genies and evil eye is given by people who have evil intentions.

- Some may believe that a handicapped individual born into the family derives from the wrath of Allah for something the family has done something to upset Allah.

- Mental illness is stigmatized and hidden.

- The culturally unacceptable illness termed **narahati** (Purnell & Paulanka, 2005) is a somatoform (mental) disorder in which a person experiences many physical complaints that cannot be explained (Purnell & Paulanka, 2005). The complaints baffle the physician but make the mental disorder culturally acceptable.

- Iranians believe in staying warm and dry to prevent illness. It is especially important to keep the feet dry in rain (Spector, 2004). Since drafts and wetness are thought to contribute to illness, an athlete may refuse to shower in order to avoid becoming ill. In some sports, such as wrestling, the athlete may need to be encouraged to take a shower and completely dry off to effectively prevent skin infections.

- Women in this society often remove all body hair, other than facial and head hair, as a way to be clean (Galanti, 2004, p. 127).

Preventive Health Practices

- Recommend the routine health care examinations and immunizations. Future-oriented thinking helps Iranians practice these positive health habits (Lipson et al., 1996); thus prevention is part of the Iranian lifestyle.

- Humoral medicine addresses maintaining one's temperament in order to maintain health. Thus learning to control one's temperament would be a supportive and preventive practice. Controlling one's temperament is done by exercising and eating a balanced diet (Gill, 1999).

- The high number of Iranian smokers may require an athletic trainer to become familiar with smoking cessation programs.
- Iranians do believe in exercising and taking vitamins. The athletic trainer should ask what form of activity the athlete prefers and what kinds of vitamins he or she takes.
- Iranians may marry their first cousins, which can result in genetic disorders such as epilepsy, anemia, hemophilia, and blindness (Purnell & Paulanka, 2005). The athletic trainer may refer athletes to a genetic counselor for preventive counseling. The athletic trainer may also want to share information with the team physician about this possibility of a genetic link to a condition.

Symptom Management

- An athlete in pain may exhibit grimacing and guarding to prevent pain. The athlete may feel able to express the level of pain on a scale of 1 to 10. However, pain is thought to be a way to purify oneself, and the athlete may choose to endure rather than treat it.
- Some athletes may accept medication for management of an illness but decide their own dosage (Purnell & Paulanka, 2005). If the athletic trainer is working with this athlete, it would be prudent to determine if the medication is being taken properly. To do this, ask the athlete to bring in his medication and count the number of pills.
- An athlete may use warm tea to assist in resolving the illness.
- Vomiting and diarrhea are considered foul and embarrassing, and it is important to give privacy to an athlete suffering these ailments (Lipson, et al.). Over-the-counter medicine may be used to remedy diarrhea.

Treatments

When you are going to perform a procedure, explain it well. Iranians respect an educated professional and may not want to work with an athletic trainer who is not authoritative; they prefer a person who can make quick diagnoses and readily decide on treatment.

Athletic trainers may be surprised that the athlete selects the most intrusive of possible treatments. It is common thinking among Iranians that the most intrusive treatment is the most effective one.

Home Remedies

The family may be involved in the care of the injured or ill person, who may allow the family to care for his or her needs and make decisions. The women will serve as the primary caregivers and may provide food at the bedside of one who is hospitalized.

Home remedies may be used in conjunction with medicines. It is believed that home remedies will more than likely resolve the illness. The athletic trainer may want to know what home remedy is being used so as to avoid adverse interactions.

Here are some remedies that may be used (Purnell & Paulanka, 2005; Spector 2004, p. 146):

- Mint tea and cilantro seed—relaxation
- Dried foxglove flowers and sugar—upset stomach
- Khakshir (mugwort seed)—stomach problems and "dirty" (infected) blood
- Razianeh (fennel)—bad breath
- Quince seeds—sore throat
- Vinegar and water—sore throat
- Honey and lemon—cough
- Baking soda and water—upset stomach from acidic food
- Alcohol rub—sore muscles
- Cornstarch—rash
- Saffron—nervous system disorders
- Sedr—dandruff
- Wheat starch and boiling water—sore throat, cough, and diarrhea
- Mint—stomach gas
- Shatareh plant—fever

Illness is a family affair, and the family may care for the ill or injured person so that he or she can focus on getting well. You may refer to the earlier portion of this chapter regarding prayer and Islam.

SUMMARY

First-generation Iranian immigrants may hold more beliefs rooted in their home country and its cultural history. Members of second and third generations in the United States are more inclined to believe in Western medicine, or at least be open to trying it.

Wars and political upheaval in the Middle East have placed a great deal of stress on many people there, and Middle Eastern people have come to the United States for opportunities—especially in jobs and education. Upon arriving in the United States, Middle Eastern people have settled in communities with other Middle Eastern immigrants, and the resulting cultural communities have eased the way for those who are learning to feel comfortable in a new country.

Middle Eastern cultures are male dominated, and it is not uncommon for a male to act as spokesperson for an ill family member. Women are expected to be modest and to follow the direction of male family members. It may be best to match the sex of the athlete with the sex of the athletic trainer. Middle Eastern people hold physicians in higher regard than they do others in the health care profession. Individuals with grey hair are also more highly regarded in the belief that they have more knowledge.

Gestures considered to be offensive include use of the left hand, which is considered unclean, and calling a person by waving. In addition, a handshake may be refused unless the person is comfortable with the athletic trainer.

A Middle Eastern person may use maalesh—that is, give a response that he or she thinks the athletic trainer wants to hear though it is not genuine. This behavior may constitute a challenge of the athletic trainer, and it must be dealt with proactively.

The religion is usually the Islamic faith, which follows the lunar calendar. Ramadan is a major holiday in the Islamic faith, during which followers are expected to fast from sunrise to sunset for 30 days. This can pose a challenge for those who are ill and require regular nutrients—and for an athletic trainer trying to convince them to eat. Food preparation must be handled in a particular way or the food will not be eaten. Certain foods, especially pork, are forbidden.

Middle Eastern people are known for having olive skin, which may make it challenging for the athletic trainer to diagnose jaundice, pallor, or cyanosis.

Some of the more common illnesses associated with Middle Eastern people include familial Mediterranean fever, malaria, trachoma, typhoid fever, Dubin-Johnson syndrome, Dyggve-Melchior-Clausen syndrome, familial hypercholesterolemia, Mediterranean glucose-6-phosphate dehydrogenase deficiency, hepatitis A, hepatitis B, schistosomiasis, sickle-cell anemia, thalassemia, and tuberculosis. Marriage between first cousins may also cause problematic conditions.

Varying beliefs about illness hold that it may be created by germs, jinns, imbalance between hot and cold, the "evil eye," environmental factors, or stress. Symptoms are handled via over-the-counter medication; if that does not work, then home remedies and medication are used.

Preventive health care practices for Middle Eastern athletes work well when the athletic trainer explains the need and the fact that it is best for the athlete's future health. Vitamins are used to supplement one's health. To support women, the athletic trainer should appreciate modesty and the need for a female athletic trainer.

Treatment for various illnesses should be based on the athlete's belief about the cause. For the evil eye or jinns, a healer may be used. For a hot–cold imbalance, foods may be changed. An environmental illness may be addressed by staying dry, and those who believe in germ theory may seek the assistance of a physician.

Understanding the information presented in this chapter will help the athletic trainer become culturally competent, which may enable greater understanding and the formation of a more productive relationship between the athletic trainer and the athlete.

Learning Aids

What Would You Do If . . . ?

1. What if you are left-handed, or have no right hand, and thus must use your left hand to provide care?

2. What if you are Jewish and a Middle Eastern athlete asks what religion you practice?

3. What if you receive a gift from an athlete but your workplace policy bars you from accepting gifts?

4. What if your Iranian athlete indicates that he fears you because of your white coat? What do you suspect is causing the problem, and how will you resolve it?

5. What if an Arab American athlete has injured her knee but refuses to remove her sweat pants so that you can examine the knee in the co-ed training room?

6. What if an Arab American woman passes out and you determine that she has not eaten all day and thus get her some food, but she refuses to eat before sundown?

7. What if an Arab American student is being taken from his room into surgery and his brother follows him into the restricted area for surgery, refuses to leave, and says, "I have to speak for my brother while he is in surgery."

Activities

1. What genetic testing is available to determine whether a gene is responsible for the illnesses that are common among Iranians or Arab-collective people?

2. Determine whether there is any merit to the home remedies listed in this chapter. To do so, you will need to identify the active ingredients, then research whether they can resolve the relevant illness.

3. Compare the home remedies common in Iran and the Arab-collective nations with those of your culture. How are they similar or dissimilar?

4. Examine your own beliefs. Do you believe that Western medicine is best? Why or why not? How might your belief keep you from incorporating new techniques?

5. If you could switch places with a Middle Eastern athlete, what might you hope the athletic trainer would ask, provide, or consider when providing care for you? Answer in terms of the following ailments: swelling, muscle soreness, genetic illness?

Key Terms

Define the following key terms found in this chapter.

Baten	Kufi	Ramadan
Garm	Maalesh	Sard
Halaal	Mashbooh	Ta'arof
Hijab	Mecca	Zaher
Imam	Narahati	Zeranghi

Questions for Review

1. How do the beliefs of Iranians and Arab-collective people affect their health?
2. Describe the health practices of men and women who have immigrated to the United States from the Middle East.
3. What role does Islam play in health care for Arab-collective and Iranian people?
4. Please describe the various cultural influences that may affect the care of a Middle Eastern athlete.
5. How can an athletic trainer support a Middle Eastern athlete's cultural needs and still use techniques of Western medicine to resolve an injury or illness?
6. How has health care improved and evolved for Iranians over time?

PART

IV

Cultural Skill and Cultural Encounters

Cultural skill is the ability to apply knowledge, collect relevant cultural data, and perform a culturally based physical assessment. Cultural encounters involve direct engagement in cross-cultural interaction. Chapter 12 discusses ways to elicit information from patients (e.g., collect relevant cultural data) by using Kleinman's explanatory model and several models of cross-cultural communication. It also addresses ways of working with an interpreter.

Chapter 13 describes the components of a culturally based physical assessment. The chapter follows the assessment process used in athletic training, which includes taking an oral history, inspecting, observing, and palpating. Cultural considerations are presented for each part of the assessment.

Chapter 14 explores ways to use Campinha-Bacote's model to assess the cultural competence of a health care organization. It explains the process of conducting an institutional cultural self-audit; using SWOT analysis to identify strengths, weaknesses, opportunities, and threats; and forging a strategic plan. It also discusses steps to take in order to gain cultural knowledge from the community and addresses the meaning of cultural skill and cultural encounters relative to the health care organization.

Eliciting Information

Learning Objectives

Upon completing this chapter, students will be able to do the following:

1. Describe Kleinman's explanatory models approach
2. Describe Kleinman and Benson's revised cultural formulation
3. Describe the LEARN and RESPECT models of cross-cultural communication
4. Explain the reasons for using an interpreter
5. List the types of interpreting services
6. Apply strategies for working with an interpreter

Paul Alvarez, PhD, ATC

Photo courtesy of Jennifer Alvarez

Ethnically, I am Mexican American and Japanese American. My paternal grandfather was from Mexico, and my paternal grandmother was born in Los Angeles. My maternal grandparents were from Japan. During World War II, my maternal grandparents were held in the Tule Lake internment camp. My parents valued education and asked me, "What college are you going to?" So I got my BS in physical education and athletic training from California State University at Sacramento in 1985 and my MS in physical education and athletic training from the University of Oregon in 1987. Since then, I have worked at the University of La Verne, in California, as an assistant athletic trainer and faculty member. I earned my PhD in education from the University of California at Riverside in 2004, and I currently serve as chair of the movement and sports science department at the University of La Verne, which includes an athletic training education program accredited by the Commission on Accreditation of Athletic Training Education (CAATE).

My advice to all people who work in environments characterized by cultural variety is to be open minded and be honest with yourself. No one is perfect, and no one is going to be perfectly at ease with all kinds of people and cultures. Being yourself is a lot more comforting than trying to put on another's skin and pretend to be someone you are not. I love watching some of the student-athletes put on "the look" and "the talk" and act like they are part of a culture they are not in fact part of, just thinking they will be accepted. I would not appreciate having a health care practitioner pretend to be something that he or she is not. However, being open-minded means accepting that there are different cultures and looking to learn about them as you look to learn about a patient.

Part III of this text discusses cultural knowledge in the form of specific information about various racial and ethnic groups. Rather than taking that information and reducing it to a set of cultural factors to be memorized, athletic trainers should use it as a guideline for understanding a patient's world view (Kleinman & Benson, 2006). It is crucial that athletic trainers learn to think globally but act locally. In other words, having a broad understanding of a cultural group is important, but an athletic trainer needs to know how an individual patient is experiencing his or her illness or injury. Acting locally also means understanding that there is more variation within cultural groups than between them (Campinha-Bacote, 2003); if an athletic trainer loses sight of this reality, then his or her ability to discern culture may not be relevant to a particular patient's problem at all (Kleinman & Benson). Thus, in order to accurately and appropriately assess and treat a patient, the athletic trainer must elicit information from that patient.

A REVISED CULTURAL FORMULATION AND THE EXPLANATORY MODELS APPROACH

One way to act locally and elicit information from the patient's perspective is to use the revised cultural formulation (Kleinman & Benson, 2006) and the **explanatory models approach** introduced by Arthur Kleinman (Kleinman & Benson; Kleinman, Eisenberg, & Good, 1978). According to the *Diagnostic and Statistical Manual of Mental Disorders* (4th edition, text revision [DSM-IV-TR]), **cultural formulation** (see "DSM-IV-TR Cultural Formulation") is a means for systematically reviewing, evaluating, and reporting a patient's cultural background and the effect of the cultural context (American Psychiatric Association, 2000). The cultural formulation includes, among other things, asking the patient to explain his or her illness (i.e., to provide an **explanatory model** which explains the epidemiology of illness). The explanatory models approach is the specific set of questions designed to elicit the patient's explanatory model (see "The Explanatory Models Approach"). For example, does the patient believe that the problem was caused by fate, bad luck, an accident, punishment by God?

Kleinman and Benson (2006) revised the cultural formulation by integrating Kleinman's (Kleinman, Eisenberg, & Good, 1978) explanatory models approach. The revised cultural formulation should be used at the beginning of the assess-

DSM-IV-TR Cultural Formulation

The athletic trainer should ask questions about the topics presented in the following list (in the order in which they are presented here). By ascertaining the information in a systematic fashion, the athletic trainer is less likely to leave out or miss anything. Once the information is obtained, the athletic trainer can review it for accuracy; use it to provide a cultural context for physical assessment, diagnosis, and treatment; and report (document) the patient's cultural background.

Cultural identity of the individual

Cultural explanations of the individual's illness

Cultural factors related to psychosocial environment and levels of functioning

Cultural elements of the relationship between the individual and the clinician

Overall cultural assessment for diagnosis and care

American Psychiatric Association, 2000.

ment process, when taking the oral history, in order to obtain relevant cultural information. By understanding what is important to the patient at the onset, the athletic trainer can integrate that information when conducting the remainder of the physical assessment. He or she should also use the information when negotiating the clinical diagnosis, treatment, or rehabilitation goals and plans.

The revised cultural formation involves six steps (Kleinman & Benson, 2006):

1. **Ethnic identity:** Ask the patient about ethnic identity and determine relevance to the patient. Explain that the information is being gathered only in order to treat her or him in an appropriate manner. The purpose is to ask if ethnicity is relevant, rather than simply to assume that it is, in order to avoid stereotyping.

2. **What is at stake:** The purpose of asking what the patient has at stake is to determine how the problem (illness or injury) will affect the patient and his or her family, team, ability to earn an income, religious or social commitments, and overall life. For example, if the patient will be unable to work due to reconstructive knee surgery, how will missing work affect the family?

3. **The illness narrative:** Ask the patient questions to help reconstruct the illness narrative. In other words, ask questions that will elicit the patient's explanatory model (page 234) in order to help you understand the meaning of the problem.

4. **Psychosocial stresses:** It is important here to determine whether the patient has psychosocial problems associated with the illness, such as family tension or

The Explanatory Models Approach

Kleinman's model addresses etiology, time and mode of onset of symptoms, pathophysiology, course of illness, and treatment (Campinha-Bacote, 2003).

1. What do you call this problem?
2. What do you believe is the cause of this problem?
3. What course do you expect it to take? How serious is it?
4. What do you think this problem does inside your body?
5. How does it affect your body and your mind?
6. What do you most fear about this condition?
7. What kind of treatment do you think you should receive?
8. What are the most important results you hope to receive from this treatment?
9. What do you most fear about the treatment?

Kleinman & Benson 2006; Kleinman, Eisenberg, & Good 1978.

work-related issues. For example, in sport, does the patient have problems with the coach or teammates because of the illness or injury? On the other hand, does the team provide support for the patient?

5. **Influence of culture on clinical relationships:** In every interaction with a patient (i.e., every cultural encounter)—whether the interaction takes place within a culture or is cross-cultural—culture is always present, operating and influencing the interchange. As part of this equation, the athletic trainer needs to understand the effects of the culture of medicine (e.g., the omnipotence of technology for the treatment of illness and injury) on the cultural encounter and recognize, for example, that technology is not always the best answer.

6. **The problems of a cultural competence approach:** This step involves taking into account the efficacy of intervention. The athletic trainer should determine whether the intervention, recommended treatment, or course of action is going to work in this particular case. Kleinman and Benson (2006) suggest that "every intervention [including the use of a culturalist approach] has potential unwanted effects" (p. e294). For example, patients and family may view a focus on cultural differences as intrusive—as serving to single out or stigmatize the patient. Similarly, an "overemphasis on cultural difference can lead to the mistaken idea that if' the cultural root of the problem can be identified, the problem can be resolved (Kleinman & Benson, p. e294).

OTHER MODELS FOR ELICITING INFORMATION

Two other models for eliciting information from patients are the **LEARN model of cross-cultural communication** (Berlin & Fowkes, 1983) and the **RESPECT model of cross-cultural communication** (Welch, 2003). Berlin and Fowkes' LEARN model recommends a process for improved communication. The RESPECT model was first used for diverse patients with alcohol and drug dependency.

LEARN Model

The acronym LEARN stands for Listen, Explain, Acknowledge, Recommend, and Negotiate (Berlin & Fowkes, 1983; Campinha-Bacote, 2003; Mutha, Allen, & Welch, 2002; Welch, 2003). In this model, the athletic trainer should "listen with sympathy and understanding to the patient's perception of the problem" (Berlin & Fowkes, p. 934). In other words, as with step 3 in the revised cultural formulation, the purpose is to elicit and listen to the patient's explanatory model (Kleinman & Benson, 2006). Explaining here refers to communicating the athletic trainer's perception of the problem (e.g., the athletic trainer's explanatory model) to the patient. Acknowledgement involves recognition by the athletic trainer of the patient's explanatory model and the ways in which the patient's model differs from or is similar to the athletic trainer's model. Differences between the explanatory models are then discussed and resolved. In the next step, the athletic trainer recommends a treatment plan, in consultation with the patient and within the constraints of the patient's and the athletic trainer's explanatory models; to enhance the patient's compliance with the plan, cultural considerations are included in this step. The final step is to negotiate the recommended plan. The athletic trainer and the patient examine the biomedical, psychosocial, and cultural options and determine the final course of action to treat the problem.

RESPECT Model

The acronym RESPECT stands for Rapport, Empathy, Support, Partnership, Explanations, Cultural Competence, and Trust. The model involves the following elements (Mutha, Allen, & Welch, 2002, p. 104; Welch, 2003, p. 124):

RAPPORT
- Connect on a social level.
- Seek the patient's point of view.
- Consciously attempt to suspend judgment.
- Recognize and avoid making assumptions.

EMPATHY
- Remember that the patient has come to you for help.
- Seek out and understand the patient's rationale for his or her behaviors or illnesses (i.e., patient's explanatory model).
- Verbally acknowledge and legitimize the patient's feelings.

SUPPORT
- Ask about and try to understand barriers to care and compliance.
- Help the patient overcome barriers.
- Involve family members if appropriate.
- Reassure the patient you are and will be available to help.

PARTNERSHIP
- Be flexible with regard to issues of control.
- Negotiate roles when necessary.
- Stress that you will be working together to address medical problems.

EXPLANATIONS
- Check often for understanding.
- Use verbal clarification techniques.

CULTURAL COMPETENCE
- Respect the patient and his or her culture and beliefs.
- Understand that the patient's view of you may be informed by ethnic or cultural stereotypes.
- Be aware of your own biases and preconceptions.
- Know your limitations in addressing medical issues across cultures.
- Understand your personal style and recognize when it may not be working with a given patient.

TRUST
- Self-disclosure may be an issue for some patients who are not accustomed to Western medical approaches.
- Take the necessary time and work consciously to establish trust.

The revised cultural formulation and the LEARN and RESPECT models of cross-cultural communication give you ways to elicit information from a patient. All of the models include tools for eliciting the patient's explanatory model. The LEARN and RESPECT models are mnemonic devices that may help athletic trainers remember the steps in the process. Regardless of which model you use to elicit information, you should use the explanatory models approach (Kleinman & Benson, 2006; Kleinman, Eisenberg, & Good, 1978) for determining the patient's explanatory model.

ELICITING INFORMATION THROUGH USE OF AN INTERPRETER

According to Bethell and colleagues, "the nurse did not identify any needs. I [an interpreter] come 5 minutes later and identify five needs" (2006, p. W3-9). As in this report by a health care provider, two critical roles played by an interpreter are to avoid miscommunication and to accurately elicit information from the patient. In fact, patient–physician communication is of significantly higher quality when physicians use interpreters than when they do not (Betancourt, Green, Carrillo, & Ananeh-Firempong, 2003). By extension, we can reasonably expect that the same is true for patient communication with other health care providers, such as athletic trainers.

In addition, organizations that receive federal funding are subject to legal requirements mandating that they provide reasonable access to health care, as written in Executive Order No. 13166: Improving Access to Services for Persons with Limited English Proficiency (Exec. Order, 2000), and in the National Standards on Culturally and Linguistically Appropriate Services (CLAS), specifically standards 4, 5, 6, and 7 (Office of Minority Health, 2001; Salimbene, 2001). One way to provide patients with reasonable access is to make an interpreter available; it also helps provide culturally competent care, which may help eliminate health disparities.

There are several types of interpreter services. Salaried professional medical interpreters provide the most comprehensive services and are available as either full- or part-time staff members. Bilingual staff members can be certified in medical knowledge and should be trained and tested in cross-cultural issues and interpreter skills; they should also demonstrate fluency in the use of everyday English and in a second language. Community volunteers can serve in a similar capacity, and contract interpreters can be arranged in advance to provide services on an as-needed basis. Remote simultaneous medical interpreting (RSMI) services can provide real-time assistance. Remote simultaneous interpreting, which is used by the United Nations, is a "near word for word running rendition performed within milliseconds of the original speech—nearly simultaneously" (Gany, Kapelusznik, et al., 2007, p. 319). Thus the interpreter does not have to wait for the provider or patient to stop speaking before interpretation can begin. With RSMI, the athletic trainer and patient use wireless headsets and microphones to communicate remotely with the interpreter (Gany, Leng, et al., 2007; Gany, Kapelusznik, et al., 2007). Telephonic interpreting services are also available; in this setup, the athletic trainer and patient are in the same room, and the interpreter joins via telephone. Thus the interpretation is not simultaneous; rather, the athletic trainer and patient must pause and wait for the interpretation to occur. The type of interpreter service should be selected based on an organization's size, the frequency of requests for service, and the success of interpretation services utilized previously (Salimbene, 2001).

Several factors should be considered when choosing an interpreter or interpreting service. First, the interpreters need to be trained in medical interpretation and in how to deal with health care situations. Second, the interpreter should be fluent in English and in a second language in the areas of reading, writing, speaking, and comprehension. Third, the interpreter should understand cultural issues related to health care, such as culture-bound syndromes and commonly used complementary and alternative medicine practices. Last, the interpreter needs to understand and demonstrate professional ethics and code-of-conduct issues, such as patient confidentiality, informed consent, and privacy (Immigrant and Refugee Health Task Force, Chicago, 1993, as cited in Salimbene, 2001).

It is inappropriate—and sometimes medically dangerous—to use family members, friends, or children as interpreters (Salimbene, 2001). Therefore, it should be avoided (Welch, 2003). For example, Asian American patients were reported to prefer trained interpreters to family members. When children were used as interpreters, the power dynamics in the family were tilted toward the child, which created discomfort for the adult patient. Patients also reported that they were concerned that the family member was not adequately trained in medical terminology and thus might not accurately or completely convey their symptoms (Ngo-Metzger, et al., 2003). In another example, a parent observed that "for a 14-year old to be translating to the mother that her [newborn] sister isn't doing too well is extremely traumatic" (Bethell, et al., 2006, p. W3-9). Thus, even if a patient insists on using a family or friend to provide interpretation, the organization should still use a trained interpreter to listen and correct any miscommunication (Salimbene).

When working with an interpreter, the athletic trainer should consider the following strategies (Welch, 2003):

- When possible, meet with the interpreter before the patient arrives in order to clarify any issues or concerns, "establish the context and nature of the visit" (p. 129), and inform the interpreter where to position him- or herself during the patient's visit.
- At the beginning of the visit, introduce the interpreter formally and inform the patient of the interpreter's role.
- Speak to the patient, not the interpreter.
- To minimize confusion, avoid the use of technical terms, abbreviations, professional jargon, and idioms.
- Ask the interpreter to "translate the patient's own words rather than paraphrasing or omitting information" (p. 129).
- In order to verify that the patient understands, ask him or her to repeat instructions with the help of the interpreter.
- Remain patient when using an interpreter; the process will take longer.

SUMMARY

One of the five components in the process of cultural competence is cultural skill, which involves conducting a culturally based physical assessment of the patient. In order to conduct the assessment, the athletic trainer must elicit information from the patient. This chapter provides several models for eliciting information, including Kleinman's cultural formulation (which encompasses the explanatory models approach) and the LEARN and RESPECT models of cross-cultural communication. Each model offers a unique way to engage the patient, thus giving the athletic trainer the information he or she needs in order to complete an assessment. When working with a patient who speaks limited English or no English at all, it may also be necessary to use an interpreter to elicit information from the patient. Several types of interpreter services are available, and the athletic trainer will benefit from using recommended strategies for working with an interpreter such as speaking to the patient, not the interpreter; verifying patient understanding; and remaining patient because using an interpreter takes longer. When athletic trainers and patients are able to communicate with each other, there is less chance for misunderstanding, misdiagnosis, mistreatment, and patient noncompliance, and more chance for obtaining accurate, complete information.

Learning Aids

What Would You Do If . . . ?

1. What if you were trying to take an oral history during the physical assessment but your patient spoke limited English?
2. What if you needed to demonstrate how to use a particular piece of equipment to a patient who spoke limited English?

Activities

For these two activities, use information from chapters 6 through 11 to create a simulated patient.

1. Working in a group of three, practice eliciting information from a simulated patient using Kleinman and Benson's revised cultural formulation. One person plays the role of the health care provider, one acts as the patient, and the third is an observer. At the end of the assessment, the patient and observer should provide feedback to the health care provider.
2. Working in a group of four, practice using an interpreter to elicit information from a simulated patient. One person plays the role of the athletic trainer, one acts as the patient, the third is an interpreter and the fourth is the observer. At the end of the assessment, the observer should provide feedback to the athletic trainer.

Key Terms

Define the following key terms found in this chapter:

Cultural formulation
Explanatory model
Explanatory models approach
LEARN model of cross-cultural communication
RESPECT model of cross-cultural communication

Questions for Review

1. What are the revised cultural formulation and the explanatory models approach?
2. How could an athletic trainer use the revised cultural formulation to elicit information from a patient?
3. How are the LEARN and RESPECT models of cross-cultural communication similar, and how do they differ?
4. Why should an athletic trainer use an interpreter?
5. What types of interpreting services exist, and why would an athletic trainer choose one over another?
6. What strategies should an athletic trainer employ when using an interpreter?

Culturally Based Physical Assessment

Learning Objectives

Upon completing this chapter, students will be able to do the following:

1. Define cultural skill
2. Describe the components of a culturally based physical assessment
3. Identify verbal communication issues associated with taking an oral history
4. Identify nonverbal communication cues
5. Describe cultural considerations associated with inspecting and observing
6. Describe cultural considerations associated with palpating

---

Nathan C. Tomson, MA, ATC

I am a graduate of Indiana State University and Central Michigan University. A certified athletic trainer since 1999, I have worked at the Walt Disney World Resort, the Disney Cruise Line, and with Work-Fit at the GM Powertrain Flint South plant. I currently work as a residence hall director, part-time instructor, and assistant conference manager at Central Michigan University. I also volunteer with the Central Michigan chapter of Thrivent Financial for Lutherans.

I have presented on multiple topics at the local, state, regional, and national levels to diverse groups of professionals including athletic trainers and residence life professionals. I most enjoy presenting to students about professional development and maximizing their benefits packages. Other topics include living and learning communities, networking, Web site development, team building, and summer conferences.

I live in Mount Pleasant, Michigan, with my partner, Wade, our son Connor Lincoln, and daughter Taylor Kennedy.

When performing a physical assessment, it is important to gather pertinent and accurate information from the patient. Evaluating patients within a cultural context helps the examiner gather more complete information and convey that he or she cares for the patient as a person and not just as a body part. Therefore, it is critical to develop cultural skill, which is "the ability to collect relevant cultural data regarding the client's presenting problem as well as accurately perform a culturally-based, physical assessment" (Campinha-Bacote, 2003, p. 35).

The physical assessment has several components: taking an oral history, inspecting and observing physical signs, and palpating.

TAKING AN ORAL HISTORY

Taking an oral history involves verbal and nonverbal communication between the health care professional and the patient. Miscommunication can result from differing cultural conventions, and it can lead to patient dissatisfaction, incorrect diagnosis, inappropriate care, noncompliance, and poor health outcomes (Betancourt, Green, Carrillo, & Ananeh-Firempong, 2003).

Verbal Communication

Verbal communication is an important part of communicating effectively with the patient; it requires the ability to express oneself clearly in words.

Greeting and Name Pronunciation

Unless directed otherwise by the patient, greet your patient formally (particularly if he or she is an adult) with an appropriate title such as Miss, Ms., Mrs., or Mr. Using a title is thought to convey respect in many cultures, including African American, Arab, Chinese, and Korean cultures. One way to avoid an inappropriate greeting is to ask the patient how she or he would like to be addressed. This can be done orally or by asking the question on a patient information form.

Learn the correct pronunciation of your patient's name. For example, a common Vietnamese family name, Nguyen, is pronounced /Wee-un/ not /Nugooen/ (Giger & Davidhizar, 1999). Some patients may adopt a Western-style name in order eliminate mispronunciation; in such cases, clarify which name is the legal name that should be used on official records. Writing the name phonetically in the patient's chart may help facilitate accurate pronunciation.

Language

Among other things, language involves grammatical structure, vocabulary, pronunciation, and intonation. Approximately 20 percent of the U.S. population over the age of 5 speaks a language other than English, and 44 percent of these individuals speak English less than well. The percentage of the population speaking a language other than English is even higher in California (about 42 percent), New Mexico (37 percent), and Texas (34 percent) (Lowe, 2008). Thus it is important for an athletic trainer to determine a patient's proficiency and fluency in speaking Standard English. It is also important to determine the patient's ability to read and, when necessary, write in Standard English. Some patients may be proficient in one aspect of communication, such as speaking, but not in another, such as reading. Some patients may speak in slang or use a dialect of Standard English, such as African American Vernacular English (also known as Black English or Ebonics), Spanglish (a mixture of Spanish and English), or Hoosier Dialect (spoken in the Midwest, particularly in Indiana).

To minimize miscommunication due to language issues, here are a few suggestions:

- Clarify words and phrases used by the patient.
- Speak slower, not louder.
- Ask about one symptom at a time.
- Avoid using medical jargon and technical terms.
- Use pictures.
- Use a trained medical interpreter who is culturally competent.

Silence

Perceptions of silence vary across cultural groups. For some, silence may be a reaction to pain, a time of reflection, or a way of listening to God. For some American Indians and traditional Chinese, silence may be used as a sign of respect or an indication that the question was worthy of contemplation. For others, such as persons of English or Arabic decent, silence may be used for privacy. Silence may also be used to organize one's thoughts so that spoken words will be more meaningful (Giger & Davidhizar, 1999).

For patients who speak English as a secondary language, silence may be needed in order to process what a person has heard. For example, a patient may hear the words spoken in English, translate them into his or her primary language, formulate a response in the primary language, and then translate the response to English in order to respond in English (see figure 13.1).

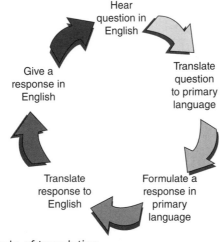

Figure 13.1 The circle of translation.

Avoid interrupting the silence. Instead, use periods of silence to assess nonverbal communication, such as body posture, facial expression, or eye contact.

Narrative Sequencing

Narrative sequencing refers to the order in which a story is told or a description is given. When a patient is injured, ill, or otherwise seeking services and tells the athletic trainer about what happened, his or her account is akin to telling a story. The patient is providing a narrative sequence of the events associated with the injury or illness. In Western culture, stories are typically organized and told temporally—that is, chronologically. Stories have a beginning, a middle, and an ending. Similarly, the taking of an oral history during a physical examination is typically temporal. For example, athletic trainers often ask about past injuries, illnesses, and treatments (i.e., patient history—"Have you injured your knee before? If so, what did you do to treat it?"). Then they ask about how the current injury or illness occurred, what signs and symptoms appeared at the time of injury, and what treatment has been used (i.e., mechanism of injury—"How did you injure your knee? Did you put ice on the knee when you hurt it?"). Finally, the patient is asked about current signs and symptoms (i.e., chief complaints and concerns—"How does the knee feel today?").

When the patient and athletic trainer share the same cultural norms for storytelling, there is no communication barrier in terms of narrative sequencing. If not, however, the "lack of shared cultural norms for telling a story, making a point, giving an explanation and so forth can create barriers to understanding" (Michaels, as cited in Reissman, 1991, p. 217). Thus, if the patient tells the story episodically, rather than temporally, the athletic trainer may experience confusion and perhaps frustration. However, if the athletic trainer tries to force the patient into a chronological or linear retelling of the story of the injury or illness, the patient may view the pressure as suggesting a lack of caring or lack of willingness to understand. Thus the responsibility of accurately deciphering the story belongs to the athletic trainer. To minimize frustration on both sides, the athletic trainer can listen with few interruptions (Reissman) and document what the patient said. He or she can then reread the story, during or after the evaluation, and, if necessary, summarize it temporally as part of the documentation.

Nonverbal Communication

Many racial and ethnic groups engage in nonverbal communication (some examples are included in the following sections). What the athletic trainer and patient do—and how they do it—can be just as important as what they say. To be in tune with nonverbal communication cues, the athletic trainer must watch for gestures, eye contact, touch, and facial expressions.

Gestures

Gestures do not have universal meaning. For instance, in American culture, when pointing at something or someone, the index finger is often used. However, in many cultures, pointing with the index finger is considered rude, and the thumb or multiple fingers are used instead. The gesture of moving one's head up and down often means "yes" or "I agree," but it may also mean "I hear you" or "I am actively listening to you" without necessarily conveying agreement.

Touch

Touch can have many meanings, and health care professionals must be aware of how and why they touch a patient and how the patient reacts to touch. It is important to demonstrate caring yet avoid being intrusive. Touch can be used to express positive feelings, such as warmth, care, love, empathy, and camaraderie. At the same time, touch can invoke fear or communicate anger, hate, or punishment. Touch may also be used for professional purposes, such as conducting a physical examination, shaking hands during a business meeting, or caring for someone's hair.

Touch has cultural meaning and significance as well. "All cultural groups have rules, often unspoken, about who touches whom, when, and where" (Giger and Davidhizar, 1999, p. 31). For instance, in African American culture, touch may be used for healing and prayer, as described by Stubbs (1995, pp. 305–306):

> *"Mrs. Stubbs, use gloves, gently wash your daughter's sores every night, and base [apply] them with the medicated salve that I prescribe." But my mother never used gloves. For three weeks, each night, her bare hands bathed my infection . . . . My mother always held a prayer service as her hands washed my head and face. . . . Sometimes . . . I could hear the words, "Heal her." . . . I finally asked if she were not worried about catching the disease. She responded, "Yes. But there is more at stake than drying up your sores. . . . Your self-esteem is being shattered; your spirit is troubled. In order to heal you, I must touch you, I must feel you. I can't use gloves." My mother was never infected. My sores disappeared. My self-confidence was restored.*

Touching someone with the left hand may be considered an obscenity in some Muslim and Asian cultures, and offering something with the left hand may be highly insulting. The reason? The left hand is used "to aid in the process of elimination" (Sue & Sue, 2008, p. 164)—that is, in wiping oneself—and thus is considered dirty or unclean. Thus the right hand, considered clean, is used for eating. Therefore, when offering something to a patient from such a culture, use your right hand or both hands.

Similarly, in Southeast Asian culture, the head is considered sacred, and touching someone's head is taboo. When an examination of the head is warranted, the athletic trainer should explain what will be done, and ask and receive permission before initiating the examination.

Smiling

In U.S. culture, smiling is generally considered a positive expression. It may represent happiness, friendliness, or a good personality and therefore is certainly appropriate in health care. However, athletic trainers should recognize that in Asian culture, smiling may convey other meanings, such as embarrassment or shyness (Sue & Sue, 2008), and may be used to "save face." Given the high value placed on dignity in Asian culture, from the patient's perspective **saving face** may prevent a loss of dignity for not understanding the athletic trainer, the diagnosis, or the treatment plan. In addition, a patient's practice of saving face may prevent a loss of dignity on the part of the athletic trainer for failing to explain in a way that the patient could understand. To avoid misinterpreting the smile of a patient of Asian descent who may be saving face, the athletic trainer should ask the patient to repeat the instructions. If the result indicates that the patient misunderstood the athletic trainer, the athletic trainer can then provide clarification, which allows the patient to save face.

Eye Contact

Purnell and Paulanka (2003) suggested that, regardless of social standing or class, "Americans maintain direct eye contact without staring" (p. 16). Maintaining eye contact may be perceived as demonstrating trustworthiness or truthfulness or indicating that the listener is paying attention to the speaker. Sue and Sue (2008, p. 165) suggested that when interaction between Black and White Americans occurs, the eye contact is different for each race:

> [W]hen White Americans listen to a speaker, they make eye contact with the speaker about 80 percent of the time. When speaking to others, however, they tend to look away (avoid eye contact) about 50 percent of the time. This is in marked contrast to many Black Americans, who make greater eye contact when speaking and make infrequent eye contact when listening!

For members of some cultures (e.g., Cubans, Egyptians, Greeks, Iranians, Italians, Mexicans, Puerto Ricans), eye contact maintained between individuals may invoke or summon the "evil eye" or "bad eye," which causes injury or illness. Different cultures have different meanings for the evil eye. "The variables include how it is cast, who can cast it, who receives it, and the degree of power that it has" (Spector, 2000, p. 102). For one interpretation of the evil eye, if an adult admires something about a baby or child, such as beautiful eyes, a spell is cast on the child and the child becomes ill (Purnell & Paulanka, 2003). Maintaining eye contact may also be seen as a sign of disrespect in some American Indian cultures. Thus, the athletic trainer should avoid attaching negative connotations to a patient's level of eye contact; it is best to follow the lead of the patient in order to determine how much eye contact to maintain.

Other Considerations

While doing the oral history portion of the cultural physical assessment, the athletic trainer should consider several other cultural phenomena besides verbal and nonverbal communication—for instance, the social organization of the family, the use of traditional or cultural health practices and folk healers, and the patient's spiritual or religious beliefs.

It is important to understand both the social organization of the family and the patient's role in the family. Is the family patriarchal? Does the father, husband, or other male figure act as the decision maker or otherwise need to be a part of the decision-making process? Is the family intergenerational, in which case elders should be consulted, or if the patient is an elder, does she need to be protected and not told about the seriousness of an illness or injury (Carrese & Rhodes, 2000)? Will members of the extended family be present during assessment, treatment, or rehabilitation, and if so will they need to be accommodated? How will the family members react to the illness or injury? What are the patient's expectations regarding duties and obligations to the family versus to self? How does family involvement affect issues of patient confidentiality?

The athletic trainer should also ascertain whether the patient is using herbal medicines, homeopathy, complementary and alternative medicine, traditional or cultural health care practices, or a folk healer. The purpose here is to determine whether the patient is receiving care that is contraindicated by or might conflict with the care given by the athletic trainer. The athletic trainer and the patient should work together to devise a care plan that is inclusive of cultural needs. For example, the athletic trainer can ask what the patient is doing to treat her- or himself, and do so without criticizing or judging the behavior or practice. If it conflicts with the treatment that the athletic trainer wants to prescribe, he or she can ask if there is a way to modify the behavior or practice to eliminate the conflict. If the behavior or practice cannot be modified, then the athletic trainer should explain that it "would be too strong if taken/done along with your recommended medication or treatment plan" (Salimbene, 2005, p. 6) and thus should be discontinued.

In addition, the athletic trainer should determine the patient's spiritual or religious preferences. During the physical assessment, note any religious symbols or amulets that may indicate the patient's religion. Ask questions about how the patient's religious or spiritual beliefs may affect care. Also, ask patients whether he or she consulted with members of the church, synagogue, or mosque or with other religious or spiritual leaders for health diagnosis or advice—and if so, what was recommended (Salimbene, 2005). Are protective prayers or ceremonies needed before any interventions are performed (Carrese & Rhodes, 2000)? If the patient refuses to share his or her religious or spiritual beliefs, then the athletic trainer must respect the patient's right to privacy. In such cases, the athletic trainer should proceed with treatment under the assumption that the patient does not have any religious or spiritual preferences that affect care.

INSPECTING AND OBSERVING PHYSICAL SIGNS

Inspecting and observing involves looking at the patient's physical structure and body movement to help determine the extent of injury or illness. Skin assessment of patients with dark skin should be done in natural light when possible in order to ascertain the condition; it may be necessary to check mucous membranes, lips, nail beds, palms, and soles of feet for accurate assessment, particularly of jaundice in some Asians and cyanosis in some patients with dark skin. Jaundice may also be observed in African Americans as generalized yellowing of the sclera. Some patients of Mediterranean descent may have blue lips, thus giving a false indication of cyanosis (Campinha-Bacote, 2003). Pallor may present as the absence of red tones in underlying tissue—"brown skin tends to appear yellow-brown and black skin tends to appear ashen" (Salimbene, 2005, p. 40). Sometimes, erythema and ecchymosis may be detected only by palpation—the skin becomes warm to the touch, tight, and edematous in the inflamed area (Campinha-Bacote; Salimbene).

PALPATING

Palpation is a form of touching that is used to medically examine a patient. The purpose is to assess the physical signs of an injury or illness. During palpation, several cultural considerations need to be addressed: space, touch, and expressions of pain.

Space

In U.S. culture, space has been defined in terms of four interpersonal distance zones. The zones are intimate (from contact to 1.5 feet, or about 0.5 meter), personal (1.5 to 4 feet, or 0.5 to 1.2 meters), social (4 to 12 feet, or 1.2 to 3.7 meters), and public (greater than 12 feet, or 3.7 meters) (Hall, as cited in Sue & Sue, 2008). The assessment process necessarily requires the athletic trainer to enter the patient's social, personal, and intimate spaces. The greeting and oral history portions may take place in the social and personal spaces, whereas the observation, inspection, and palpation all occur in the patient's personal and intimate spaces. The athletic trainer should note the patient's level of comfort with the spatial arrangements during the greeting and the taking of the oral history. If the patient continues to lean into the athletic trainer, then he or she typically prefers a smaller distance. In contrast, a patient who steps back or leans away from the athletic trainer may need more distance. The athletic trainer must resist the urge to move away from a patient who is moving in or toward a patient who is moving out. If a patient is uncomfortable with proximity, the athletic trainer should not linger in the intimate space during palpation. To do so may make the patient feel very uncomfortable. The athletic trainer should ask permission to palpate and tell the patient what to expect.

Touch

When touching a patient during palpation, the athletic trainer should consider religious and gender issues. The patient's religious or cultural beliefs may dictate that the assessment be performed by an athletic trainer of the same sex. When a health care provider of the same sex is not available, it may be necessary to have another member of the staff or a family member be present during the assessment. When in doubt, ask the patient.

Expressions of Pain

During palpation, the health care provider may purposely elicit pain, and expressions may vary culturally. Some patients may remain stoic because they believe that emotion should be restrained or because they view pain as an inevitability or a fact of life that must be endured. Other patients may express pain emotively or even see the expression of pain as a pain-relieving act. Thus, accurately assessing pain not only involves deciphering an expression of pain but also taking into account nonverbal cues which may provide a better indication of the patient's level of pain.

SUMMARY

All patients "deserve a cultural assessment," not just those who "look" like they need one (Campinha-Bacote, 2003, p. 47). Conducting a culturally based assessment is about establishing a good rapport with the patient. It is about learning what the patient needs—not what the health care provider needs. For example, there is a "direct correlation . . . between patient satisfaction and the amount of time a physician spends with hypertensive African Americans. [Likewise, there was] . . . increased compliance with nursing interventions among Hispanic and Haitian mothers once the provider explored and demonstrated respect for the client's belief system" (Niemeier, Burnett, & Whitaker, 2003, p. 1243).

Knowledge about variations between groups does not allow one to assume that everyone in a group shares common beliefs, values, and practices. However, knowledge about variations does enhance an athletic trainer's ability to ask better questions and to focus on assessment more effectively (Schim, 2005, p. 256).

Learning Aids

What Would You Do If . . . ?

1. What if you had a patient with very dark skin and severe ecchymosis on the posterior thigh due to a third-degree hamstring strain? How would you accurately diagnose the injury?
2. What if your patient is prone to keloid formation and is scheduled for shoulder surgery. What would you tell the surgeon? What would you do to reduce postoperative scarring?

Activities

1. Develop an assessment tool to use during physical assessment to elicit cultural information from the patient.
2. How do you touch patients? What might your touch say to a patient? Try this exercise (with permission, of course). Pretend that your partner is a patient. Touch the "patient" in different ways that you think convey each of the following: (a) warmth, (b) caring, (c) a feeling that you do not want to touch him or her but have to do so. Discuss the different ways that you touched your "patient"—and how the "patient" felt or responded.

Key Terms

Define the following key terms found in this chapter:

Narrative sequencing
Saving face

Questions for Review

1. What are the components of a culturally based physical assessment?
2. What verbal and nonverbal communication cues should an athletic trainer attend to while taking an oral history? How should the verbal and nonverbal cues be addressed?
3. What social organizational factors might a health care provider need to know?
4. Explain how the patient's skin color can affect skin assessment during inspecting and observing.
5. Describe cultural considerations associated with palpating (space, touch, expressions of pain).

14

Working in a Culturally Competent Health Care Organization

Learning Objectives

Upon completing this chapter, students will be able to do the following:

1. Apply Campinha-Bacote's cultural competence model to the health care organization
2. Explain the components necessary for assessing the cultural competence of a health care organization
3. Explain the process for conducting an institutional cultural self-audit
4. Explain the process for conducting a cultural SWOT analysis and formulating a strategic plan
5. Identify steps to gain cultural knowledge of the community
6. Describe what cultural skill and cultural encounters mean in regard to the health care organization

Angela Shannon

I am a forty-something, African American, female pastor in the Evangelical Lutheran Church in America (ELCA). I currently work with a large, predominately White congregation in Fort Wayne, Indiana, where I serve as the associate pastor for mission, outreach, and evangelism. Pastoral ministry is my second career, on which I embarked after holding various positions in governmental assistance programs and in the nonprofit sector. I have worked as a family services caseworker, a child protective services caseworker, and a correctional officer. These career choices have contributed immensely to my pastoral formation.

Photo courtesy of Colette Slyby.

I was born in Gary, Indiana, which was known as a "Chocolate city" because it was predominately African American and was led by one of the nation's first African American mayors. This character of the city had tremendous implications for a young Black girl coming of age in the 1970s. African American experience was normative. Our educators and other professionals looked like me. My parents were very conscientious about self-image in the midst of the intra-color caste system that Blacks often inflicted on each other. Black in all of its expressions was beautiful to my parents and consequently to my younger brothers and me. Most of my dolls were Black—only because my Christie doll often hung out with Barbie and friends.

My upbringing gave me a sense of self-worth, loving self-acceptance, and the confidence to venture out into the world and connect with people regardless of cultural background. I would internalize the words of Jesus that direct us to love our neighbors as ourselves. I accept myself and therefore I can embrace others in kind. For a brief time, I lived in India. There, I gained a palpable understanding that there are myriad ways of being in this world. Extensive travel widens one's perspective.

I am not a health care provider. But as a pastoral caregiver, I understand that the fullness of shalom includes health, peace, and all that is needed to sustain life. I often visit members in hospitals awaiting surgery or recovering from illness. Unfortunately, many people hold to the belief that God visits them with illness for a variety of sins and other reasons. Clergypersons labor against this belief that runs counter to the gospel that seeks shalom for all humanity.

Congregants tend to ask questions of ethical responsibility in response to burgeoning advances in health care—questions that were inconceivable twenty years ago! I get questions about stem cell research, in vitro fertilization, cloning, abortion, and the like. The ELCA teaches that congregations are communities of "moral deliberation." We are to carefully discern the issues at hand in the light of the gospel of Jesus Christ.

Mourning and funeral practices point out significant cultural differences. In an Atlanta hospital where I completed a unit of clinical pastoral education, there was a "cry room" or "quiet room." I am accustomed to outward emotional expressions of grief, so in my mind the "cry room" was a place where one could go to air those feelings. Thus I thought the room was soundproof. I later found out that the "cry room" was a place where the bereaved could go to *quietly* "collect" themselves—and therefore not soundproof.

When getting to know persons from other cultures, listen more than you speak, and exercise patience and reverence. It takes time to build a trusting relationship. A dear friend held me at arm's length for nearly 2 years because she thought I was trying to convert her from Islam to Christianity. Find an interfaith or intercultural discussion group. Read books like *Multicultural Manners* and *How to Be a Perfect Stranger*. But this is not substitute for the honest encounter with one another.

It is not enough for athletic trainers to "engage in the process of becoming culturally competent" (Campinha-Bacote, 2002, 2003). Health care organizations must do the same. They should be responsive to all patients, staff, and providers and deliver culturally and linguistically competent health care services, including athletic training services. In fact, according to standard 8 of the National Standards on Culturally and Linguistically Appropriate Services (CLAS), "Health care organizations should develop, implement, and promote a written **strategic plan** that outlines clear goals, policies, operational plans, and management accountability/ oversight mechanisms to provide culturally and linguistically appropriate services" (Office of Minority Health, 2001). CLAS standard 9 states that, "Health care organizations should conduct initial and ongoing organizational self-assessments of CLAS-related activities and are encouraged to integrate cultural and linguistic competence-related measures into their internal audits, performance improvement programs, patient satisfaction assessments, and outcomes-based evaluations" (Office of Minority Health).

What does an organization need to do in order to begin addressing how it provides culturally and linguistically appropriate services? How does an organization "engage in the process of becoming culturally competent" (Campinha-Bacote, 2002, 2003)? More specifically, how do athletic training organizations and other organizations that employ athletic trainers become culturally competent? Certified athletic trainers are employed in a variety of health care organizations and settings. The top three are clinics (27 percent; includes hospital-owned clinics; outpatient, ambulatory, and rehabilitation clinics); colleges and universities (23 percent); and secondary schools (17 percent) (National Athletic Trainers' Association, 2009). Using Campinha-Bacote's model (as outlined in chapter 1), this chapter describes how an organization can assess and develop cultural desire, cultural awareness, cultural knowledge, and cultural skill, as well as engage in cultural encounters.

CULTURAL DESIRE IN THE HEALTH CARE ORGANIZATION

Cultural desire is a moral commitment (Campinha-Bacote, 2003) to providing high-quality services to all patients regardless of race, ethnicity, class, values, beliefs, or practices—even when they differ from those of the provider or organization. The organization that engages in cultural desire recognizes that all patients are part of the human race. An organization that has cultural desire genuinely cares about the patients served as the main priority—not just about the financial gain from treating the patient. Simply put, developing cultural desire in the health care and athletic training environment is about the organization's motivation in "wanting to" rather than "having to" engage in becoming culturally competent (Campinha-Bacote, 2002, 2003).

CULTURAL AWARENESS IN THE HEALTH CARE ORGANIZATION

Cultural awareness involves the process of self-assessing the organization's own biases toward certain cultures. The self-assessment involves in-depth exploration of the organization's cultural and professional background. "Cultural awareness also involves being aware of the existence of documented racism and other 'isms' in healthcare delivery" (Transcultural C.A.R.E Associates, 2010). In other words, health care organizations should evaluate what they are, or are not, doing to provide culturally competent services to their patients and staff members. To this end, Salimbene (2001) recommends gathering data about the organization by conducting an **institutional cultural self-audit**. After the self-audit, conduct a cultural SWOT analysis; that is, determine the organization's overall strengths, weaknesses, opportunities, and threats. Finally, develop a strategic plan for implementing and fostering cultural competence (Mutha, Allen, & Welch, 2002).

Conducting an Institutional Cultural Self-Audit

Multiple people in the organization, including the athletic trainer, should be involved in the cultural awareness process. For example, in hospitals or hospital-based clinics, the people involved may include the executive officers and administrators, upper- and middle-level managers, clinicians, technicians, support staff, patients, and community members. In secondary schools, the following parties may be included: central administration (e.g., school board members, superintendent), school administration (e.g., principal, athletic director), other health care providers (e.g., school nurse, psychologist, counselor), support staff, student-athletes, parents, and boosters. In colleges and universities, the people involved might include central administrators (e.g., vice presidents, student affairs personnel, affirmative action officer, diversity officer), athletics administrators (e.g., athletic director), other health care providers (e.g., health services clinicians, psychologists, counselors), faculty, support staff, athletic training students, student-athletes, parents, and boosters. The institutional cultural self-audit should be conducted from the top down, from the bottom up, and horizontally across peer employee groups. The purpose is to clarify what the organization is doing to provide culturally competent care and what areas need the most attention.

To begin the process, the organization should seek to answer the following questions related to cultural competence: Who are we as an organization? What is our vision, mission, and philosophy? What are our beliefs, attitudes, and values? What are we doing to promote cultural competence through the structure of the organization, staff recruitment and development, delivery of clinical services, administration responsibility, and leadership commitment (Mutha et al., 2002)? Table 14.1 provides a synopsis of the checklists used by Salimbene (2001) to help answer the questions.

Table 14.1 Questions for the Institutional Cultural Self-Audit

Question	Data needed	Analysis
Who are we as an organization?	Patient demographics (present*, future**) Staff demographics*** (by race or ethnicity and position: e.g., administrator, clinician, clerical, technical)	How well do staff demographics match patients served? At what employment level are most people of color employees?
What are our vision, mission, and philosophy? What are our beliefs, attitudes, and values?	Current copy of organizational vision, mission, and philosophy statements.	Are staff diversity and culturally competent care mentioned or integrated throughout? Are beliefs, attitudes, and values regarding the provision of culturally competent care mentioned or integrated throughout?
What are we doing to promote cultural competence through . . .		
Structure of the organization	Organizational chart	Is there a department or specific person assigned to promote cultural competence or diversity? If so, to whom does the person or department report? Is the person or department empowered to make decisions about policy and implementation?
Staff recruitment, retention, promotion	Human resources strategic plan Hiring policies and procedures Recruitment and retention statistics across employee groups by race or ethnicity Promotion statistics across employee groups by race or ethnicity Affirmative action goals and timetables	Is there a plan to recruit, retain, and promote diverse staff across all employment levels of the organization? Is there a plan to recruit employees who have received cultural competence training or demonstrated cultural competence? What specific strategies are being used? Are the strategies effective? Which groups are being retained or promoted? Which are not?
Staff development	Types of staff development activities offered by the organization	Do staff development activities include cultural competence and workplace diversity training? If so, how often does the training take place (e.g., one time vs. ongoing)? Which employee groups are involved in the training? Who facilitates the training?

(continued)

Table 14.1 *(continued)*

What are we doing to promote cultural competence through . . . *(continued)*		
Delivery of clinical services (Mutha, Allen, & Welch, 2002)	Policy and procedure manual or standard operating procedures associated with clinical services	Are policies and procedures germane to the diversity of the patient population? Examples of issues to consider include appropriate use of trained medical interpreters, how to work with traditional healers, and use of complementary and alternative medicine (Mutha et al.).
Administration responsibility (Mutha et al.)	Strategic plan Marketing plan Physical space (tour of the physical space)	Do strategic plans and marketing plans integrate cultural competence throughout? Is the physical space welcoming and posted with signage in languages used by the community (Mutha et al.)?
Leadership commitment (Mutha et al.)	Board- or trustee-level policies and procedures	Does the leadership support and participate in cultural competence activities? How are CLAS standards implemented?
Funding	Budget	Are there permanent line items in the budget for culturally competent services, including staffing, staff development, and clinical services?

*Estimated from patient records (race or ethnicity)
**From U.S. Census Bureau data for race and ethnicity by community
***Estimated from personnel records

Conducting a Cultural SWOT Analysis

The **cultural SWOT analysis** (figure 14.1) involves synthesizing what was learned during the institutional cultural self-audit. The written analysis should be short, simple, and as specific as possible (Marketing Teacher, 2010; Salimbene, 2001). Strengths and weakness are determined by factors internal to the organization, whereas opportunities and threats are determined by external factors.

Strengths are those areas where cultural competence is being demonstrated well. Weaknesses are the areas where cultural competence is demonstrated poorly or not at all. Opportunities include interesting trends. For example, are there changes in social patterns, population (Mind Tools, 2008), or health issues in the community served? Opportunities can also be created by eliminating weaknesses (Mind Tools). Threats include obstacles that could have dire consequences for the organization. For example, if there is an influx of immigrants to the community, or the university increases the number of international students who speak

Figure 14.1 Example of a Cultural SWOT Analysis

Strengths	Weaknesses
Vision and mission statements reflect a commitment to cultural competence.	Staff demographics are not representative of patient population.
People of color hired in the last 3 years have been retained at a rate of 70%.	Most people of color work in lower-level support staff positions.
	Cultural competence training is required only at the time of hire—no continuing staff development activities regarding cultural competence.
Opportunities	**Threats**
U.S. Census data projections include a 5% increase in Latinos and 3% increase in Middle Easterners in the community.	State appropriations are expected to decrease by 5% in the next fiscal year.
$100,000 from unfilled positions is available for use.	Patient satisfaction scores have dropped in regard to delivery of culturally competent care.

limited English, and the organization is unable to adequately communicate with potential patients, those potential patients may choose other services or choose not to seek services at all.

In another example, if a new fitness, physical therapy, or sports medicine facility opens in the community and offers the same services, then it threatens the existing organization because of increased competition for patients or clients. Other possibilities include a change in governmental regulations (e.g., Medicare, Medicaid, other insurance regulation) or a downturn in the economy, either of which could affect how the organization receives funding, as well as the patient's ability to pay for services.

The final SWOT analysis will be used to guide strategic planning. Strengths should be maintained, built upon, or leveraged. Weaknesses should be remedied. Opportunities should be prioritized and optimized, and threats need to be defended against or opposed (Decide-Guide, 2009).

Developing a Strategic Plan

Once the cultural self-audit and SWOT analysis have been conducted, the 3- or 5-year strategic plan can be written. Organizations must be responsive to the changing dynamics of the environment. Thus, for smaller or nonprofit organizations (e.g., a secondary school athletic training room), 3 years is appropriate, whereas 5 years may be more appropriate for organizations (e.g., hospitals, colleges, universities) with large service constituencies (Alliance for Nonprofit Management, 2004). The purpose of the strategic plan is to outline the long- and short-term goals (to do), lay out the strategies and timelines for achieving the goals (when), and identify the staff or department responsible for achieving the goals (by whom) (Salimbene, 2001). An example of an abbreviated strategic planning document is provided in table 14.2.

Table 14.2 Example of an Abbreviated Strategic Plan

To Do	Strategy	By Whom	When	Other Considerations
Increase staff diversity based on affirmative action goals and timetables	Post job announcements in ethnic-minority publications and Web sites Attend job fairs at colleges and universities with diverse student populations	Human resources department	2nd year of plan	
Hire director of diversity	Post job announcements in ethnic-minority publications and Web sites Contact organizations that provide cultural competence training to ask for referrals	Human resources department	1st year of plan	Funding from unfilled positions
Develop ongoing cultural competence training	Determine training needs and objectives Select mode of delivery Develop curriculum Establish training schedule for all employee groups	Staff development department in conjunction with director of diversity	2nd year of plan	
Fully implement ongoing cultural competence training	Initiate daily reminders and (bi)monthly lectures	Staff development department	4th year of plan	

Salimbene (2001) recommends that "no more than one major task or four minor tasks per year" be assigned to one person or department. The reason is that the person or department may not have sufficient time to complete the task successfully if inundated with other duties. Characteristics of major tasks include substantial budget, creation of new infrastructure, and multiple or ongoing intervention(s); they may also be considered difficult to implement. One example of a major task is the creation of a department for institutional diversity and cultural competence, for which a budget (salaries, benefits, operating expenses) and infrastructure (capital expenses, office space) could be needed. Characteristics of minor tasks, in contrast, include little expense to the organization, use of existing infrastructure, and one-time intervention; they may be considered easy to implement. A minor task might include ensuring that all job announcements are posted in publications and on Web sites that target people of color.

CULTURAL KNOWLEDGE IN THE HEALTH CARE ORGANIZATION

The focus of cultural awareness is internal to the organization, whereas the focus of cultural knowledge is external. Cultural knowledge involves the process of obtaining information on the "health-related beliefs, practices and cultural values [of the community]; disease incidence and prevalence [in the community]; treatment efficacy" (Campinha-Bacote, 2003, p. 27); and health care services needed by the community. Organizations should gather the information in order to implement a successful plan.

One way to gain cultural knowledge is by establishing partnerships in the served community that involve community members (Health Resources and Services Administration, 2001); community, religious, or culture-based organizations (Mutha et al., 2002; Salimbene, 2001); and community leaders (Mutha et al.). By involving community partners, health care organizations can identify the community's needs, assets, and barriers to care, and then work collaboratively to create appropriate responses (Health Resources and Services Administration). Possible steps include the following:

- Identifying important community members, organizations, and leaders among the patient populations served (may include parents, booster club members, student council leaders) (Salimbene, 2001)
- Making direct contact with identified individuals and organizations (Salimbene, 2001)
- Inviting identified individuals and organization representatives to serve on a community advisory council (Mutha et al., 2002), the health care organization's governing board, or other advisory boards or committees (Salimbene, 2001)
- Requesting information from community partners pertinent to each community group (see the sidebar for sample questions adapted from Salimbene, 2001)
- Participating in or sponsoring community health fairs and initiatives and school health events (Mutha et al.)
- Establishing "a 'good neighbor' policy that encourages activities such as providing meeting space for community events, serving on community committees, [and] promoting personal relationships between organization staff and [the] community" (Mutha et al., p. 159).

It is also important to gather cultural knowledge through independent reading and research. Community members and student-athletes may identify only the information that is immediately noticeable to them. In addition, they will not mention factors that are so ingrained as to pass out of conscious notice for members of the culture (and that cause the most confusion to outsiders) (Salimbene, 2005).

Gaining Cultural Knowledge from Community Partners

Health-Related Beliefs, Practices, and Cultural Values of the Community (Campinha-Bacote, 2003)

1. When a member of your community (racial or ethnic group) enters a health care facility, how does he or she want to be treated by the person at the front desk or the receptionist? How is courtesy defined or measured within this group? How is politeness measured? How does one show caring and concern?

2. How might a person wish to be addressed by an athletic trainer? Does the form of address differ for women and men; adults and children?

3. What criteria might a patient or patient's family use to rate the care received (i.e., greeted patient with appropriate title or followed cultural "rules of touching")?

4. Are there any tests, treatments, or surgeries that some members of your community (racial or ethnic group) find inappropriate?

5. Is there a language spoken and understood by all members of your community (racial or ethnic group)? If so, what is the language?

6. Are other languages spoken and understood by all members of your community (racial or ethnic group)? If so, what are the languages?

7. Can you recommend a professional interpreter of the language?

8. Is there a common language written and understood by all members of your community (racial or ethnic group)? If so, what is the language?

9. Are other languages written and understood by all members of your community (racial or ethnic group)? If so, what are the languages?

10. Can you recommend a professional who can translate the written language?

11. What is the estimated level of literacy of the racial or ethnic group? Will some members need pictorial signs?

Disease Incidence and Prevalence in the Community (Campinha-Bacote, 2003)

1. What are your community (racial, ethnic, or cultural group) members' three primary concerns related to general health, fitness, exercise, or sport?

2. How well do the members of your community (racial, ethnic, or cultural group) feel that Mountain Top Sports Medicine (fictional) addresses these concerns? (Very well, well, somewhat well, not well at all)

3. What steps might Mountain Top Sports Medicine take to better address these concerns?

4. How might Mountain Top Sports Medicine and your community (racial, ethnic, or cultural group) partner to address these concerns?

Reputation of Health Care Organization and Attracting and Retaining Patients (Salimbene, 2001)

1. In general, what is the reputation of Mountain Top Sports Medicine among members of your community?

2. How might Mountain Top Sports Medicine improve that general reputation?

3. What five qualities or criteria do members of your community (racial, ethnic, or cultural group) consider most important in choosing a health care organization?

4. How might Mountain Top Sports Medicine make the patient's visit more pleasant?

5. What are the five major reasons that members of your community (racial, ethnic, or cultural group) feel dissatisfied or leave a health care organization?

6. How can Mountain Top Sports Medicine and your community (racial, ethnic, or cultural group) partner to do the following:

   • Improve health care access
   • Improve health outcomes
   • Reduce common illnesses or epidemiological problems through educational efforts
   • Other suggestions for partnering?

CULTURAL SKILL
IN THE HEALTH CARE ORGANIZATION

According to Campinha-Bacote, "Cultural skill [during the patient–athletic trainer interaction] is the ability to collect relevant cultural data regarding the client's presenting problem, as well as accurately perform a culturally based physical assessment in a culturally sensitive manner" (2003, p. 35). On an organizational level in the health care and athletic training environment, cultural skill means collecting relevant cultural data about the patients and community served and about the athletic trainers and other health care providers who work in the environment.

These cultural data are collected in order to determine whether the organization is meeting the cultural needs of patients, community members, and employees.

For example, the organization should ask these question: Have we assessed our policies, procedures, and documents to determine whether they are appropriate for collecting relevant cultural data from the patient? Have we adequately prepared the athletic trainer or assessed the athletic trainer's ability to conduct a cultural assessment of the patient? Have we examined the physical spaces, decor, signage, and language services to determine whether they meet the patient's or community's needs and language preferences?

CULTURAL ENCOUNTERS IN THE HEALTH CARE ORGANIZATION

Cultural encounters are the basis of "the process which encourages the healthcare provider [athletic trainer] to directly engage in face-to-face interactions with clients from culturally diverse backgrounds" (Campinha-Bacote, 2003, p. 48). Within the health care organization and athletic training setting, cultural encounters mean that the organization engages in face-to-face interactions with the community. Because there is more variation within groups than across groups, cultural encounters may allow participants to experience the in-group variations. Having a better understanding and appreciation for the in-group variations may help modify participants' behaviors and beliefs and minimize stereotyping (Campinha-Bacote, 2002, 2003). We need to remember that each patient is a unique individual who may or may not subscribe to or participate in the behaviors or beliefs that would be generally attributed to group membership (Salimbene, 2001). Cultural encounters, therefore, add perspective and context for understanding a patient's uniqueness.

To assess cultural encounters, the organization should determine what types of encounters are occurring, how often, and to what degree. Regardless of whether the organization is a hospital, an outpatient rehabilitation clinic, or a university or high school athletic training room, here are several examples of the kind of questions to ask: Is the organization involved in community-led health fairs? Does the organization sponsor health fairs or clinics that address the needs of the community for particular community partners? Does the organization work with religious, social, civic, and service organizations in planning and in delivering health information? Does the leadership of the organization regularly meet, both formally and informally, with community leaders and members? Is the organization an integral partner with and part of the community?

SUMMARY

Cultural competence involves ongoing assessment and active efforts to listen to the needs of the patient and the community; it also engages them in the creation of solutions and adapts to change (Health Resources and Services Administration, 2001). It is important to understand how the assessment process is tied to cultural desire, cultural awareness, cultural knowledge, cultural skill, and cultural encounters. For example, the cultural self-audit, SWOT analysis, and strategic plan help the organization look internally to examine current practices and organizational structure in order to make meaningful decisions that are responsive to environmental changes. Gaining cultural knowledge from and about the community, on the other hand, allows the organization to look externally in order to determine needs of the community as defined by the community. When an organization determines how well it provides cultural services and engages with the patient and community, it positions itself to become an integral partner in the community. Cultural competence is about providing high-quality services to all patients, and assessing the organization's services is a critical step.

Learning Aids

What Would You Do If . . . ?

1. What if you were the athletic trainer at a high school whose demographics shifted to include an influx of people from a culture with which you are unfamiliar, such as Middle Easterners of Chaldean descent?
2. What if you were asked to develop the cultural competence initiatives for the local urgent care facility? How would you proceed?

Activities

1. Develop a vision and mission statement that addresses cultural competence in terms of organizational philosophy, clinical care, language services, staffing, administration, and leadership.
2. Using the information provided in this chapter, visit a health care setting on your campus or wherever you provide clinical services (e.g., doctor's office, athletic training room, hospital unit, wellness center, university health service) and conduct an institutional cultural self-audit. Meet with health care providers, administrators, and (where possible) patients in order to complete the audit.
3. Using the information gained in your institutional cultural self-audit, conduct a cultural SWOT analysis.
4. Using your cultural SWOT analysis, develop a mini strategic plan.
5. Using the questions in the sidebar on pages 260-261, interview two community leaders or members in order to gain cultural knowledge.
6. Using the cultural knowledge you gained from your interviews, develop a mini strategic plan for addressing this new information in the organization's planning and operations.

Key Terms

Define the following key terms found in this chapter:

Cultural SWOT analysis   Institutional cultural self-audit   Strategic plan

Questions for Review

1. Define cultural desire, cultural awareness, cultural knowledge, cultural skill, and cultural encounters within the context of a health care organization.
2. What is an institutional cultural self-audit?
3. Describe the cultural SWOT analysis.

Appendix

Common Illnesses
and Conditions

Some of the illnesses and conditions discussed in the book is listed here along with a brief description. Nongenetic illnesses may be common only in the home country and in first-generation immigrants to the United States.

ALCOHOLISM (AMERICAN INDIANS, IRISH, NATIVE ALASKANS)

Alcoholism is addiction to alcohol. One faces increased risk of alcoholism if a family member has addiction; there may be a genetic link to alcoholism.

A person who is becoming an alcoholic will drink to excess with or without a particular reason or occasion and may hide alcohol. When the person stops drinking, withdrawal symptoms occur. As the disease progresses, the person will need to drink more and more in order to get the same effect from alcohol.

Drinking in excess may be a risk factor, as is having blackouts, which occur when a person drinks enough that, despite being conscious, he or she does not remember a period of time.

Treatment can be inpatient or outpatient. It usually requires the support of a physician because withdrawal can cause nausea, chills, sweating, and seizure and can even be life threatening. Native Americans have the highest number of years of potential life lost due to use of alcohol (Centers for Disease Control and Prevention, 1985).

AMOEBIC DYSENTERY (MEXICANS)

Entamoeba histolytica causes infection of the intestine. The amoebas enter the body through contaminated water or food (or by means of unwashed hands that have been in contact with infected feces), then infect the intestine.

This form of dysentery causes intestinal bleeding, stomach cramps, dehydration, and diarrhea. The amoebas burrow through the intestine and can get into the bloodstream; from there, they can attack any organ and cause serious consequences.

Diagnosis is made through examination of the feces, and treatment involves a course of antibiotics. About 10 percent of Mexicans are infected with amoebas (Medindia, 2008).

ANEMIA (VIETNAMESE)

The anemia that most often effects Vietnamese people is iron deficiency. Prevention involves eating red meat or taking iron pills.

ARTHRITIS (FILIPINOS)

Arthritis is an inflammation of the joints that may be caused by injury or old age. The articular cartilage is damaged, and ultimately the bones rub against each other without a cushion. Signs and symptoms include swelling, redness, pain, and stiffness.

Many Filipinos believe that using yoga will keep a person flexible and ease the pain of arthritis; they may also believe that use of hot or cold packs provides relief.

ASTHMA (PUERTO RICANS)

An asthma attack involves narrowing of the air passages, thus making it difficult to breathe. The cause of asthma is unknown; attacks arise in many situations. For some people, an attack can be initiated by an irritant, such as smoke, cold air, medication, exercise, or dust.

During an asthma attack, the sufferer may wheeze, cough, and experience anxiety, shortness of breath, and chest tightness. It is possible to treat the attack by having the person sit up, breathe humidified air, use his or her medication, and get to a physician. Prevention consists of removing the irritant and taking medication.

BIRTHMARKS (AFRICAN AMERICANS)

Birthmarks are more prevalent among African Americans. The causes of birthmarks are unknown; possibilities include genetics and cellular damage during the fetal stage. It is possible to remove birthmarks with lasers or via surgery. They come in several varieties. Port-wine stains, which are permanent, are made of dilated blood capillaries; these birthmarks are usually large. Salmon patches, caused by blood vessels, tend to be small and are usually found on the head and back. A hemangioma, caused by blood vessels near the skin, may develop over time and may disappear as the child gets older.

BLOUNT'S DISEASE (AFRICAN AMERICANS)

Orthopedic health care providers have heard of Blount's disease, which is actually a condition—specifically, bowleggedness. It is also known as tibia vara, because the medial side of the tibia stops growing while the lateral side continues. As this condition progresses, the patient will become unable to touch the knees together in the middle. The cause of this condition is unknown, but MedlinePlus, 2008 indicates the cause may be attributed to a child walking too early or being overweight. Treatment involves surgical intervention to remove a portion of the tibia so that the knee joint surface aligns correctively.

BOUFÉE DELIRANTE (HAITIANS, SUB-SAHARANS)

This condition consists of a sudden outburst of agitated and aggressive behavior, marked confusion, and psychomotor excitement. It may sometimes be accompanied by visual and auditory hallucinations or paranoid ideation.

The episode resembles a psychotic disorder. This is a cultural-bound syndrome most commonly found among Haitians. The cause is stress or postpartum depression (Windmill Perception, 2009). The episode lasts about one day and is treated with medication.

BRAIN FAG OR BRAIN FOG (SUB-SAHARAN AFRICANS)

This condition is experienced by high school and university students. Symptoms include difficulty in concentrating, remembering, and thinking. Additional symptoms center on the head and neck and include pain, pressure, tightness, blurring of vision, heat, or burning. The experience may be described by sufferers as brain "fatigue." Brain fag is treated with medication (Morakinyo, 2002).

BREAST CANCER (GERMANS)

Breast cancer can be caused by external factors or by factors that cannot be controlled. Risk factors include family history, being overweight, being Caucasian, exposure to radiation, high-fat diet, incidence increases with age, hormone replacement, use of birth control pills, and early onset of menstruation.

The most common signs of a cancerous tumor are discharge from the nipple, palpation of a tumor, redness of the breast, or a change in the contour of the breast. If a lump or discharge is noticed, one should seek the assistance of a physician. In some instances, a doctor may recommend waiting to go through another menstrual cycle to help determine if the lump is related to the cycle before doing a biopsy or other intervention.

If a women has breast cancer, the physician will decide what kind of treatment is necessary. In most instances, treatment will include surgery to remove the tumor and the primary lymph node; it may also involve chemotherapy and radiation.

Being proactive and doing monthly breast self-examinations can help catch a cancerous tumor in the early stages. Women should also have mammograms once a year. Prevention includes eating a high-fiber diet, avoiding fatty foods, and taking flaxseed oil.

CANCER (PUERTO RICANS)

Malignant neoplasm is another name for cancer. Puerto Ricans have a higher incidence of cancer. Puerto Ricans are modest and may not seek preventative health care (Lipson, et. al, 1996) or care in enough time to prevent the cancer from spreading.

CERVICAL CANCER (VIETNAMESE)

Vietnamese women are more prone to cervical cancer because they do not practice preventive annual examination, and even when cervical cancer is found the afflicted woman sometimes fails to appear for follow-up for treatment. Modesty impacts the lack of early diagnosis of cervical cancer. Having unprotected sex makes one more prone to cervical cancer. It has been reported that 55 percent of sexually active, unmarried Vietnamese women have unprotected sex (Centers for Disease Control and Prevention, 2007c).

CHOLERA (HAITIANS, IRANIANS, VIETNAMESE)

Cholera is caused by the bacteria Vibrio cholerae. The infection occurs when a person consumes food or water infected with the bacteria, which infect the intestine and cause diarrhea, vomiting, and leg cramps. If left untreated, the diarrhea causes dehydration and shock.

Improperly handled sewage and drinking water treatment increases the risk of cholera. The bacteria is carried in feces of the infected person.

Treatment involves rehydration, and the best combination is water with salt and sugar. Antibiotics can also be used to reduce the symptoms.

To prevent cholera, a person should drink only boiled or chlorine-treated water and eat only foods that have been thoroughly cooked. There is also a cholera vaccination. Cholera has been found in Africa, Asia, and Eastern Europe. The 35 cases found in the United States all involved travelers from foreign countries (Centers for Disease Control and Prevention, 2005).

CHORIOCARCINOMA (VIETNAMESE)

Choriocarcinoma is cancer of the placenta. It spreads to the lungs, kidneys, and brain. There is a high rate of cure through chemotherapy, but this cancer is almost always fatal once it has spread to the kidneys or brain.

CIRRHOSIS OF THE LIVER (AFRICAN AMERICANS, NATIVE ALASKANS)

Cirrhosis of the liver is most often caused by hepatitis and excessive use of alcohol. Common signs and symptoms include weight loss, abdominal pain, fatigue, and loss of appetite. If the cause is alcoholism, the drinking must stop. If it is hepatitis, medication is necessary. In severe cases, a liver transplant may be the only possible treatment.

COCCIDIOIDOMYCOSIS (AFRICAN AMERICANS, CHINESE, CUBANS, PUERTO RICANS)

This illness is caused by the fungus Coccidioides immitis. The Coccidioides immitis fungus is transmitted via the inhalation of fungus spores. Fungus spores are common to desert areas and inhalation is more common among those having an occupation that exposes one to dust. The incubation period is at least 7 days. Some people show no signs or symptoms and go untreated as the illness resolves without a problem. An acute form can be resolved through use of antifungal medication.

In some instances, a person can develop a lung infection (chronic pulmonary coccidioidomycosis). Signs include coughing, bloody sputum, muscle soreness, headache, and fever. If chronic pulmonary coccidioidomycosis is left untreated, the infection can spread to other organs (MedlinePlus, 2009a). This illness is not common in the United States, and only first-generation immigrants are likely to show signs of coccidioidomycosis.

CYSTIC FIBROSIS (GERMANS, ENGLISH)

Cystic fibrosis is more common among those with a family history of the illness and those of white European background. It is a genetically inherited disease in which a defective gene alters the body's ability to move salt in and out of cells. The lungs accumulate fluids, which causes the tissue to stick together and makes breathing difficult.

The first signs and symptoms of cystic fibrosis occur at birth. The baby will have wheezing or coughing along with foul-smelling feces. The infant's skin will also be salty.

Treatment of cystic fibrosis includes using medication to reduce fluid in the lungs. Antibiotics are used for infections. Sometimes breathing becomes so difficult that the lungs must be drained. In the most extreme cases, a lung transplant is needed.

DENGUE (HAITIANS, MEXICANS, PUERTO RICANS, VIETNAMESE)

Dengue is caused by a virus transmitted by mosquitoes. Signs and symptoms include fever, rash, headache, vomiting, enlarged lymph glands, and muscle aches. Treatment of dengue involves taking fluid for rehydration. Additional treatments target the symptoms. Prevention involves wearing clothing to protect against bites and implementing spraying programs that kill mosquitoes. Dengue is endemic in Africa, Asia, the Caribbean, and the South Pacific (Centers for Disease Control and Prevention, 2010a). First-time immigrants are the most likely to have dengue.

TYPE 1 DIABETES (AMERICAN INDIANS, FILIPINOS, HAITIANS, MEXICANS, PUERTO RICANS)

Type 1 diabetes is caused by lack of circulating insulin produced by the pancreas. Insulin is a hormone that decreases the amount of sugar in the bloodstream. Signs and symptoms of type 1 diabetes include thirst, excessive urination, and weight loss.

In Filipinos, diabetes may be traced to their carbohydrate-based diet. Treatment usually focuses on resolving symptoms rather than attempting to cure the disease. Treatment is based upon the severity of the illness. In many cases the patient will need insulin and learn how to control their diet, which should be low in carbohydrates.

Treatment for type 1 diabetes includes injections of insulin and changes in diet. Treatment depends on the cause and severity of the disease. Cases that are severe or left untreated can lead to poor circulation, blindness, decreased function of kidneys, heart disease, and poor healing. Those who have type 1 diabetes and those with type 2 who have trouble controlling their blood sugar with diet and exercise alone require insulin shots or oral hypoglycemic medication.

TYPE 2 DIABETES (AFRICAN AMERICANS, NATIVE ALASKANS)

Type 2 diabetes is found most often in adulthood. This form of diabetes is related to insulin resistance. It is characterized by increased frequency of urination, fatigue, slow healing time, and possible visual impairment (MedlinePlus, 2009b). It is diagnosed through a fasting test in which the patient drinks a high-carbohydrate beverage, then undergoes a blood test to determine how quickly the blood glucose level returns to normal. If it stays high, then diabetes is suspected. Treatment normally involves exercise, weight loss, and a change in diet. The revised diet generally consists of foods that take a long time to process, such as meat, high-fiber grains, and nonstarchy vegetables. People with diabetes are encouraged to limit their intake of food that has simple carbohydrate (i.e., starchy or sugary foods) and little nutritional value, such as cake, pie, white bread, white rice, french fries and other fried foods, and candy.

DUBIN-JOHNSON SYNDROME (ARAB-COLLECTIVE MIDDLE EASTERNERS, IRANIANS)

Dubin-Johnson syndrome is a genetic disorder that must be inherited from both parents. It is caused by failure to process bilirubin (a product of red blood cells) out of the body. The resulting buildup of bilirubin causes jaundice (yellowing skin and conjunctiva) (MedlinePlus, 2006a).

Diagnosis is made by testing the bilirubin via a urine test and a liver biopsy. Treatment is necessary only when jaundice becomes worse or other illnesses exacerbate the syndrome (MedlinePlus, 2006a). This syndrome is found most often among Iranian Jews and the Japanese (PatientPlus, 2006).

DUPUYTREN'S DISEASE (GERMANS)

Dupuytren's disease is a thickening of the tissue of the palm of the hand, which causes the fingers to stay flexed. Northern Europeans are the most likely to have Dupuytren's disease. The cause is not known. A lump generally develops first at the base of the ring finger (Penn State, 2006).

Since there is no known cause, preventing the disease is not possible at this time. Surgical intervention can be done to release the contraction of the fingers.

DYGGVE-MELCHIOR-CLAUSEN SYNDROME (ARAB-COLLECTIVE MIDDLE EASTERNERS)

Dyggve-Melchior-Clausen syndrome is a genetic disorder that results in mental retardation and abnormal skeletal development (Cigna, 2005).

DYSENTERY (SUB-SAHARAN AFRICANS, MEXICANS, IRANIANS, VIETNAMESE)

Dysentery is a sign of an intestinal tract infection or a parasite. Signs and symptoms include bloody stool, abdominal cramping, weight loss, and high fever. Dysentery is transferred from one person to another through contact with feces. In some instances, feces get into the food chain or water supply; foods grown with tainted water become infected. An entire village can get dysentery by drinking contaminated water or food.

Treatment involves rehydrating the ill person and determining the nature of the intestinal infection or parasite; then antibiotics or other medications can be given to stop the diarrhea. Once the source of the dysentery is found, it (food, water) needs to be treated to prevent further contamination.

EAR ANOMALIES (AMERICAN INDIANS)

Navajos are more likely to have ear anomalies. The Children's Health System (2007) reports that more males than females have ear anomalies and that the anomaly is more likely to be on the right side. The anomaly may mean the absence of the external ear or a mild form of lop ear, in which the outside rim of the external ear is tightened down upon itself. Ear anomalies can be addressed through surgery.

EPILEPSY (AFRICAN AMERICANS, IRANIANS)

Iranians are prone to epilepsy from genetics rather than from the other possible causes (head injury, high fever, reaction to medication). The epileptic shaking of the body is known as a seizure. Some seizures result in nothing more than a vacant stare, while in other cases the body may shake for several minutes. Treatment involves medications (HealthScout, 2001a).

FALLING OUT (AFRICAN AMERICANS)

Falling out is a response to hearing shocking news. The affected person collapses and continues to hear but cannot speak and may suffer hysterical blindness. This is a mental disorder.

FAMILIAL HYPERCHOLESTEROLEMIA (ARAB-COLLECTIVE MIDDLE EASTERNERS)

This disease is inherited (MEDPED, 2005), and the person who has it will not know this unless his or her cholesterol is tested. High cholesterol causes a higher incidence of heart attack, cardiac arrest, transient ischemic attack, and stroke (MEDPED).

Diagnosis may result from investigating the premature death of a parent and then testing the offspring. It is unfortunate that many who have this disease go untreated simply because they do not know they have it. Treatment involves medication and diet modification.

FAMILIAL MEDITERRANEAN FEVER (ARAB-COLLECTIVE MIDDLE EASTERNERS)

This inherited disorder commonly occurs in persons of Jewish, Arab, Armenian, and Turkish heritage (National Center for Biotechnology Information, 2007a). It is inherited when both parents carry the gene. The most common symptoms are abdominal pain (which may include peritonitis), enlarged joints, rash, and high fever (National Center for Biotechnology Information). Diagnosis is most commonly made over time after repeated flare-ups. The physician will run blood tests that check for elevated white blood cell counts. Treatment involves anti-inflammatory and gout medications.

GASTROINTESTINAL DYSENTERY (IRANIANS)

Gastrointestinal dysentery is an inflammation of the intestines, especially the large colon. It may be caused by a parasite, bacteria, or protozoa. It causes dehydration, and it is important for the affected person to drink plenty of fluids, especially water. Specific treatment depends upon the cause, but antibiotics will be used.

GHOST SICKNESS (AMERICAN INDIANS)

This condition involves a preoccupation with death and the deceased; it is sometimes associated with witchcraft, meaning someone has inflicted this condition upon the person (McCajor Hall, 1998). Symptoms may include bad dreams, weakness, feelings of danger, loss of appetite, fainting, dizziness, fear, anxiety, hallucination, loss of consciousness, confusion, feelings of futility, and a sense of suffocation (McCajor Hall, 1998).

GINGIVITIS (CUBANS)

Gingivitis involves inflammation of the gums. Affected gums bleed easily and may be bright red, and the person's teeth may have visible plaque buildup. To prevent gingivitis, a patient must brush after every meal, avoid sweets, and floss daily. If the condition persists, it can progress to periodontitis.

Risk factors include diabetes, smoking, and hormone change (as a result of puberty, menopause, or pregnancy). During times of hormonal change, one should be encouraged to stay on top of dental care. It is good preventive care to have one's teeth cleaned twice a year.

GLUCOSE-6-PHOSPHATE DEHYDROGENASE DEFICIENCY (BLACKS, CHINESE, FILIPINOS)

Glucose-6-phosphate dehydrogenase deficiency (G6PD) is an enzyme deficiency that results in the destruction of the red blood cells, thus creating anemia (MedlinePlus, 2007b). It is an X-linked recessive genetic disorder that is typically found among males. Some foods, drugs, and illnesses can cause a person with G6PD to have an anemic reaction and jaundice (Carter & Gross, 2005). This disorder is found among those from Africa, the Middle East, and Asia. In the United States, 10 to 14 percent of Blacks are affected by G6PD (Matsui, 2007).

Diagnosis is made by means of a red blood cell count and a check of liver enzymes. Recommended treatment is to avoid broad bean and drugs that cause oxidative reactions (Carter & Gross, 2005).

GOUT (FILIPINOS)

This disorder causes crystallization of uric acid in muscles. These deposits can affect the joints, causing inflammation or arthritis. If the gout goes untreated or is not cared for properly, it can lead to kidney stones, kidney failure, and arthritis. Gout is normally an inherited disorder in which the body fails to properly process uric acid, though an elevated level of uric acid in the blood, called hyperuricemia, does not mean that a person will necessarily develop gout. Filipinos are more prone to hyperuricemia.

HEART DISEASE (AMERICAN INDIANS, CUBANS, ENGLISH, GERMANS, IRISH, MEXICANS, NATIVE ALASKANS)

Heart disease refers to a number of diseases of the heart, including coronary artery disease, irregular heartbeat, and valve disorders. It can involve high blood pressure, buildup of plaque inside the blood vessels, or a decrease in oxygen supply to the heart. It can be caused by high cholesterol, genetics, smoking, lack of exercise, being overweight, and diabetes.

Diagnosis of heart disease depends upon the cause of the problem. High cholesterol is to be treated with medication to reduce the person's cholesterol level. If smoking is part of the problem, smoking cessation will be recommended. Overweight persons will be placed on a plan of exercise. Dietary changes are important in decreasing cholesterol and controlling diabetes. Blood thinners may be necessary, as well as medication for high blood pressure.

A doctor may perform angioplasty by inserting a thin plastic tube into the arteries around the heart to identify any blockages; if so, a stint may be placed inside a partially closed artery to allow blood to flow properly. If the heart is not protected via medication, or if the heart disease is not discovered, the first sign may be a heart attack or even a cardiac arrest.

HEPATITIS A (ARAB-COLLECTIVE MIDDLE EASTERNERS)

Hepatitis A is caused by the hepatovirus and infects the liver. Transmission of the virus goes from fecal matter to the mouth, usually by way of infected food or water (WebMD, 2005-10). The body makes antibodies against hepatitis A, and one can take a series of shots as a preventive. Those at higher risk for hepatitis A include intravenous drug abusers, international travelers, and non-monogamous gay sex participants.

HEPATITIS B (ARAB-COLLECTIVE MIDDLE EASTERNERS, CHINESE, FILIPINOS, HAITIANS, SUB-SAHARAN AFRICANS, VIETNAMESE)

Each of these countries or cultures has a hepatitis B prevalence of at least 2 percent (Centers for Disease Control and Prevention, 2006b). "Hepatitis B virus (HBV) causes an infection of the liver. The HBV tends to persist in the blood of the infected patient and can be transmitted by [means of] contact with [the] infected blood, including dried blood. Those who are infected with HBV have it for a lifetime and are more prone to cirrhosis (liver disease)—they may feel tired and nauseated and experience a lack of desire for food. Some infected individuals may be carriers of the disease . . . [without being ill] themselves. . . . The signs and symptoms of hepatitis B are not unlike those of a cold or flu. The patient will have signs of jaundice—yellowing of the skin and sclera. Immediate medical attention is critical to control the damage from hepatitis B. It is possible to result in chronic problems and possibly die" (Cartwright & Pitney, 2005).

"The good news is that hepatitis B is totally preventable through a series of shots. Because healthcare providers are in contact with blood on a regular basis, they should consider receiving the shots. Exposure to this condition can be limited by observing the universal precautions" (Cartwright & Pitney, 2005). Universal precautions include wearing a barrier such as latex gloves, a mask, and eyewear when working with bodily fluids.

HEREDITARY HEMOCHROMATOSIS (GERMANS)

This inherited disorder involves absorption of iron into the body, and excess iron deposits cause disease in various internal organs. In the liver, the disorder causes cirrhosis or even cancer (National Center for Biotechnology Information, 2007b). Pancreatic deposits can lead to diabetes, and the lungs can become hypertensive from iron overload. Treatment is to reduce the intake of iron-rich foods. This disorder is most common among Caucasians.

HIV/AIDS (AFRICAN AMERICANS, HAITIANS, MEXICANS, PUERTO RICANS, SUB-SAHARAN AFRICANS)

Acquired immunodeficiency syndrome (AIDS) is characterized by weight loss, easy bruising, lung infections, and damage to the immune system. When the immune system fails, opportunistic infections can lead to life-threatening situations.

The human immunodeficiency virus (HIV) can lead to AIDS. It can be transferred via ejaculate, vaginal secretions, breast milk, and blood. People who know they carry HIV should not have unprotected sex, share needles, or breastfeed newborns. HIV can be treated with antiviral medication; however, there is no cure. AIDS is a pandemic in Africa.

HOOKWORM (IRANIANS)

Hookworms are parasites that are about half an inch (about 1.25 centimeters) long. They invade the body by burrowing through the skin, then moving into the bloodstream. From there, they go to the lungs and cause coughing; eventually, they go into the intestinal tract and multiply. Antibiotic treatment is used to resolve the issue.

HYPERCHOLESTEROLEMIA (FILIPINOS)

Hypercholesterolemia literally means "high cholesterol in the bloodstream." Cholesterol is a waxy substance made in the body or ingested in food. High-cholesterol foods include shellfish, red meat, dairy, and egg yolk.

Cholesterol is used in making hormones and aids in the digestion of dietary fat. However, it can build up within blood vessels, and a blocked vessel can cause a heart attack or stroke. Prevention involves controlling one's level of cholesterol through diet and medication. A person with hypercholesterolemia should avoid eating foods that are high in cholesterol. Cooked Filipino food is generally very high in cholesterol.

HYPERTENSION (CHINESE, FILIPINOS, HAITIANS, IRANIANS, MEXICANS, PUERTO RICANS)

Hypertension is also known as high blood pressure. There is no known cause for primary hypertension; it may be related to one's genetics. Another form of hypertension can be caused by kidney damage or over-the-counter medication. Blood pressure is considered high at a level of 160 over 100 (Mayo Clinic, 2007). Increasing age can bring a gradual increase in blood pressure. Treatment involves dietary changes (in particular, avoiding salt) and medication.

INTESTINAL PARASITES (MEXICANS, PUERTO RICANS)

Intestinal parasites infect the intestine when introduced into humans. Most often, they enter the body through the mouth on food or through poor hygiene (e.g, not washing ones hands) that allows fecal contamination. The typical parasites are worms or protozoans (single-celled parasites). They cause diarrhea, gas, bloating, cramping, and diarrhea. If the infection becomes more serious, the parasites can travel to other parts of the body and cause coughing, vomiting, and bloody stools (University of Maryland, 2009)

Diagnosis is done through examination of feces. Treatment involves the use of antibiotics effective against the form of parasite that is found.

JAPANESE ENCEPHALITIS (VIETNAMESE)

Japanese encephalitis is a viral disorder that affects the central nervous system. Most often found in rural areas, it is carried by mosquitoes from person to person and thus occurs with higher incidence during the spring and summer when mosquitoes are around. Japanese encephalitis is found in Asia, which experiences thirty to fifty thousand annual cases (Centers for Disease Control and Prevention, 2003).

Common signs and symptoms include fever, chills, confusion, headache, and vomiting. It takes about a week after a mosquito bite for signs to occur. Diagnosis usually involves a blood test. The disorder can be fatal or cause brain damage and paralysis.

Prevention includes programs to eliminate standing water and treatments to kill mosquitoes to contain the spread of the disease. Treatment is symptomatic.

KELOID FORMATION (AFRICAN AMERICANS, SUB-SAHARAN AFRICANS)

Keloid is an overgrowth of scar tissue usually occurring after surgery, rash, acne, or vaccination. The keloid continues to grow even after the injury has healed. The keloid skin formation is thicker than unaffected skin and may be shiny. There are no preventive measures other than to avoid injury to the skin. Keloid formation is more prevalent among African Americans and sub-Saharans.

KIDNEY STONES (FILIPINOS)

Kidney stones are formed in the kidneys and are generally caused by decreased urine and or an increase in stone-forming minerals (Medicinenet.com, 2010). Some conditions can increase a person's chance of having kidney stones, including gout, high calcium in the urine, diabetes, kidney disease, and high blood pressure (Medicinenet.com, 2010).

A person who has kidney stones can experience blood in their urine and severe pain in the abdomen, the side of the abdomen, or the groin (Medicinenet.com, 2010).

Kidney stones are treated by allowing them to pass in urine. Increasing hydration is important to increase the likelihood that the stone will pass naturally in urine. Pain medication can provide comfort. If the stone is too large or will not exit naturally, then lithotripsy (shock waves to break up the stone) or surgery are used (Medicinenet.com, 2010).

LACTOSE INTOLERANCE (AFRICAN AMERICANS, CHINESE, CUBANS, FILIPINOS, MEXICANS, NATIVE ALASKANS, VIETNAMESE)

Lactose intolerance involves an inability to digest lactose, which is a sugar found in milk and milk products. Intolerance to lactose can appear at birth or over time. Lactose is broken down for use in the body by the enzyme lactase, which is produced in the small intestine. A person who is deficient in the enzyme is lactose intolerant and experiences bloating, indigestion, and gas upon ingesting lactose.

The people primarily predisposed to lactose intolerance are Africans, Native Americans, and Asians. Prevention and treatment entail either avoiding milk-based products (e.g., cheese, milk, ice cream) or taking an over-the-counter lactose enzyme supplement before eating them. One can also eat soybean products as an alternative.

LEUKOEDEMA (AFRICAN AMERICANS)

Leukoedema is a white or gray discoloration of the mucosa of the mouth. When the oral mucosa is stretched, the normal color returns. This is not a disease or disorder but a normal variation found in Blacks. There is no need for treatment.

LUNG CANCER (IRISH)

The Irish have a higher number of smokers in their culture making them, as a people, more prone to lung cancer; secondhand smoke also causes lung cancer. Another cause involves inhalation of toxins such as radon or asbestos (Irish Cancer Society, 2010).

Signs and symptoms include persistent cough, coughing up of blood, wheezing, breathing difficulty, and repeated lung infections. Diagnosis can be made via a CAT scan or lung biopsy.

Treatment may include surgery, chemotherapy, and radiation. There is a belief that lung cancer can be prevented by not smoking, stopping smoking, avoiding secondhand smoke, checking for radon, eating fruits and vegetables, exercising, and protecting oneself from toxic chemicals (Mayo Clinic, 2010).

LYME DISEASE (GERMANS)

White Europeans are more likely to get Lyme disease, which is a bacterial illness transmitted by the deer tick. In order to transfer the disease, the tick, which is small, must stay attached to the person for at least half a day.

Signs and symptoms include rash, chills, nausea, headache, joint pain and stiffness, swollen lymph nodes, and a red spot at the area of the bite. If the disease is caught in its early stages, antibiotics can be used to resolve it. If not, however, complications can include memory loss, heart arrhythmias, fatigue, paralysis, inflammation of the brain, arthritis, and nerve abnormalities.

Prevention entails wearing long pants and insect repellent when walking in tall grasses, checking oneself for ticks after being outdoors, and, if a tick is found, remove it with tweezers.

MALARIA (ARAB-COLLECTIVE MIDDLE EASTERNERS, FILIPINOS, HAITIANS, IRANIANS, MEXICANS, SUB-SAHARAN AFRICANS, VIETNAMESE)

Malaria is an infectious disease caused by a parasite that is spread by mosquitoes. The parasites grow inside of the infected person's red blood cells. Symptoms include high temperature, chills, vomiting, and anemia (Centers for Disease Control and Prevention, 2010b). Diagnosis is done by means of a blood test. Treatment involves antimalarial drugs (Centers for Disease Control and Prevention, 2009).

Malaria is found primarily in Africa, Asia, and the Middle East. It is endemic in several islands of the Philippines, and prophylactic medications are highly recommended before traveling to these areas.

Malaria is not common in the United States and is found here only in persons who have traveled to countries with the disease. Sub-Saharan African travel accounts for 62 percent of U.S. cases, whereas 19 percent of U.S. cases come from Asian countries and 16 percent from Central and South America (Centers for Disease Control and Prevention, 2009).

To reduce the spread of malaria, one must reduce the contact between mosquitoes and people. The primary prevention techniques involve use of netting and insecticides.

MAL DE PELEA (PUERTO RICANS)

This condition involves a dissociative episode characterized by a period of brooding followed by an outburst of aggressive, destructive, violent, or even homicidal behavior (McCajor Hall, 1998). The treatment of mal de pelea is a referral to a mental health professional. Once the medical professional confirms the symptoms, then medication and mental health therapy can be used for treatment (Saint Martin, 1999).

MALI-MALI OR SILOK (FILIPINOS)

This condition, which goes by either name listed here, involves hypersensitivity to sudden fright; it often involves repetitive movements, repetititive vocalization (not words), command obedience, and dissociative or trancelike behavior (Saint Martin, 1999). Treatment consists of medication.

MALNUTRITION (SUB-SAHARAN AFRICANS, VIETNAMESE)

Malnutrition is caused by not having food, not eating the proper food, or eating an unbalanced diet. Malnutrition is likely in areas where food is not available. Contributing factors can include natural disaster and war. Likely results include decreased skinfold fat and, in children, stunted growth.

If malnutrition goes on for a long time, organs can be damaged. Signs and symptoms include weight loss, abdominal swelling, fatigue, swollen eyelids, retention of water, lack of desire to eat, dry skin, and brittle hair.

Treatment of a mild form of malnutrition includes gradual increase of food and vitamins. A person who is suffering from severe malnutrition may need intravenous food support and hospitalization.

MEDITERRANEAN GLUCOSE-6-PHOSPHATE DEHYDROGENASE DEFICIENCY (ARAB-COLLECTIVE MIDDLE EASTERNERS, IRANIANS)

This enzyme deficiency destroys red blood cells, thus resulting in anemia (MedlinePlus, 2007b). It is an X-linked recessive genetic disorder typically found in males. Those most likely to have G6PD include Sephardic Jews (who originated in Spain) and Middle Eastern Kurds (MedlinePlus, 2007b). Some foods, drugs, and illnesses can cause destruction of red blood cells, which can exacerbate the intensity of the illness (MedlinePlus, 2007b).

Diagnosis is made based on red blood cell count and a check of liver enzymes. Treatment involves avoiding the food and drugs that instigate incidences in people with G6PD.

MENINGITIS—VIRAL AND BACTERIAL (IRANIANS)

Meningitis is inflammation of the fluid surrounding the brain and spinal cord; it can be viral or bacterial. Viral meningitis is the less serious of the two illnesses and resolves without medical intervention. Bacterial meningitis is severe. It is treated with antibiotics; if left untreated, bacterial meningitis can result in brain damage or death. The illness is spread through saliva and can be transmitted during a cough or a kiss. Typical signs and symptoms include high fever, headache, and a sore neck.

METHEMOGLOBINEMIA (NATIVE ALASKANS)

Methemoglobinemia is a blood disorder. Methemoglobin is a portion of the blood that does not carry oxygen. It is formed when hemoglobin, which carries oxygen, is oxidized. When a person has methemoglobinemia, his or her blood does not carry as much oxygen as necessary. As a result, the person's skin tone will be bluish (MedlinePlus, 2009c). This disorder can be caused genetically or by medication side effects; treatment is based on the cause. Oxygen therapy is necessary to support care.

MYOTONIC MUSCULAR DYSTROPHY (GERMANS)

This inherited disorder occurs most commonly in Caucasians of German decent. Signs and symptoms can arise shortly after birth or as late as adulthood. They include weakness of facial muscles, drooping eyelids, muscle loss in the forearms and lower legs, heart arrhythmias, cataracts, constipation, insulin resistance, low motivation, low IQ, balding, skin disorders, and cataracts (Penn State, 2004).

Because there is no cure, treatment is symptomatic. Surgery may be required to correct heart conditions, and physical therapy may be needed to improve range of motion and strength. Genetic testing can help determine the possibility that a person might transfer the defective gene.

NAVAJO NEUROPATHY (AMERICAN INDIANS)

Navajo neuropathy is a genetically inherited disease found in children. Clinical signs and symptoms include sensory loss for temperature and pain, inability to tolerate heat, inability to sweat normally, failure to thrive, short stature, inability to fight infection, and corneal ulcerations. Fractures can occur without pain. Sufferers often die within the first 10 years of life (Wrong Diagnosis, 2010).

ONCHOCERCIASIS (SUB-SAHARAN AFRICANS)

This illness is caused by a parasitic worm. The parasite is transmitted by black flies, usually found along rivers, that pick up the parasite from infected people.

Signs and symptoms include skin rash, visual impairment (including blindness), itching, depigmentation of the skin, lymphadenitis, skin nodules, and lesions (Merck, 2007). Onchocerciasis is the second leading cause of blindness worldwide. It is treated with oral medication, and pesticides are used to treat waterways affected by the parasites. People who live along the waterways can take pills to prevent them from getting onchocerciasis.

OSTEOPOROSIS (CHINESE, IRISH)

Osteoporosis is a disorder in the uptake of calcium into the bloodstream that leaves bones frail and vulnerable to breaking. It can result from lactose intolerance, failure to take in calcium in the diet, or poor eating habits; inhibited calcium uptake can also be caused by an increase in phosphorus in a person's diet. It is best to modify eating habits before osteoporosis takes effect. People with osteoporosis can monitor their bone density by means of a bone density scan. Prevention and care involve taking calcium, with vitamin D, at a rate of 1000 milligrams per day. If osteoporosis becomes severe, the physician may prescribe medication.

PERIODONTITIS (CUBANS)

Periodontitis is an inflammatory disease of the gums and underlying bone in which bacterial buildup causes teeth to become loose. It results from poor dental care. Diabetes and smoking are risk factors. Prevention includes brushing after every meal, using dental floss, avoiding sweets, and seeing a dentist twice a year. Failure to prevent the bacterial growth will result in tooth loss.

PIBLOKTOQ (NATIVE ALASKANS)

Pibloktoq is an abrupt dissociative episode that has been described by Landy, 1985 as "artic hysteria." Landy explains that the cause can be ecological, nutritional, psychological, biological, or related to vitamin intoxication. The treatment will depend upon the cause found.

PSEUDOFOLLICULITIS (AFRICAN AMERICANS)

Pseudofolliculitis involves irritation of the skin by hair that is growing back after shaving; the hair grows into the face instead of outward and may cause infection. The pustules may make ones face appear to have pimples. To prevent pseudofolliculitis, some men just grow beards. Other treatments include laser therapy, topical antibiotics, and chemical depilatories. African American males are most commonly affected.

QIGONG PSYCHOTIC REACTION (CHINESE)

This is an acute, time-limited episode characterized by dissociative, paranoid, or other psychotic or nonpsychotic symptoms that occur after participating in the Chinese folk health-enhancing practice of qigong.

SALMONELLA (AMERICAN INDIANS)

Salmonella is a group of bacteria that cause vomiting, abdominal pain, and diarrhea. It is typically contracted by consuming undercooked foods; antibiotics can be used to resolve it. American Indians are more likely to get salmonella because of poor sanitary conditions on reservations.

SARCOIDOSIS (GERMANS, IRISH)

Germans and Irish are more likely to develop sarcoidosis, which is believed to be caused by an immune system reaction to a toxin that enters through the lungs. Because the toxin itself is surrounded by a granuloma, it does not affect the body, but the granuloma causes the lungs to scar and thus decreases lung capacity.

Signs and symptoms include a cough that will not go away, fatigue, high temperature, loss of weight, and red watery eyes (Mayo Clinic, 2006). Diagnosis is made through lung function tests, lung biopsy, and blood tests. Treatment involves the use of the medication prednisone and may continue for many years.

SCABIES (SUB-SAHARAN AFRICANS)

Scabies is a skin infection caused by mites that burrow into and lay eggs in the skin; more mites then hatch and live in and on the skin of the host. The mites travel from one human to another by skin contact or through shared use of items such as hair brushes, bed linens, and clothing. Patients experience intense itching and infections. It may be possible to see the burrowing sites. Treatment consists of oral or topical antibiotics.

SCHISTOSOMIASIS (ARAB-COLLECTIVE MIDDLE EASTERNERS, FILIPINOS, SUB-SAHARAN AFRICANS)

This illness is typically found in Africa, Asia, the Caribbean, Latin America, and the Middle East. The rate among sub-Saharans can be as high as 50 percent (Centers for Disease Control and Prevention, 2004). It caused by a parasite (Centers for Disease Control and Prevention, 2004) whose eggs are released into fresh water when an infected person urinates or defecates.

The parasitic eggs develop in a snail's foot (Centers for Disease Control and Prevention, 2004) and are eventually released into the water. The parasite lives for 48 hours in the water, seeking a person to serve as a host. It lives on the host's skin, burrows its way in, and then enters the circulatory system, by means of which it takes up residence in the lungs, liver, and gastrointestinal system (Centers for Disease Control and Prevention, 2004).

Typical symptoms include abdominal pain, coughing, enlarged liver, enlarged spleen, diarrhea, high temperature, and fatigue (Centers for Disease Control and Prevention, 2004). Diagnosis is made through stool and urine testing. Treatment involves antibiotics. Prevention entails avoiding contact with infected water and killing the snails that are likely carriers.

SEXUALLY TRANSMITTED DISEASES (HAITIANS)

Common types of sexually transmitted disease include chlamydia, syphilis, gonorrhea, HIV, genital herpes, human papillomavirus (HPV), and trichomoniasis. Each of the sexually transmitted diseases has its own signs and symptoms, which can vary between men and women. Each also has its own course of treatment; in some instances (e.g., HIV and herpes), there is no cure—only symptomatic treatment. Preventive measures include using protection during sexual intercourse.

SHENJING SHUAIRUO (CHINESE)

Shenjing shuairuo is also known as "neurasthenia." Symptoms include physical and mental fatigue, dizziness, headache and other pain, difficulty with concentrating, sleep disturbance, and memory loss (McCajor Hall, 1998). Fatigue is the symptom most often treated. Treatment consists of rest and medication (Yew Schwartz, 2002).

SHENKUI (CHINESE)

This condition is marked by anxiety or panic symptoms accompanied by somatic complaints for which no physical cause can be demonstrated. Symptoms include dizziness, backache, fatigability, general weakness, insomnia, frequent dreams, and complaints of sexual dysfunction (e.g., premature ejaculation, impotence). Symptoms are attributed to excessive semen loss from frequent intercourse, masturbation, nocturnal emission, or passing of "white turbid urine" believed to contain semen. Excessive semen loss is feared because it represents the loss of one's vital essence and can thereby be life threatening.

SHIGELLA (AMERICAN INDIANS)

The most common cause of this food poisoning is the use of water contaminated by shigella bacteria—for example, using contaminated water to wash fruits and vegetables. Signs and symptoms include diarrhea, vomiting, abdominal cramps, fever, and bloody stool. American Indian reservations may be more prone to shigella because of poor sanitary conditions. The condition can be resolved through use of antibiotics.

SICKLE-CELL ANEMIA (AFRICAN AMERICANS, ARAB-COLLECTIVE MIDDLE EASTERNERS)

Cartwright and Pitney, 2005 indicate "sickle-cell anemia is a chronic inherited disease. Although it is often thought of as an illness of African-Americans, it also occurs in those of other races. People of eastern European descent are also at high risk for sickle-cell anemia.

"The normal red blood cell is round and has a large surface area for carrying oxygen. The red blood cells of a patient with sickle-cell anemia look like sickles or crescents, with points on each end. The sickling of the cells causes them to hook onto the sides of the blood vessels, producing a logjam of cells in the capillaries. Also, the sickle cell is not capable of carrying as much oxygen as a normal red blood cell. The result is that oxygen is not carried efficiently to all parts of the body. The patient with sickle-cell anemia who is in crisis may have a blue skin tone, feel nauseated and weak, and have abdominal pain. Most often the patient can be treated with high-flow oxygen from an oxygen tank. Preventing a sickle-cell crisis includes taking in fluids, avoiding high altitudes (above 4,000 feet [1.2 kilometers]), warming up well, and avoiding short bursts of activity" (Cartwright & Pitney, 2005).

SKIN CANCER (GERMANS, IRISH)

Being fair-skinned races, Germans and Irish are more prone to skin cancer because the ultraviolet rays of the sun penetrate fair-skinned people more easily than it does those with darker skin. Thus a person with fair skin should use sunscreen to add a layer of protection if the skin cannot be covered with clothing during exposure to the sun.

Signs and symptoms of skin cancer include a change in a mole or in the pigmentation of the skin; it can also be indicated by a lump under the skin. If any of these signs or symptoms are found, a physician should be consulted. The most serious form of skin cancer is melanoma, which can be fatal.

STROKE (AMERICAN INDIANS, ENGLISH, GERMANS)

Stroke results from the loss of blood flow to the brain—the longer the loss lasts, the greater the damage to the brain. If left untreated or if occurring in a significant part of the brain, stroke can result in death. Strokes can be caused by blood clots, blockage, or a rupture in a blood vessel.

Treatment entails immediate emergency care. Clot-busting drugs may be given to relieve a clot, or surgery may be necessary. Angioplasty can be used to open an area of the brain affected by a clot. In some cases, treatment may not resolve the damage and a person may have to live with the resulting deficits.

Risk factors include high blood pressure, heredity, smoking, obesity, high cholesterol, hormone therapy, diabetes, age, fibrillation, diabetes, and transient ischemic attacks. The risk can be reduced by controlling high blood pressure, eating a proper diet, and taking medication for fibrillation. Prevention includes exercising, reducing intake of fat and cholesterol, stopping smoking, and stopping hormone therapy.

SUICIDE (CUBANS, NATIVE ALASKANS)

The suicide rate is higher among Native Alaskans and Cubans. Contributing factors include economic woes, unsanitary conditions, lack of opportunity, drug abuse, depression, and alcohol use. Males are more likely to succeed at suicide, but more females attempt suicide unsuccessfully. Signs and symptoms include depression, giving away items, and forming a suicide plan. If a health care provider comes into contact with a person who is suicidal, he or she should call for a professional who specializes in mental health issues.

SYSTEMIC LUPUS ERYTHEMATOSUS (AFRICAN AMERICANS)

This is a genetic autoimmune disorder, which means that the immune system does not know the difference between healthy or unhealthy substances and thus attacks healthy ones. During a lupus outbreak, skin lesions are common, the skin is very sensitive to the sun, and the sufferer often experiences joint pain, nausea, and fever. Severe cases can affect the kidneys, lungs, central nervous system, and heart. There is no cure for systemic lupus erythematosus; it is treated symptomatically.

THALASSEMIA (ARAB-COLLECTIVE MIDDLE EASTERNERS, CHINESE, FILIPINOS, IRANIANS)

This genetic disorder causes anemia due to an abnormality in the production of the alpha or beta hemoglobin chain. Thalassemia comes in different forms and degrees of illness. Those most likely to have thalassemia live in Africa, Asia, and the Middle East (HealthScout, 2001b, 2001c). Symptoms include enlarged spleen, pale skin, and tiredness. Diagnosis is made through blood testing. Treatment is dictated by the severity of illness and may include intake of iron for mild cases and removal of the spleen for severe cases (HealthScout 2001b, 2001c).

THYROID CANCER (FILIPINOS)

The thyroid gland is found in the front of the throat and produces thyroid hormones. Thyroid cancer is first found as a nodule in the neck. These nodules are curable if found early enough (Medicinenet, 2007).

Those who are more prone to thyroid cancer include Filipinos, women, people over 30, those exposed to radiation, and those with a family history of thyroid cancer (Medicinenet, 2007). Treatment of this form of cancer can include surgery, radiation, radioactive iodine therapy, or chemotherapy (Medicinenet, 2007).

TOOTH DECAY (ENGLISH)

The standard stereotype of the English is that they have poor dental hygiene, and, unfortunately, they do not have the best dental care practices. Specifically, there is no fluoridation of the water in England due to a belief that it creates higher incidence of Alzheimer's disease.

Tooth decay occurs when food is left on or between the teeth, thus enabling the growth of bacteria that break down tooth enamel and cause tooth cavities and gum disease. To prevent tooth decay, a person should brush after every meal. Flossing to clear any debris between the teeth helps reduce the material that starts the process of decay. It is also wise to avoid sugary foods, which contribute to bacterial growth in the mouth. Dental check-ups should be done at least twice per year.

TRACHOMA (ARAB-COLLECTIVE MIDDLE EASTERNERS, SUB-SAHARAN AFRICANS)

This infectious disease, caused by chlamydia bacteria, accounts for the blindness of 6 million people worldwide. Children in African countries make up 10 to 40 percent of the carriers of the active disease (Centers for Disease Control and Prevention, 2008). Trachoma is transmitted from an infected person's nose and eye fluids to another person (International Trachoma Initiative, 2007). It is also possible for flies to transfer the disease by touching an infection person's fluid and then touching a healthy person's eye. Person-to-person transmission is enabled by unhealthy living conditions within a home or community.

Symptoms include irritation of the conjunctiva, fluid discharge from the eyes, swollen eyelids, inward curling of the eyelashes, and, if the disease is left untreated, corneal scarring and eventual blindness (Subramanian, 2006). Antibiotics can cure the disease if it is caught early.

The areas of the world most often afflicted with trachoma are Africa, Asia, Latin America, and the Middle East (International Trachoma Initiative, 2007). Improved sanitary conditions can prevent trachoma. Health care providers must wash their hands between patients.

TRYPANOSOMIASIS (SUB-SAHARAN AFRICANS)

This illness, found primarily in Africa and sometimes called sleeping sickness, is spread from one person to another by the tsetse fly, which carries a parasite and transmits it upon biting a person. Signs and symptoms of trypanosomiasis include a chancre, headache, fatigue, long periods of daytime sleep, rash, weight loss, sore joints, and swollen lymph glands. Left untreated, the illness can result in death. If it attacks the central nervous system, the person exhibits seizures, difficulty with speaking and walking, and confusion (Directors of Health Promotion and Education, 2007). If caught early enough, the illness can be resolved through use of medicine.

TUBERCULOSIS (AMERICAN INDIANS, ARAB-COLLECTIVE MIDDLE EASTERNERS, CHINESE, FILIPINOS, HAITIANS, SUB-SAHARAN AFRICANS, VIETNAMESE)

Tuberculosis is an infectious bacterial disease that is currently on the rise. Commonly called TB, it is caused by a mycobacterium (MedlinePlus, 2007a) and most often affects the lungs. About nine million people around the world get tuberculosis each year (Centers for Disease Control and Prevention, 2007a). Tuberculosis has a higher incidence in southern Africa than in the Middle East and Asia (MedlinePlus, 2007a). In the United States, Blacks account for 45 percent of all cases (Centers for Disease Control and Prevention, 2007a).

TB is an airborne disease that is transferred when a person coughs, sneezes, or talks. For prevention, infected persons should cover their mouths when coughing or sneezing to avoid spreading the disease. Those with lowered immune systems are more susceptible to TB.

Typically, a person is diagnosed after a prolonged bout of coughing or pain in the chest. In the past, anyone who worked in schools, with food, or in hospitals was tested by means of a TB tine test or a chest X ray. A person diagnosed with TB is given one of several medicines to kill the bacterial infection. Signs and symptoms of tuberculosis mimic other illnesses, such as thalassemia, melioidosis, and paragonimiasis (Purnell & Paulanka, 2005).

TYPHOID FEVER (ARAB-COLLECTIVE MIDDLE EASTERNERS, SUB-SAHARAN AFRICANS, VIETNAMESE)

Typhoid fever is a bacterial illness caused by Salmonella Typhi (Centers for Disease Control and Prevention, 2006a). It is transmitted by ingestion of food or water contaminated with feces from an infected person (Centers for Disease Control and Prevention, 2006a). Typhoid fever can be transferred very easily by people who are food handlers. In many food service establishments, signs can be seen that require workers to wash their hands before returning from the rest room.

The common symptoms of typhoid fever include general malaise, high fever, loss of appetite, stomach pains, and headache (Centers for Disease Control and Prevention, 2006a). Diagnosis is made through a blood test, and antibiotics are used to treat typhoid fever. Typhoid fever is seen most commonly in Africa, Asia, Latin America, and the Middle East. Industrialized nations such as the United States do not have it.

VITAMIN A DEFICIENCY (FILIPINOS)

Vitamin A deficiency is usually caused by the failure to eat enough foods containing the vitamin. Vitamin A is found in leafy green vegetables, eggs, liver, milk, and some fruits. Failure to take in enough Vitamin A can lead to blindness or a compromised immune system. Poverty in the Philippines, especially in urban areas, may lead to Vitamin A deficiency.

VITAMIN B$_{12}$ AND FOLIC ACID DEFICIENCY (IRANIANS)

Vitamin B$_{12}$ and folic acid are important in red blood cell formation, development of DNA, and tissue repair (Vitamin Diary, 2007). Deficiency of vitamin B$_{12}$ or folic acid can lead to anemia, which in this instance results in production of red blood cells that are larger than normal but unable to transport oxygen efficiently. The deficiency takes months or even years to develop because the body is able to store both B_{12} and folic acid. Signs and symptoms include confusion, diarrhea, dizziness, increased heart rate, numbness in extremities, and shortness of breath. Resolution of the deficiency is achieved by increasing one's levels of vitamin B_{12} and folic acid.

VITILIGO (AFRICAN AMERICANS)

Vitiligo involves destruction of the skin cells that make pigment. As a result, white patches of skin appear on parts of the body, most commonly the hands, knees, face, lips, and arms. It is believed, but has not been proven, that vitiligo is inherited. It is more obvious in African Americans, but many Caucasians have it as well. Medications are available to bleach the rest of the skin so that the skin color is more uniform throughout the body. Other treatment options include steroids, ultraviolet A therapy, and surgery.

WHEAT INTOLERANCE (FILIPINOS)

Wheat intolerance means that the body is unable to digest wheat. It is thought that the intolerance is actually to gluten, which is found in many grains (Food intol, 2007). The intolerance is associated with an increased incidence of diabetes, osteoporosis, colon cancer, and anemia. It is important for those with wheat intolerance to be diagnosed early so that treatment can begin early as well. The treatment is to avoid gluten-containing foods.

YELLOW FEVER (SUB-SAHARAN AFRICANS)

Yellow fever is a virus carried by mosquitoes. Suffers experience fever, nausea, vomiting, fatigue, muscle aches, headaches, and chills. The patient's skin turns yellow because of liver infection, and he or she may also suffer bleeding from the mouth, nose, and gastrointestinal tract ("Yellow Fever," 2006). In severe cases, a person can go into shock or coma and experience multiple organ failure.

Treatment of yellow fever is symptomatic; there is no treatment for the virus itself. Prevention takes the form of a vaccine and the use of measures to prevent being bitten by mosquitoes. Yellow fever is endemic in sub-Saharan countries. The last outbreak of yellow fever in North America occurred in 1905 (Centers for Disease Control and Prevention, 2007d).

ZAR (IRANIANS, SUB-SAHARAN AFRICANS)

This is a condition in which people have an experience of spirit possession. Spirits are generally male and females are more likely to be possessed (Hall, 2010). This condition is believed in this culture to be inherited (Hall, 2010). Symptoms may include dissociative episodes characterized by laughing, shouting, hitting the head against a wall, singing, or weeping. Individuals may show apathy and withdrawal, refusing to eat or carry out daily tasks. Some may develop a long-term relationship with the possessing spirit. Treatment is done with a Zar ritual healing dance. The dance is not an exorcism of Zar, but a way to placate the spirit (Hall, 2010).

Glossary

advantage—Condition in which one occupies a superior position or enjoys a benefit.

Akasan—Haitian food made of evaporated milk, cream, cinnamon, vanilla extract, salt, cornmeal, and sugar—a food that encourages eating.

Aleut—Indigenous people who live on the Aleutian Islands in Alaska. Aleuts can also be found in Russia.

Allah—The ultimate highest power in Islam. A "word used to describe the God worshiped by Muslims, Christians, and Jews" (Purnell & Paulanka, 2008, p. 351).

allopathic medicine—Based on proven, scientific methodology to determine value in the treatment of disease and practiced by medical doctors (MDs).

alternative medicine—Practices used in place of conventional medicine.

am—In Vietnam, the female principle, considered to be dark as well as cold or cool.

am duc—In Vietnam, accumulation of good deeds by ancestors.

American Indian—Member of a group who (or whose ancestors) inhabited the area referred to today as the continental United States.

amok—"Dissociative episode characterized by a period of brooding followed by an outburst of violent, aggressive, destructive, even homicidal behavior; typically seen in males" (American Psychological Association, 2000, p. 899). See chapter 2 for specific countries.

albularyo—Herbalist in the Philippines.

Ayurveda—Translates as the science or knowledge of life. Hindu holistic medicine that originated in India more than 4,000 years ago.

bahala na—Filipino belief that the world is controlled by God and supernatural forces.

baten—One's private thoughts—Iranian.

biological-based practice—CAM approach using herbs, foods, and vitamins found in nature.

braucher—A powwow doctor in German culture.

caida de la mollera—In Mexico, refers to a folk illness in children and babies in which a fallen fontanel of the skull occurs by what is believed to be dehydration and vomiting caused by someone touching a person's head. In reality, the dehydration of the child can cause a serious illness and death, but the dehydration is more often caused by diarrhea.

cao gio—Home remedy, common in Asian cultures and given the name listed here in Vietnam, wherein one uses the edge of a spoon, dish, or coin to scrape the skin.

Caucasian—Of or relating to White European, North African, or Southwest Asian peoples with light skin color.

chant—Verbal rhythmic utterance used to maintain good health without offense against any entity.

chi (or **qi**)—In Chinese belief, the natural life force or energy that exists in all living things.

cho— In the Haitian belief system, the body becomes ill when exposed to too much heat.

class—Socially constructed category associated withone's economic position in society based on a combination of their income, wealth, education, occupation, and social connections.

complementary medicine—Practices used in conjunction with conventional medicine.

conventional medicine—Practice used by medical doctors (MDs) and doctors of osteopathy (DOs) and their allied health professionals.

Creole language—Pidgin communication that is spoken and passed on to members of the next generation as their primary language.

crystal gazing—Divination practice of looking into a crystalline gem or crystal ball.

cultural awareness—In-depth self-examination for the purpose of exploring one's personal and professional cultural values, beliefs, biases, and prejudices and how these factors affect clinical judgment.

cultural competence—Involvement in and appreciation of cultural differences. "The ongoing process in which the health care professional continuously strives to achieve the ability and availability to work effectively within the cultural context of the patient (individual, family, community)" (Campinha-Bacote, 2007, p. 15).

cultural desire—Health provider's motivation to want to (rather than have to) provide care that is culturally responsive (Campinha-Bacote, 2007).

cultural encounter—Direct engagement in cross-cultural interaction for the purposes of refining and modifying one's beliefs about a cultural group and preventing stereotyping (Campinha-Bacote, 2007).

cultural formulation—Means for systematically reviewing, evaluating, and reporting a patient's cultural background and the impact of the cultural context.

cultural knowledge—Learning about cultural values and beliefs, health disparities, and treatment efficacy.

cultural skill—Ability to collect relevant cultural data, apply knowledge gained, and perform a culturally based physical assessment (Campinha-Bacote, 2007).

cultural SWOT analysis—Tool for determining an organization's strengths, weaknesses, opportunities, and threats relative to cultural competence.

culture—The sum total of socially inherited characteristics of a human group that comprises everything which one generation can tell, convey, or hand down to the next (Spector, 2000).

culture-bound syndrome—"Features of an illness that vary from culture to culture" (Campinha-Bacote, 2003, p. 32).

curandero (or curandera)—Spiritual healer in Latino culture, particularly Mexican.

dao—Body in balance with itself and environment. A balance between yin and yang.

dirt—African American concept closely related to germs.

disadvantage—inferior or prejudicial condition; loss or damage, particularly to one's reputation or finances.

duong—In Vietnam, the male principle, associated with heat and light.

Ebonics—African American dialect of Standard English, also known as African American Vernacular English and Black English.

empacho—Ball of food stuck or perceived to be stuck in the lining of the stomach.

energy medicine—Therapies involving the purported use of two types of energy fields (biofields and bioelectromagnetic fields).

envidia—Term for envy in Latino culture.

Eskimo—Member of one of a group of indigenous peoples living primarily in Alaska.

espanto—Term for shock in Latino culture.

espiritism—Belief in God and spirits in Mexican religion.

ethnicity—Cultural heritage of a group (thus distinct different from race).

evil eye—Glance believed to be capable of creating illness; person believed to use such a glance.

explanatory model—Patient's or healthcare provider's explanation of why an illness occurred (explains the epidemiology of illness).

explanatory models approach—Set of questions designed to elicit the patient's explanatory model.

falling out—Response to shocking news wherein a person retains hearing but collapses, falls mute, and cannot see.

financial barrier—Type of factor (e.g., lack of sufficient health insurance, refusal of clinicians to accept an insurance plan, general lack of income) that limits one's ability to access health care.

fire burning—Practice of heating a stick, then applying it to the skin to cure an illness.

Five Pillars of Islam—Five duties considered incumbent on every Muslim, including profession of faith (shahada), prayer (salat), giving (zakat), fasting (sawm), and pilgrimage (hajj).

fret—In the Haitian belief system, the body becomes ill when exposed to too much cold.

garm—In Iranian culture, a food that is considered hot, causing one to become overheated.

gender—Set of social constructed practices, rituals, and learned behaviors historically considered as either feminine or masculine.

generalization—Statement presented as a general truth but based on limited or incomplete evidence.

halaal—Arabic term meaning *lawful*; used to designate food permissible under Islamic law (e.g., a sacrificed animal that was healthy before being killed quickly by means of throat slitting after the name of Allah was said).

hand trembler—Navajo traditional healer who waves a hand over an ill person to diagnose illness.

haram—Food prohibited for Muslims.

health disparities—"Differences in the incidence, prevalence, mortality, burden of disease, and other adverse health conditions or outcomes that exist among specific population groups" (Michigan Department of Community Health, 2007, p. 1).

heterosexism—Institutionalized structures and beliefs that define and enforce heterosexual behavior as the only natural and permissible form of sexual expression.

high blood—Term used in African American culture to describe having too much blood in the body.

hijab—Head covering often worn by Muslim women.

hilot—In Filipino culture, a healer who uses massage, manipulation, and herbs to treat muscles, joints, and ligaments.

hiya—In Filipino culture, the feeling of shame that would lead one to want to save face.

homeopathic medicine—Type of healing that originated in Germany. Based on the law of similars; in other words, like cures like. In this practice, patients are given a very small dose of a highly diluted medicinal substance that in larger, more concentrated doses would cause the symptoms or disease. The small dosage is believed to provoke a healing response.

Imam—A Muslim leader of prayer who recites words of the Quran for relief from illness or injury.

injera—Bread made by sub-Saharan Africans from grains containing high levels of iron.

institutional cultural self-audit—Tool for determining what an organization does to provide culturally competent care.

integrative medicine—Combines conventional and CAM treatments for which there is evidence of safety and effectiveness.

Juneteenth—Annual celebration of the freeing of slaves in Texas.

kufi—Head covering worn by some African or Muslim men.

kulam—Witchcraft in Filipino culture.

laying on of hands—Practice wherein a person places his or her hands on another person and prays; may be used to give support to one who is ill.

LEARN model of cross-cultural communication—Model hinging on five practices: listen, explain, acknowledge, recommend, and negotiate.

lok—Laxative mixture of tea leaves, juice, syrup, and oil used in Haitian culture to maintain health.

low blood—Term used in African American culture to describe having too little blood in the body; associated with weakness and anemia.

maalesh—Arabic attitude in which one says what another wants to hear even though it is not genuine.

mal aire—Bad air, usually from drafts, that results in illness in Mexican culture.

mal de ojo—In Latino culture, term for the "evil eye."

manipulative and body-based practices—CAM approaches that focus on structures and systems of the body (including bones and joints, soft tissues, and circulation and lymphatic systems) and that are based on manipulation (a passive, quick thrust of one articulating surface on another).

mashbooh—Term indicating foods with doubtful or uncertain status under Islamic law.

Mecca—In Islam, the holiest site in the world; located in Saudi Arabia.

median household income—Income level determined by dividing households into two equal categories, with half above the median and half below it (U.S. Census Bureau, 2007, p. 1).

meridian—In various Asian cultures, electrical pathway along which energy flows through the body (six yin and six yang).

mien—The act of saving face or maintaining family honor in Chinese culture.

mind–body medicine—Variety of CAM techniques designed to enhance the mind's capacity to affect bodily function and symptoms.

mitch—Term for mental illness in sub-Saharan Africa.

narahati—Culturally unacceptable illness by Iranians.

narrative sequencing—Telling of a story about the history of an illness or an injury.

Native Alaskan—Person indigenous to Alaska.

Native American—Person indigenous to North America.

naturopathic medicine—Type of medicine that originated in Europe. Predicated on the belief that nature has the power to heal. In other words, it posits that self-healing occurs and that the body can establish, maintain, and restore health. Naturopaths use botanical medicine (biological-based practice), homeopathy (whole medical system), and nutrition (biological-based practice) to prevent and treat illness by identifying and removing the underlying cause of illness rather than by suppressing symptoms.

nomadic—Moving from place to place based on availability of food.

observation—Process in which a Chinese physician examines skin tone, eyes, nails, and tongue.

osteopathic medicine—The art of curing without the use of surgery or drugs and takes into account the relationship between body structure and organ functioning.

pakikisama—In Filipino culture, going along with whatever is being talked about.

passing through—In German folk belief, component of powwowing in which a child rotates around the leg of the table three times or in multiples of three in order to resolve an illness.

personal barrier—Type of factor (e.g., cultural and spiritual differences, language, sexual orientation, and concerns about confidentiality and discrimination) that makes it hard to access health care.

pidgin—Speech form created for intergroup communication between groups who do not share a language.

poverty—Condition in which total family income is less than a particular threshold.

prejudice—Preconceived judgment or opinion, usually based on limited information.

privilege—Right or immunity granted as an advantage or favor, especially to some and not to others.

qi—see entry for *chi*.

qigong—Therapy that involves breathing, exercise, and meditation to improve one's qi (chi).

Quran—Islamic sacred text that includes the Five Pillars of Islam.

race—Social marker of difference serving as the grounding for differentiation in treatment based on perceived physical characteristics.

Ramadan—Annual sacred holiday in Islam that involves a month of fasting (date changes dependent on the cycle of the moon).

religion—Organized set of beliefs, practices, and ethical values focused on a divine or superhuman power or powers to be obeyed and worshiped as the creators and rulers of the universe.

RESPECT model of cross-cultural communication—Model hinging on seven conditions: rapport, empathy, support, partnership, explanation, cultural competence, and trust.

rootwork—Haitian diagnostic system for determining and curing illness. May also be an illness as the result of hexing, witchcraft, voodoo, or the influence of an evil person.

sand painting—Artwork done by an American Indian medicine man in various colors of sand. The patient then sits on the painting to help draw out or transfer the illness out of a patient.

sard—Food considered to be cold in Iranian culture.

saving face—Avoiding embarrassment; preserving the dignity of either the health care provider or the patient.

sexuality—A continuum of behaviors, identities, ideologies; includes, among others, gay, lesbian, bisexual, transsexual, down low, straight, questioning.

sezisman—In Haitian culture, a fright suffered upon hearing bad news.

shaman—Medicine man or woman consulted to determine what has caused an illness or injury.

siesta—Period of rest during the middle part of the day in the Latino world.

social location—One's position in society based on the intersection of race, class, gender, sexuality, religion, nationality, ability, age, and geography.

socially constructed—Having a meaning that changes over time based on systems of privilege and oppression; said of a social category (e.g., race, gender, sexuality).

spirituality—"As primarily relational—a transcendent relationship with that which is sacred in life (Walsh, 2000) or with something divine beyond the self (Emmons, 1999)" (as cited in Miller & Thoresen, 2003, p. 27).

stargazer—Native American diagnostician who uses stargazing to diagnose illness and determine needed treatment.

stereotype—An undifferentiated, simplistic attribution that involves a judgment of habits, traits, abilities, or expectations assigned as characteristic of all members of a group.

strategic plan—Document that outlines clear goals, policies, operational plans, and management accountability and oversight mechanisms to provide culturally and linguistically appropriate services.

structural barrier—Type of factor (e.g., lack of proximity to facilities and primary care providers or other health care providers) that makes it hard to access health care (U.S. Department of Health and Human Services, 2000a, 2000b).

susto—Fright sickness in Latino culture.

ta'arof—In Iran, form of expressed courtesy, or the public persona one puts on with those outside one's intimate circle.

traditional Chinese medicine (TCM)—The current term for the ancient system of medical practices that originated in China. It is based on the belief that qi or vital energy that flows throughout the body must remain balanced in order to maintain health.

tribe—Group of people (e.g., among American Indians) usually related by blood ties.

whole medical systems—Comprehensive health care systems based on theory and practice, include (from Eastern cultures) traditional Chinese medicine (TCM) and the Indian practice of Ayurveda and (from Western culture) homeopathic medicine and naturopathic medicine.

yang—The force that opposes yin in Asian culture and is hot or warm.

yin—The force that opposes yang in Asian culture and is cold or cool.

zaher—Outward appearance generated through behavior by Arabs in order to keep outside people at a distance.

zeranghi—Arab term indicating the ability to manipulate people.

References

PREFACE

Office of Minority Health (U.S. Department of Health and Human Services). (2001). *National standards for culturally and linguistically appropriate services [CLAS] in health care.* http://minorityhealth.hhs.gov/assets/pdf/checked/finalreport.pdf.

CHAPTER 1

Andersen, M.L., & Collins, P.H. (2007). *Race, class and gender* (6th ed.). Belmont, CA: Wadsworth.

Andrews, M.M., & Boyle, J.S. (1995). *Transcultural nursing.* Philadelphia: Lippincott-Raven.

Boyle, J.S., & Wenger, A.F. (2002). A summary of the panel discussion: Comments from the moderators. *Journal of Transcultural Nursing, 13,* 200–201.

Bureau of Primary Health Care (Health Resources and Services Administration of the U.S. Department of Health and Human Services). (2000). *Cultural competence: A journey.* (SuDoc: HE 20.9102: C 89). Bethesda, MD: Author.

Campinha-Bacote, J. (2002). The process of cultural competence in the delivery of healthcare services: A model of care. *Journal of Transcultural Nursing, 13,* 181–184.

Campinha-Bacote, J. (2007). *The process of cultural competence in the delivery of healthcare services: The journey continues.* Cincinnati: Transcultural C.A.R.E.

Clark, S. L. & Weismantle, M. (August, 2003). *Employment status 2000: Census 2000 brief.* www.census.gov/prod/2003pubs/c2kbr-18.pdf

Collins, P.H. (1994). Foreword. In M. Baca Zinn & B.T. Dill (Eds.), *Women of color in U.S. society* (pp. xiv–xv). Philadelphia: Temple University Press.

Frankenberg, R. (2008). Whiteness as an 'unmarked' cultural category. In K.E. Rosenblum & T.C. Travis (Eds.), *The meaning of difference: American constructions of race, sex and gender, social class, sexual orientation and disability.* (5th ed.). Boston: McGraw-Hill.

Funderburg, L. (2006, April). Our town. *O: The Oprah Magazine,* 277–279.

Giger, J.N., & Davidhizar, R.E. (1999). *Transcultural nursing: Assessment and intervention.* (3rd ed.). St. Louis: Mosby.

Giger, J.N., & Davidhizar, R.E. (2007). *Transcultural nursing: Assessment and intervention.* (5th ed.). St. Louis: Mosby.

Health Resources and Services Administration (U.S. Department of Health and Human Services). (2001). *Cultural competence works: Using cultural competence to improve the quality of health care for diverse populations and add value to managed care arrangements.* Washington, DC: Author.

Jamieson, K. (1995). Latinas in sport and physical activity. *Journal of Physical Education, Recreation and Dance, 66*(7), 42–47.

Lattanzi, J.B., & Purnell, L.D. (2006). *Developing cultural competence in physical therapy practice.* Philadelphia: Davis.

Leininger, M. (1978). *Transcultural nursing: Theories, research, and practice* (2nd ed.). New York: Wiley.

Lowe, S. (2008). New Census Bureau Data Reveal More Older Workers, Homeowners, Non-English Speakers. Washington, DC: U.S. Census Bureau (U.S. Department of Commerce). www.census.gov/Press-Release/www/releases/archives/american_community_survey_acs/010601.html.

National Athletic Trainers' Association. (2006). *Athletic training educational competencies* (4th ed.). Dallas: Author.

National Center for Education Statistics (U.S. Department of Education, Institute of Education). (n.d.). Integrated Postsecondary Education Data System. *Definitions for new race and ethnicity categories.* http://nces.ed.gov/ipeds/reic/definitions.asp

Office of Minority Health (U.S. Department of Health and Human Services). (2001). *National standards for culturally and linguistically appropriate services* [CLAS]. http://minorityhealth.hhs.gov/assets/pdf/checked/finalreport.pdf

Perrin, D. (2003). William E. "Pinky" Newell Memorial Address, Eastern Athletic Trainers' Association Annual Meeting. January 5, 2003. www.uncg.edu/kin/faculty/perrinNewellAddress.pdf

Purnell, L.D., & Paulanka, B.J. (2003). *Transcultural health care: A culturally competent approach* (2nd ed.). Philadelphia: Davis.

Purnell, L.D., & Paulanka, B.J. (2005). *Guide to culturally competent health care.* Philadelphia: Davis.

Purnell, L.D., & Paulanka, B.J. (2008). *Transcultural health care: A culturally competent approach* (3rd ed.). Philadelphia: Davis.

Salimbene, S. (2005). *What language does your patient hurt in? A practical guide to culturally competent patient care* (2nd ed.). St. Paul, MN: EMC Paradigm.

Shingles, R.R. (2001). *Women in athletic training: Their career and educational experiences.* Doctoral dissertation, Michigan State University, East Lansing.

Smallwood, S.R. (1997). *Cultural diversity: Self-learning module.* Unpublished manuscript, Wake Forest University Baptist Medical Center.

Spector, R.E. (1996). *Cultural diversity in health and illness* (4th ed.). Stamford, CT: Appleton and Lange.

Spector, R.E. (2000). *Cultural diversity in health and illness* (5th ed.). Upper Saddle River, NJ: Prentice Hall.

Spector, R.E. (2004). *Cultural diversity in health and illness* (6th ed.). Upper Saddle River, NJ: Prentice Hall.

Spector, R.E. (2009). *Cultural diversity in health and illness* (7th ed.). Upper Saddle River, NJ: Prentice Hall.

Tatum, B.D. (1997). *"Why are all the black kids sitting together in the cafeteria?" And other conversations about race.* New York: Basic Books.

Taylor, R. (2005). Addressing barriers to cultural competence. *Journal for Nurses in Staff Development, 21*(4), 135–142.

Weston, K. (1991). *Families we choose: Lesbians, gays, kinship* (pp. 2, 7–17). New York: Columbia University Press.

CHAPTER 2

Alternative Medicine Foundation. (2006). *Naturopathic medicine: An alternative and complementary medicine resource guide.* www.amfoundation.org/naturopathinfo.htm#introduction.

American Psychiatric Association. (2000). *Diagnostic and statistical manual of mental disorders* (4th ed., text revision). Washington, DC: Author.

Andrews, M.M., & Boyle, J.S. (2007). *Transcultural concepts in nursing care* (5th ed.). Philadelphia: Lippincott, Williams & Wilkins.

Barnes, P.M., Bloom, B., & Nahin, R.L. (2008, December 10). Complementary and alternative medicine use among adults and children: United States, 2007. *National Health Statistics Reports, 12.* Hyattsville, MD: National Center for Health Statistics. www.cdc.gov/nchs/data/nhsr/nhsr012.pdf.

Barnes, P.M., Powell-Griner, E., McFann, K., & Nahin, R.L. (2004, May 27). Complementary and alternative medicine use among adults: United States, 2002. *Advance Data From Vital and Health Statistics, 343.* Hyattsville, MD: National Center for Health Statistics. www.cdc.gov/nchs/data/ad/ad343.pdf.

Berman, B.M., Lao, L., Langenberg, P., Lee, W.L., Gilpin, A.M.K., & Hochberg, M.C. (2004). Effectiveness of acupuncture as adjunctive therapy in osteoarthritis of the knee: A randomized, controlled trial. *Annals of Internal Medicine, 141*(12), 901–910.

Campinha-Bacote, J. (2003). *The process of cultural competence in the delivery of healthcare services: A culturally competent model of care.* Cincinnati: Transcultural C.A.R.E.

Choi, Y.J., & Lee, K.J. (2007). Evidence-based nursing: Effects of a structured nursing program for the health promotion of Korean women with Hwa-Byung. *Archives of Psychiatric Nursing, 21*(1), 12–16.

Hall, T.M. (2006). *TMH: Index of culture-bound syndromes by culture.* http://homepage.mac.com/mccajor/cbs_cul.html.

Hosick, M.B. (2005, April 29). Latest athlete drug-use data continue downward pattern. *NCAA News*. Indianapolis: National Collegiate Athletic Association. www.ncaa.org/wps/ncaa?key=/ncaa/ncaa/ncaa+news/ncaa+news+online/2005/association-wide/latest+athlete+drug-use+data+continue+downward+pattern+-+8-29-05+ncaa+news.

Kim, H.R., Rajaiah, R., Wu, Q.L., Satpute, S.R., Tan, M.T., Simon, J.E., et al. (2008, November). Green tea protects rats against autoimmune arthritis by modulating disease-related immune events. *The Journal of Nutrition*, *138*(11), 2111–2116.

McPhee, S. (2002, January 23). Caring for a 70-year-old Vietnamese woman [Electronic version]. *The Journal of the American Medical Association*, *287*(4), 495–504.

National Center for Complementary and Alternative Medicine (NCCAM). (2005, September). *Rheumatoid arthritis and CAM* (NCCAM Publication No. D282). Bethesda, MD: Author. http://nccam.nih.gov/health/RA/.

National Center for Complementary and Alternative Medicine (NCCAM). (2007). *CAM basics: What is CAM?* (NCCAM Publication No. D347). http://nccam.nih.gov/health/whatiscam/.

National Center for Complementary and Alternative Medicine (NCCAM). (2009a). *Acupuncture for chronic back pain*. http://nccam.nih.gov/research/results/spotlight/062109.htm.

National Center for Complementary and Alternative Medicine (NCCAM). (2009b). *The use of complementary and alternative medicine in the United States*. http://nccam.nih.gov/news/camstats/2007/camsurvey_fs1.htm.

Nichols, A.W., & Harrigan, R. (2006). Complementary and alternative medicine usage by intercollegiate athletes. *Clinical Journal of Sports Medicine*, *16*(3), 232–237.

Reznik, M., Ozuah, P.O., Franco, K., Cohen, R., & Motlow, F. (2002). Use of complementary therapy by adolescents with asthma. *Archives of Pediatric Adolescent Medicine*, *156*, 1042–1044.

Roberts, M.E., Han, K., & Weed, N.C. (2006). Development of a scale to assess Hwa-Byung, a Korean culture-bound syndrome, using the Korean MMPI-2. *Transcultural Psychiatry*, *43*(3), 383–400.

Simons, R.C. (2001, November 1). Introduction to culture-bound syndromes. *Psychiatric Times*, *18*(11). www.searchmedica.com/resource.html?rurl=http%3A%2F%2Fwww.psychiatrictimes.com%2Fdisplay%2Farticle%2F10168%2F54246%3FpageNumber%3D2&q=Culture-bound+syndromes&c=ps&ss=psychTimesLink&p=Convera&fr=true&ds=0&srid=1

Spector, R.E. (2004). *Cultural diversity in health and illness* (6th ed.). Upper Saddle River, NJ: Prentice Hall.

Spector, R.E. (2009). *Cultural diversity in health and illness* (7th ed.). Upper Saddle River, NJ: Prentice Hall.

Turner, R.B., Bauer, R., Woelkart, K., Hulsey, T.C., & Gangemi, J.D. (2005). An evaluation of *Echinacea* angustifolia in experimental rhinovirus infections. *The New England Journal of Medicine*, *353*(4), 341–348.

CHAPTER 3

Agency for Healthcare Research and Quality (U.S. Department of Health and Human Services). (2005, May). *Health care disparities in rural areas: Selected findings from the 2004 national healthcare report* (AHRQ Publication No. 05-P022). Rockville, MD: Author. www.ahcpr.gov/research/ruraldisp/ruraldispar.htm.

Agency for Healthcare Research and Quality (U.S. Department of Health and Human Services). (2007, January). *Key themes and highlights from the National Healthcare Disparities Report*. Rockville, MD: Author. www.ahrq.gov/qual/nhdr06/highlights/nhdr06high.htm.

American Physical Therapy Association (APTA). (2009). *APTA minority membership statistics*. www.apta.org/AM/Template.cfm?Section=Resources5&CONTENTID=57574&TEMPLATE=/CM/ContentDisplay.cfm.

Asian Nation. (2008). Socioeconomic statistics & demographics. www.asian-nation.org/demographics.shtml.

Beach, M.C., Price, E.G., Gary, T.L., Robinson, K.A., Gozu, A., Palacio, A., et al. (2005,

April). Cultural competence: A systematic review of health care provider educational interventions. *Medical Care, 43*(4), 356–373.

Betancourt, J.R., Green, A.R., Carrillo, J.E., & Ananeh-Firempong, O. (2003). Defining cultural competence: A practical framework for addressing racial/ethnic disparities in health and health care. *Public Health Reports, 118*, 293–302.

Brach, C., & Fraserirector, I. (2000). Can cultural competency reduce racial and ethnic health disparities? *Medical Care Research and Review, 57*(1), 181–217.

Carter-Pokras, O., & Baquet, C. (2002). What is a health disparity? *Public Health Reports, 117*, 426–434.

Giles, W.H. (2007). *Addressing racial and ethnic health disparities.* Presentation given at the SOPHE Annual Meeting. www.cdc.gov/reach/pdf/giles_sophe.pdf.

Horner, R.D., Salazar, W., Geiger, H.J., Bullock, K., Corbie-Smith, G., Cornog, M., et al. (2004). Changing healthcare professionals' behaviors to eliminate disparities in healthcare: What do we know? How might we proceed? *The American Journal of Managed Care, 10,* SP12–SP19.

Michigan Department of Community Health. (2007). *2007 health disparities report to the Michigan legislature.* www.michigan.gov/documents/mdch/Response_to_Legislature.final_228597_7.pdf.

National Athletic Trainers' Association (NATA). (2006). *Athletic training educational competencies* (4th ed.). Dallas: Author.

National Athletic Trainers' Association (NATA). (2008). *Ethnicity 2005-2008 membership trend.* www.nata.org/members1/documents/membstats/2008EOY-stats.htm

National Collegiate Athletic Association (NCAA). (2006). *1999–2000 to 2004–2005 NCAA student athlete race and ethnicity report.* Indianapolis: Author.

Starfield, B. (1992). Effects of poverty on health status. *Bulletin of the New York Academy of Medicine, 68*(1), 17–24.

U.S. Census Bureau. (2005, August 11). Texas becomes nation's newest "majority-minority" state, Census Bureau announces.

Press release. www.census.gov/Press-Release/www/releases/archives/population/005514.html.

U.S. Census Bureau. (2006, August 29). Income climbs, poverty stabilizes, uninsured rate increases. Press release. www.census.gov/Press-Release/www/releases/archives/income_wealth/007419.html.

U.S. Census Bureau. (2007a). *Population profile of the United States: Dynamic version.* www.census.gov/population/www/pop-profile/profiledynamic.html.

U.S. Census Bureau. (2007b, September 12). New Census Bureau data reveal more older workers, homeowners, non-English speakers. Press release. www.census.gov/Press-Release/www/releases/archives/american_community_survey_acs/010601.html.

U.S. Department of Health and Human Services (DHHS). (2000a). *Healthy People 2010 Volume I: Understanding and improving health: Access to quality health care.* www.healthypeople.gov/Document/HTML/Volume1/01Access.htm.

U.S. Department of Health and Human Services (DHHS). (2000b). *Healthy People 2010 Volume I: Understanding and improving health: Leading health indicators.* www.healthypeople.gov/Document/html/uih/uih_bw/uih_4.htm#accesshealth.

CHAPTER 4

Agency for Healthcare Research and Quality (U.S. Department of Health and Human Services). (2007, January). *Key themes and highlights from the National Healthcare Disparities Report.* www.ahrq.gov/qual/nhdr06/highlights/nhdr06high.htm.

Andersen, M.L., & Collins, P.H. (1995). *Race, class and gender* (2nd ed.). Belmont, CA: Wadsworth.

Baca Zinn, M., & Dill, B.T. (2005). Theorizing difference from multiracial feminism. In M. Baca Zinn, P. Hondagneu-Sotelo, & M.A. Messner (Eds.), *Gender through the prism of difference* (3rd ed.). New York: Oxford University Press.

Baca Zinn, M., Hondagneu-Sotelo, P., & Messner, M. (Eds.). (2005). *Gender through the prism of difference* (3rd ed.). New York: Oxford University Press.

Barrett, J.E., & Roediger, D. (2005). How white people became white. In P.S. Rothenberg (Ed.), *White privilege: Essential readings on the other side of racism* (2nd ed.). New York: Worth.

Beauboeuf-Lafontant, T. (2005). Strong and large black women?: Exploring relationships between deviant womanhood and weight. In M. Baca Zinn, P. Hondagneu-Sotelo, & M.A. Messner (Eds.), *Gender through the prism of difference* (3rd ed.). New York: Oxford University Press.

Biddington, C. (2007, Winter). Teaching diversity awareness. *Academic Exchange Quarterly, 11*(4), 71–75.

Brodkin, K. (2005). How Jews became white folks. In P.S. Rothenberg (Ed.), *White privilege: Essential readings on the other side of racism* (2nd ed.). New York: Worth.

Bull, C. (February 16, 2004). The healer. *ESPN The Magazine*, pp 90–95.

Burton, M.G. (1995). *Never say nigger again: An antiracism guide for white liberals.* Nashville: Winston.

Coakley, J. (2004). *Sports in society: Issues and controversies* (8th ed.). Boston: McGraw-Hill.

Collins, P.H. (1991). Learning from the outsider within: The sociological significance of black feminist thought. In J.E. Hartman & E.M. Davidow (Eds.), *(En) gendering knowledge.* Knoxville: University of Tennessee Press.

Connell, R.W. (1992). A very straight gay: Masculinities, homosexual experience, and the dynamics of gender. *American Sociological Review, 57*, 735–751.

Crooks, R., & Baur, K. (2008). *Our sexuality* (10th ed.). Belmont, CA: Wadsworth, Cengage Learning.

Curlin, F.A., Lantos, J.D., Roach, C.J., Sellergren, S.A., & Chin, M.H. (2005, July). Religious characteristics of U.S. physicians: A national survey. *Journal of General Internal Medicine, 20*(7), 629–634.

Davis, J. (2005). *Who is black? One nation's definition* (10th anniversary ed.). University

Park, PA: Pennsylvania State University Press.

DeMark, J.F. (2007). Cultural competency: Making the invisible visible—lesbian, gay, bisexual, transgender identities. Paper presented at the 6th Annual CMU Campus Diversity Forum, Central Michigan University.

Denny, D., Green, J., & Cole, S. (2007). Gender variability: Transsexuals, crossdressers, and others. In A. F. Owens & M. S. Tepper, M. S. (Eds.), *Sexual health: State-of-the-art treatments and research* (Vol 4). Westport, CT: Praeger.

Diller, J.V. (2007). *Cultural diversity: A primer for the human services* (3rd. ed.). Belmont, CA: Thomson Brooks/Cole.

Egan, M., & Swedersky, J. (2003). Spirituality as experienced by occupational therapists in practice. *American Journal of Occupational Therapy, 57*(5), 525–533.

Ehrenreich, B. (1995). Are you middle class? In M.L. Andersen & P. Hill Collins (Eds.), *Race, class, and gender* (2nd ed.). Belmont, CA: Wadsworth.

Griffin, P. (1998). *Strong women, deep closets.* Champaign, IL: Human Kinetics.

Info Please. (2007). *Self-described religious identification among American adults.* www.infoplease.com/ipa/A0922574.html.

Johnson, A.G. (2001). *Privilege, power, and difference.* New York: McGraw-Hill.

Jordan, J. (1995). A new politics of sexuality. In M.L. Andersen & P. Hill Collins (Eds.), *Race, class, and gender* (6th ed.). Belmont, CA: Wadsworth.

Langston, D. (2007). Tired of playing monopoly? In M.L. Andersen & P. Hill Collins (Eds.), *Race, class, and gender* (2nd ed.). Belmont, CA: Wadsworth.

Lorber, J. (1994). Night to his day: The social construction of gender. In J. Lorber, *Paradoxes of gender.* New Haven, CT: Yale University Press.

Messner, M., & Sabo, D. (1990). Toward a critical feminist reappraisal of sport, men, and the gender order. In M. Messner & D. Sabo (Eds.), *Sport, men and the gender order: Critical feminist perspectives.* Champaign, IL: Human Kinetics.

Miller, W. R., & Thoresen, C. E. (2003). Spirituality, religion and health: An emerging research field. *American Psychologist, 58*(1), 24-35.

Omi, M., & Winant, H. (1994). *Racial formation in the United States from 1960s to the 1990s.* (2nd ed.). New York: Routledge.

Perkins, M.V. (1995). Exploring new spaces: A dialogue with black women on religion, culture, and spirituality. In G. Wade-Gayles (Ed.), *My soul is a witness: African-American women's spirituality.* Boston: Beacon.

PEW Forum on Religion and Public Life. (2008, June). *U.S. religious landscape survey: Religious beliefs and practices: Diverse and politically relevant.* http://religions.pewforum.org/pdf/report2-religious-landscape-study-full.pdf.

Powers, R. (1989, October). Fat is a black woman's issue. *Essence, 75,* 78, 134, 136.

Robert Wood Johnson Foundation. (1998, December 1). *Opening doors: A program to reduce sociocultural barriers to health care.* www.rwjf.org/reports/npreports/opendoorse.htm

Roscoe, W. (1992). *The Zuni man-woman.* Albuquerque: University of New Mexico Press.

Rubin, L.B. (2007). "Is this a white country, or what?" In M.L. Andersen & P. Hill Collins (Eds.), *Race, class, and gender* (6th ed.). Belmont, CA: Wadsworth.

Schaefer, R.T. (2007). *Race and identity in the United States* (4th ed.). Upper Saddle River, NJ: Prentice Hall.

Shingles, R.R. (2001). *Women in athletic training: Their career and educational experiences.* Unpublished doctoral dissertation, Michigan State University, East Lansing.

Smith, Y.R. (1992, August). Women of color in society and sport. *Quest, 44*(2), 228–250.

Spector, R.E. (2000). *Cultural diversity in health and illness* (5th ed.). Upper Saddle River, NJ: Prentice Hall.

Spector, R.E. (2004). *Cultural diversity in health and illness* (6th ed.). Upper Saddle River, NJ: Prentice Hall.

Sue, D.W., & Sue, D. (2008). *Counseling the culturally diverse: Theory and practice* (5th ed.). Hoboken, NJ: Wiley.

Taylor, E., Mitchell, J.E., Kenan, S., & Tacker, R. (2000, July–August). Attitudes of occupational therapists toward spirituality in practice. *American Journal of Occupational Therapy, 54*(4), 421–426.

U.S. Census Bureau. (2006, August 29). Income climbs, poverty stabilizes, uninsured rate increases. Press release. www.census.gov/Press-Release/www/releases/archives/income_wealth/007419.html.

U.S. Census Bureau. (2010). United States Census 2010: The questions on the form. http://2010.census.gov/2010census/how/interactive-form.php

CHAPTER 5

Abrums, M.E., & Leppa, C. (2001). Beyond cultural competence: Teaching about race, gender, class and sexual orientation. *The Journal of Nursing Education, 40*(6), 270–275.

Andersen, M.K. (1991). *Pioneer women in athletic training: Their oppression and resistance as viewed from a feminist perspective.* Unpublished doctoral dissertation, University of Iowa, Iowa City.

Asian Nation. (2008). Socioeconomic statistics & demographics. www.asian-nation.org/demographics.shtml.

Baca Zinn, M., & Dill, B.T. (2005). Theorizing difference from multiracial feminism. In M. Baca Zinn, P. Hondagneu-Sotelo, & M.A. Messner (Eds.), *Gender through the prism of difference* (3rd ed.). New York: Oxford University Press.

Biddington, C. (2007, Winter). Teaching diversity awareness. *Academic Exchange Quarterly, 11*(4), 71–75.

Campinha-Bacote, J. (2003). *The process of cultural competence in the delivery of healthcare services: A culturally competent model of care.* Cincinnati: Transcultural C.A.R.E.

Campinha-Bacote, J. (2007). *The process of cultural competence in the delivery of healthcare services: The journey continues.* Cincinnati: Transcultural C.A.R.E.

Diller, J.V. (2007). *Cultural diversity: A primer for the human services* (3rd. ed.). Belmont, CA: Thomson Brooks/Cole.

Ferber, A. (2007). What white supremacists taught a Jewish scholar about identity. In

M.L. Andersen, & P.H. Collins (Eds.), *Race, class, and gender* (6th ed.). Belmont, CA: Wadsworth.

Frankenberg, R. (2008). Whiteness as an 'unmarked' cultural category. In K.E. Rosenblum & T.C. Travis (Eds.), *The meaning of difference: American constructions of race, sex and gender, social class, sexual orientation and disability.* (5th ed.). Boston: McGraw-Hill.

Griffin, P. (1998). *Strong women, deep closets.* Champaign, IL: Human Kinetics.

Hossfeld, K.J. (1997). "Their logic against them": Contradictions in sex, race, and class in Silicon Valley. In M. Baca Zinn, P. Hondagneu-Sotelo, & M.A. Messner (Eds.), *Gender through the prism of difference: Readings on sex and gender* (pp. 388–406). Needham Heights, MA: Allyn & Bacon.

Johnson, A.G. (2001). *Privilege, power, and difference.* Boston: McGraw-Hill.

Johnson, A.G. (2006). *Privilege, power, and difference* (2nd ed.). Boston: McGraw-Hill.

Lai, T. (1995). Asian American women: Not for sale. In M.L. Andersen & P. H. Collins (Eds.), *Race, class, and gender* (2nd ed.). Belmont, CA: Wadsworth.

Lambda 10 Project. (n.d.). *Gender normative privilege.* www.lambda10.org/transgender/GenderNormativePrivilege.pdf.

Lattanzi, J.B., & Purnell, L.D. (2006). *Developing cultural competence in physical therapy practice.* Philadelphia: Davis.

Ligutom-Kimura, D.A. (1995, September). The invisible women. *Journal of Physical Education, Recreation and Dance, 66*(7), 34–41.

McIntosh, P. (2007). White privilege and male privilege: A personal account of coming to see correspondences through work in women's studies. In M.L. Andersen & P.H. Collins (Eds.), *Race, class, and gender* (6th ed.). Belmont, CA: Wadsworth.

Oglesby, C. (1993). Issues of sport and racism: Where is the white in the rainbow coalition? In D. Brooks & R. Althouse (Eds.), *Racism in collegiate athletics: The African American athlete's experience* (pp. 251–267). Morgantown, WV: Fitness Information Technology.

Purnell, L.D., & Paulanka, B.J. (2003). *Transcultural health care: A culturally competent approach* (2nd. ed.). Philadelphia: Davis.

Salimbene, S. (2001). *CLAS A-Z: A practical guide for implementing the National Standards for Culturally and Linguistically Appropriate Services (CLAS) in Health Care.* Northampton, MA: Inter-Face International.

Schaefer, R.T. (2007). *Race and identity in the United States* (4th ed.). Upper Saddle River, NJ: Prentice Hall.

Shingles, R.R. (2001). *Women in athletic training: Their career and educational experiences.* Unpublished doctoral dissertation. Michigan State University, East Lansing.

Spector, R. (1996). *Cultural diversity in health and illness* (4th ed.). Stamford, CT: Appleton and Lange.

St. Clair, A., & McKenry, L. (1999). Preparing culturally competent practitioners. *Journal of Nursing Education, 38*(5), 228–234.

Sue, D.W., & Sue, D. (2008). *Counseling the culturally diverse: Theory and practice* (5th ed.). Hoboken, NJ: Wiley.

Takaki, R.T. (2007). A different mirror. In M.L. Andersen & P.H. Collins (Eds.), *Race, class, and gender* (6th ed.). Belmont, CA: Wadsworth.

Tatum, B.D. (1997). *"Why are all the black kids sitting together in the cafeteria?" And other conversations about race.* New York: Basic Books.

Welch, M. (2003). *Teaching diversity and cross-cultural competence in health care: A trainer's guide* (3rd ed.). San Francisco: Perspectives of Differences Diversity Training and Consultation Services for Health Professionals (PODSDT).

CHAPTER 6

American Indians and Alaska Natives and Immunizations. (2006). In *The provider's guide to quality and culture.* Cambridge, MA: Management Sciences for Health. http://erc.msh.org/mainpage.cfm?file=1.0.htm&module=provider&language=English.

Anthro4n6. (2004a). Chants and their uses. www.anthro4n6.net/navajosandpainting/table2.html.

Anthro4n6. (2004b). Navajo sand painting: The art of healing. www.anthro4n6.net/navajosandpainting.

Black, L.T., and Liapunova, R.G. (2004). Aleut. Washington, DC: Arctic Studies Center. www.mnh.si.edu/arctic/features/croads/aleut.html.

Diller, J.V. (2007). *Cultural diversity: A primer for the human services* (3rd. ed.). Belmont, CA: Thomson·Brooks/Cole.

Downes, N.J. (1997). *Ethnic Americans for the health professional* (2nd ed.). Dubuque, IA: Kendall/Hunt.

Encyclopedia Britannica. (2009). Eskimo: People. www.britannica.com/EBchecked/topic/192518/Eskimo.

Eskimo-Aleut. (2007). *The Columbia Electronic Encyclopedia* (6th ed.). New York: Columbia University Press. www.infoplease.com/ce6/society/A0817692.html.

Eskimo-Aleut religion. (2010). Division of Religion and Philosophy, University of Cumbria. http://philtar.ucsm.ac.uk/encyclopedia/nam/inuit.html.

Griffin, S. (2010) Eskimos—The People of the Artic. www.workersforjesus.com/esk.htm

Gropper, R.C. (1996). *Culture and the clinical encounter.* Yarmouth, ME: Intercultural Press.

Hendrix, L. (2002). *Health and health care of American Indian and Alaska Native elders.* Stanford, CA: Stanford University. www.stanford.edu/group/ethnoger/americanindian.html.

Intercultural Cancer Council. (2001). American Indians/Alaska Natives and cancer. http://iccnetwork.org/cancerfacts/cfs2.htm.

Kennett, F. (1976). *Folk medicine fact and fiction.* New York: Marshall Cavendish.

Kiva Trading. (2007). American Indian symbols dictionary. www.kivatrading.com/symbol1.htm.

Lipson, J., Dibble, S., & Minarik, P. (1996). *Culture and nursing care: A pocket guide.* San Francisco: UCSF Nursing Press.

Livesay, N. (2002). *Understanding the history of tribal enrollment.* American Indian Policy Center. St. Paul, MN. www.airpi.org/pubs/enroll.html.

McCabe, M. (2001, November/December). Treating American Indians/Alaskan Native elders. *Geriatric Times*, 2(6).

Management Sciences for Health. (2003) Reducing health disparities in Asian American and Pacific Islander populations: An interactive virtual seminar for providers.

Marbella, A.M., Harris, M.C., Diehr, S., Ignace, G., & Ignace, G. (1998). Use of Native American healers among Native American patients in an urban Native American health center. *Archives of Family Medicine*, 7(2), 182–185.

Native Languages of the Americas. (2007). Native American hairstyles. www.native-languages.org/hair.htm.

Oropeza, L. (2002). Clinician's guide: Working with Native Americans living with HIV. Oakland, CA: National Native American AIDS Prevention Center. http://www.ihs.gov/medicalprograms/hivaids/docs/Cliniciansguide.pdf.

Perrone, B., Stockel, H.H., & Krueger, V. (1989). *Medicine women, curanderas, and women doctors.* Norman, OK: University of Oklahoma Press.

Purnell, L., & Paulanka, B. (2003). *Transcultural health care: A culturally competent approach* (2nd ed.). Philadelphia: Davis.

Purnell, L., & Paulanka, B. (2005). *Guide to culturally competent health care.* Philadelphia: Davis.

Robinson, B. (2002). *Native American spirituality.* Ontario, CA: Consultants on Religious tolerance. www.religioustolerance.org/nataspir.htm.

Salimbene, S. (2005). *What language does your patient hurt in? A practical guide to culturally competent patient care* (2nd ed.). St. Paul, MN: EMC Paradigm.

Schrefer, S. (Ed.). (1994). *Quick reference to cultural assessment.* St. Louis, MO. Mosby.

Scott. (2005). Berdaches—two spirits. eTransgender Forum. http://etransgender.com/viewtopic.php?f=9&t=5.s

Spector, R.E. (2004). *Cultural diversity in health and illness* (6th ed.). Upper Saddle River, NJ: Prentice Hall.

Spectrum Center. (2009). LGBTQ ally program participant manual. Ann Arbor: University of Michigan.

U.S. Census Bureau. (2000). The American Indian and Alaska Native Population: 2000. www.census.gov/prod/2002pubs/c2kbr01-15.pdf.

U.S. Department of Health and Human Services. (2000). Healthy people 2010: Understanding and improving health (2nd ed.). Washington, DC: U.S. Government Printing Office. www.healthypeople.gov/Document/tableofcontents.htm#under

Walter, M., & Fridman, E.J. (2004) *Shamanism an encolyopidia of world beliefs, pracitices and cultures.* Santa Barbara, CA: ABC-CLIO, Inc.

Yehieli, M., & Grey, M. (2005). *Health matters.* Yarmouth, ME: Intercultural Press.

CHAPTER 7

Accredited Language Services (2010) Chinese. www.alsintl.com/resources/languages/Chinese/

Acupuncture Today. (2007). Moxibustion. www.acupuncturetoday.com/abc/moxibustion.php.

Adler, L., & Mukherji, B. (1995). Spirit versus scalpel, traditional healing and modern psychotherapy. London, England: Bergin and Garvey.

Ampalaya.com. (2004). Momordica charantia. www.ampalaya.com/.

Anderson, J.N. (1983). Health and illness in Pilipino immigrants. *Western Journal of Medicine, 139*(6), 811–819.

Anisman-Reiner, V. (2007, April 3). Sedate the triple warmer meridian. Suite101.com. http://naturalmedicine.suite101.com/article.cfm/sedate_the_triple_warmer_meridian.

A World of Chinese Medicine. (2006). Traditional Chinese medicine diagnosis methods. www.aworldofchinesemedicine.com/chinese-medicine-diagnosis.htm.

Axtell, R. (1993). *Gestures: The do's and taboos of body language around the world,* 3rd ed.). New York: Wiley.

Central Intelligence Agency. (2009) The World Factbook. China. www.cia.gov/library/publications/the-world-factbook/geos/ch.html

Central Intelligence Agency. (2009) The World Factbook. Macau. www.cia.gov/library/publications/the-world-factbook/geos/mc.html

Chinese Society for the Study of Sexual Minorities. (2003, December 30). Gay rights in China: An update. *CSSSM News Digest.* www.csssm.org/English/e9.htm.

Chmelik, S. (1999). *Chinese herbal secrets.* Garden City Park: Avery Group.

Complementary Healthcare Information Service—UK. (2007). Aromatherapy. www.chisuk.org.uk/bodymind/whatis/aromatherapy.php.

Curry, J., & Nguyen, C. (1997). *Passport Vietnam.* San Rafael, CA: World Trade Press.

Dharmananda, S. (1999) Cupping. www.itmonline.org/arts/cupping.htm

Downes, N.J. (1997). *Ethnic Americans for the health professional* (2nd ed.). Dubuque, IA: Kendall/Hunt.

Erickson D'Avanzo, C., & Geissler, E. (2003). *Pocket guide to cultural health assessment* (3rd ed.). St. Louis, MO: Mosby.

Francia, L. (1997). *Passport Philippines.* San Rafael, CA: World Trade Press.

Friends of Tibet (NZ). (2008). Brief history of Tibet. www.friends-of-tibet.org.nz/tibet.html.

Ji, S.D. (2007). Chinese food therapy. www.dhyansanjivani.org/chinese_food.asp.

Kaptchuk, T. (2000). *The web that has no weaver.* Linwood, IL: Contemporary Books.

Kennett, F. (1976). *Folk medicine fact and fiction.* New York: Marshall Cavendish.

Leininger, M., & McFarland, M. (2002). Transcultural nursing. New York: McGraw-Hill.

LifeEvents.org. (2001). Shamanic lunar calendar. www.shamancalendar.com/.

Lipson, J., Dibble, S., & Minarik, P. (1996). *Culture and nursing care: A pocket guide.* San Francisco: UCSF Nursing Press.

Lowell, W. (1996). Chinese immigration and Chinese in the United States. Records in the Regional Archives of the National Archives and Records Administration. www.archives.gov/locations/finding-aids/images/chinese-immigration.gif.

Lucas, R. (1987). *Secrets of the Chinese herbalists* (2nd ed.). West Nyack, NY: Parker.

McCabe, V. (2005). *Household homeopathy.* North Bergen, NJ: Basic Health.

Nielsen, A. (2001). Welcome to Gua Sha. www.guasha.com/index.html.

Pich, L. (2005, November 16). Cao gio (coin rubbing or coining). Vanderbilt University Psychology Department (Health Psychology Home Page). http://healthpsych.psy.vanderbilt.edu/CAOGIO.htm.

Purnell, L., & Paulanka, B. (2003). *Transcultural health care: A culturally competent approach* (2nd ed.). Philadelphia: Davis.

Purnell, L., & Paulanka, B. (2005). *Guide to culturally competent health care.* Philadelphia: Davis.

Radhika, M. (2000, October 8). A tradition of bone setting. *The Hindu Folio.* www.hinduonnet.com/folio/fo0010/00100380.htm.

Rangzen. (1995). Tibet: A brief history. www.rangzen.com/.

Rastogi, N.S. (2008). Why does China care about Tibet? www.slate.com/id/2187567/.

Reed, M. (1990). Immune system boosting. www.acupressure.com/articles/immune-sys.htm.

Rundle, A., Carvalho, M., & Robinson, M. (Eds.). (1999). *Cultural competence in health care: A practical guide.* San Francisco: Jossey-Bass.

Salimbene, S. (2005). *What language does your athlete hurt in? A practical guide to culturally competent athlete care* (2nd ed.). St. Paul, MN: EMC Paradigm.

Seligman, S.D. (1999). *Chinese business etiquette.* New York. Warner Business Books.

Schrefer, S. (Ed.). (1994). *Quick reference to cultural assessment.* St. Louis, MO: Mosby Year Book.

Spector, R.E. (1996). *Guide to heritage assessment and health traditions.* Stamford, CT: Appleton and Lange.

Spector, R.E. (2004). *Cultural diversity in health and illness* (6th ed.). Upper Saddle River, NJ: Prentice Hall.

U.S. Census Bureau. (2000). United States Census 2000. www.census.gov/main/www/cen2000.html.

Wood, A.J.J. (1997). Pharmacogenetic and ethnic differences in opiate response. Meeting of the American Chemical Society, Las Vegas.

CHAPTER 8

Adherents.com. (2007). Santeria. www.adherents.com/Na/Na_581.html.

Apple Inc. (2005-2007) Dictionary Version 2.0.3

Centers for Disease Control and Prevention. (2007). U.S. Public Health Service Syphilis Study at Tuskegee. www.cdc.gov/nchstp/od/tuskegee/time.htm.

Common beliefs and cultural practices: Sub-Saharan Africans. (2007). In *The provider's guide to quality and culture.* Cambridge, MA: Management Sciences for Health. http://erc.msh.org/mainpage.cfm?file=5.3.0b.htm&module=provider&language=english.

Dessio, W., Wade, C., Chao, M., Kronenberg, F., Cushman, L.E., Kalmuss, D. (2004). Religion, spirituality, and healthcare choices of African-American women: Results of a national survey. www.ncbi.nlm.nih.gov/pubmed/15132203.

Downes, N.J. (1997). *Ethnic Americans for the health professional* (2nd ed.). Dubuque, IA: Kendall/Hunt.

Erickson D'Avanzo, C., & Geissler, E. (2003). *Pocket guide to cultural health assessment* (3rd ed.). St. Louis, MO: Mosby.

Essortment. (2002). Islam—the lawful (halaal) and the prohibited (haram). http://iaia.essortment.com/islamhalaalhar_rdep.htm.

Foster, D. (2002). *The global etiquette guide to Africa and the Middle East.* New York: Wiley.

Haiti. (2007). *The Columbia Electronic Encyclopedia* (6th ed.). New York: Columbia University Press. www.infoplease.com/ce6/world/A0858544.html.

Infoplease. (2007). The Tuskegee syphilis experiment. www.infoplease.com/ipa/A0762136.html.

Juneteenth Newsletter. (2007). www. juneteenth.com/.

Lipson, J., Dibble, S., and Minarik, P. (1996). *Culture and nursing care: A pocket guide.* San Francisco: UCSF Nursing Press.

McQuillar, T.L. (2003). *Rootwork.* New York: Simon & Schuster.

Miller, L. (2003) Proclamation on Immigration Quotas (28 April 1938). www. encyclopedia.com/doc/1G2-3401804817. html

Molaligne, A.K. (1996). Voices of the Ethiopian community. Seattle: The Cross Cultural Health Program. www.xculture.org/files/ETHIOPIAN.pdf.

Parkinson, R. (2010). Yin and Yang in Chinese Cooking. http://chinesefood.about.com/library/weekly/aa101899.htm

Purnell, L., & Paulanka, B. (2003a). *Transcultural health care: A culturally competent approach, 2nd ed.).* Philadelphia: Davis.

Purnell, L., and Paulanka, B. (2003b). *Transcultural health care: A culturally competent approach* [CD] (2nd ed.). Philadelphia: Davis.

Purnell, L., & Paulanka, B. (2005). *Guide to culturally competent health care.* Philadelphia: Davis.

Rundle, A., Carvalho, M., & Robinson, M. (Eds.). (1999). *Cultural competence in health care: A practical guide.* San Francisco: Jossey-Bass.

Salimbene, S. (2005). *What language does your athlete hurt in? A practical guide to culturally competent athlete care* (2nd ed.). St. Paul, MN: EMC Paradigm.

Schrefer, S. (Ed.). (1994). *Quick reference to cultural assessment.* St. Louis, MO. Mosby Year Book.

Spector, R.E. (2004). *Cultural diversity in health and illness* (6th ed.). Upper Saddle River, NJ: Prentice Hall.

Turbitt, S. (2008). When you must select among versions of the same language. *Global Advisor Newsletter* (18th ed.). www. intersolinc.com/newsletters/newsletter_18. htm.

U.S. Census Bureau. (2000). United States Census 2000. www.census.gov/main/www/cen2000.html.

Wiener, J.M., and Dulcan, M.K. (2004). *Textbook of child and adolescent psychiatry* (3rd ed.). Arlington, VA: American Psychiatric.

World Book Dictionary, version 1.0.2.1. (2005). The Software MacKiev Company: World Book, Inc.

Yehieli, M., and Grey, M. (2005). *Health matters.* Yarmouth, ME: Intercultural Press.

CHAPTER 9

Axtell, R. (1993). *Gestures: The do's and taboos of body language around the world.* New York: Wiley.

Bird, S. (2004). *Sticks, stones, roots and bones.* St. Paul, MN: Llewellyn.

Chong, N. (2002). *The Latino athlete.* Yarmouth, MA: Intercultural Press.

Downes, N.J. (1997). *Ethnic Americans for the health professional* (2nd ed.). Dubuque, IA: Kendall/Hunt.

Erickson D'Avanzo, C., & Geissler, E. (2003). *Pocket guide to cultural health assessment* (3rd ed.). St. Louis, MO: Mosby.

New Orleans Mistic. (2007). Espiritismo/spiritism,. www.neworleansmistic.com/spells/primer/espiritismo.htm.

Kennett, F. (1976). *Folk medicine fact and fiction.* New York: Marshall Cavendish.

Library of Congress. (1998). Jones Act. www. loc.gov/rr/hispanic/1898/jonesact.html.

Lipson, J., Dibble, S., & Minarik, P. (1996). *Culture and nursing care: A pocket guide.* San Francisco: UCSF Nursing Press.

Malat, R. (2003). *Passport Mexico* (2nd ed.). Navato, CA: World Trade Press.

Ngai, M. (2004). Impossible subjects: Illegal aliens and the making of modern America. Princeton, NJ: Princeton University Press.

Purnell, L., & Paulanka, B. (2003). *Transcultural health care: A culturally competent approach* (2nd ed.). Philadelphia: Davis.

Purnell, L., & Paulanka, B. (2005). *Guide to culturally competent health care.* Philadelphia: Davis.

Rundle, A., Carvalho, M., & Robinson, M. (Eds.). (1999). *Cultural competence in health care: A practical guide.* San Francisco: Jossey-Bass.

Schrefer, S. (Ed.). (1994). *Quick reference to cultural assessment.* St. Louis, MO: Mosby Year Book.

Spector, R.E. (1996). *Guide to heritage assessment and health traditions.* Stamford, CT: Appleton and Lange

Spector, R.E. (2004). *Cultural diversity in health and illness* (6th ed.). Upper Saddle River, NJ: Prentice Hall.

U.S. Census Bureau (2000). United States Census 2000. www.census.gov/main/www/cen2000.html.

Vela, L. Written document 2/5/08.

Yehieli, M., & Grey, M. (2005). *Health matters.* Yarmouth, ME: Intercultural Press.

CHAPTER 10

Bryant, J. (1999). Immigration in the United States, Yale-New Haven Teachers Institute.www.yale.edu/ynhti/curriculum/units/1999/3/99.03.01.x.html.

Chao, A., and Spencer, D., (2008). Immigration: The Journey to America; The English http://library.thinkquet.org/20619/English.html.

Downes, N.J. (1997). *Ethic Americans for the health professional, 2nd ed.).* Dubuque, Iowa: Kendall/Hunt.

Erickson D'Avanzo, C., & Geissler, E. (2003). *Pocket guide to cultural health assessment, 3rd ed.).* St. Louis, MO: Mosby.

Foster, D. (2000). *The global etiquette guide to Europe.* New York: Wiley.

Kennett, F. (1976). *Folk medicine fact and fiction.* New York: Marshall Cavendish.

Kriebel, D (2007) Powwowing among Pennsylvania dutch: a traditional medical practice in the modern world. University Park: Penn State Press.

Leininger, M., & McFarland, M. (2002). Transcultural Nursing. New York: McGraw Hill.

Loveland, B. (2005) Hilite for the Month of October 2005. Mrs., Ms, or Miss? www.biochakra.com/archives/oct_05.htm

Purnell, L., & Paulanka, B. (2003). *Transcultural health care a culturally competent approach* (2nd ed.). Philadelphia: Davis.

Purnell, L., & Paulanka, B. (2005). *Guide to culturally competent health care.* Philadelphia: Davis.

Rich, T. (2007). Judaism 101 Kashrut: Jewish Dietary Laws www.jewfaq.org/kashrut.htm.

Schrefer, S. (Ed.). (1994). *Quick reference to cultural assessment.* St. Louis, MO. Mosby Year Book.

Spector, R.E. (1996). *Guide to heritage assessment and health traditions.* Stamford, Conn: Appleton and Lange.

Spector, R.E. (2004). *Cultural diversity in health and illness, 6th ed.).* Upper Saddle River, NJ: Prentice Hall.

University of Virginia Health Care System. (2006). Protestant beliefs and practices affecting health care. www.healthsystem.virginia.edu/internet/chaplaincy/protestant.cfm.

U.S. Census Bureau (2000). United States Census 2000. www.census.gov/main/www/cen2000.html.

CHAPTER 11

Atallah, R. (1996). Voices of the Arab communities. The Cross Cultural Health Care Program. www.xculture.org/files/ARAB.pdf.

Erickson D'Avanzo, C., & Geissler, E. (2003). *Pocket guide to cultural health assessment* (3rd ed.). St. Louis, MO: Mosby.

Essortment. (2002). Islam—the lawful (halaal) and the prohibited (haram). http://iaia.essortment.com/islamhalaalhar_rdep.htm.

Galanti, G. (2004). *Caring for athletes from different cultures* (3rd ed.). Philadelphia: University of Pennsylvania Press.

Gill, N.S. (1999) Four Humors. http://ancient-history.about.com/cs/hippocrates/a/hippocraticmeds.htm

Holes, C. (2000). *Dialect, culture, and society in eastern Arabia, Volume 1: Glossary.* Boston: Brill.

Islamic Services of America. (2004). What is halaal? www.isaiowa.org/content.asp?ID=1677.

Lipson, J., Dibble, S., & Minarik, P. (1996). *Culture and nursing care: A pocket guide.* San Francisco: UCSF Nursing Press.

Muslims. (2006). In *The provider's guide to quality and culture.* Cambridge, MA: Management Sciences for Health. http://erc.msh.org/mainpage.cfm?file=1.0.htm&module=provider&language=English.

Purnell, L., & Paulanka, B. (2003). *Transcultural health care: A culturally competent approach* (2nd ed.). Philadelphia: Davis.

Purnell, L., & Paulanka, B. (2005). *Guide to culturally competent health care.* Philadelphia: Davis.

Ramadan. (1992). *The Islamic Bulletin, 7.* www.islamicbulletin.com/newsletters/issue_7/ramadan.aspx.

Salimbene, S. (2005). *What language does your athlete hurt in? A practical guide to culturally competent athlete care* (2nd ed.). St. Paul, MN: EMC Paradigm.

Spector, R.E. (2004). *Cultural diversity in health and illness* (6th ed.). Upper Saddle River, NJ: Prentice Hall.

U.S. Census Bureau. (2000). United States Census 2000. www.census.gov/main/www/cen2000.html.

Young, C., & Koopsen, D. (2005). *Spirituality, health, and healing.* Boston: Jones and Bartlett.

CHAPTER 12

American Psychiatric Association. (2000). *Diagnostic and statistical manual of mental disorders* (4th ed., text revision). Washington, DC: Author.

Berlin, E., & Fowkes, W.A. (1983). Teaching framework for cross-cultural health care. *Western Journal of Medicine, 129*(6), 934–938.

Betancourt, J.R., Green, A.R., Carrillo, J.E., & Ananeh-Firempong, O. (2003). Defining cultural competence: A practical framework for addressing racial/ethnic disparities in health and health care. *Public Health Reports, 118,* 293–302.

Bethell, C., Simpson, L., Read, D., Sobo, E., Vitucci, J., Latzke, B., et al. (2006). Quality and safety of hospital care for children from Spanish-speaking families with limited English proficiency. *Journal for Healthcare Quality Web Exclusive, 28*(3), W3-2–W3-16. www.nahq.org/journal/online/pdf/mayjune2006.pdf.

Campinha-Bacote, J. (2003). *The process of cultural competence in the delivery of healthcare services: A culturally competent model of care.* Cincinnati: Transcultural C.A.R.E.

Exec. Order No. 13166, 3 C.F.R. 50119-50122 (2000), *Improving access to services for persons with limited English proficiency.*

Gany, F., Kapelusznik, L., Prakash, K., Gonzalez, J., Orta, L.Y. Tseng. C., et al. (2007). The impact of medical interpretation method on time and errors. *Journal of General Internal Medicine, 22*(Suppl. 2), 319–23.

Gany, F., Leng, J., Shapiro, E., Abramson, D., Motola, I., Shield, D.C., et al. (2007). Patient satisfaction with different interpreting methods: A randomized controlled trial. *Journal of General Internal Medicine, 22*(Suppl. 2), 312–318.

Kleinman, A., & Benson, P. (2006). Anthropology in the clinic: The problem of cultural competency and how to fix it. *PLoS Medicine, 3*(10): e294. DOI: 10.1271/journal.pmed.0030294.

Kleinman, A., Eisenberg, L., & Good, B. (1978). Culture, illness, and care: Clinical lessons from anthropological and cross-cultural research. *Annals of Internal Medicine, 88*(2), 251–258.

Mutha, S., Allen, C., & Welch, M. (2002). *Toward culturally competent care: A toolbox for teaching communication strategies.* San Francisco: Center for the Health Professions, University of California, San Francisco.

Ngo-Metzger, Q., Massagli, M., Clarridge, B.R., Manocchia, M., Davis, R.B., Iezzoni, L.I., et al. (2003). Linguistic and cultural barriers to care: Perspectives of Chinese and Vietnamese immigrants. *Journal of General Internal Medicine, 18,* 44–52.

Office of Minority Health (U.S. Department of Health and Human Services). (2001). *National standards for culturally and linguistically appropriate services [CLAS] in health care.* http://minorityhealth.hhs.gov/assets/pdf/checked/finalreport.pdf.

Salimbene, S. (2001). *CLAS A-Z: A practical guide for implementing the National Standards for Culturally and Linguistically Appropriate Services [CLAS] in Health Care.* Northampton, MA: Inter-Face International.

Welch, M. (2003). *Teaching diversity and cross-cultural competence in health care: A trainer's guide* (3rd ed.). San Francisco: Perspectives of Differences Diversity Training and Consultation Services for Health Professionals (PODSDT).

CHAPTER 13

Betancourt, J.R., Green, A.R., Carrillo, J.E., & Ananeh-Firempong, O. (2003). *Defining cultural competence: A practical framework for addressing racial/ethnic disparities in health and health care.* Boston: Harvard Medical School.

Campinha-Bacote, J. (2003). *The process of cultural competence in the delivery of healthcare services: A culturally competent model of care.* Cincinnati: Transcultural C.A.R.E.

Carrese, J.A., & Rhodes, L.A. (2000). Bridging cultural differences in medical practice: The case of discussing negative information with Navajo patients. *Journal of General Internal Medicine, 15*(2), 92–96.

Giger, J.N., & Davidhizar, R.E. (1999). *Transcultural nursing: Assessment and intervention* (3rd. ed.). St. Louis, MO: Mosby.

Lowe, S. (2008). New Census Bureau data reveal more older workers, homeowners, non-English speakers. U.S. Census Bureau. www.census.gov/Press-Release/www/releases/archives/american_community_survey_acs/010601.html.

Niemeier, J.P., Burnett, D.M., & Whitaker, D.A. (2003). Cultural competence in the multidisciplinary rehabilitation setting: Are we falling short of meeting needs? *Archives of Physical Medicine and Rehabilitation, 84:* 1240–1245.

Purnell, L.D., & Paulanka, B.J. (2003). *Transcultural health care: A culturally competent approach* (2nd. ed.). Philadelphia: Davis.

Reissman, C.K. (1991). When gender is not enough: Women interviewing women. In J. Lorber & S.A. Farrell (Eds.), *The social construction of gender* (pp. 217–236). Newbury Park, CA: Sage.

Salimbene, S. (2005). *What language does your patient hurt in? A practical guide to culturally competent patient care* (2nd ed.). Amherst, MA: Diversity Resources.

Schim, S.M. (2005). Cultural diversity: A picture on the front of the box. *Journal of Professional Nursing, 21*(5), 255–256.

Spector, R.E. (2000). *Cultural diversity in health and illness* (5th ed.). Upper Saddle River, NJ: Prentice Hall.

Stubbs, M.A. (1995). "Be healed": A black woman's sermon on healing through touch. In G. Wade-Gayles (Ed.), *My soul is a witness: African American women's spirituality* (pp. 305–313). Boston: Beacon.

Sue, D.W., & Sue, D. (2008). *Counseling the culturally diverse: Theory and practice* (5th ed.). Hoboken, NJ: Wiley.

CHAPTER 14

Alliance for Nonprofit Management. (2004). Frequently asked questions. www.allianceonline.org/content/index.php?pid=172

Campinha-Bacote, J. (2002). The process of cultural competence in the delivery of healthcare services: A culturally competent model of care. *Journal of Transcultural Nursing, 13,* 181–184.

Campinha-Bacote, J. (2003). *The process of cultural competence in the delivery of healthcare services: A culturally competent model of care.* Cincinnati: Transcultural C.A.R.E.

Decide-Guide.com. (2009, May 15). The SWOT model: Strengths, weaknesses, opportunities and threats. www.decide-guide.com/swot/

Dresser, N. (2005). *Multicultural manners: Essential rules of etiquette for the 21 century* (rev. ed.). New York: Wiley.

Health Resources and Services Administration. (2001). *Cultural competence works: Using cultural competence to improve the quality* of health care for diverse populations and add value to managed care arrangements. U.S. Department of Health and Human Services.

Marketing Teacher. (2010). SWOT analysis: Lessons. www.marketingteacher.com/Lessons/lesson_swot.htm.

Matlins, S.M., & Magida, A.J. (2006). *How to be a perfect stranger: The essential religious etiquette handbook.* Woodstock, VT: Skylight Paths.

Mind Tools. (2008). SWOT analysis: Discover new opportunities. Manage and eliminate threats. www.mindtools.com/pages/article/newTMC_05.htm.

Mutha, S., Allen, C., & Welch, M. (2002). *Toward culturally competent care: A toolbox for teaching communication strategies.* San Francisco: Center for the Health Professions, University of California, San Francisco.

National Athletic Trainers' Association. (2009). *June 2009 NATA certified membership by setting and district.* www.nata.org/members1/documents/membstats/2009%2006.htm.

Office of Minority Health (U.S. Department of Health and Human Services). (2001). *National standards for culturally and linguistically appropriate services [CLAS] in health care.* minorityhealth.hhs.gov/assets/pdf/checked/finalreport.pdf.

Salimbene, S. (2001). *CLAS A-Z: A practical guide for implementing the National Standards for Culturally and Linguistically Appropriate Services [CLAS] in Health Care.* Northampton, MA: Inter-Face International.

Salimbene, S. (2005). *What language does your patient hurt in? A practical guide to culturally competent patient care* (2nd ed.). Amherst, MA: Diversity Resources.

Transcultural C.A.R.E. Associates. (2010). *The process of cultural competence in the delivery of healthcare services.* www.transcultural-care.net/.

APPENDIX

American Psychiatric Association. (2000). *Diagnostic and statistical manual of mental disorders* (4th ed., text revision). Washington, DC: Author.

Carter, S., & Gross, S. (2005). Glucose-6-phosphate dehydrogenase deficiency. www.emedicine.com/med/topic900.htm.

Cartwright, L., & Pitney, W. (2005). *Athletic training for student assistants* (2nd ed.). Champaign, IL: Human Kinetics.

Centers for Disease Control and Prevention. (1985). Current trends alcohol-associated premature mortality—United States, 1980. www.cdc.gov/mmwr/preview/mmwrhtml/00000592.htm.

Centers for Disease Control and Prevention. (2003). Japanese encephalitis fact sheet. www.cdc.gov/ncidod/dvbid/jencephalitis/facts.htm.

Centers for Disease Control and Prevention. (2004). Schistosomiasis. www.cdc.gov/NCIDOD/DPD/parasites/schistosomiasis/factsht_schistosomiasis.htm.

Centers for Disease Control and Prevention. (2005). Cholera. www.cdc.gov/nczved/divisions/dfbmd/diseases/cholera/.

Centers for Disease Control and Prevention. (2006a). Typhoid fever. www.cdc.gov/ncidod/dbmd/diseaseinfo/typhoidfever_g.htm.

Centers for Disease Control and Prevention. (2006b). Viral Hepatitis. www.cdc.gov/ncidod/diseases/hepatitis/bcountry_listing.htm#mideast.

Centers for Disease Control and Prevention. (2007a). Malaria. www.cdc.gov/malaria/faq.htm.

Centers for Disease Control and Prevention. (2007b). Tuberculosis in blacks. www.cdc.gov/tb/WorldTBDay/resources_TB_Blacks.htm.

Centers for Disease Control and Prevention. (2007c). Vietnamese American Women. www.cdc.gov/cancer/nbccedp/publications/cc-strategies/vietnamese.htm.

Centers for Disease Control and Prevention. (2007d). Yellow Fever Fact Sheet. www.cdc.gov/ncidod/dvbid/yellowfever/YF_FactSheet.html.

Centers for Disease Control and Prevention. (2009). Cholera. www.cdc.gov/nczved/divisions/dfbmd/diseases/cholera/

Centers for Disease Control and Prevention. (2008). Trachoma. www.cdc.gov/ncidod/dbmd/diseaseinfo/trachoma_t.htm.

Centers for Disease Control and Prevention. (2009) Guidelines for treatment of malaria in the United States. www.cdc.gov/malaria/resources/pdf/treatmenttable73109.pdf

Centers for Disease Control and Prevention. (2010a). Dengue Fever. www.cdc.gov/Dengue/.

Centers for Disease Control and Prevention. (2010b). Malaria. www.cdc.gov/malaria/about/index.html.

Children's Health System. (2007). Congenital ear anomalies. http://pedsent.chsys.org/default.aspx?id=9.

Cigna. (2005). Dyggve Melchior Clausen syndrome. www.cigna.com/healthinfo/nord874.html.

Directors of Health Promotion and Education. (2007). African trypanosomiasis. www.dhpe.org/infect/Trypano.html.

Foodintol. (2007). Wheat intolerance and wheat sensitivity. www.foodintol.com/wheat.asp. Gonsalves, W., Chi, A., & Neville, B. (2007, February 15). Common oral lesions: Part II. Masses and neoplasia. *American Family Physician*, 75(4), 509–512. Martin, J.L. (1992).

Hall, L. (2010) Conceptions of mental illness: cultural perspectives and treatment implications. www.fcas.nova.edu/current-students/quadrivium/vol1/conception-of-mental-illness/index.cfm

HealthScout. (2001a). Epilepsy. www.healthscout.com/ency/1/000694.html.

HealthScout. (2001b). Thalassemia. www.healthscout.com/ency/1/000587.html.

HealthScout. (2001c). Thalassemia—symptoms, treatment and prevention. www.healthscout.com/ency/68/477/main.html.

International Trachoma Initiative. (2007). About trachoma. www.trachoma.org/core/sub.php?cat=trachoma&id=trachoma /.

Irish Cancer Society. (2010) Cancer of the lung. www.cancer.ie/cancerInfo/lung_different_types.php#causeslungcancer?

Landy, D. (1985). Pibloktoq (hysteria) and Inuit nutrition: possible implication of hypervitaminosis. www.ncbi.nlm.nih.gov/pubmed/4049004

Matsui, W. (2007). Glucose-6-phosphate dehydrogenase deficiency. www.nlm.nih.gov/medlineplus/ency/article/000528.htm.

Mayo Clinic. (2006). Sarcoidosis. www.mayoclinic.com/health/sarcoidosis/DS00251/DSECTION=3.

Mayo Clinic. (2007). High blood pressure. www.mayoclinic.com/health/high-blood-pressure/DS00100/DSECTION=8.

Mayo Clinic. (2010) Lung cancer; prevention. www.mayoclinic.com/health/lung-cancer/ds00038/dsection=prevention

McCajor Hall, T. (1998) Glossary of Culture-Bound Syndromes: http://homepage.mac.com/mccajor/cbs_glos.html#top

MedicineNet.com. (2007) Thyroid cancer symptoms and warning signs. www.medicinenet.com/script/main/art.asp?articlekey=53303

MedicineNet.com. (2010). Kidney Stones www.medicinenet.com/kidney_stone/article.htm

Medindia. (2008). Amoebic dysentery/amoebiasis. www.medindia.net/patients/patientinfo/AmoebicDysentery.htm.

MedlinePlus. (2006a). Congenital adrenal hyperplasia. www.nlm.nih.gov/medlineplus/ency/article/000411.htm.

MedlinePlus. (2006b). Dubin-Johnson syndrome. www.nlm.nih.gov/medlineplus/ency/article/000242.htm.

MedlinePlus. (2007a). Disseminated tuberculosis. www.nlm.nih.gov/medlineplus/ency/article/000624.htm.

MedlinePlus. (2007b). Glucose-6-phosphate dehydrogenase deficiency. www.nlm.nih.gov/medlineplus/ency/article/000528.htm.

MedlinePlus. (2008). Blount's disease. www.nlm.nih.gov/medlineplus/ency/article/001584.htm

MedlinePlus. (2009a) Chronic pulmonary coccidioidomycosis. www.nlm.nih.gov/medlineplus/ency/article/000096.htm

MedlinePlus. (2009b) Type 2 diabetes. www.nlm.nih.gov/medlineplus/ency/article/000313.htm

MedlinePlus. (2009c) Methemoglobinemia. www.nlm.nih.gov/medlineplus/ency/article/000562.htm

MEDPED. (2005). Familial hypercholesterolemia—high cholesterol. www.medped.org/MEDPED-What-is-FH.html.

Merck. (2007) Onchocerciasis. http://www.merck.com/mmhe/sec17/ch196/ch196m.html

Morakinyo, P. (2002) "Brain Fag" symptoms and apprentices in Nigeria. Psychopathology, Nov-Dec; 35(6):382-6.

National Center for Biotechnology Information. (2007a). Familial Mediterranean fever. www.ncbi.nlm.nih.gov/disease/FMF.html.

National Center for Biotechnology Information. (2007b). Hereditary hemochromatosis. www.ncbi.nlm.nih.gov/books/bv.fcgi?rid=gnd.section.251.

PatientPlus. (2006). Dubin-Johnson syndrome. www.patient.co.uk/showdoc/40001223/.

Penn State College of Medicine. (2004). Muscular dystrophy. www.hmc.psu.edu/healthinfo/m/musculardystrophy.htm.

Penn State College of Medicine. (2006). Dupuytren's disease. www.hmc.psu.edu/healthinfo/d/dupuytren.htm.

Purnell, L., & Paulanka, B. (2005). *Guide to culturally competent health care*. Philadelphia: Davis.

Saint Martin, M. (1999) Running amok: amodern perspective on a culture-bound syndrome. www.ncbi.nlm.nih.gov/pmc/articles/PMC181064/

Subramanian, M. (2006). Trachoma. www.nlm.nih.gov/medlineplus/ency/article/001486.htm#Treatment.

University of Maryland Medical Center. (2009). Intestinal parasites. www.umm.edu/altmed/articles/intestinal-parasites-000097.htm

Yellow Fever. (2006). *The Merck manual of medical information—Second home edition*. www.merck.com/mmhe/au/print/sec17/ch198/ch198k.html.

Vitaminsdiary.com (n.d.). What are vitamin B12 injections? And how to administer it? www.vitaminsdiary.com/vitamins/vitamin-b12-injection.htm

WebMD. (2005-10) Heptatits A Guide. www.webmd.com/hepatitis/hepa-guide/hepatitis-a-topic-overview

Windmill Perception. (2009) Boufee delirante. www.windmillperception.posterous.com/?tag=psychoticdisorders

Wrong Diagnosis (2010). Prognosis of Navajo neurohepatopathy. www.wrongdiagnosis.com/n/navajo_neurohepatopathy/prognosis.htm

Yes Schwartz, P. (2002) Why is neurasthenia important in Asian cultures. West J Med. 2002 September; 176(4): 257–258 www.ncbi.nlm.nih.gov/pmc/articles/PMC1071745/

GLOSSARY

Andersen, M.L., & Collins, P.H. (1995). *Race, class and gender* (2nd ed.). Belmont, CA: Wadsworth.

Campinha-Bacote, J. (2003). *The process of cultural competence in the delivery of healthcare services: A culturally competent model of care*. Cincinnati: Transcultural C.A.R.E.

Campinha-Bacote, J. (2007). *The process of cultural competence in the delivery of healthcare services: The journey continues*. Cincinnati: Transcultural C.A.R.E.

Carter-Pokras, O., & Baquet, C. (2000). *What is a health disparity?* Public Health Reports, 117, 426–434.

Coakley, J. (2004). *Sports in society: Issues and controversies* (8th ed.). Boston: McGraw-Hill.

Diller, J.V. (2007). *Cultural diversity: A primer for the human services* (3rd. ed.). Belmont, CA: Thomson Brooks/Cole.

Michigan Department of Community Health. (2007). *2007 health disparities report to the Michigan legislature*. www.michigan.gov/documents/mdch/Response_to_Legislature.final_228597_7.pdf.

Miller, W. R., & Thoresen, C. E. (2003). *Spirituality, religion and health: An emerging research field*. American Psychologist, 58(1), 24-35.

National Center for Complementary and Alternative Medicine (NCCAM). (2007). *CAM basics: What is CAM?* (NCCAM Publication No. D347). http://nccam.nih.gov/health/whatiscam/.

Purnell, L.D., & Paulanka, B.J. (2008). *Transcultural health care: A culturally competent approach* (3rd ed.). Philadelphia: Davis.

Spector, R.E. (2000). *Cultural diversity in health and illness* (5th ed.). Upper Saddle River, NJ: Prentice Hall.

Tatum, B.D. (1997). *"Why are all the black kids sitting together in the cafeteria?" And other conversations about race.* New York: Basic Books.

U.S. Census Bureau. (2007). Population profile of the United States: Dynamic version (Internet release). www.census.gov/population/www/pop-profile/profiledynamic.html.

U.S. Department of Health and Human Services. (2000a). Healthy People 2010 Volume I: Understanding and improving health: Access to quality health services. www.healthypeople.gov/Document/HTML/Volume1/01Access.htm.

U.S. Department of Health and Human Services. (2000b). Healthy People 2010 Volume I: Understanding and improving health: Leading health indicators. www.healthypeople.gov/Document/html/uih/uih_bw/uih_4.htm.

Index

Note: The italicized *f* and *t* following page numbers refer to figures and tables, respectively.

protection
  African Americans 142
  Asian Americans 109-110, 126
  Europeans 198
  Latinos 170, 176, 181-182
  Native Americans 87
Protestantism 190
pseudofolliculitis 138, 158
Puerto Ricans
  biocultural traits 174
  CAM usage 30
  cultural information 172-174
  demographics 172
  first-generation 174
  health beliefs and practices 174-176
  language and communication 172
  origins and immigration 171-172, 171*f*
Pujalte, George 47
purification 84
Purnell, L.D. 10-12, 13*f*

Q
qi (chi) 103
qigong 29, 109
qi-gong psychotic reaction 21, 103

R
race and ethnicity
  defined 49
  group terminology 15-17
  history 49-50
  implications in health care 51
Ramadan 214
Reiki 30
religion or spirituality
  Asian Americans 102, 122
  Blacks 137, 147, 154
  Europeans 189-190, 195-196, 198, 201, 202
  Filipinos 114
  Latinos 166, 170, 173-174, 179, 182
  Middle Easterners 213-214, 221
  Native Americans 81, 89
  oral history and 247
  in social location 56-57
remote simultaneous medical interpreting
    (RSMI) 237
RESPECT model 235-236
rootwork 25, 142
Rootwork (McQuillar) 142
RSMI 237

S
sacred medicine 223
Salmonella 82
sand painting 86
Santeria 173, 176, 180, 182
sarcoidosis 190, 196
sard 221
saving face 99, 112, 113, 246
scabies 148
scapular 191
schistosomiasis 115, 148
seizures 83, 139

self-assessment
  individual 62-63
  organizational 253, 254, 255*t*-256*t*
semen loss syndromes 21-22
sexuality 55
sexually transmitted diseases 155, 156, 168
sezisman 155
shamans 85, 91-92
Shannon, Angela 251-252
shenjing shuairuo 21, 103
shen k'uei (shenkui) 21-22, 103
Shigella 82
shin-byung 22
sickle-cell anemia 138
siesta 168
silence 243-244
silok 23
Simons, R. C. 26
skin assessment 247-248
skin cancer 190, 191, 196
salimbene 139
Smallwood, Sheila 131-132
smiling 245-246
smoking 197, 222, 224
social class 51-53
social location
  components of
    gender 53-55
    intersection of 57-58
    race and ethnicity 49-51
    religion and spirituality 56-57
    sexuality 55
    social class 51-53
    "unpacking" 48*f*, 49
  defined 48
space (distance zones) 248. *See also specific*
    cultures
Spector, Rachel 10-12, 12*f*
spell 25
spirit possession 23
spirituality. *See* religion or spirituality
Sri Lanka 22. *See also* Asian Americans
stargazer 85
stereotypes 65-66, 165
strategic plans 253, 257-259, 258*t*
stroke 190, 191, 202
structural barriers to health care 41
student athletes
  CAM usage 27, 29
  demographics 37
sub-Saharan Africans
  biocultural traits 148
  cultural information 145-147
  culture-bound syndromes 23
  demographics 144
  health beliefs and practices 148-150
  language and communication 144-145
  origins and immigration 143-144, 143*f*
suicide 90, 180
sukra prameha 22
sun exposure 191, 197
susto (fright) 24-25, 167

About the Authors

Photo courtesy of Erin Cole.

Lorin A. Cartwright, MS, ATC, is assistant principal and athletic director at Pioneer High School in Ann Arbor, Michigan. As a teacher and the school's head athletic trainer for more than 15 years, she has extensive experience with all aspects of instruction of student athletic trainers. She was an adjunct professor in athletic training at the University of Michigan for three years. Cartwright earned a bachelor's degree in physical education from Grand Valley State College and a master's degree in education from the University of Michigan.

Cartwright is the author of three books, including the popular *Preparing for the Athletic Trainers' Certification Exam,* and was the first woman and first high school athletic trainer to serve as the president of the Great Lakes Athletic Trainers' Association. She served as the investigative chair on the Ethics Committee for the National Athletic Trainers' Association (NATA) from 1998 to 2004 and was also an active member of NATA's National Membership Committee and the National Review Committee for Misconduct from 1988 through 1992. Highly regarded in her field, she was the recipient of the Great Lakes Athletic Trainers' Association Outstanding Educator Award in 2010, the Athletic Trainer Award from the Great Lakes Athletic Trainers' Association in 2002, the Most Distinguished Athletic Trainer Award from the Michigan Athletic Trainers' Society in 1999, and the Distinguished Service Award from the National Athletic Trainers' Association in 1998.

Her travels have taken her to Alaska, Italy, Nova Scotia, Sweden, Finland, and the Caribbean. Cartwright has been the athletic trainer for the amateur and semipro summer basketball league and the Michigan men's basketball all-star team, and she worked at the Olympic Trials for wrestling.

Cartwright resides in Ann Arbor, Michigan, where she enjoys woodworking, creating stained glass, and gardening in her free time.

René Revis Shingles, PhD, ATC, is director and associate professor in the department of physical education and sport at Central Michigan University in Mt. Pleasant. She received her doctorate from Michigan State University. Her doctoral studies in sport sociology and program design and evaluation provide the theoretical framework for her continued research in cultural competence. Revis Shingles has presented extensively on cultural competence and diversity and has over 20 years of experience in teaching at the collegiate level.

Revis Shingles is a member of the National Athletic Trainers' Association's (NATA) Ethnic Diversity Advisory Council, serving as chair from 1995 until 2000.

She also served on the NATA Education Council Executive Committee from 2004 through 2009. In addition to her athletic training experience, her work with these committees provided firsthand knowledge of diversity and educational issues in athletic training. In 2010, she received the Great Lakes Athletic Trainers' Association Outstanding Educator Award and the NATA's Most Distinguished Athletic Trainer Award.

As an athletic trainer and researcher, she has traveled to Malaysia, Singapore, Thailand, Japan, Mexico, Aruba, Puerto Rico, Dominican Republic, and throughout the Caribbean. Revis Shingles also served as an athletic trainer for the 1996 Atlanta Olympic Games.

She and her husband, Stan, reside in Mt. Pleasant, Michigan, where she enjoys spending time with family and friends, reading, and traveling.